D1597223

FOOD IN VOGUE

FOOD IN VOGUE

Six Decades of Cooking and Entertaining

Edited by
BARBARA TIMS

Harrap  London

in association with
The Condé Nast Publications Ltd

First published in Great Britain 1976
by George G. Harrap & Co. Ltd
182–184 High Holborn, London WC1V 7AX
Reprinted 1976

© *The Condé Nast Publications Ltd* 1976

All rights reserved. No part of this publication may be reproduced in any form or by any means without the prior permission of the publishers.

ISBN 0 245 52945 4

Designed by Michael R. Carter.

Composed in Plantin type and printed
by Billing and Sons Limited
Guildford, London and Worcester
Made in Great Britain

Colour reproduction by Pinepoint Ltd

Contents

Acknowledgments

Over the past sixty years many people have written about food and entertaining in *Vogue*. Apart from contributions from the professionals there have been innumerable suggestions, ideas and hints on cooking, party-giving, drinking, from a host of expert and knowledgeable amateurs. It would be impossible to acknowledge them individually but to all of them we are grateful. Special thanks are due to Elizabeth David, Robert Carrier, Arabella Boxer and Veronica Maclean for permission to reprint their articles from the magazine, and to J. D. and S. B. B. Stamm for permission to quote "The Rainbow Sauces of Toulouse-Lautrec" from *La Cuisine de Monsieur Momo, Célibataire*.

Wherever possible the original illustrations accompanying the text have been used, supplemented when appropriate with the work of other artists and photographers. Their names appear next to the pictures except in a few cases where authorship could not be established. Our thanks go to them all and indeed to the many gifted people who work for the Condé Nast Publications worldwide whose skills over the decades have been distilled into our magazines and now further into this book.

Introduction

Browsing through old copies of *Vogue* is as compulsive as eating almonds and the difficulty with this book has been not what to put in but what to leave out.

British Vogue celebrates its diamond anniversary this year. Sixty years of reporting and reflecting changes more crowded and more violent than in any other century. Nowhere have the changes been greater than in food and entertaining. Air travel, frozen food, women's suffrage and women's lib, plus two world wars and rationing, have changed the whole concept of living and eating.

When the first issues of *British Vogue* appeared in 1916 you could, just, tell there was a war on: "By the way, for an informal dinner party, some hostesses are now serving a light white wine 'en carafe', throughout the meal.". . . "If seen with one's friends at a restaurant, however festive and décolletée, onlookers might charitably suppose that one's cook had gone to make munitions, or that one had rushed in for a hurried snack between good works. The girls who frivol so gaily and decoratively at supper-time have, many of them, put in an eight-hour shift canteening in a draught, or munitioning at the risk of T.N.T. poisoning."

Fish

And an anonymous writer asked: "Could not some one of the Powers that Be pass a law forbidding the retention of more than two or three cooks and scullions in the houses of the truly rich, in consideration of the many worthy people who have to do without cooked food (or obtain it in bottles) for lack of someone to cope with the gas range?" Both tinned and bottled food was obtainable—though perhaps not to everyone's taste: "Stuffed Field Larks, Guinea Hens in Aspic Jelly, and Such Dainties as Snail in Sauce Ravigote come from the Unexpected Resources of Tins and Glasses." "The Pleasures of the Tea Table" were important to *Vogue* readers: "Tea is the excuse for so many pleasant things—cigarettes, and gossip, and afternoon frocks.". . . "Of all hours of the day perhaps Tea-Time is the most fraught with pleasurable impressions and charming intimacies. It comes at such a cosy time in the energies of life, when most of the day's disagreeable duties or necessities having been accomplished, people are ready to be entertained and entertaining, soothed and soothing, confidential or sympathetic, as opportunity demands.". . . And in 1919: " 'Now that the war is over,' said the tea-gowns jubilantly, 'we can be as luxuriously draped and voluminous and feminine as ever.' "

During the twenties progress of *British Vogue* was "rocky"—according to Edna Woolman Chase, Editor-in-Chief of all *Vogues*. But Harry Yoxall, business manager

Norman Parkinson

of *Vogue* from 1923, guided the magazine into calmer seas. It was he who, in the General Strike of 1926 when the entire country was paralysed, had the foresight to pack his office with 7,000 copies of *Vogue* and sent his staff out to sell them to the bookstalls. One of the dealers said: "Now there ain't no newspapers, people will read anything, even Vogue."

It was Harry Yoxall who really started *Food in Vogue* when he commissioned Marcel Boulestin to write his Finer Food series, which is why this book starts with the twenties. Boulestin was followed by June Platt, Doris Lytton Toye, Elizabeth David (the first cookery writer to be awarded the O.B.E.), Mapie de Toulouse-Lautrec, Robert Carrier and Arabella Boxer (winner of the 1976 Glenfiddich award for Cookery Writer of the Year). Alongside their articles and recipes were photographs and drawings by the great photographers and artists: Cecil Beaton, McKnight Kauffer, Francis Marshall, Denton Welch, John Minton, Eric, John Ward, Dali, Picasso, Anthony Denney, Penn, Lester Bookbinder. . . . As Peter Ustinov said: "If Botticelli were alive today he'd be working for *Vogue*. . . ."

Decade by decade food and entertaining in *Vogue* has mirrored the life of the times and the best of everything. Each article and each recipe in this book is reprinted as it first appeared. Ingredients are given in imperial measures and the table on page 250 will convert them to metric and American measures. There are altogether some 750 recipes to choose from but remember, as *Vogue* remarked in 1947, "most good figures are carved with knife and fork".

Karen Radkai

avec mes
excuses
a Marty
Brissaud
et Simon
BENITO

20s

Menus were elaborate and recipes scanty at the beginning of the twenties. There were hints "For the Hostess"—"Mandarin Oranges are welcome in all their many *rôles*, but are more than usually interesting when they are filled with pheasant", while the menu for a "Charming Candle-lit Dinner for Two" consists of eleven dishes:

Hors d'Œuvres Variés
Consommé aux Pointes d'Asperges
Truite Saumonée, Sauce Bordelaise
Mousse de Volaille aux Champignons
Quartier d'Agneau Rôti
Pommes de Terre Nouvelles
Epinards au Beurre
Bavaroise à la Vanille
(or Bavaroise aux Pistaches)
Sauce Chaude au Chocolat
Petites Crèmes d'Anchois
Dessert

There were seasonal features. In August 1922: "OUT-OF-DOOR ENTERTAINING—Lured by the Loveliness of Modern Lawn and Garden, the Fête Champêtre Reappears as a Leading Motif in Summer Entertaining". Readers learnt that, "When one's heart is set upon using the precious warmth of a summer evening to its last breath, and giving one's friends a few hours of enchantment under the open sky, more than ordinary forethought is needed.

"If the barometer is at set fair and there seems every prospect of a moon it will not be necessary to take much trouble over lighting the garden itself; and if it is hot enough one may start the evening with an out-of-doors dinner, to which the performers and a few chosen guests are bidden. For this it is well to have a long table near a fountain, to deck it with a runner of heavy Italian lace and a lavish

Fish

Woodruff

centrepiece of fruit and flowers, and to light it from above with Japanese lanterns in soft colours and fantastic shapes, slung from long bamboo poles. The late summer fruits and those that are imported from Southern climes—pomegranates, persimmons, ripe figs and clusters of grapes, both purple and white—have a luxurious air when they are arranged in a high crystal dish. The flowers of late summer are also capable of much beauty. One may mass quantities of old-fashioned red roses in the centre of the table, or combine antirrhinums, mignonette and tiger lilies, long spikes of montbretia and some of the early flowering chrysanthemums in a bouquet that is almost Chinese in colour and feeling.

"The dinner itself should be planned so as to simplify service as much as possible. Hors d'œuvres such as canapés of olives stuffed with anchovies may be set ready in each place. The soup may be easily served as hot as it should be by having it kept (behind a rhododendron bush for choice) in a tureen set above a spirit lamp, and poured into little marmite pots just before it is handed. An aspic of sole or mullet or turbot; a casserole of Poulet Henri Quatre; a salad of very cold vegetable marrow decorated with mushrooms, tomatoes and green peas, dressed with mayonnaise and served as a separate course; little open tartlets of mulberries and whipped cream and the hottest of coffee—here is a menu of which the hot dishes are not likely to suffer from being out-of-doors, and the cold courses of which are attractive and easily prepared."

The twenties, it appears, was one glorious round of parties: "There was a good party at the Marchesa Malacrida's one afternoon . . . tea in the dining-room with its iron lilies and red brocades; upstairs (up the Botticelli stairs) cocktails and trays of caviare and cheese straws carried round to us by Sir Edward Worthington."

"A party we enjoyed was Mrs William Jowett's serious musical party, and her other entirely frivolous one for her more intimate friends, who had a children's party all dressed as children, the Fauntleroys, Alices in Wonderland and Struwwelpeters we all love. There were sugar cakes, crackers, presents and a conjuror, all the things appealing to children—some Bloomsburys and some members of the Russian Ballet were there, for have they not the childish spirit stronger than any? And they helped the more grown up to take the fences, as we used to say in Leicestershire!"

"At tea the other day Lady Ossulston's drawing-room was discussing parties and dance parties in particular, and why people feel it necessary to disguise the waiters as farmers to go in coster guise and dance to a barrel organ to get a proper thrill. As she says, the surprise element is always there without any need to supply it. Had she not been the night before to Sir Crisp English's dance and felt that there was something familiar about one or two of her partners? Where had she met them? Then a vague remembrance of white coats, rubber gloves, a curious whiff of—what? —crept back. They had operated on her!"

"The best party of the past fortnight—in its own genre, of course—has been Mrs Somerset Maugham's in her famous house in Chelsea, which is next to Lady Colefax's and almost opposite the Sitwells. Her parties are not made, they are designed. They are just one large social cocktail. For your wise hostess in these days knows it is as important to mix one's guests as one's drinks."

"Next Wednesday sees the grand climax of a record run of large-scale dances in the Santa Claus Ball at the Kit-Cat. A really witty pageant has long been needed, because so many of the parades have become a trifle pompous and pretentious. The characters will present a typical Christmas Dinner. Lady Grant will be Plum Pudding. Mrs Redmond McGrath Red Wine, Lady Dunn White Wine, Lady Ashley, Lady Jean Dalrymple, Dorothy Bethell, Lady Scarsdale, are all parts of the menu; while Lady Patricia Douglas is Mince Pie and Mrs McCorquodale, who is organising the pageant, is to be Champagne."

The decade ended with "one of the strangest parties ever given": "The great Shell-Mex Oil Company was host to four hundred at a sit-down supper at the May Fair on December 4th. After a cabaret, headed by Norah Holt and the Houston Sisters, all the great racing aces went round the floor in toy-cars! This idea of a great industrial organisation playing with night-life deserves to be encouraged and developed. It opens vast new possibilities."

But every Party was not perfect: ". . . it may be well in warning to detail the Worst Party. This took place last summer. On arriving I was handed the wrong ticket for my hat, and made to sit on the stairs outside closed doors. When the seemingly endless piece of music finished, the doors opened and I was shot into a large red drawing-room where the heat beat down in waves from the lustre chandelier, and desperate guests fought for window space. Supper brought no relief, for the hostess was so busy eating a hearty sit-down meal with royalty that we were left to snatch fearfully from a buffet groaning with heavy and unsuitable 'eats'. Clean plates or glasses there were none; and to our petitions the hired waiters returned an untimely hilarity. A painful scene followed in the cloakroom."

The twenties saw the blossoming of the fashion for eating out, and in May 1929 *Vogue* reasoned why: "Those who have taken houses for the Season have by now had trying experiences below stairs, which well explains the entirely modern vogue of the smart restaurant or club. Never were good cooks scarcer, or perhaps our taste is better travelled nowadays."

There were "terrible problems" about where to eat: "Gourmets have reported to *Vogue* that the notorious difficulty of finding the delights of the Russian table in London is no more, for a famous *maître d'hôtel* from St Petersburg is now in charge at the Green Park, so that you need not travel to the caveaux of Montmartre or the rue de la Bourse to taste good vodka and find real *zakuski*." "We are once again faced with that terrible problem of where to dine or sup during the season at Covent Garden. Those who intend to see the whole cycle of *The Ring* will have to decide whether they will go as usual to the Savoy for their hasty dinner, or to that convenient restaurant which M. Boulestin has provided for us. What a lot we have learnt from M. Boulestin; in fact, cooking in London has improved beyond belief since he started to tell us all about it."

Boulestin by Max Beerbohm

X. Marcel Boulestin had been persuaded to close his Leicester Square Restaurant and move to Southampton Street to open the Restaurant Boulestin because of its proximity to Covent Garden, and when *The Ring* was performed he had a trumpeter from the Opera House to sound Siegfried's fanfare ten minutes before the end of the dinner interval so that his diners could get to their seats on time. M. Boulestin had come to London before the First World War and was well known as a theatre critic. After serving as an interpreter with the British Forces he set up a shop called Modern Decoration and edited a book of pictures and articles—neither of which were a success. To stave off bankruptcy he gave French lessons and wrote articles on food and drink which were so good that friends persuaded him to write a book of recipes, which he did.

Boulestin's,
Southampton Street

In 1923 he began his *Finer Cooking* series for *Vogue*. And Finer Cooking it still is. Although it was written over fifty years ago, the menus and recipes are appropriate today. As are his complaints about the cost of food and his attitude to it: "No one, these days, can afford to waste materials, for materials are always more or less costly. Even if money did not count waste is stupid and wicked. It is immoral. But most people waste perfectly good things not out of wickedness but simply because they do not care; they do not realise the value and the sport of economy. For it becomes an amazing sport to make things do, to 'manage' this week on less than you did the week before." He wrote about food in a light and entertaining way, although he took the art of eating very seriously. He deplored "strong cocktails two seconds before you sit down to dinner, smoking between courses, hurried meals, let alone noise, bustle and jazz bands, typical evils of post-war civilisation".

He thought "The mellowing influence of good food on civilised beings cannot be under-rated, or its importance exaggerated. It is conducive to success and, which is more important, to happiness. . . . *Cuisine* should be taken seriously first of all by the cook (obviously, that is if she is worthy of the name) and also by both hostesses and guests. Yet the income tax and the servant problem combine in making life complicated, and that is where the personal element comes in tactfully and changes what might have been an indifferent dinner indifferently cooked into a delicious one with just that touch of the 'unexpected' which makes for success."

His menus were seldom more than three courses and he was constantly urging his *Vogue* readers to cook and serve vegetables *à la française* as a separate dish and complaining about "That queer English tradition, Sunday supper, responsible for more bad meals than it is possible to imagine—which seems surprising in a country where the *buffet froid* for luncheon is usually admirable; for a good 'veal and ham pie', a well-flavoured 'steak and kidney pudding', a noble roast beef are perfect of their kind, both as dishes and as national symbols."

The Finer Cooking

By X. MARCEL BOULESTIN

Food is of all times. A good dinner served in 1830 would be as good served to-day.

It goes deeper still: if you read today the *Memoirs of Casanova*, it is still a marvellous book, but a book of its period; while if you eat today the *filets de perdreaux aux bigarades* prepared as for the court of Versailles in the XVIIIth century it strikes you as exquisite; but simply as a dish it certainly has no XVIIIth century character. But if good food is of all times, the way of serving it changes according to the period. Horace Walpole is interesting on the subject:

"The last branch of our fashion into which the true observation of nature has been introduced is our desserts. Jellies, biscuits, sugar plums and crèmes have long since given way to harlequins, gondoliers, Turks, Chinese and Shepherdesses of Saxon China. By degrees meadows of cattle, of the same brittle materials, spread themselves over the table; cottages rose in sugar and temples in barley-sugar; pigmy Neptunes in cars of cockle shells triumphed over oceans of looking-glass or seas of silver tissue. At last even these puerile puppet-shows are sinking into disuse. Gigantic figures succeed to pigmies; and it is known that a celebrated confectioner (Lord Albemarle's) complained that, after having prepared a middle dish of gods and goddesses eighteen feet high, his lord would not cause the ceiling of his parlour to be demolished to facilitate their entrée. '*Imaginez-vous,*' said he, '*que milord n'a pas voulu faire ôter le plafond!*' "

Let this be the *morale* in the summing-up of our good resolutions: we must be prepared to *ôter le plafond*—or resolve to have things less ambitious, which, on the whole, is perhaps simpler.

Soupe à l'oignon gratinée

Get some large white onions, cut them in thin slices, melt some butter in a pan, and cook them till they are a nice brown colour. Then add a pinch of flour, a teaspoonful of beef stock, salt and pepper and sufficient water. Stir well, bring to the boil, and let it simmer till reduced by a quarter—that is to say, about twenty minutes.

Meanwhile, you have cut some thin slices of French bread, the long roll kind being the best, and dried them till very crisp in the oven. Now pour your onion soup into little earthenware soup tureens, one for each person; put two or three pieces of dried bread on the top of each, sprinkle freely with grated cheese (Gruyère preferably), and put them to *gratiner* in the oven.

Potage au cresson

Take one pound of floury potatoes and cook them in salt water, also take a bundle of watercress, clean it, remove the stalks, chop the leaves and add them to the potatoes when these are about three-quarters cooked. Squeeze through a wire sieve and put back in the saucepan with a certain quantity of water: cook a few minutes more without bringing to the boil; then add a little cream, see that it is well seasoned, bind with the yolk of an egg in which you have stirred a little lemon juice, and add just before serving a few leaves of watercress and chervil cut fine (not chopped, as they would look bruised). This refreshing soup, which must be the consistency of rather thin thick soup, is served with small croûtons of bread, fried perfectly crisp.

Soupe au poisson
Most people usually associate the fish soup either with Marseilles or with America; indeed, both the "bouillabaisse" and the "chowder" are well known and remarkably good when well prepared. But I came across some quite good fish soup at Boulogne last autumn during the famous "fish week", and I tasted a very pleasant one only the other day in a small village near Dinard. Needless to say, these dishes never appear on the menu of even the smallest hotel, probably because the patron thinks, rightly or wrongly, that they are not civilised enough for visitors; as a matter of fact, the food the patron and his wife have on a corner of the kitchen table is often better than the more elaborate dishes which are sent to the *table d'hôte*.

The fish soup, which is very popular with Breton fishermen, is simple to make and very pleasant. It is very different from the Provençal dish of the same type as no oil is used for the cooking and it does not contain crab, saffron, tomato or any of the ingredients which give the "bouillabaisse" its special flavour. You simply chop very fine and brown well in a good piece of the best butter what the Bretons call "*des herbes*", that is, spring onions and sorrel (about a handful), one carrot, one potato, a little parsley, chives and (unexpectedly) mint; add salt and pepper, boiling water, bring to the boil, put in some fish (it does not matter very much which as long as it is not a flat fish) and cook about twenty minutes. They eat it with bread and boiled potatoes, and as the man said all too modestly: "*Ça aide à faire passer le pain.*"

For a more civilised table, it will of course be better to pass it through a sieve, and remove the skin and bones of the fish before serving, but "*les herbes*" should be served with the pieces of fish.

Potage aux herbes maigres
Take a handful of sorrel, remove the stalks, and cut it very thin. Do the same to two lettuces and to a handful of chervil, and cook all these in butter till thoroughly soft and almost "melted"; then add hot water, salt and pepper, bring to the boil, and let it simmer for half-an-hour or so. Just before serving "bind it" by adding the yolks of two eggs, stirring them in quickly. If both sorrel and chervil are unobtainable, which sometimes happens in London, use instead spinach and parsley treated in the same fashion, but it should be remembered that spinach takes a little longer to cook than sorrel.

Soupe de chasse
Put in a saucepan three or four onions finely chopped, with a piece of butter the size of an egg. Melt the onions over a slow fire but do not let them get brown.

Add water (enough for five or six people, allowing a little more for reducing), bring to the boil, then put in one leek, a head of celery, parsley, thyme, bay leaf, clove and a little garlic, salt and pepper, also a pinch of sugar; let it boil gently for at least two hours.

Cut thin slices of stale bread, fry them in butter, and dispose them two or three deep in a warm soup tureen. Take a tablespoonful of potato flour, add to it a small quantity of good stock, mix well and see that it is smooth. To this you add, stirring quickly, the yolks of three eggs; mix well again and pour this into the soup, stir once more and pour the finished mixture over the bread in the soup tureen. Serve at once.

Potage à la purée de marrons
This is an old provincial recipe for chestnut soup; it is rather out of the ordinary and a pleasant change from the better-known kind of soups. Take a pound of chestnuts (for five or six people), remove the outer skin and boil them in a narrow and deep saucepan in salted water till the water begins to boil, after which you can easily remove the thin skin; then put at the bottom of a saucepan a clove, a bay leaf, a few small pieces of bacon, one large potato and a carrot cut in slices, salt and pepper; over this the chestnuts and water and cook them till they are soft. Drain them and pound them well, add a sufficient quantity of good stock, breadcrumbs (one slice of stale bread will do) the potato which has boiled with the chestnuts, and pass the whole thing through a sieve, so that it is as smooth as cream. Bring it to the boil and let it simmer a little while. Just before serving you can, if you like, "bind" it with either cream or the yolk of an egg. It should be served with croûtons crisply fried in butter and the consistency should be that of an ordinary thick soup.

Purée de marrons
Boil the peeled chestnuts in salted water, strain them and pass them through a sieve into a small saucepan. Add a piece of butter and some consommé. The purée should be a little thicker than potato purée.

Potage printanier
This soup, which is an adaptation of the soup beloved of the French peasant of the South, will be found pleasant and comforting for a typical English summer day. Get some young carrots and turnips, wash them well and scrape them lightly; their skin is still very thin and will come off easily. Also get a white cabbage, remove all the outside leaves and use the heart only; cut it in four quarters and the other vegetables in thin narrow slices; add the white part only of two or three leeks and cook all this very slowly in butter in a fireproof dish, keeping the lid on all the time. When tender, add some good clear soup, the heart of a lettuce cut in four, a handful of small fresh peas and a little chopped chervil. You should add clear soup in sufficient quantity so that there is enough for your purpose when it has been reduced by one-third, on a slow fire.

Taste it to see if it is properly seasoned and, just before serving, add in the yolk of one egg well beaten and mix it well with this pleasant mixture of spring vegetables.

Martin

Fish

The new cry now in England is "Eat more fish!" as it was about two years ago in France when the famous *Semaine du poisson* was started in seaside places. And the Ministry of Agriculture and Fisheries seem to have awakened to the real situation. They state in their recent report that "it is clear that fish as presented to the consumer is not sufficiently attractive to be given a permanent position as a principal item in the menu; and that if the home market is to expand it is essential to educate the consumers to the dietetic value of good fresh fish, and at the same time ensure that supplies of such fish, at prices which will enable it to compete with all classes of meat, are continuously available."

As a matter of fact, good fish in England is expensive, and, moreover, there is very little choice; when you have had in turn sole, turbot, lobster and salmon, you have exhausted the list of most fishmongers. It is rare to find either grey or red mullet or langouste, and almost impossible to obtain freshwater fish and lamprey—all of which are great delicacies. Yet the last specially used to be much appreciated in England, and one of the kings died of having too much of that good thing. There is no danger of that nowadays; indeed only twice in six months have I been able to have lampreys, and they had to be sent specially from Worcestershire; but I must say it was worth the trouble.

The Romans thought very highly of fish and were very particular about the way it should be cooked and served. Dr King, in one of his letters to Dr Lister on the subject of Apicius's gastronomic work, says: "It seems that Seneca the Philosopher (a Man from whose morose Temper little good in the Art of Cookery could be expected) in his third Book of Natural Questions, correcting the Luxury of the Times, says, the Romans were come to that Daintiness that they would not eat a Fish unless upon the same Day it was taken, that it might taste of the Sea, as they express it; and therefore had 'em brought by Persons who rode Post, and made a great Out-cry, whereupon all other People were oblig'd to give them the Road. It was an usual Expression for a Roman to say, In other Matters I may confide in you, but in a thing of this Weight it is not consistent with my Gravity and Prudence, I will trust nothing but my own Eyes, bring the Fish hither, let me see him breathe his last."

I understand that in Jamaica it was customary for the people who live in the mountains to have their fish brought straight from the sea by relays of negroes running all through the night so that the fish arrived delightfully fresh for breakfast. These negroes usually died young or of heart failure. The whole thing is truly Roman and no doubt this custom dates from the days of slavery.

In England trains and lorries help us in these matters, and as London is very near the sea, it seems a pity that you cannot find at the fishmongers all the variety of fish which you find, for instance, in Paris.

Poisson poché aux groseilles

Having poached your fish or cooked it in a court bouillon (you can use cod, mackerel or turbot), prepare the following sauce to serve with it. Put a quarter of a pound of green gooseberries in hot water till they become soft, drain them well and put them in a small saucepan with half a glass of veal stock, seasoning, a little *jus*; cook a little, bind with a puddingspoonful of potato flour; add little by little small pieces of butter and cook a few minutes longer.

Poisson farci au vin blanc

Take a good-sized carp, or a pike, and remove the head; wash the fish and clean it and wipe the inside. Sprinkle it with salt and pepper, both inside and out, and leave it in a cloth till the following day.

Prepare the stuffing as follows: streaky bacon and ham, a little cold roast veal, a small slice of stale bread, parsley, two shallots, salt and pepper, all passed through a sieve or a mincing machine; add a drop of white wine and stuff the fish with this mixture.

Put the fish in a fireproof dish, cover it with white wine and cook it in the oven. When it is about half-cooked sprinkle over it some of the stuffing and a few breadcrumbs and finish cooking, being careful to regulate the heat so that the wine sauce does not evaporate altogether.

Crab jambalaya

Chop two onions very fine and brown them in a pan; add a puddingspoonful of flour (and stir well), also, chopped together, thyme, bay leaf, parsley, one head of garlic; fry these for a few minutes, then add chili pepper and three large tomatoes cut in very small pieces; let the mixture simmer for about ten minutes, after which you add the necessary quantity of boiling stock, that is, about half a pint, also a glass of dry white wine.

Bring to the boil, throw in your already cooked rice, about half a pound, the flesh of two crabs (previously boiled, of course), see that it is highly flavoured and seasoned and cook for about twenty minutes, stirring occasionally. Serve very hot.

Coquilles St Jacques

This recipe comes from the famous *Chapon Fin* at Bordeaux. It is a delicious dish and by far the best way of serving a shellfish already delicious, and which, judging from the prices it fetches at fishmongers, as compared with those of crab and lobster, seems unfairly despised in England. Wash the scallops well, boil them in salted water and chop the red part and the white part together with a tomato, a little onion, parsley, a few mushrooms, salt and pepper. Cook this for a few minutes in butter, bind it with a little béchamel sauce, fill the shells with the mixture and brown in the oven.

Homard crème au porto

Cut in sections the tail of a lobster and cut in two the rest. This should be done over a small basin so as not to lose the water contained in the shell; you must also add to it the "insides", which will be used later for the "binding" of the sauce. Season the pieces of flesh with salt and pepper and fry them in very hot oil, turning them on all sides. Remove the pieces of lobster, keep them hot; remove also the oil from the pan and put instead a piece of butter the size of a walnut. Put in a puddingspoonful of very finely chopped onions, let them get brown; add then two shallots also finely chopped. Put back the pieces of lobster, a glass of good port wine, let it reduce by half, after which you add a tumblerful of cream previously heated.

Cook about twenty minutes, remove the lobster once more, add the insides of the lobster, a drop of brandy, a few pieces of butter, leave this on a slow fire a few minutes, add a little more butter and squeeze through a muslin over the pieces of lobster. Serve with this a dish of rice. This way of cooking lobster or *langouste* is, of course, a little more complicated than boiling or grilling it, but it is worth the extra trouble.

Baked mackerel

Slit some mackerel down the middle, having first cut off the heads and tails. Remove the backbone, scrape the fish with a blunt knife and dry them well. Roll them and place them in a deep baking dish with salt, pepper and one or two black peppercorns. Fill the dish with a mixture of three parts vinegar to one of water, and add one bay leaf, one capsicum, and a little grated nutmeg. Bake in a very slow oven for at least four hours. The vinegar must not be allowed to reach the boiling point as the fish should remain firm and unbroken. Serve quite cold.

Martin

Rougets au fenouil

Take some red mullets, dry and score them; put in a fireproof dish a mixture of butter and oil and a few pieces of fennel and two tomatoes cut in quarters, dispose your mullets over these and bake in the oven. Season them with salt and pepper and when cooked remove them to another dish and keep them hot. Add a glass of white wine and a glass of Madeira to the stock in the first dish, and go on cooking till well reduced. Pass through a fine sieve.

Prepare a *maître d'hôtel* butter (there should be a good amount of lemon juice in it), with this you bind your sauce; see that it is well seasoned and pour it over the red mullets in the serving dish.

Rougets marseillaise

Take several mullets (one large one is enough for two people) and put them in hot olive oil in a flat saucepan; season them and cook a few minutes on both sides. Peel two or three tomatoes, remove the seeds, cut them in small pieces, and add chopped onion, parsley and a little garlic. Cover the mullets with this mixture and add half a glass of dry white wine. Bring to the boil, put the lid on the saucepan and finish cooking in the oven. The sauce should reduce by half. When cooked carefully move the mullets to a serving dish and pour the sauce over them.

Sole bretonne

Skin the sole, remove the fins and slice it the whole length in the middle; lift the fillets and insert little pieces of salt butter worked with a little parsley and lemon juice. Cook it in butter in a frying-pan, turning it once; add before serving more salt, pepper and a little more lemon. This way of cooking a sole is very simple and delicious, being a little more than a fried one and a little less than a sole *meunière*.

Filets de sole Dorothée

The sole having been filleted, put in a small saucepan the head and bones, one onion in slices, one carrot, thyme, bay leaf, clove, salt and pepper, a glass of water and a glass of dry white wine, bring to the boil, and reduce it on a slow fire for about twenty minutes. Pass it through a muslin and keep it warm. Sprinkle the fillets with salt and paprika and cook them in butter, then *flambez* them with a little good brandy; mix together this butter and brandy and the sauce previously prepared, add small mushrooms, a glass of fresh cream, a little lemon juice, and pour it very hot over the fillets. It is advisable for this dish, as for all dishes which are *flambés*, to use really good brandy, and not the kind generally sold as cooking brandy, which is useless for the purpose, having no strength and no flavour.

Paupiettes de sole Elisabeth

Take some fillets of sole, roll them and fill them with the stuffing described below; tie them and cook them slowly in Chablis or any other dry white wine mixed with fish stock. Drain them well and keep them hot.

Cook the stock a little longer till it has reduced by half, then add a glass of béchamel sauce and a glass of fresh cream, a little grated Parmesan and a few pieces of butter.

Season well, cook a few minutes and squeeze through a muslin. Keep hot in a *bain marie*.

Have as many *fonds d'artichauts* as there are fillets, previously sautéed in butter (tinned *fonds d'artichauts* do not need poaching first), put on each a few chopped truffles, lay over this one paupiette of sole, pour some sauce over, sprinkle with a little grated cheese, brown quickly and serve at once.

The stuffing to be prepared in the following manner: take some stale breadcrumbs and soak them in milk, reduce to a pulp and "bind" with the yolk of an egg; add double the quantity of raw fish (pike or whiting), salt it and pound well together for a few minutes; add one or two more yolks of eggs according to quantity of stuffing wanted, fresh butter worked to a cream and seasoning; and before using see that the stuffing is perfectly smooth.

For the fish stock necessary for this dish (also very useful for cooking other kinds of fillets of sole), put in a small saucepan the head and bones of the fish, slices of mushroom and carrot, thyme, bay leaf, parsley, cloves, salt and pepper, a glass of water, a glass of white wine, bring to the boil and reduce on a slow fire.

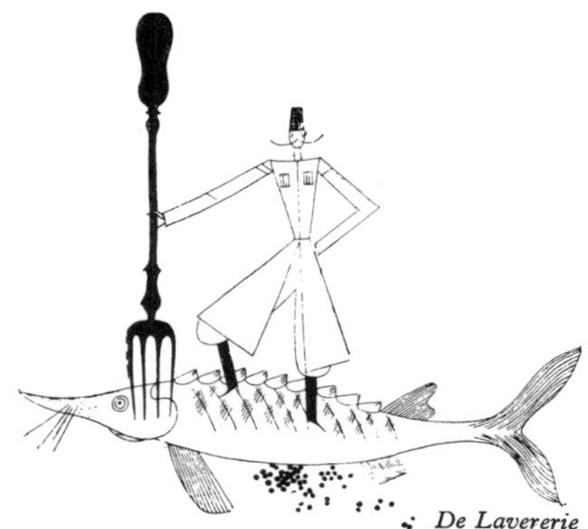

De Laverie

Sole normande

Take a fine sole, skin it and put it in a fireproof dish with several pieces of butter, salt, pepper, a little grated nutmeg and a glassful of good white wine. Bake it in a moderate oven for about half an hour, basting occasionally, then remove it and keep it warm while the sauce is being made. For this you want a few prawns (shelled), a dozen or so of mussels already cooked (which means simply boiling them for a few minutes in salt water with a *bouquet*, when they open and you can easily remove them from the shells), and the stock in which the mussels have been cooked.

Put in a small saucepan all the gravy from the sole, two spoonfuls of the mussel stock, the mussels and the prawns, cook it for a few minutes, bind it with butter in which you have cooked a little flour, cook a little more, add a small quantity of cream, pour the sauce over your sole and serve very hot.

Sole en matelote

This dish, although it has not the reputation of the *sole normande*, is a very favourite dish both in Brittany and Normandy. Skin the sole, put it in a fireproof dish, cover the sole with a mixture in equal parts of water and dry cider, salt, pepper, and a *bouquet*. Cook about twenty-five minutes, then put the gravy in a small saucepan, remove the *bouquet*, bind as described above, pour it over the fish and sprinkle over it very fine brown breadcrumbs and serve at once.

Filets de sole à la crème

Take some fillets of sole, fold them in two and poach them for a few minutes in a glass of Chablis or Graves with a tablespoonful of chopped mushrooms, salt and pepper. Remove these and the fish and keep them hot. Let the wine reduce by half, add a glass of cream, mix well, cook a little, see that it is well seasoned, add a few small pieces of butter and pour over the fillets of sole. Serve at once.

For all these *liaisons* with cream, it is better to do the mixing not by stirring with a spoon, but simply by shaking the dish till the sauce is perfectly smooth.

Filets de sole Robin

Have some fillets of sole fried quite crisp and not coated with breadcrumbs, and serve very hot with the following icy cold sauce by way of contrast.

Whip some fresh cream to a stiff froth, season well with salt, pepper and a little wine vinegar, and mix with it a tomato sauce well reduced and thick; stir well, whip a little more and stand in ice for about one hour.

The contrast and the lightness of that sauce, which is really a mousse, are delicious, but see that it is served on a cold plate, otherwise it will "thaw" in the most disastrous manner, and the effect will be *raté*.

Filets de sole Veron

Put in a small saucepan a tumblerful of wine vinegar with two chopped shallots and a bouquet of thyme, bay leaf and tarragon, reduce it by half and add two tablespoonfuls of good béchamel sauce; bind with three yolks of eggs and cook very slowly till the mixture has the consistency of a rather stiff mayonnaise sauce. Add then a little less than a quarter of a pound of butter divided into small pieces, see that it is properly seasoned and squeeze through a muslin, after which you add a tablespoonful of parsley, chervil, and tarragon leaves, chopped very fine, also a tablespoonful of good tomato sauce.

This delicious sauce is to be served with either fillets of sole or fillets of brill, which then should be cooked not only nicely browned in butter, but literally swimming in butter. It gives the fish an incomparable richness which is happily counter-balanced by the pleasant sharpness and the spicy taste of the sauce.

Truites au chablis

Have some small trout, dispose them in a small fireproof dish, with, all round, tomatoes cut in quarters, one banana cut in thin slices, tarragon and shallots finely chopped. Pour over all this a glass of Chablis (or Pouilly), season well, and cook very slowly; turn them carefully when they are about half done. When they are ready, remove the skins and keep the fish hot; let the sauce reduce a little more, then pass it through a fine sieve. Dispose the trout in the fireproof dish; add some *sauce hollandaise* to the sauce, little by little, over a very slow fire and whipping all the time. When it has the right consistency pour over the trout and serve at once.

Meat, Poultry, Game

The English habit of not talking about food strikes the foreigner, however long he may have stayed in England, as a very queer one—indeed, as a quite unnatural custom. It seems somehow so aloof and so ungrateful—that is, needless to say, if the dinner has been good (in other cases, on the whole, silence is better than any exhibition of peevishness or pained surprise).

But think of a pleasant and successful dinner-party of, say, twelve people. Try to visualise the preparations: the hostess carefully supervising the menu; the cook up at dawn (at least, I like to think so) all eagerness and ingenuity, the kitchenmaid trying to peel the vegetables even better than she usually does; the husband bringing up the wine after breakfast so that it should be *chambré* to perfection; five women in their own houses wondering what to wear and if the meal will be up to the mark; five men thinking dreamily about that vintage port or that '65 brandy they have a remembrance of being offered. Then, the last few moments before the curtain (or rather the kitchen lift) goes up: anxiety, peace, despair, hope, felt in turn with equal intensity, bring the cook to the verge of a nervous breakdown; of course if "they" are late the fillets of sole will be "burnt to a cinder, dear, and the cream sauce curdled . . ." a strong cup of tea specially brewed by the faithful kitchenmaid brings her round. . . . And the meal, *on a fait des folies*, even *primeurs* sent by aeroplane from Paris. Then, not one word, not one about the whole affair. Dish after dish is carelessly eaten as if the performance was rather a bore, the *mot d'ordre* being: not to pay any attention to anything so gross as food.

In fact, twelve people "upstairs" and at least four "downstairs" have been thinking of nothing else for some time and have, no doubt, immensely enjoyed the evening, yet they remain strangely and inhumanly silent. No one made a remark, even condescendingly, about that specially delicious sauce, and even the Cheval Blanc 1911 was offered without any introduction. (No doubt it was drunk in beautiful old cut glass goblets filled to the brim and entirely wrong for the wine.) Not so in France; you know at least what you are drinking and eating. It is true that the epicure who said that when you were eating a fine dish "*il faut en parler, avant, pendant, après*" was perhaps slightly overdoing it. But one should talk about food and wine; they taste better if you do. For words have an occult power which we cannot afford to overlook: and there is no doubt that good food likes to be praised.

Côtelettes d'agneau au four

Take two large onions, cut them in thin slices and cook them in butter for a few minutes only; cut also in thin slices about half a pound of good potatoes (the long yellow kind being in this case preferable to the large white floury ones); put potatoes and onions in a well-buttered fireproof dish; add salt and pepper and a claret glassful of beef stock. Cook for about one hour in a moderate oven.

Take six lamb cutlets well trimmed and brown them in butter both sides, then bury them in the bed of potatoes and onions, adding here and there a few small pieces of butter and finish cooking in the oven. You must put in the cutlets just at the right moment, so that they are nicely done just when the potatoes are getting a golden brown colour. It is also essential to put in the correct amount of beef stock, which should have entirely disappeared when the dish is ready: if you put too little, the potatoes will probably "catch"; if you put too much they will be sodden instead of being in that state which is an agreeable mixture of softness and crispness.

Gigot d'agneau aux pointes d'asperges

Prepare a nice leg of lamb, place it in a casserole on a bed of carrots, onions, bacon rind and broken bones, and put the casserole on a slow fire for about twenty minutes, put it aside a little while and then add a glassful of good stock, salt and pepper, cover it with buttered paper and cook it in the oven, basting often.

Prepare a béchamel sauce with very little milk, add to it the gravy from the braised lamb (having skimmed off the fat), some asparagus tips cooked in the ordinary way, and sautéed in butter, and cover the lamb with this sauce. Have some more asparagus tips round the dish or at each end.

Gigot Pravaz

Having secured a fine leg of lamb or mutton, prepare in a port glass the following mixture: two liqueur glasses of good brandy, one bay leaf, two cloves, one small piece of garlic, one sprig of thyme, six peppercorns coarsely broken —all this to soak undisturbed for twelve hours. Then take a hypodermic syringe for intra muscular injections (it should be large enough to contain the above, and the needle rather strong), and inject the solution very slowly in the meat in four or five places, taking care not to shake the deposit at the bottom of the glass. The meat must then rest for at least two hours, to give the solution time to penetrate and flavour. The preparations finished, we come to the actual cooking of the piece. There are two ways:

1. Boiled in the manner called in France *à l'anglaise*, for which you wrap the leg of mutton in a white cloth, put it in boiling water with salt, pepper (unbroken), carrots, onions, bay leaf, and cook it a quarter of an hour to the pound.
2. Roasted on a bed of potatoes, onions, carrots, all sliced, and mixed together.

Brochettes

Cut in pieces about one inch and a half square some lean veal and some liver, also cut some very thin pieces of streaky bacon and one or two truffles in slices. Put them on silver skewers—so that each person has his little *brochette*—in the following order: a slice of bacon, a piece of veal, a slice of bacon, a slice of truffle, a slice of bacon, a piece of liver, a slice of bacon and so on. Grill for a few minutes, if possible on a charcoal fire (it really makes the whole difference in the world), exposing in turn each side to the fire, and sprinkling with salt and pepper during the process.

Paupiettes de veau

Have some well trimmed, thin escalopes of veal, flatten them well and season with pepper, salt and a little paprika.

Prepare also a stuffing in the following way: a few *cèpes*, a rasher of bacon, two truffles chopped finely (the *cèpes* and the bacon should, of course, be fried first), very little bread-crumbs, a small piece of *foie gras* reduced to a purée—all this well mixed together, well seasoned and bound with a yolk of egg.

Each escalope to be spread all over with this mixture, rolled and tied, then cooked in a fireproof dish or a copper *sauteuse* with a little butter.

When they are ready, remove them to a serving dish, put in the *sauteuse* a glass of white wine and a glass of sherry, reduce quickly and pour over the escalopes. Add as garniture a few mushrooms and slices of truffles.

Escalopes de veau Tzarine

Take some thin escalopes of veal, flatten them well and cook them in butter; they should be well browned; remove them and keep them hot. Put in the pan about a glassful of cream, mix well, add a tablespoonful of good chicken stock, a few pieces of butter and let all this reduce. Squeeze this sauce through a muslin, add to it a little fennel chopped and previously poached, pour it on the escalopes and serve with slices of cucumber *à la crème*. The cucumber for this dish should be cooked slowly in butter till soft, after which you add a little cream, salt and pepper and a very little grated nutmeg—and arranged around the escalopes of veal in the serving dish.

Veau au citron

Take a good piece of veal, trim it well and put it in a casserole with salt, pepper, a little chopped parsley, and no more than a puddingspoonful of water. Add a sprinkling of cinnamon and nutmeg, keep covered and cook slowly. One hour afterwards add the juice of several lemons (about two lemons to each pound of veal) and go on cooking slowly with the lid on till ready.

Rôti de veau braisé

Get a good piece of veal, preferably in the ribs, but see that the butcher does not cut it into chops. Bone it and trim it carefully, flatten it. If there is a kidney place it in the middle, and, having sprinkled the whole thing both sides with salt and pepper, roll it like a galantine and tie it well. Brown it in butter.

At the same time prepare in a buttered fireproof dish a bed of vegetables, carrots, onions cut in small pieces, a little bacon, and parsley finely chopped, water it with a glass of dry white wine, add a drop of vinegar and let your veal rest on this. Bake in a moderate oven, basting often.

Before serving squash the vegetables and pass the gravy obtained through a sieve; remove the string, serve the veal, covered with the gravy.

Poulet sauté à la crème

Joint a young chicken and put it in a casserole with about one ounce of butter, two small onions, thyme and a bay leaf. Salt and cook, with the lid on, on a moderate fire. When the chicken is nearly done, remove thyme, bay leaf and onions, add a pinch of flour and cook another ten minutes, stirring often. Then add one tablespoonful of water, three of dry white wine, let it simmer and add little by little about one shilling's worth of cream (about $\frac{1}{2}$ pint) cook again for about twenty minutes on a very slow fire, sprinkle with freshly ground pepper and serve. The addition of either small mushrooms or *fonds d'artichauts* is recommended, but not necessary.

Poulet sauté à la crème *another version*
Take a spring chicken and cut in five pieces, wings, legs and breast, and season it with salt and pepper. Melt some butter in a saucepan with one head of garlic and two shallots (these should not be chopped); cook the chicken for ten minutes; remove it, add to the butter a glass of port wine, let this reduce a little, then add a tumblerful of cream, put back the chicken and cook another ten minutes or a little more, by which time it should be ready. Remove it, dispose it in a serving dish and keep it hot. Add to the sauce a piece of *foie gras* the size of an egg and a little lobster butter, whip well so that it is perfectly smooth and pour over your chicken through a fine strainer.

Crêpes Nicole
This dish and the following one are extremely useful for utilising remnants of chicken. Although they belong, so to speak, to the bargain basement, they are worthy of a place of honour in the shop window.

Take whatever meat is left out of a roasted chicken or of a poached one as the case may be, cut in small cubes and toss these lightly in butter, season and sprinkle with paprika. Do the same to a few fresh mushrooms; mix together mushrooms and pieces of chicken, add a little cream, just enough to moisten the mixture, and keep it hot.

Prepare a good béchamel sauce and a few pancakes, done in the classical French manner (omitting the small quantity of sugar which is usually put in the batter). Dispose on each pancake some of the mixture, roll it, and arrange all the pancakes in a long fireproof dish. Add a yolk of egg to the béchamel sauce, mix well, pour over the pancakes, sprinkle a little grated cheese, and brown quickly in a salamander or under the grill. Serve at once.

Timbales landaises
Take remnants of roasted chicken and cut these in small pieces; toss them in butter and season well. Make a little roux (not too much of it and not too much flour), add small pieces of bacon, chopped olives, a little fried onion (also chopped) and a few sweet peppers cut in thin pieces. Cook all this on a slow fire in a saucepan. See that it is well seasoned, and just before serving bind with a yolk of egg and add a little lemon juice. Serve in little *timbales,* one or two for each person according to size and appetite.

De Lavererie

Coq au vin
Take a young chicken and cut in six pieces. Put in a casserole three rashers of streaky bacon cut in dice, a good piece of butter and a dozen button onions—all this to melt slowly over the fire: then, the classical *bouquet,* a tiny piece of chopped garlic, a few sliced mushrooms and the chicken well seasoned. Cook on a quick fire with the lid on, so that the chicken is a nice golden colour; shake occasionally. See that it is well cooked and when ready season the pieces of chicken and keep them hot. Skim off from the gravy the excess of fat and prepare a small brown roux, just enough to "bind" the gravy (it should not be thickened too much); mix well together, add a glass of brandy and a tumblerful of claret or burgundy; put back the pieces of chicken and and let the whole thing reduce over a slow fire.

Capon au chablis
Take a fine capon and cut it, according to the size, in six or eight pieces, fry it lightly in butter and season it; when it is about three-quarters cooked drain the butter from the saucepan and put instead a glass of Chablis and the juice of a lemon, also a few fresh mushrooms. Cover the saucepan and finish cooking with the lid on all the time. Then remove the bird and the mushrooms and add to the sauce a small quantity of *velouté* and a glass of fresh cream; sprinkle a little nutmeg and let the same reduce for a little while. Dispose the pieces of capon nicely in a serving dish, pour the sauce over and serve, as a garniture, braised endives.

TWO ESSENTIALS
The two dishes described above are not really difficult to prepare; they only require a little attention and quickness, also a certain lightness of touch. One of the essential things is to keep really hot the pieces of chicken or capon, as, if they are allowed to grow too cold, it will mean that the sauce which is added at the last stage of the process will have to be cooked too long at the end. As for these sauces themselves, it is absolutely useless for the cook to attempt them with success if she will not taste them until they are perfectly right. The idea, unfortunately prevalent in England, that you can cook by the clock and the thermometer is utterly ridiculous—you must taste.

Nantais au chambertin
An exquisite dish, in the making of which the best duck from Nantes and the best wine from Burgundy collaborate harmoniously. Prepare a duck as for roasting and wrap it in thin fat bacon. Put in a cocotte two onions, two carrots, a little celery and one piece of garlic, all chopped fairly fine, also a *bouquet,* a quarter of a pound mixed of veal and beef cut in small squares and a calf's foot. (All these must first be sautéed in butter.) Cook on a slow fire for about ten minutes, then add a bottle of Chambertin (or Pommard) and a bottle of consommé. Add the duck and cook about thirty-five minutes or so, according to its size. Drain it well, remove the bacon and keep it warm. Keep the sauce simmering till reduced by half, then bind it with butter well worked with a wooden spoon. Bring to the boil, keep it on about a quarter of an hour, then remove it from the fire, add small pieces of fresh butter and pass through a fine muslin. add as garniture a few small onions (previously prepared) little button mushrooms, a rasher of bacon and

the calf's foot, these last two ingredients being cut in thin slices. This dish should be served without any accompaniment of vegetable.

Faisan poché au céleri

Prepare as for roasting a fine pheasant and cook it in a stock made in the following manner, which must have cooked already one hour before using.

Put in a saucepan two onions and two carrots finely chopped, a *bouquet garni*, half a head of celery and half a pound of beef and veal and two pints of consommé; salt and pepper. When properly cooked put in the pheasant and cook it about half an hour according to size.

Remove it, drain it and keep warm. With the stock prepare a *velouté*. Remove to the corner of the stove and add, whipping all the time, three ounces of butter (in small pieces) and two tablespoonfuls of cream. See that it is hot. Put the pheasant in a cocotte dish, garnish with braised celery and pour over the sauce squeezed through a muslin.

Pigeons marocaine

Take several pigeons, allowing a half for each person, and cook them slowly in butter (cut in two or four pieces according to size) for a few minutes. Take also a handful of button onions, cut them in four and add them to the birds. Shake the pan occasionally, season with salt and freshly ground pepper and add, a little later, a tumblerful of white wine, a handful of blanched almonds and Malaga raisins (the pips should be removed) and a pinch of mixed spices. Let all this simmer till the pigeons are really well cooked and serve very hot.

Cailles fourrées

Take some fat quails and stuff them with minced meat prepared as described below. Put in a deep fireproof dish or a cocotte two or three rashers of fat bacon, one onion and one carrot cut in slices, salt, pepper, and a pinch of mixed spice, also two juniper berries crushed. Dispose the quails on this bed and cook very slowly till ready (about a quarter of an hour). Pour the gravy through a muslin over the quails in the serving dish.

Farce.—There are many ways of stuffing quails, but on the whole the best are the following:

1. Mince finely remnants of roast chicken, one or two mushrooms, add very little breadcrumbs, mix well, season with pepper and salt and bind together with marrow fat.

2. Mash some *foie gras,* season it with salt and pepper, a pinch of mixed spice, add a little fresh cream, a teaspoonful of port wine, the yolk of an egg, and mix well.

When the quails are stuffed with either of these preparations, the opening should be sewn (the thread to be removed before serving). Some people cook the birds for a minute or two in butter before putting them in the cocotte.

Râble de lièvre à la crème

Marinade for forty-eight hours a saddle of hare in vinegar, with salt, peppercorns, a *bouquet* and a little piece of garlic. Take it out and dry well, and put it in a saucepan with some butter and a little paprika. When it is three parts cooked remove it and keep it hot. Add to the saucepan a teacupful of cream, stir well and cook until you have a thick sauce; see that it is well seasoned and pass it through a fine sieve into a clean saucepan with a few pieces of butter. Put the hare into this sauce and simmer gently until it is well cooked.

Civet de lièvre

Cut the hare in smallish pieces and fry them a few minutes in a saucepan. Put in another saucepan a *hachis* made with shallots, parsley and streaky bacon, cook a few minutes, then add a little flour, a tablespoonful of good stock, salt and pepper, a little grated nutmeg and a tumblerful of claret. Add the hare, stir well, and let it simmer with lid on at least three hours. Halfway through add the liver and the lungs of the hare, finely chopped, and a few minutes before serving add a few button mushrooms and a drop of brandy. It should be remembered that the hare should not weigh more than about six pounds, as the flesh of bigger hares is liable to be tough.

Here is a recipe in its original splendour together with several others for preparing rabbit, dating from the year 1805.

A rabbit pye

"Truse two small Rabbits, then Season 'em with pepper and salt, put 'em in a Pye, raised oval or square. Then put to 'em a little strong broth and a little butter, close your Pye and bake it, and against it comes out of the oven, have redy made a Ragoo, brown, with butter and flower (a little brown only) good gravy, Morrells, Truffels, Mushrooms and Cocks Combs, Pallets, Sweetbreads, Asparagus topps boyld tender, put to 'em a little Melted Butter. Shake these well together, poure it in our Pan. Garnish with ye Lidd Cutt and Serve it hott."

Lapereau à la minute

Having cleaned the rabbit and wiped it well with a cloth, cut it in pieces; put a quarter of a pound of butter in a saucepan; when it has melted put in the pieces of meat together with salt and pepper, spices and grated nutmeg. Cook on a quick fire, ten minutes will do. Two minutes before it is ready throw in the saucepan two or three shallots and parsley finely chopped. Shake well, see that it is well seasoned, and serve.

Lapereau sauté au chablis

Cook the rabbit in the same way as directed above. When it is ready, remove the saucepan from the fire, sprinkle the meat with flour (not more than a puddingspoonful) and add a good glass of Chablis (or Graves or any dry French white wine—not sherry or Madeira, which are too full flavoured and would change the character of the dish). Shake and stir well, put on a slow fire to cook a few minutes. See that the sauce is well *liée* and smooth, also that it does not reach the boiling point.

Cuisses de lapereau en papillotes

The legs of rabbit can be utilised in this pleasant way. First make some lardons the size of your larding needle, roll them well in salt, pepper and spices and insert them in the legs. Put these in a saucepan with butter and cook them about half an hour, turning them once or twice. Sprinkle them with *fines herbes à papillotes*; cook slowly ten minutes; then dispose your legs of rabbit on a board well coated with the *fines herbes* and let them grow cold.

Meanwhile, prepare the paper for the *papillotes*. Take a sheet of paper large enough, and paint it with melted butter or oil; put in the middle of it a thin rasher of streaky bacon, on the top of it one leg of rabbit with its *fines herbes*: fold the paper over, pleat the ends together, gather and tie them well so that the butter and the gravy cannot escape. Cook in a slow oven for about half an hour, turning the *papillotes* once (the original recipe, of course, says grill on charcoals). The heat of the oven should be well regulated so that the paper does not burn. Serve if you like with a *sauce diable* or sharp sauce of some kind.

FOR VEAL OR RABBIT

Fines herbes à papillotes

The *fines herbes* should be prepared as follows: chop very finely three rashers of streaky bacon, four mushrooms, and cook these a few minutes in a small saucepan with butter; a few minutes later add two or three shallots also finely chopped, cook two minutes more and add a tablespoonful of chopped parsley, salt, pepper, spices and grated nutmeg. Mix well. Your *fines herbes* are ready for your *papillotes*. Veal cutlets are also very good treated and cooked *en papillotes* and you can, if you like, add a little tomato purée to the preparation.

There are many other ways of cooking leveret or rabbit; it is delicious *en purée* as a *gibelotte* or *en filets sautés* with mushrooms and a well-flavoured cream sauce, but the thing to remember is that it must be well seasoned as the flesh is rather tasteless. Rabbit indifferently cooked, needless to say, is not worth eating.

Cecil Beaton

Aïoli

This sauce is given here *à titre de curiosité* or for the few English people who are not afraid of a strong smell of garlic. It is a classical sauce in Provençe and really delicious. Take four heads of garlic, pound them in a mortar and add the yolks of two eggs, then olive oil (the very best) drop by drop, stirring meanwhile with the pestle as you would do for a mayonnaise sauce with a spoon. Stop occasionally to squeeze in the sauce a little lemon juice. When you have used about four tablespoonfuls of oil, put in a puddingspoonful of warm water, which ought to give the sauce the right consistency, which must be that of a stiff, smooth mayonnaise. Serve with the boiled fish together with plain boiled potatoes, and retire from your most British friends for a day or so. The taste is marvellous, but the bouquet, so to speak, strong and persistent.

Béchamel sauce

Put in a saucepan on a slow fire a piece of butter the size of a small egg and a tablespoonful of flour; cook for a few minutes and add a little beef stock, stirring all the time. Then add a glass of milk, salt, pepper and a little nutmeg. Mix well and cook for a quarter of an hour, stirring occasionally, after which you add a few pieces of butter and pass through a sieve.

Beurre d'anchois

Take four fillets of anchovy, pound them well in a mortar with a good piece of butter.

Sauce Bercy

Chop very finely together parsley, chives and two shallots, add a little lemon juice; work all these well with a good piece of butter.

For these *beurres* you want a piece the size of an egg for a steak large enough for three. There are other sauces often served in France with grillades; one of the best is the *sauce bordelaise* which comes from Bordeaux.

Sauce bordelaise

Put in a small saucepan a chopped shallot and half a glass of white wine, cook it so that it reduces to a spoonful, also poach the marrow of a bone and cut in small cubes, add these to the sauce with a little piece of butter, seasoning and chopped parsley. Cook for a minute or so and either pour it over your entrecote or serve in a small (and very hot) sauceboat.

Sauce aux grenouilles

Take twelve frogs, wash and clean them well under the cold tap. Put in a saucepan a good-sized piece of butter, melt it, add two small onions, chopped, salt and pepper and the frogs. Cook all this on a moderate fire for ten minutes without browning. Meanwhile mix well in a bowl a tablespoonful of flour and a cup of bouillon, see that it is smooth and add it to the saucepan. Cook rather slowly, and stirring occasionally, about half an hour. Pass, then, the whole mixture through a fine sieve; the small bones of the frogs ought to come off easily, remove them and mash the flesh through the sieve into a bowl. Stir well, add a piece of butter, stir again, then bind with a yolk of egg and add at the same time a little chopped parsley.

This curious sauce has a remarkably fine and indefinable taste. It is served with macaroni or any kind of pasta or Alsatian *farinages*.

Sauce Armando

Prepare a béchamel sauce well seasoned, see that it is very soft—if in doubt, squeeze through a muslin and about five minutes before it is ready add a little lemon juice and a spoonful of shredded watercress, and just before serving a few pieces of fresh butter. Only the tenderest leaves should be used and they should not be chopped, but cut with a knife.

Sauce hollandaise

This is the simplest way of making a good *sauce hollandaise*: put in a small saucepan two tablespoonfuls of wine vinegar and a little pepper, reduce it by three-quarters. Put in a basin the yolks of four eggs, mix them well with about one ounce of butter, and pour over the mixture the hot vinegar you have reduced. Stir all the time on a slow fire while the butter melts; the mixture should be very smooth. Squeeze through a muslin into another saucepan and cook *au bain marie*, whipping all the time and adding occasionally small pieces of butter till the sauce is thick enough and well "bound". The butter used should be absolutely fresh and really the best.

Sauces pour viandes froides

Should you want any sauces to eat with cold meat, there are other things than mayonnaise sauce. To a mayonnaise you add mustard, parsley, gherkins, capers and tarragon chopped together and you have a *sauce tartare* far less sickly and with a pleasant sharp taste. Another sauce which is very easy to prepare is the *ravigote*: chop a hard-boiled egg and mix it well with salt, pepper, mustard, parsley, oil and vinegar. The proportions should be two tablespoons of vinegar to three and a half of oil, that is if your wine vinegar is of average strength; they vary a great deal. And a very good dressing for salads is a plain one made with wine vinegar, salt and pepper, and a little mustard mixed with the crushed yolks of hard-boiled eggs; these should be well crushed and mixed in the vinegar till the dressing has the consistency of a smooth thick cream; the white of the eggs should be finely chopped and added afterwards when dressing the salad.

Farce aux marrons

This stuffing is remarkably good for roast goose or duck. Take a quarter of a pound of onions, cut them in thin slices and cook them slowly in pork fat or butter till golden brown. Peel about a pound of chestnuts (both skins should be carefully removed), add them to the onions, also salt, pepper and a little more fat or butter. Cook very slowly till the chestnuts are reduced to a pulp and stir well before stuffing the bird.

Velouté

Make a white roux with flour and butter and add little by little some stock, bring it to the boil and cook about half an hour (in fact a *velouté* is a béchamel sauce, but made with stock instead of milk, and it should have the same consistency).

AT THE 500 CLUB

(Left) So important are cocktails that we must have a club for them —where one can get all the delightful accessories to the drink as well, but where one naturally only expects caviare or lobster Neuburg before hurrying to the first night of a new play, a function for which one simply must be on time. This young woman, who is terrified of being late, is wearing a beautiful flame-coloured evening coat of velvet made for her by Ospovat with a luxurious collar of black and white foxes

AT THE CAFE ANGLAIS

It is naturally most amusing to dine and dance where one meets the greatest number of amusing people; no place answers this description better than the Café Anglais, where one goes "just as one is," or dresses to the fullest: the woman in white is wearing Chanel 668 from Lady Victor Paget, destined to be one of the dresses of the year, in chiffon. The Norman Hartnell black lace dress is such a success because it dines, goes to the theatre and dances

WHERE THE SMART WORLD MEETS

AT THE RITZ

At lunch-time the green and gold dining-room of the Ritz is so crowded that one speaks to Aletto to make sure of a table before daring to have a cocktail. The woman on the left wears Jean Patou's smartest suit of men's suiting in brown and white with a white satin blouse, made for her by the Misses Wilson. The chic young woman with her wears a crêpe satin dress of dull green, beneath a green cloth coat collared with grey fox: from Norah Crampton

AT THE BERKELEY

(Right) Cocktails are so necessary a part of the fabric of social existence that it seems one must always be having them: sometimes one rushes in before lunch on the way to some hair-raising spectacle, such as dirt-track racing, dressed like this young woman. She is wearing a new model from Paris Trades' collection made of beige and white tweed, collared smartly in white piqué with a brown leather belt. In such a run-about costume one is perfectly sure to be right for either town or country

OR LUNCHEON, COCKTAILS, DINNER

Vegetables

The summer is the time when a hostess' fancy turns lightly to thoughts of vegetable dishes. We are "off" butcher's meat, there is no game and we want lighter fare. Can there be anything better than vegetables pleasantly cooked and served *à la française* as a separate dish? It will excite even the most jaded appetite.

Indeed, at this time of the year every possible young vegetable is at its tenderest best and it seems, somehow, a ghastly tragedy to see these admirable raw materials cooked ever so primitively in plain water, or allowed to grow till over-mature by a gardener more anxious of size than of flavour. However, if we live in London we must be content with what we can get at the greengrocer's, but if we have a garden we must be firm and not be afraid of breaking the gardener's heart: our peas must be small, our broad beans under age and our lettuces gathered in their youth.

Fonds d'artichauts saintengeoise

These are artichokes stuffed with a purée of broad beans. Take the hearts of some globe artichokes, cook them "*au blanc*"—as you do salsify (it means that you put in a saucepan a little flour, a drop of vinegar and salt, also, little by little, water which you stir well in till you have enough for your purpose). When the artichokes are cooked drain them well, put them in a fireproof or silver dish, each stuffed with purée of broad beans, pour a little *mornay* sauce (rather light and thin), sprinkle with grated cheese and brown under the gas grill or in the oven. The broad beans are to be cooked like fresh haricot beans—that is, in plenty of salt water with an onion and a *bouquet* and then mashed into a purée with salt and pepper, butter and fresh cream.

Artichauts à la barigoule

Take some artichokes, cut off three-quarters of the leaves and remove the smaller ones which are nearer the stalk. Put them in boiling water and cook them about ten minutes. Remove them and dip them in cold water. Then remove all the inside, only leaving the heart and the outer circles of leaves and fill them with a mixture prepared as follows:

Put in a saucepan one onion, one shallot and a few mushrooms very finely chopped, a piece of butter the size of a small egg, a little olive oil and cook on a moderate fire about ten minutes; then add parsley and a rasher of bacon chopped together, salt and pepper, a "drop" of white wine, a tablespoonful of beef stock, a teaspoonful of purée of tomatoes.

Fill the artichokes with this mixture; place over each a very thin rasher of bacon and tie them with some thread.

Put in a fireproof dish pieces of carrot and onion, one bay leaf and whatever scraps of meat and small bones you have by you; add a tablespoonful of beef stock. Place your artichokes on this bed and bring to the boil, keeping the dish covered. Put it aside a few minutes, remove the lid, baste the artichokes, cover them with oiled paper and finish cooking in a moderate oven, basting occasionally.

When ready, remove the strings and bacon. Serve the artichokes covered with gravy, obtained by squashing through a sieve all the ingredients in which they have cooked.

Asperges à la royale

Cut the tips of a bundle of small green asparagus, cook them in salted water, drain them well and pass them through a sieve to obtain a purée. Put in a small saucepan a piece of butter the size of a walnut, and a puddingspoonful of flour; mix well, add half a tumblerful of milk, salt, pepper and a little nutmeg. Bring to the boil, whipping all the time, put in the purée of asparagus and a little more butter. Let it simmer a little while and serve in a sauceboat as an accompaniment to large asparagus.

Aubergines sautées
Take some aubergines (egg-plant is, I am told, the correct English name), cut them in thin slices, sprinkle them with salt and leave them on a plate for an hour or so. This will bring out the water they contain. Drain them well, fry them in a mixture of oil and pork fat, and keep them hot. Then cut a few tomatoes in quarters, fry them in very little of the same mixture, till soft, pass through a sieve and pour the sauce thus obtained over your aubergines. Cook the whole a few minutes longer, add pepper (more salt will not be necessary) and serve very hot.

Aubergines à la crème
Peel the aubergines and cut them lengthways in thin slices; fry these in oil and when cooked drain them well, also sprinkle them with salt. Meanwhile, prepare a fairly thick béchamel sauce; pour a little of it into a fireproof dish (adding a little gravy or *jus*) then put in a layer of aubergines, more béchamel, more aubergines, and so on, finishing by a covering of sauce. Cook slowly in the oven. You can, if you like, add a little grated cheese or incorporate with the sauce a little purée of tomatoes for a change.

Carottes sautées
Take a dozen smallish carrots, scrape and wash them well and cook them in boiling salted water. When they are tender remove and drain them well. Melt some butter in a saucepan, add two onions finely chopped and brown them; add the carrots cut in pieces and sprinkle them with flour; when they become brownish add stock (not too much, it should be a fairly dry dish), salt, pepper and a little chopped parsley; simmer for about a quarter of an hour and serve.

Croquettes de céleri
This is an extremely good accompaniment to roast veal or to a saddle of mutton. Take the same quantity of potatoes and celery. Boil them in salted water and mash them thoroughly well (for safety pass the purée obtained through a hair sieve). The mixture should be then prepared like a potato purée, that is, over the fire so that it gets quite dry, with pieces of butter and hot milk, whipping all the time. Season well and add, mixing quickly one (or two according to quantity) yolks of egg. The mixture should be fairly stiff. Shape it into little balls or quenelles when partly cold, roll them in breadcrumbs and fry them like any croquettes in deep fat. Drain well, of course, before serving.

Chou à la crème
Take a good-sized savoy cabbage, remove the coarse outer leaves and cut the cabbage into four pieces; wash them well and cook them in boiling salted water till quite tender. Then remove the cabbage, drain off all the water, season it and put it in a serving dish with the following sauce poured over: Put a tablespoonful of flour in a small saucepan with a good piece of butter and cook it a little, then add a little milk, salt and pepper. Bring to the boil, stirring constantly, add a little more butter, and if too thick more milk; also, just before serving some fresh cream.

Chou farci à la russe
Take a large white cabbage, remove the outside leaves and boil the best and largest leaves carefully, being careful not to break them. Chop together a few slices of rump steak, and fry this (with minced onion and shallots) in butter; also fry about same quantity of pork sausage meat. Mix together on a board, chop again, season well and add about the same quantity of boiled rice. Mix again, add a little gravy and put some of the mixture on each cabbage leaf. Roll and shape it like a fat sausage and dispose in a fireproof dish. Cover with bouillon and simmer till almost all the bouillon has reduced. Serve with a tomato sauce. This dish is one that requires to be highly seasoned.

Choux-fleurs frits
Prepare and boil the cauliflower in the usual manner but remove it before it is too soft; break it into pieces and soak these for about a quarter of an hour in half cold water, half vinegar, salt and pepper. Dip the pieces in a batter and fry them in the ordinary way. A tablespoonful of olive oil added to the batter two hours before it is to be used is a considerable improvement.

Concombres au blanc
Take some cucumbers (two would do for about four people), peel them, cut them in two and remove the seeds, then cut them in pieces about two inches long and cook them in boiling water (with salt and a little wine vinegar) for about one hour. Drain them well and be careful not to break them. Put in a saucepan a good piece of butter, and a tablespoonful of flour; cook a few minutes, stirring well with a wooden spoon; add a glass of boiling water, salt and pepper and boil this a few minutes till the sauce is the proper consistency, put in the pieces of cucumber, chopped parsley, a drop of lemon, bind with two yolks of eggs and serve at once. Some people use milk instead of water, and the addition of fresh cream at the last minute is very pleasant.

Concombres farcis
Peel some cucumbers, cut them in two or three pieces according to size, scoop out the inside, which you fill with a mixture made of a little cucumber flesh, one onion, one rasher of bacon, a few mushrooms, one tomato, breadcrumbs, salt and pepper, all finely chopped together and cooked in butter. Place the cucumbers on a bed of bacon rind, onions and tomatoes in a fireproof dish, add meat stock, and cook on a moderate fire, finishing in the oven. Serve when the flesh is soft in an entrée dish, and pour over them the gravy through a sieve.

Concombres au jus
Peel and cut the cucumbers as above, place them raw in a dish, sprinkle them with salt and add a few slices of onion. An hour later remove the onions and drain the cucumbers which you place in a saucepan over a bed of fat bacon, on a

slow fire. Meanwhile, make a brown roux (flour and butter cooked to the browning point and the addition of stock and a little tomato sauce instead of water or milk), pour this over the cucumbers which should be cooked about half-an-hour on a slow fire. Serve the sauce, passed through a sieve, over the cucumbers.

Endives meunière and **endives au fromage**

For about four people get two pounds of these delightful endives (it must be remembered when ordering these that most London greengrocers call endives "chicory" and chicory "endives"). Remove the outer leaves, refresh them in cold water for twenty minutes and put them in boiling salted water. When they are cooked—they should be quite soft—drain them well and put them in a fireproof dish with butter melted to a light brown colour. Cook them in the oven, basting often with the butter till they are slightly browned. Sprinkle with a good deal of salt, which is necessary to correct the slight natural bitterness of the endives. They are also very good cooked in the same way, but *gratinées* with grated cheese, the usual mixture of half Parmesan, half Gruyère being the best.

Epinards au gratin

Take some spinach; wash and clean it well and cook it in salted boiling water; drain it well and put it in a fireproof dish with a good piece of butter, salt and pepper.

Take about a quarter of a pound of mushrooms, peel them and cook them in a small saucepan, with water, a little vinegar and a small piece of butter. When cooked, chop them very fine. Add a teaspoonful of flour, a liqueur-glassful of sherry and a tumbler of milk. Cook for about twenty minutes. Then add the yolks of two eggs and a little cream, stirring well.

Pour this over the spinach, sprinkle with breadcrumbs and grated cheese, with here and there a few small pieces of butter, and brown in the oven.

Fèves maître d'hôtel

Take some broad beans (they should be young and tender) and throw them in salted boiling water, to which you add a *bouquet* composed of the heart of a lettuce, parsley and one small onion. Cook on a quick fire and drain well. Put in a saucepan a good piece of butter, a tablespoonful of the water in which the beans have cooked, salt, pepper; bring to the boil, put in the beans and go on cooking for a few minutes. Just before serving add a little more butter, a teaspoonful of cream and chopped parsley.

Haricots verts à la crème

Do not cut them after the English fashion, but break both ends, tearing off the part which is "stringy" and throw them in boiling water with salt and pepper. When cooked (they should be still quite firm) drain them well and keep them hot.

Meanwhile, you have cooked a wineglassful of red wine vinegar till reduced by one-third, and also removed it from the fire. Now, in another small saucepan mix some cream and the yolks of two eggs; cook this over a slow fire till it just begins to thicken adding the vinegar little by little and stirring all the time. Pour this mixture over the French beans, mix well, season, add chopped parsley and cook for a few minutes more. Squeeze a quarter of a lemon over it just before serving.

Haricots verts bonne dame

Take six *fonds d'artichauts* already boiled and cold, cut them in quarters and cook them in butter with parsley and chervil chopped; add, when they are hot, a pound of French beans (carefully drained), mix well but lightly, toss over the fire, add one or two more pieces of fresh butter, see that it is well seasoned, put in the serving dish and sprinkle over the yolks of two hot hard-boiled eggs, finely chopped.

Haricots mange-tout

Take some fresh haricot beans of the kind called *mange-tout*, the pod of which is still tender, although the bean has reached its normal size. Break off the ends, removing at the same time the stringy parts, then break them in two and wash them well. Prepare a saucepan of boiling water (with salt and a *bouquet* of parsley and thyme), throw your haricots in this and add to it the juice of some tomatoes (four to a pound of *mange-tout*), cooked in very little water and squeezed through a sieve. Let it reduce a good deal, and just before serving add a piece of fresh butter.

In the South of France, instead of adding butter, they add a small amount of bacon, parsley and garlic finely chopped together. The taste is delicious. But it must be remembered, if trying this Southern way, that the garlic which grows in the North is much more powerful than the one from the South and very little of it is sufficient to give it the right taste.

Purée de haricots blancs

You can use either the small or the large variety; wash them well in running water, and soak them for twelve hours, then put them in a saucepan with lots of salted water, coarsely broken pepper, one onion, one carrot and the usual *bouquet* of thyme, bay leaf and parsley. Start them on a quick fire, skim well, let them simmer till perfectly tender, and mash them through a sieve. Add seasoning and fresh butter just before serving. The consistency should be that of a potato purée.

Laitues au four

Take some lettuces and remove the outside green leaves. Throw them in salted boiling water and cook for a few minutes. Remove most of the water and finish cooking in a closed dish on a slow fire. Drain them well and put them in a buttered fireproof dish, cover with a béchamel sauce, sprinkle with breadcrumbs and brown in the oven.

Purée de navets

Peel and wash five or six turnips and cook them in boiling salted water; drain them well first, chop and then mash them well with a fork. Melt a good piece of butter in a frying-pan, add the turnips, well seasoned, and fry them for a few minutes, stirring well. You may add a little Devonshire cream just before serving; it gives a pleasant mellow flavour to the turnips.

Petits pois au lard

Cut two rashers of streaky bacon in little cubes, cook them in butter with six small onions and a pinch of flour; add a tablespoonful of beef stock and a tumblerful of water, salt, pepper and a *bouquet* (of parsley, chives and one bay leaf). Bring to the boil; throw in your peas and cook till tender. Remove the *bouquet* before serving.

Purée de pommes soufflée

Cook in salted water some white floury potatoes, drain them well, put them in a clean saucepan and dry them over the fire so that they are not watery. Mash them well—there must not be a single lump left—put in salt and pepper, a good piece of butter and a tablespoonful of hot milk. Beat this well and work it over the fire, add the yolks of two eggs and another tablespoonful of milk, more even if it looks too thick, then put in the whites of the two eggs well whipped. Mix thoroughly, and bake in a hot oven for about a quarter of an hour.

Another attractive way of serving this dish is the following: instead of boiling the potatoes, bake them in their skins in the oven, then cut them in two, scrape out the inside, prepare as described above and refill the empty skins with the purée instead of putting it in a dish. Finish baking in the same way.

Pommes de terre au lard

Cut in pieces about ten or twelve medium-sized potatoes (the yellow kind being for this dish better than white floury ones), dry them well and keep them wrapped in a cloth. Cut in small cubes a quarter of a pound of lean bacon and put them in a casserole with a good piece of butter. When they are getting brown add a tablespoonful of flour and mix well. Simmer for a few more minutes, add a little stock, salt and pepper and the classical *bouquet* (to be removed before serving). Then put in the potatoes and cook them gently for about an hour or so till they are well done. Some people fry the potatoes a few minutes in butter before putting them in the casserole. There is something to be said for this process.

Pommes frites paysanne

This way of frying potatoes is, so to speak, against all rules, yet they come out of the pan crisp and delicious. Cut the potatoes in cubes about half an inch square and fry them in very little fat, so that there is none left at the end of the process (a piece the size of an egg would be enough for a pound and a half of potatoes), shaking them often. When they are nearly done add chopped parsley, salt and, if you like, a little garlic very finely chopped. Serve at once.

Devonshire fried potatoes

First boil the potatoes, then put a little fat in a pan and your potatoes; chop them over the fire, shaking them well, add seasoning, and give them the shape of a flat cake about half the size of the frying-pan. Put a plate over them. They should be fried over an even glowing fire till they begin to smoke; by then they should be nicely browned. Turn them over in the plate and serve at once.

Pommes paille

Cut some yellow potatoes as thin as straw, dry them well, and throw them into a deep dish full of boiling fat. In a few minutes they will be crisp and golden, after which you drain them well and sprinkle with salt.

Purée of sweet potatoes

Boil two or three large sweet potatoes in salted water, strain and mash them and put them in a clean saucepan with a piece of butter, salt and pepper. Stir well over the fire and add the grated flesh of half a small coconut and plenty of black pepper. Just before serving pour in sufficient milk to give the purée the consistency of thick cream and beat it for a minute with a fork.

Ragoût landais

Cut into cubes two small vegetable marrows and two aubergines, season well and toss for a few minutes in butter, add a little later four sweet peppers, two tomatoes (also cut in cubes and with seed removed), one head of garlic well pounded. Cook for about twenty minutes, or less, according to the tenderness of the vegetable, and serve very hot.

Raw fry

In the Cornish villages this dish is usually made of turnips, potatoes and onions. Cut them in slices and fry them in butter till they are half cooked, then add water, just enough to cover the vegetables, salt and pepper, a few small pieces of streaky bacon; cover the frying-pan and let the whole thing simmer till thoroughly cooked, by which time it should be fairly dry.

Squab pie

The story goes that there was once an old man and his wife who lived quietly in their little cottage. They had a tiny garden in which he grew onions, leeks, potatoes, wallflowers and hollyhock, and she cooked some of these (not the flowers) for their modest meals. She never complained and he never grumbled; they only quarrelled at dinner time because the one liked sweet pie, the other savoury pie; and, as they were old people without money or children, their daily food was their only interest in life. So that the squabble about the pie became every day more noisy and passionate. In fact, they were on the verge of what the daily press would call a "domestic tragedy" when, one day while cooking the famous pie, the wife had an inspiration—why not mix the ingredients and make a combined pie, partly sweet, partly savoury? The ingredients were good, thought she, the result ought to be good. Indeed it was, and so was born the "squab pie," and they lived happily for ever after, the old man, his wife and the squab pie—of which here is the genuine recipe:

Put in a pie dish leeks and potatoes cut in slices and a few pieces of either beef or mutton, salt, pepper and a little water, and cook on a moderate fire till it is partly cooked; then add apples cut in quarters, and sugar (it should be noticeably sweet), finish cooking, cover with pastry of a flaky kind, and bake the pie in a quick oven. The apples should be put in so that they are cooked precisely at the same moment as the meat and vegetables.

Salade Carmen

A mixture of endives, celery and beetroot. The sauce to be prepared with very little oil, salt and pepper, fresh cream, lemon instead of vinegar, and tomato ketchup, which gives it a pleasant pink colour and a peculiar taste, also pleasant if you like it.

Salade de concombres aux œufs durs

Take a good-sized cucumber, peel it, cut in very thin slices and put them in a flat dish; sprinkle with a good deal of salt and let it rest for about one hour and a half. The salt draws the moisture out of the cucumber making it tender and more digestible. Throw away the water which has come out and wash the slices of cucumber in water, otherwise they are likely to be too salt. Then dry them.

By then your hard-boiled eggs should be ready; that is, cooked and cold. (Do not forget after they have been boiled to put them in cold water, otherwise the shell will be difficult to remove.) Cut them in quarters and put aside two-thirds of the yolks; these you crush with a fork and add to the salad dressing, which should be made as follows: melt the salt in the vinegar (red wine vinegar, of course), add pepper, oil (the best olive oil, of course) in the proportion of three tablespoonfuls of oil to two of vinegar. Beat all this well with the cucumber and hard-boiled eggs. Put the mixture in a salad bowl and dispose round it the white leaves from the hearts of several lettuces, over which you squeeze a little juice of lemon.

It should be remembered that the lettuce, having been well washed, must be equally well dried. Many good salads are spoilt by leaving the leaves wet with water. The best way is to use the wire basket specially made for that purpose; or failing that, shake the leaves lightly in a thin dry cloth.

Salade d'endives à l'orange

Wash and clean the endives, and remove carefully all the outside leaves which are not perfect and white, cut them in two, lengthways. Peel thinly two oranges and cut the pieces of skin *en julienne* (that is, very thin and fine as you do for vegetables in a *potage julienne*). Boil these for about five or six minutes (this in order to remove the bitter taste), drain and let grow cold. Mix a tablespoonful of mustard with a glass of fresh cream, season well and add a little cayenne pepper. Dispose the endives in a dish and sprinkle with the julienne of oranges.

Salade parisienne

Mix in equal parts watercress, batavia and beetroot, season with salt, pepper, oil and vinegar, add parsley, chervil and tarragone finely chopped together.

Salade lorraine

Cut in thin slices some cold boiled potatoes (the yellow Dutch kind which is not floury), season with oil, vinegar and a little claret, add chopped beetroot, chopped gherkins and *fines herbes*.

Salade algérienne

Take some tomatoes and some sweet peppers, either green or red, cut them in two, remove the seeds and grill them; then cut them in very fine slices and add two small onions, one shallot and parsley finely chopped; season with pepper, salt, oil and vinegar.

Salade de thon

Take a tin of tunny fish, empty the contents in a soup plate and cut the fish finely, *en julienne*, add the juice of a lemon and a little chopped chervil to the oil and mix well. As a rule it is not necessary to add salt.

Anchois monégasque

Take some sweet peppers, grill and cut them *en julienne*, add some fillets of anchovies and simply dress with plain olive oil.

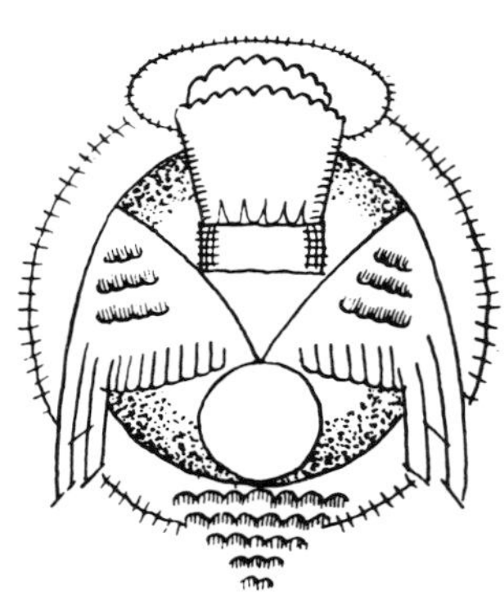

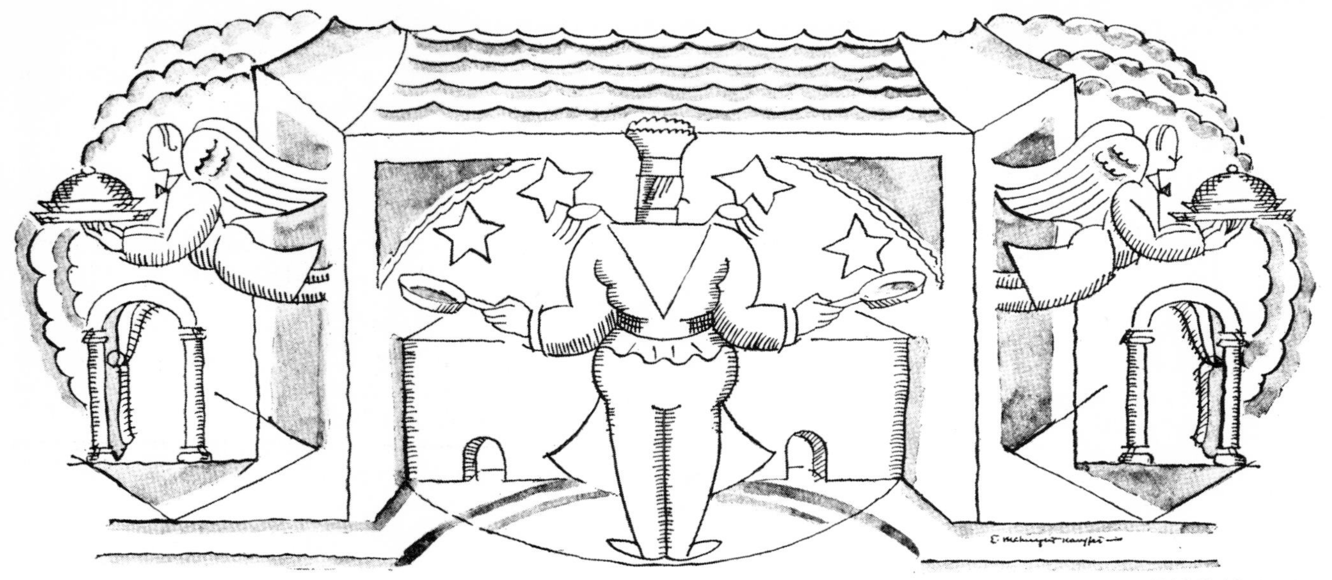

E McKnight Kauffer

Puddings

Sweets are indeed a comparatively modern invention. In the treatise of Apicius Cœlius—probably the earliest work on cookery known, and what we have of it is no doubt as apocryphal as parts of the "Satyricon"—according to Dr Lister, commentator of Apicius, the Fifth Book "is of Pease Porridge under which are included Frumentary, Watergruel, Milk Porridge, Flumary, Stirabout and the like", which seems a very dull collection of sweets. Though it may be said that sweets are apt to be dull unless they are of a complication which is even worse than dullness. Puzzles are out of place at the dinner table. And the choice of a sweet for dinner, formal or informal, is conducive to extreme perplexity.

Ananas au kirsch

Get a good-sized pineapple, as ripe as it is possible to get in England, and scoop out the flesh with a silver knife and fork; also cut in small quarters two grapefruit, being careful there is none of the inner skin left. Sprinkle with sugar and pour over it a port glassful of Kirschwasser (Maraschino can also be used, but it is rather too sickly) or of Quetsch, which is plum brandy and has a pleasant sharp taste and a subtle flavour. Let it stand for at least half an hour on ice in a hollow dish. You should, of course, be careful not to waste the juice which has come out of the fruits during the initial operation.

Serve well covered with the following *crème fouettée*: fresh cream, to which you have added castor sugar and Kirschwasser (or Quetsch, or Maraschino) whipped to a stiff consistency. This should be served very cold and, as Brillat-Savarin says when describing a dish, "*on verra des merveilles*".

Crème aux bananes

Bring to the boil a pint of milk flavoured with half a vanilla pod, and keep it hot. Put into a saucepan two tablespoonfuls of flour, a quarter of a pound of sugar, four yolks of eggs and two whole eggs; mix well with a whip and add, little by little, the hot milk. Bring to the boil and go on cooking, whipping all the time till it reaches the right consistency, which should be that of thick cream. Add, then, a liqueur glassful of Kirschwasser or Curaçao and remove the vanilla pod.

Peel four bananas, cut them in small pieces and mash them with a fork, after which you beat them, first stirring, then whipping; they soon become a frothy, smooth mixture. This should be done in a large bowl, so that you can add, little by little, the *crème* you have prepared. Stir well all the time, see that it is sweetened and flavoured.

There are two ways of serving this; either you pour the *crème* (through a fine colander) into little custard pots or you pour the lot (also through a fine colander) into a fireproof dish. Then sprinkle with sugar and brown in the oven or under the gas grill. In either case serve very cold.

Bananes créole

Peel six bananas and put them in a fireproof dish. Sprinkle over them three tablespoonfuls of Demerara sugar, squeeze the juice of a lemon and add three tablespoonfuls of water. Bake brown in a slow oven and halfway through the baking add a sherryglassful of Jamaica rum. Should you require more bananas the other ingredients, including water, should be increased proportionately. Serve with cream, whipped and flavoured with either rum or lemon.

Bananas créole *another version*

Put in half a pint of milk about eight lumps of sugar and bring to the boil; when cold stir in the yolks of two eggs. Peel six bananas and scoop out the flesh of two sweet oranges (the pith and skin having been carefully removed), mash this together, add a little castor sugar, and beat it well with a fork till foamy. Then add it to the milk, and add, last, the whites whipped to a froth. All this to be put in a soufflé dish, baked *au bain marie* till set and brown, and served at once.

Crème frite

Take a quart of milk and bring it to the boil and put in one vanilla pod for flavouring. Meanwhile work well together two eggs, twelve yolks, about half a pound of castor sugar and a quarter of a pound of flour passed through a hair sieve; add a pinch of salt. When all this is well mixed add little by little the boiling milk and cook on a slow fire till the mixture has sufficiently thickened. Then remove the vanilla pod and pour the mixture on a greased marble board or tin and let it grow cold. It should be then quite thick cream about the consistency of batter, and you will find that in falling on the board it will spread slowly and stop of its own accord and be then about half an inch thick. When quite cold cut the batter in smallish squares, coat them lightly with whipped egg and breadcrumbs, fry these in clarified butter (they should be crisp outside and creamy inside), and serve either with a hot chocolate sauce, or better still, with a manner of *sabayon* done in the following way:

Put in a small saucepan six yolks of eggs, a quarter of a pound of castor sugar and about a wineglassful of liqueurs; the best mixture is brandy and Curaçao, but of course there are many other combinations like brandy and Kummel (or, should you wish to be economical, use sherry or Madeira as you would for an Italian Zablione). Cook *au bain marie*, whipping all the time. The consistency of this sauce should be that of cream, not more. The quantities quoted are ample for six to eight people.

Crêpes à l'anis

These pancakes are very different from any other pancakes, either French or English, and really delicious. Prepare the batter in a basin in the usual manner, but using for two pints of cold boiled milk, four eggs, and not quite a quarter of a pound of flour. Add the classical pinch of salt and two tablespoonfuls of olive oil. As for the flavouring, *anis*, you can use powder of aniseed or, better still, two tablespoonfuls of that liqueur called "*anis*" (not *anisette*) which in France has now taken the place of *absinthe*. Have your pan very clean and put in it very little oil and butter mixed, then some of the batter, which must be fairly liquid. Cook in the ordinary way but on one side only, sprinkling castor sugar meanwhile on the pancake. Then roll it in the pan and serve. The result is a rich *crêpe* beautifully soft and perfumed.

Croûte aux fruits

First stew some apples in very little water, and sugar, till reduced to a pulp; also stew some pears cored and cut in halves in water flavoured with half a vanilla pod till they are soft (they should keep their shape); also chop very fine a few slices of pineapple. Mix together the chopped pineapple, the mashed apples, a tablespoonful of apricot jam, castor sugar, and add a portglassful of good brandy. Fry slices of *brioche* in butter till they are nicely browned and crisp; put them standing up all round a soufflé dish; fill it half way up with your mashed fruit; dispose the pears over it; sprinkle freely with castor sugar, add a few breadcrumbs and brown in the oven. It should be served *flambé* with brandy. It is, by the way, advisable in these days of 30 under proof spirits to warm the brandy before lighting it, otherwise it may not burn—a tragic failure on the dining table.

Brioche—To make the batter for the necessary *brioche* use, say, one pound of flour and pass it through a fine sieve, take a quarter of it and make a heap on the board; melt, in the middle, a small quantity of yeast with lukewarm water; mix it gradually with the flour, adding water if necessary, so as to make a fairly firm mixture. Put it aside in a bowl, and keep it fairly warm.

Work the rest of the pound of flour with a pinch of salt, two of sugar, a quarter of a pound of butter (well worked) and six eggs. Mix and beat this well for about twenty minutes on the board. Flatten it, add the quarter of pound previously put aside, and put the whole thing away in a bowl sprinkled with flour; keep it at the same slightly warm temperature for six or seven hours; it should rise to double its original size. Then put it once more on the board, work it a little while, let it rest a few minutes, and bake your *brioche* in a very hot oven, the crown shape being the best for your purpose.

Ile flottante

Take four eggs, beat the whites to a stiff froth, add four tablespoonfuls of castor sugar, put this in a tin mould previously coated with caramel and cook in the oven, *au bain marie*, about twenty minutes. Make a liquid custard by boiling some milk flavoured with vanilla and sweetened, and adding the yolks, cooking on a slow fire till it thickens. Turn the whites out of the mould in a hollow dish, and pour the custard round it.

Mango fool

Take six green mangoes and remove every particle of green peel, cut them into four, steep in clean water and throw stones away. Boil the fruit until perfectly tender, pulp and pass through a sieve. Sweeten to taste, and add very gradually, stirring all the time, as much milk as will make it the consistency of thick custard. Set on ice and serve very cold. A little port wine much improves the flavour.

Omelette au kummel

Prepare the omelette in the ordinary way, and put in some tomato jam instead of ordinary jam. Place the omelette in a hot silver dish, sprinkle with sugar, using the rather coarse kind, and pass over it a red-hot salamander. Warm some Kummel, pour it over the omelette, and set it alight. Be careful to keep the flame alive by stirring it with a spoon, otherwise the flavour of Kummel will be overpowering; prick the omelette occasionally with a fork. The flame must die out naturally in spite of your constantly stirring.

Pêches Barbara

Take some fine peaches, peel them, cut them in half, and cook them in water and sugar (and half a vanilla pod) till they are soft. The water should just cover them. When they are cooked, remove them, add a liqueur glassful of Grand Marnier to the juice, and go on cooking it till it is reduced to the consistency of thick syrup. Then remove the vanilla pod and let the syrup get tepid.

Dispose the peaches in a hollow dish all round, and fill the centre with tomato jam, pour over the peaches the syrup, and "drape" them with cream flavoured with *eau-de-vie de framboises* (or Kirschwasser), whipped to a stiff froth, and sprinkle over the cream crushed pistachio nuts.

The whipped cream to be done in the following manner:—First beat a white of egg then add fresh cream (about $\frac{1}{4}$ pint for four people), whip till stiff, add the flavouring, whip a little more, then, and only then, add the castor sugar; mix it well in but do not whip any more. Let the mixture rest half an hour in a cool place; dispose it over the peaches, sprinkle with the crushed nuts, and keep on ice till wanted. If you have no tomato jam (which seems incredible) you may use quince jelly, or, better still—have another sweet.

Poires au caramel

Get some good sound pears, peel them and leave them whole, put them standing in a saucepan, just covered with water: add sugar, half a vanilla pod and cook till soft on a moderate fire. When cooked remove the pears carefully, add to the juice a glass of good port wine and let it reduce till it has the consistency of syrup; then remove it from the fire for a few minutes and add a tumblerful of fresh cream. Cook a few minutes, pour it over the pears and serve.

Poires au chocolat

Peel and cut some pears in quarters, cook them in a large saucepan with very little water to which you add sugar and a piece of vanilla pod. When they are nearly ready remove them, also the vanilla. Put in a small saucepan two sticks of good chocolate finely grated and a drop of the water in which the pears have cooked. When thoroughly melted pour it into the large saucepan, add a little butter, the pears and more sugar if necessary. Cook slowly. When finished the pears should be quite soft and the chocolate juice the consistency of cream. Serve hot.

Locher

Poires au four

Take some fine sound pears, wash them, put them whole in a fireproof dish—they should stand in about half an inch of sugared water, and cook them very slowly in the oven until they are quite soft. By that time they will look quite "bloated" and just a little shrivelled after a few minutes' exposure to the air.

Take also another pear, peel it, cut it in quarters, and cook it in water to which you have added a sufficiency of sugar so that it becomes a thick syrup when cold. When the water is sufficiently reduced and flavoured, add a sherry glass of Cointreau or Grand Marnier and cook it a little more. Then pour the syrup through a muslin over your pears, mix it well with whatever juice may be already in the dish, put back in the oven for a few minutes, and put away to cool. Serve quite cold.

It is also very pleasant to put in, instead of liqueur, a portglassful of good claret.

Compote de pommes à l'ananas

Peel and cut your apples in quarters in the ordinary way and cook them in cold water, the proportions to be about two pounds of apples, a tumblerful of water and a handful of lump sugar (more if the apples are very sour) to four or five people. By the time they are quite soft there should be very little water left, if any.

Add a piece of butter the size of an egg, and cook a few minutes more. Then remove the compote from the fire, add two tablespoonfuls of pineapple jam, mix well and put the mixture in a fireproof dish. Sprinkle well with castor sugar and put in the oven, where it should be left till an icing of caramel has formed on the top. Serve very cold.

Pommes Borzoi

Take some eating apples, peel them and cut them in quarters. Melt a good piece of butter in a pan and when it is foaming put in the quarters of apples. Cook them slowly, turning them carefully one by one, so that they are browned on all sides; by that time they are soft all through. Then sprinkle them with Demerara sugar and a little powdered cinnamon. Cook two minutes more. Meanwhile you rub half a dozen lumps of sugar on the skin of one or two oranges, so that the sugar is saturated with the zest (that is, with the fuller perfume of the orange), moisten them with a little orange juice, and squash them with a spoon; add a piece of fresh butter (about one ounce) and mix it thoroughly with the flavoured sugar; dispose a few pieces of this prepared butter here and there on the apples, which you have arranged nicely on a serving dish, put the dish a few minutes in the oven or over the fire till the butter has melted, pour over it a tablespoonful of Curaçao or Grand Marnier, previously warmed, set it alight and serve if possible before the flames die out. Serve with this sauce the kind of delicious wafers known as *Crêpes mousseline*.

Soufflé aux pommes
Put in a saucepan three tablespoonfuls of sugar, one of flour, four yolks of egg and a glass of milk. Cook over the fire, as you would a *crème pâtissière*, bringing to the boil, stirring all the time with a whip till it has the consistency of thick cream. Flavour it with a liqueur glassful of Calvados and put the mixture to cool.

Meanwhile, bake slowly in the oven two good eating apples, peeled and sprinkled with sugar; bake them till they are very soft. Also whip to a stiff froth in a copper bowl the whites of five eggs, and add these, little by little, to the batter you have prepared before. See that it is properly sweetened.

Butter a soufflé dish, sprinkle with fine sugar so that there is a coating all round, put in a layer of batter, then your apples cut in two, cover with the rest of the mixture and cook like any soufflé, that is, about twelve to fourteen minutes, according to the oven. A few minutes before it is ready sprinkle with fine sugar so that it is, at the end, nicely *glacé*.

Tarte aux pommes
Peel and cut two pounds of apples and cook them on a slow fire, adding a tumblerful of water, and sugar. When they are reduced to a pulp, by which time there should be no water left at all, add a good piece of butter and two tablespoonfuls of apricot jam. Whip the mixture well and cook a few minutes more.

Prepare some paste as for shortcrust, put in a flat mould a thin lining, fill with the apple mixture, cover with another thin layer of paste (leaving in it about one dozen holes the size of a sixpenny piece), bake in a moderate oven. When the tart has cooled a little, introduce through the holes a glassful of rum and one of port.

Pommes Balbec
Take some fine eating apples, peel them and cut them in quarters. Melt some good butter in a frying-pan and put in the quarters one by one carefully. They should be turned so that they become brown on all sides, with great precaution as, when the flesh becomes soft, they might break. When they are well cooked, sprinkle them with castor sugar, shake the pan well, pour in a glass of Calvados, set it alight and serve at once. Serve at the same time icy cold whipped cream.

Compote de pommes aux marrons
Peel and cut in quarters some cooking apples and cook them in a tumblerful of water with half a vanilla pod and about a quarter of a pound of sugar (this for about two pounds of apples), and when cooked, by which time it should all be reduced to a pulp and no water left, add a good piece of butter and cook a few minutes more. When cold, add three tablespoonfuls of chestnut jam or, if this is not available, one pound of steamed chestnuts mashed through a sieve. Sweeten to taste, mix well. Whipped cream flavoured with vanilla or orange goes well with this.

Plum pudding
This is the recipe for the English "pouding" in an old French book: Take one pound of raisins and currants mixed, six eggs, a portglassful of rum, a quarter of a pound of suet (chopped), same quantity of butter, one pound of flour, two glasses of milk, two ounces of sugar, the peel of half a lemon, finely chopped, nutmeg, a little salt; also, to improve it, a few blanched almonds and small pieces of candied peel such as lemon, orange, lime, angelica and mixed spices. Mix with breadcrumbs so that it is a fairly stiff mixture. Sew it in a cloth and either boil it or steam it. It is usually served in slices well moistened with rum which you will set alight "*le mets en devient plus délicat, outre le plaisir que ce feu de joie répand parmi les convives*."

The sauce is made as follows: Put in a bowl a small quantity of fine castor sugar, a tablespoonful of rum and butter just melted; beat well, adding more rum and more butter. All this to be done quickly, and when finished, should have the consistency of sauce mayonnaise—which seems to be a version of the famous "brandy butter."

Pruneaux au whisky
Soak your prunes for at least twelve hours and cook them slowly in water, adding sufficient sugar. When they are quite soft and the water well reduced, add a pinch of cinnamon and a claret glassful of good whisky and cook about twenty minutes more. The juice, of course, should have the consistency of syrup. This is one of the few sweets in which whisky can be used with great success; the taste of the prunes and the flavour of the whisky blend admirably. Devonshire cream goes well with this.

Soufflé chinois
Chop very fine about two ounces of ginger, mix it with two tablespoonfuls of fresh pineapple or pineapple jam (or preserved pineapple as a last resource). Cook a handful of ground rice in about half a pint of milk, slowly, till it thickens. Add the yolks of three eggs and cook a little more, also on a slow fire. Let this get cold, then add the mixture of ginger and pineapple and the whites of the eggs beaten to a stiff froth. Cook in a buttered soufflé dish in the ordinary way. The quantities quoted above are about enough for four people.

Crêpes Suzette
Put in a basin half a pound of flour, make a hole in the middle of the heap, add a pinch of salt, a little sugar, three eggs one after the other, a glass of rum, brandy or Curaçao; mix well and add warm water little by little until it is very smooth; let this rest for three hours, then add a glass of fresh cream, mix well again; it should have the consistency of cream.

Put in a frying-pan a very small piece of butter; when it is getting brown put in quickly a tablespoon of the batter, move the pan so that it covers the bottom (it should be very thin) and cook on a quick fire, tossing once.

Melt in a silver dish over a spirit lamp a piece, the size of a walnut, of the special butter you have prepared beforehand (butter well worked with castor sugar and the juice of an orange), put in your pancake, a liqueur glassful of brandy and one of Curaçao, set alight, *flambez* your pancake well, fold it in four and serve at once.

Savouries

It is always difficult to think of a new savoury—that is, one which is not either too banal or too freakish. Of course, in French cooking there is no word to translate "savoury", no doubt because the corresponding dish simply does not exist. Yet, if one looks up old cookery books, books published, say from about 1720—when cooking, emerging out of its grossness, became civilised and more subtle—up to about 1806, one finds under the heading *Entremets* not only what are known now as "sweets" and "puddings", but practically all vegetable dishes (I mean the more elaborate ones served separately), also a certain number of dishes having cheese, bacon or mushrooms as basis, and which really correspond to the English savoury.

These dishes are now used in France as *Entrées*, but there is no reason why in England they should not appear in their original place. It seems as if most of these were inspired by, or indeed absolutely copied from, traditional dishes of the French provinces. There is about them an unmistakable "local" flavour.

These few *entremets* will no doubt be found useful, being a pleasant finish to a dinner—one cannot all the time have fruit salads and ices, and also they are for good claret an admirable background.

Far lorientais

All that is wanted for four to six persons is: A pint and a third of milk, a quarter of a pound of sugar, a quarter of a pound of flour and two eggs. Mix together the flour, the sugar and the eggs till the mixture is absolutely smooth, and add little by little, stirring all the time, the milk, which must be almost boiling. Pour this on a buttered fireproof dish (neither too deep nor too flat), and put in a few fine raisins, or if you prefer, fat prunes, sliced and stoned. Cook in a very slow oven for one hour or a little more.

Croque-monsieur

Melt a piece of butter the size of a walnut in a saucepan, and add, before it gets brown, little by little, and stirring well, two tablespoonfuls of flour, then a teacup of boiling milk. Cook this mixture for a quarter of an hour, and let it rest ten minutes. Then add two eggs, pepper and salt, and a quarter of a pound of grated cheese, preferably Gruyère and Parmesan, mixed in equal quantities.

Cut small pieces of stale bread, about two inches square and half an inch thick, put on each a thin piece of lean ham and over it about a teaspoonful of the mixture previously described. Fry in very hot fat till golden brown (without turning them), drain well, sprinkle with a little red pepper and serve at once. The best fat to use is that part of the beef fat which is round the kidney.

Croûte bayonnaise

First fry some smoked Bayonne ham, then fry a few mushrooms in the remaining fat, then some pieces of bread also fried crisply. Dispose on these the mushrooms, then sprinkle with the fried ham chopped finely. Finish under a gas grill and season with a little cayenne pepper.

Champignons au lard

Wash and prepare some nice mushrooms and cook them in butter; also cook some very thin slices of streaky bacon about the same size as your mushrooms; put each mushroom between two slices of bacon and enclose the whole in thin batter of the *feuilletée* type used for vol-au-vent, and bake in the oven.

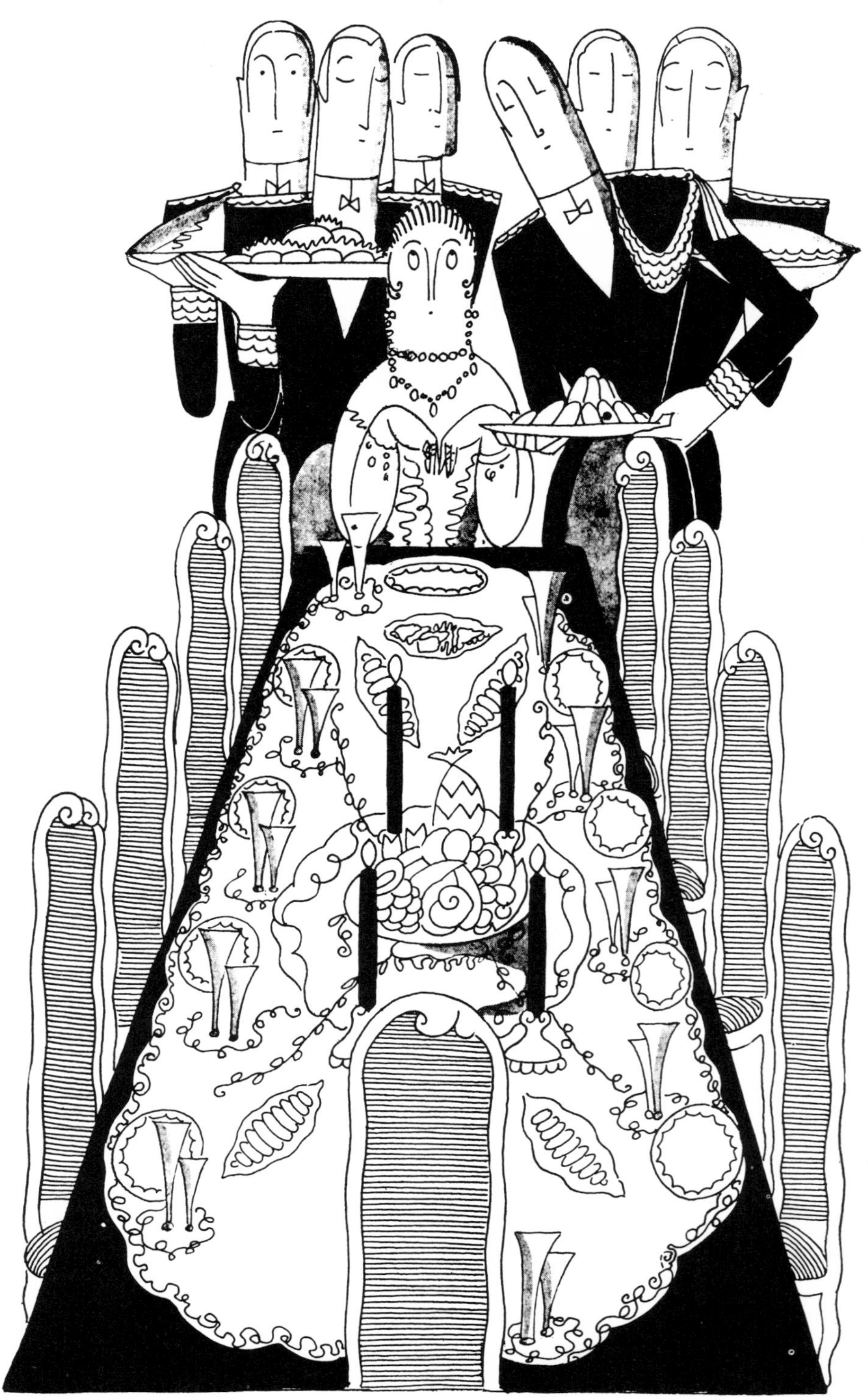

Mrs. Dummer keeps open house, two chefs, and a cockney accent. Mrs. Dummer's dinner-parties would be the pleasantest in London if Mrs. Dummer did not always insist on being present herself. Mrs. Dummer asked twenty-nine of her dearest friends to dinner last week. No one nowadays takes the trouble to send regrets, so the nine who answered all accepted. They were asked for 9.15. Mrs. Dummer waited an hour, and then sat down to dinner alone. A letter about the bad manners of our age has just appeared in all the newspapers. Mrs. Dummer wrote it: but it is signed "A Retired Lady-in-Waiting"

Mrs. Dummer Gives a Very Fashionable Dinner Party

Nine Guests Accepted: None Turned Up. Why? The Wine is Copious, the Food French, at Mrs. Dummer's. Look at the Opposite Page—it Reveals the Reasons. Those Whom the Gods Love Dine Alone

LORD REGINALD

Lord Reginald went into Buck's for a drink on his way. There he heard the Cesarewitch result. A more fortunate friend stood him a drink to console him. And another. And another. And another. Lord Reginald forgot all about Mrs. Dummer's dinner. In fact dinner was the last thing he wanted to think about

HIGHER THINGS

The Watsons are famous climbers. Her dearest friend says that when the London traffic is hushed in the small hours, you can hear the Watsons still persistently climbing. A duchess asked them at the last moment to dine. So they went to Mrs. Dummer's the following evening, and pretended they had mistaken the date

THE BARBAROUS BARBER

Poppaea Beehank perhaps should be forgiven. The famous actress asked for an Eton-cut. But the barber gave her a Borstal-bob. She tells the world she has German measles, and lies in bed, repeating hopefully "My hair grows longer and longer every day in every way"

A BOX OF SWEETS

Pierre Fichu and little Flopsy Flayre had no excuse except each other. He called in a taxi for her at his flat, and took her to see Charlie Chaplin. "He's much funnier than old Dum-Dum: besides it's dark there, and we can dance afterwards." He wrote afterwards that he had been detained at the Embassy. True enough, but not at the one in Albert Gate

INSPIRATION

The famous Wilhelmina Wallington has just discovered that "policeman's" rhymes with "Huysmans." Oblivious of all but her art, she rushed to the rhyming dictionary and wrote a poem called "Bow Street à rebours." She is going to dedicate it "To my oldest friend, Dahlia Dummer." The "oldest" will not help matters

CUTS AND CATS

Lady Isington went to a new epidermatologist. He lifted her face and straightened her nose, but the treatment left traces. She wrote to Mrs. Dummer that she had been assaulted by a cat burglar

Fish

THE LOTTERY

Captain Babe Devereux is too tired to make a choice among his numberless invitations. He puts all the cards he gets into a hat—a silk one, of course—and languidly picks one out with his eyes shut. The one he picked was not Mrs. Dummer's

Douglas Pollard

Recipes Old and New

The mellowing influence of good food on civilised beings cannot be under-rated, or its importance exaggerated. It is conducive to success and, which is more important, to happiness. This must not be overlooked even by dancers who jazz between courses and by men who eat only for the sake of feeding. It was the opinion even in the days when Markham was writing his *English Housewife*: "To speak then of the Knowledges which belong to our British House-wife—I hold the principal to be a perfect skill in Cookery. She that is utterly ignorant therein may not by the Lawes of strict Justice challenge the freedom of Marriage—because indeed She can perform but half her vow. She may love and obey but she cannot cherish and keepe her Husband."

These are grave words, but not graver than the subject itself, I mean, not the British housewife, but cooking, considered, so to speak, from the higher point of view. *Cuisine* should be taken seriously first of all by the cook (obviously, that is if she is worthy of the name) and also by both hostesses and guests.

Yet the income tax and the servant problem combine in making life complicated, and that is where the personal element comes in tactfully and changes what might have been an indifferent dinner indifferently cooked into a delicious one with just that touch of the "unexpected" which makes for success. In fact, the modern hostess should have that principal knowledge which Markham values so highly even if not for the ultimate end which he appraises.

The French have many defects; so I am assured by people who know, but no one will dispute the fact that they can cook. That makes up for many things. When I speak of French cooking, I mean of course the *real* French cooking which knows nothing of hotel chemistry and cosmopolitan concoctions; the cooking which is represented at its best by provincial food of the south and centre of France, and home recipes, which ignores substitutes and remembers traditions. So I hope that the following dishes will be found both useful and pleasant, and will be appreciated because either they are old favourites or new variations on well-known themes.

Omelette paysanne

This omelette can be made in different ways. First fry a few small pieces of bacon, one potato, cut also in very small pieces; add this to your beaten eggs, together with chopped parsley, and cook the omelette in bacon fat preferably. It should be about half an inch thick and tossed like a pancake, not rolled. Another pleasing combination is bacon, parsley and sorrel instead of potatoes; you can also add chopped spring onion to the mixture.

Omelette à la crème

This is a more ambitious and civilised omelette and when *réussie* a delicious one. Beat the eggs as usual, add to the mixture a few fresh mushrooms, previously cooked in butter, fry quickly, fold it in the usual way, pour over your omelette—which must be light, soft and not too well cooked—a béchamel sauce, well seasoned, and to which cream (and if you like, a little grated cheese) has been added, and brown lightly under a gas grill (if you have not got a salamander). Needless to say, all these operations must be done in a few minutes. No omelette should be made slowly or kept waiting a second. You can decorate it, if you want it more elaborate, with a few slices of truffles.

Chou rouge flamande

The red cabbage, which is not much used except as salad in France, and, I am told, still less in England, can be treated to great advantage and served as a kind of nondescript course which is, so to speak, half a vegetable, half a sweet.

I. Cut the cabbage in quarters, remove all the hard parts, wash well in several waters and cut it like a fine *julienne*. Put in an earthenware saucepan a good piece of butter and begin to melt it, add salt, pepper and a tablespoonful of wine vinegar, then your cabbage, stir well, put the lid on and cook very slowly for about an hour and a half. At this stage of the cooking add a few eating apples cut in small pieces and a tablespoonful of castor sugar and go on cooking slowly for another hour. Serve very hot in the casserole.

II. Cut and prepare the cabbage as before, put in a saucepan with enough water to cover it, add several eating apples cut in small pieces, salt, pepper, a little piece of butter and two cloves. Cook for two hours and a half with the lid on, on a slow fire, stirring occasionally. When it is nearly ready, prepare a *liaison* with very little potato flour, a tablespoonful of red currant jelly and same quantity of wine vinegar. Stir it in well, cook for a few minutes more and serve.

For both these variations of the same dish, the quantity of apples is rather a matter of taste, but there should be at least two apples for a medium-sized cabbage. The whole thing must be very soft and well cooked, and distinctly sweet, yet with a distinct vinegary sharpness.

Bananes gratinées

An "amusing" dish which is neither a sweet nor a savoury: melt some butter in a fireproof dish, add salt and a little paprika and cook it for a few minutes, stirring well; then put in some bananas, sprinkle with breadcrumbs and grated cheese (Gruyère and Parmesan mixed), add a few small pieces of butter here and there, and cook in the oven. You may like it or dislike it, but it is at least worth trying. It "grows" on some people like a bad habit.

Banana jam

The ingredients required are: 1 lb ripe bananas, three cups sweet orange juice, juice of one lemon, $\frac{3}{4}$ lb of white or brown sugar. Cut the bananas into slices one quarter-inch thick, add the sugar and the juice of oranges and lemon, boil slowly till it thickens and becomes a rich red colour. Care must be taken that the mixture does not catch.

Pain de gênes

This excellent cake will be useful either for tea or served with a crème. Peel half a pound of almonds (and five or six bitter ones), pound them well; add four eggs, one at a time, mix; then two tablespoonfuls of ground rice, a piece of butter the size of an egg (it is advisable to cut it in small pieces) and about three tablespoonfuls of castor sugar; mix well together, add a sherry glassful of Kirschwasser and mix well again. Prepare a tin lined with buttered paper—the flat kind for open tarts being the best shape—put in your batter and cook it in a hot oven for about twenty-five minutes; let it get cold before you take it out of the tin.

Galette de Gannat

Put on the pastry board half a pound of flour, make a batter with half a pound of grated Gruyère cheese, mix well; add then six eggs, one by one, and mix well till the batter is perfectly smooth. Flatten it on a buttered paper to the shape of a galette about one inch thick, paint the top with yolk of egg and bake in a moderate oven for about an hour.

Galette à la crème

A very simple galette: take a certain quantity of fresh cream, work in smoothly as much flour as it will absorb to make a fairly stiff batter, flavour with essence of orange or lemon, add sugar. Make a galette about half an inch thick, sprinkle over it coarse sugar, bake in a quick oven. The result is, or ought to be, a kind of blistered galette very light and delicious.

Tarte au jambon

Beat four eggs (allowing two for each person) add some milk, salt and pepper and a few rashers of streaky bacon, fried crisply and cut into tiny pieces. Mix this well and pour the mixture into a flat dish lined with pastry. Bake in a very quick oven for about ten minutes and serve at once.

Œufs brouillés au safran

Beat the eggs well (two for each person), add about a puddingspoonful of milk, salt and pepper and beat again. Mix in a pan a little butter, a teaspoonful of concentrated beef stock, a pinch of saffron, and cook it for a few minutes; then put in the eggs, stirring all the time. They should be done on a slow fire so that they remain light and creamy, and, of course, served the moment they are ready.

Œufs landaise

Grill or fry a pork sausage and chop it finely, also fry in the fat onion and parsley chopped finely; put all this in a fireproof dish and break your eggs over it, add salt and pepper, a little grated cheese; begin cooking on the fire, finish quickly in the oven. The right proportion is one medium-sized sausage to two eggs. In some places they also fry with the rest one small tomato cut in small pieces (the pips should be removed).

Lait cuit à la crème

Fill a fireproof saucepan with milk and leave it about three days without even touching it; then skim it, cut it in square pieces (it has then the consistency of junket) and cook it on a very little fire for about two hours so that it does not get really hot. Let it get cold, put in a hollow dish and cover it with a mixture of cream and milk. This *laitage*, which does not seem to be very well known, has a rather special taste, and those who like it like it very much. As for those who do not . . .

Beurre de sardines

This is a delicious and unusual hors d'œuvre. Take one or two tins of sardines, carefully remove the skin and bones and pound in a mortar; add the same quantity of butter, a little salt and pepper and mix thoroughly so that it becomes a very smooth paste. Serve with toast. You can, if you like, add to the mixture a few cooked soft roes. The mixture will keep for several days in an ice chest, but it should always be served very cold, the consistency being that of butter on a cold day. You can either give it a shape or keep it in a terrine. It is also delicious for sandwiches.

Blinis

Caviare is at its best served with blinis, which are simply small buckwheat pancakes. They should be about the size of a small saucer (there are special pans for frying them or you can make them in a larger pan and cut them with a tumbler), rather thick and tossed like an ordinary pancake. Put one on a plate, pour over a little hot melted butter, spread with caviare, cover with another pancake, more melted butter, and serve sour cream with it.

The batter is prepared in exactly the same way as batter for an ordinary pancake, only buckwheat flour is used instead of ordinary flour, and a little yeast is added. This batter should be prepared a few hours before using. As for the sour cream, a few drops of lemon juice added to the cream will do, if real sour cream is not obtainable.

While on the subject of caviare, it is also very good served on a crumpet cut in two (in the thickness), slightly toasted and treated with melted butter exactly like blinis.

Pipérade

Take sweet peppers, cut them in slices and remove the seeds, and cook them in pork fat. If you are not certain of the quality of your pork fat (so few people nowadays fatten and kill their own pigs!), use a mixture of butter and olive oil, or butter and a little bacon fat. Cook in the same way the same quantity of tomatoes (peeled), adding them later, as they do not take so long to cook. Mix well, season, let it simmer till it is all soft, melted and juicy. This mixture having been reheated or kept hot, when you want to finish the *pipérade* you simply break in, one by one and without beating them, four or five eggs (this would do for, say, half a pound of each vegetable and for about six people), stir them in quickly over the spirit lamp or the electric stove "full on." After a few minutes you will get an exquisite mixture in which the eggs have entirely disappeared and with which, should you like to make this your main supper dish, you can add some slices of Bayonne ham lightly tossed in butter and fried bread.

A delightful hat for a delightful tea-party.
Posed by Gertrude Lawrence

Moussaka

This is a pleasant luncheon dish, oriental in character, and easy to make. Take two aubergines, peel them and cut them in slices and fry them either in bacon fat or in butter. Also peel and cut in quarters six tomatoes, remove the seeds and cook them in the same fat you have used for the aubergines. Pass through a fine mincing machine one pound of lean mutton, season well with pepper, salt, spices, add two shallots and parsley chopped together. Take a terrine or any deep fireproof dish, butter it well and put in alternate layers of minced mutton and aubergines and tomatoes till the dish is full. Cover with a buttered paper and cook *au bain marie* in a moderate oven for about forty minutes. Serve with it a tomato sauce made with fresh tomatoes in the following manner.

Cut four tomatoes in quarters, remove the seeds, put the quarters in a small saucepan with one carrot and one onion finely chopped, salt and pepper; cover with water and bring to the boil; cook it well, then squeeze through a muslin. Add a brown roux—a little stock, a drop of wine vinegar and cook again, whipping well, to proper consistency. Add a few small pieces of butter at the last minute. Should be fairly thick.

The preparations given above are for a *moussaka* large enough for four or five people.

Saucisses aux choux

Put a piece of bacon, about half a pound in weight, in a large saucepan with water, broken pepper, salt and the classical bay leaf, thyme and parsley tied together; cook it for about one hour and a half. Then remove it if you are a careful person and want to use it at its best for something else (or cold in the Irish peasant fashion)—or recklessly leave it in if you do not mind. Anyhow, the water is sufficiently flavoured by now for our purpose. Bring it once more to the boil and then throw in your cabbage, previously well washed and cut in smallish pieces.

While the cabbage is cooking grill the sausages (the long French ones made of pork are the only possible ones for this dish) and keep them warm. Drain the cabbage well, add more salt and pepper, a little grated nutmeg, a small piece of butter, and put half of it in a fireproof dish, then the sausages on this bed, then the rest of the cabbage. Pour a cupful of good beef stock over it. Cook in a moderate oven with the lid on for about half an hour or so. This dish, if properly prepared, is quite delicious.

Howard and Joan Costa

The young and newly-shingled Countess of Seafield gives a dinner party at the Embassy Club, which includes her friends Miss Maureen and Miss Oonagh Guinness, to celebrate her return from South Africa. Her lovely white moiré dress (Mr Viner leaning over the table a little overshadows it) was bought at the shop of Lady Evelyn Graham. Miss Maureen Guinness wears black velvet with exquisite gardenias

People and Places

Casting one's pearls before the cook is not so profligate as it seems, if one has a literary salon, for literary lions are as hungry for filet mignon as for knowledge, and a cook is to be prized above rubies

There is a buffet upon which pyramids of cakes tower amid battalions of bottles of fine wine. This may be a delight to the gourmand, but it is too sumptuous. Nothing is more fatal to spirited conversation than an excess of cakes

MRS CONGREVE, *Congreve Manor, Staffordshire*

Pollo con arroz

Cut a fowl into neat joints and fry in a wineglassful of olive oil in a stewpan. When nearly cooked, add some chopped onions and fry with it. Then add about 4 tomatoes cut into quarters (skinned first) and a teacupful of rice. Add a little broth and stew until the rice is cooked and the broth dried up. Serve in a deep dish with chopped parsley over. Serve without lid as the steam must not be left in.

MISS V. SACKVILLE-WEST *(Mrs Harold Nicolson), who is a connoisseur of recipes as well as winner of the Hawthornden prize gives this recipe for an intriguing Persian dish*:

Khoresche fesanjan

1 lb meat or 1 fowl, 8 oz walnut kernels, 8 oz pomegranate juice, 3 oz butter.

Cut the meat into cubes (or joint the fowl) and boil till cooked. Strain off the liquid. Pound the nuts *very finely* and lightly fry them in the butter (about 5 minutes), then add the pomegranate juice and 1 pint of water. When it comes to the boil, add the cooked meat and simmer all together *very gently* till it is the consistency of custard. (Care must be taken not to let it boil fast, or it will stick to the sides of the saucepan.) Serve with boiled rice, on a separate dish. The meat can also be pounded into small balls.

MRS EDWARD NEVILLE *of Skellingthorp Manor introduces an unusual but excellent method for*

Hungarian paprika huhn

Either leave the chicken whole or cut it up. Put 4 to 5 oz of butter into a pan, and when the butter is hot fry in it about a handful of sliced onion and cook till delicately coloured. Now lay in it either a large fowl or two young ones, well dusted with paprika, and let all cook well together till the fowl is tender and the sauce of a nice consistency. Serve with macaroni or noodles round the dish.

LADY GROVE, *of Sedgehill Manor, Shaftesbury*

Game pie

Take 2 lb of calf's liver cut in pieces about 1 in square, 1 lb bacon, not too fat.

Cut up a small piece of butter. Take salt, pepper, spices, parsley and shallot, all chopped fine. Fry all these ingredients, often stirring them gently. When thoroughly done, drain off the grease and put cold into a mortar and pound them. Bone and skin your game, cut into pieces but not too small; lay it in a stewpan with a little butter to make it firm; do not let it brown. When done enough, season with cayenne and salt. Lay some of the forcemeat at the bottom of the dish and then a layer of game until the dish is full—the forcemeat always at the top. Put the dish into a stewpan of warm water on the fire for 2 or 3 hours. When done, squeeze and flatten the meat into the dish. Pour hot butter over it when cold.

Here you see a picnic in progress. The Marchioness of Queensberry and Miss Carley Robinson enjoy China tea out of a sprigged teapot, and sit gossiping and watching the hovering butterflies

This photograph of the Marquess and Marchioness of Blandford was taken in Yorkshire.

The Wedding Breakfast

by Aldous Huxley

Aldous Huxley was a regular contributor to Vogue from 1923 to 1929 having joined Condé Nast Publications in 1922 as a sub-editor.

In the day of Queen Elizabeth a bride would eat on her wedding morning a breakfast consisting of roast beef, stewed rabbits and a loaf of bread, washed down with beer and possibly a nip of Canary wine. At the end of the church ceremony, while the congregation was scrambling for the favours sewn on her dress, and even (modesty assist me!) for her garters, she had to partake deeply of a huge loving cup filled with something like sherry, after which she was expected to go home and eat a dinner the like of which, for richness and sheer solidity, it would be impossible to meet with in these present days of leanness.

Ah, those dinners of the English golden age! Nobody now living has eaten anything remotely like them. . . .

A Grecian dinner, on the other hand, was quite different: To begin with, the Athenians confined themselves almost exclusively to fish, considering that there was something rather coarse and barbarous about the consumption of joints of meat. Their luxury was the delicious Friday luxury of the "maigre" menu. A curious feature about the Athenian banquet was that it was not cooked by one's own domestics, but by professional caterers. It was not till after the days of Athenian glory that the Greeks began keeping really skilled cooks in their houses. Before that time it was customary, when a good dinner was required, for the host to go out into the market place and shout "Who wants to take a dinner contract?" He would immediately be surrounded by a score of professional caterers. With one of these he would strike a bargain, and would then go off to another contractor to arrange about the supply of plate and ornaments for the table. It is curious to note that these professional cooks always spoke and wrote their menus in the Doric, as opposed to the Attic, dialect of Greek. Doric was the gastronomic language then, just as French is today. *Pré salé* always sounds so much better than mere mutton; even the intelligent Greeks were taken in by the rich sound of an unfamiliar appellation. "A rose by any other name would smell as sweet." Fried whiting, however, appears to smell much sweeter when it is called *merlan frit*.

Erté designs for "George White's Scandals", New York, 1926

VOGUE

Early August Issue
1926

ONE SHILLING

Condé Nast & Co Ltd
Proprietors

ROUND THE CLOCK *in* MAYFAIR

Drawings by
MARK OGILVIE GRANT

11.30 A.M.
Viscountess Curzon, divinely fair, arrives with Miss Georgina Curzon for the Eton and Harrow match at Lord's and no one troubles to look at the cricket

1.30 P.M.
Lady Loughborough, lunching with Miss Poppy Baring at Sovrani's, broods on the wrongs of the modern woman, to whom all puddings are taboo

3.30 P.M.
Any of these ladies at Roehampton might be the Marquise de Casa Maury, but the one in the left-hand corner is the most like her

6.30 P.M.
Stephen Tennant and a young friend who is resplendent in a tartan tie snatch a hurried cocktail at the Five Hundred Club

12.30 A.M.
(Left) A magnificent Marchioness at the Embassy does not observe her fried egg, while in the background you may see Lady Massereene and Ferrard greeting the Brinsley Plunkets and Lady Lettice Lygon

1.30 A.M.
(Right) "Don't drink all that lemonade before I come back," says blithe Miss Maureen Guinness to Miss Rosemary Hope-Vere before she picks her Ward twin at the "Bat"

Meserole

The atmosphere of practicality pervades this dining-room in Mrs St John Hutchinson's London house. A sideboard, a set of chairs and a table on which a modern design is painted furnish a room designed for purposes of eating and not of lounging

In Lady Sackville's dining-room deep orange walls with a ceiling shaded to pale apricot colour have been chosen as a background to walnut furniture and a green marble table supported by urn-shaped silver pedestals

This small dining-room shows how a limited space may be utilised to great advantage by the careful selection of appropriate and decorative pieces. Decorated by Mr Allan Walton

The Cheerful Dining-room

by Aldous Huxley

At what date and for what reason the dining-room came into vogue it is difficult precisely to determine. Certainly the fashion is not older than the early-middle of the nineteenth century. It was then, on the flowing tide of Victorianism, that the gloomy thing came in. The dark room, wainscoted with fumed oak, hung with deep crimson paper and carpeted to match, had some connection—vital, if obscure—with the prevailing spirit of the times. "Life is real, life is earnest," those rich, severe glooms seem to proclaim.

But we—though life to us may be quite as real and earnest as it was to the best Bostonians of an older generation—we find that reality and earnestness need not necessarily be associated with darkness and ponderosity. Moreover, we know that sunlight is the best germicide, and that cheerful surroundings act through the mind most favourably on the digestion. Hence our altered views on house planning and interior decoration—views which find expression nowhere more closely than in our dining-rooms.

As the place in which we satisfy the two most important of our instincts—the instinct of self-preservation and of the herd—as the place, in other words, where we eat and talk most agreeably with our friends and relations, the dining-room deserves to be well treated by the architect and decorator. It should be a warm, bright, cheerful room, a room conducive to talk and quick digestion, enlivening and not depressing.

E J Mason

Top: The dining-room in the Rt Hon. Sir Samuel and Lady Hoare's house has interesting arrangements for light and heat. Silver-grey satin, stretched below the ceiling, conceals a circuit of lights which illuminate walls and ceiling. The walls are orange, and the carpet a deep garter blue. The heat is radiated from the mirror

Above: Tappa cloths from Fiji and Samoa in dull tones of beige, grey and black make a decorative wall treatment which is startlingly modern in effect. French Provincial chairs of the Directoire period and examples of African wood carvings complete an unusual and stimulating interior. Mr. X. M. Boulestin was the decorator

The Newest Note IN TABLE DECORATION

From Paris come many different kinds of crystal trees and other glass table decorations, such as the fantastic fish shown in the centre of this table on a mirror tray

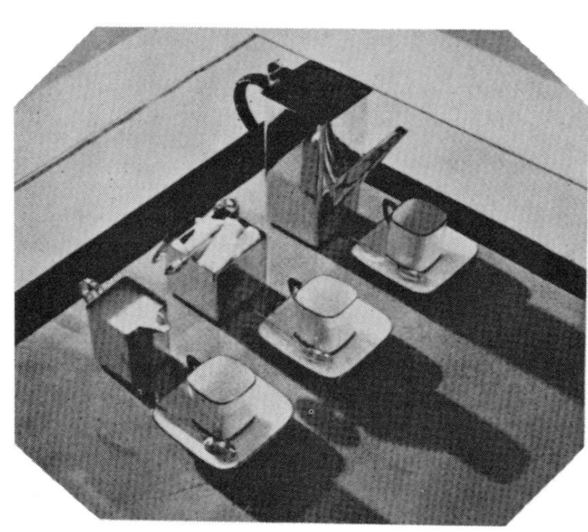

A square coffee service is distinctly of the modern school. The cups are of white porcelain with black handles; the coffee pot, cream jug and sugar bowl are of silver

"BENSON" WARE

(Late W. A. S. Benson and Co., of 82-3 New Bond Street, W.1)

B.C. 3223 A.D. 1923

" BENSON" WARE is known the world over for its elegant appearance and is the absolute replica of Sheffield Plate

Manufactured by

THE HAMMERSMITH FOUNDRY & METAL WORKS

1a Westville Road, Shepherds Bush

Obtainable at

Harrods, Barkers, Selfridges, A. & N. Co-op. Society, Civil Service, Shoolbreds & other leading Stores, Jewellers, etc.

Miss Tilly Losch, Miss Olga Lynn, Lord Berners, Lady Jersey and their hostess, Lady Castlerosse

30s

Everyone who was anyone was a Hostess in *Vogue* in the thirties. If you were Lady Portarlington, Mrs Reginald Fellowes, Mrs Syrie Maugham, Lady Mendl, Miss Elsa Maxwell, Lady Colefax or Lady Louis Mountbatten, you were a Famous Hostess and it was worth recording and photographing how you presented food ("Mrs Gordon Leith serves cheeses on leaf-shaped slabs of wood") and what you ate ("of course, it would be Mrs Ernest Simpson who first thought of the wonderful combination of seeded white grapes with little cubes of Dutch cheese, stuck through with a wooden toothpick").

Lady Mendl welcomes her guests

You didn't cook, you had a cook—"One of my friends devotes as much as an hour a day giving directions, even though her chef is one of the best known in France. She does it to keep his pride and ambition at their peak." *Vogue* ran a series: "My Cook is a Chinaman" ". . . a Russian" ". . . an Arab" ". . . three Mexicans", concluding with "My cook is a catastrophe", by Lesley Blanch.

In March 1930 *Vogue* said: "The cook one cares to have and to keep is the kind who appreciates the mistress of the house having knowledge and likes to be given books that increase her own knowledge of dishes." This was by way of explanation for devoting a whole page to THE COOKERY BOOKSHELF: "It is strange that the art of eating is not a more important feature of our daily newspapers. Books, plays, sport, all have their regular solid columns and their great names, but where shall we find the art of eating given a permanent place, and when will the title of Reviewer of Food be one of dignity, accepted by the most celebrated? This comparative lack of comment on the art of eating is the more surprising since interest in food is common to all. The population of Great Britain is over forty millions. All these people do not read the new novels and biographies, or our publishers would be millionaires, nor do they visit the theatre, or there would be no poor producers. But all of them eat meals, and are contented or dissatisfied as those meals are good or bad, and yet, though there are great book reviewers and celebrated stage critics, there are no food reviewers, and columns on the Art of Good Living are meagre and infrequent."

The reason for this page in *Vogue* was to talk about Marcel Boulestin's "good new book" *Herbs, Salads and Seasonings*. "Though a welcome addition, it will not be one of the first acquisitions for the cookery library of either mistress or

maid. The same author's two earlier books of recipes and advice, *Simple French Cooking for English Homes* and *A Second Helping* and his *Conduct of the Kitchen* might come in the first half dozen. Add also to either shelf Lady Jekyll's *Kitchen Essays*, if you are lucky enough to light on a copy, and a very good recent book by a woman, *Kitchen Ranging*, by Pearl Adam, which is full not only of recipes but of good talk about good food from all over the world. André Simon's *Art of Good Living* will certainly be found on the mistress's shelf, along with *Clarissa or the Old Cook*. G. B. Stern's *Bouquet* is another volume that will have its place there, and certainly George Saintsbury's *Notes on a Cellar Book* and P. Morton Shand's *Book of Wine* as well as his *Book of Food*. Others that must be included are Mrs Martineau's *Caviare to Candy* and A. H. Adair's *Dinners Long and Short*, both of which the mistress of the house will want at hand when she is planning meals."

Meanwhile, back in the drawing-room with *Vogue* in October 1931: "There is one thing about these crises, reflects the hostess, it causes people to stay at home, to give their minds to the real things of life in place of—what shall we call it?—the flummery. All the unnecessary rush of life, this hurrying back from Biarritz, this spending of Christmas in Switzerland, this rushing down south, with perhaps a trip to America thrown in, that is gone and done away with. The eternal telephoning, the fixing of restaurant parties, that too has faded from us. And there is left behind the real life of England, its home, its entertaining, its dining-rooms and kitchens.

"In these days we know false gaiety from true and we plan for a more stable happiness. The woman who will socially be most popular this winter is the hostess who keeps a good table. That old-fashioned phrase has always been the perfect compliment. Such a hostess entertains with dignity in her own house, understands the cuisine, orders in alliance with her cook, sees to the choosing, chambering and right serving of the wines; sees to the perfection of her table decorations as well as to the perfection of her food."

And in May 1932: "Of course big parties have been comparatively rare, but clever hostesses are always able to find a new excuse to invite a few friends to enjoy a good evening together.

"Some of the most exciting evenings we have had of late grew out of the recent rage for old-fashioned games. The craze started with the revival of such nursery favourites as Musical Chairs, Blindman's Buff, Sticking the Pig, and Bobbing for Apples. The latter game went out of favour very quickly as none of the women could play at it and risk losing their new eyelashes."

ONE BARTENDER IS A NECESSITY

Later in the year came THE NEW ENTERTAINING—The Diner-Out Reviews the Present Season in Paris: "The cocktail party, instead of being a spread of little nonsenses to eat with cocktails, has now become a real feast. Every experienced hostess has begun to realize that the fashionable world is dining at her cocktail buffet, and has resorted to giving more substantial things than olives, potato chips and caviare sandwiches. In fact, she has succumbed to the inevitable and now supplies hot dogs, hot ham sandwiches (of the quick-lunch variety), and, I doubt not, will be serving eggs and bacon, beans and corned-beef hash before she has finished the season.

"You see, entertaining is in our blood, so that if we can't entertain in the prescribed manner, we go on entertaining in the manner we can afford—but entertain we must.

"The thing that every one enjoys most this season is the afternoons at home that five Paris hostesses have adopted as their own. The Comtesse Mercati has Monday afternoon; the Princess Cito, Tuesday; Lady Mendl, Wednesday; Madame Ralli, Thursday; and the young Princess Faucigny-Lucinge, Friday. We all have standing invitations to these houses on those days, and all Paris turns up. There is a sort of friendly rivalry over the food, each one of them usually springing something new in order not to be outdone by the others.

"The Comtesse Mercati has a chocolate cake that no one could duplicate without the recipe—and she can't remember the recipe.

"The Princess Cito's chef experiments with chutneys and curried tit-bits on toast which are, to say the least, original. Also she has another thing I find very good: enormous dishes of crisp grilled bacon, which you eat in your fingers like potato chips. Lady Mendl has something she calls 'Marbury Rolls', and also a delicious mixture of Roquefort cheese paste seasoned with tomato chutney, Worcester sauce, and onion, spread thickly on squares of bread, and grilled in the oven with a garniture of bacon. And sometimes she has big dishes of hot French fried potatoes instead of the usual potato chips. Madame Ralli thought up the idea of having whitebait and courgettes and aubergines fried like potato chips. The latest thing is to get the Comte Stanislas de la Rochefoucauld to be bartender and make the cocktails. I don't know where he learned to make them, but they are wonderful, and I feel he could only have acquired the trick from some expert American bartender over the Mexican border."

In January 1933 the Hostess was told: "Unlimited expense is not the first requisite of successful entertaining. An enormous house and a retinue of servants are by no means a necessary part of successful hospitality. Frequently, in fact, such an establishment seems out of step with the times. Money must be mixed with brains. Economy of time is as necessary as economy of money, especially to the typical woman of the period, who has many duties and pleasures. One hour of the day, one person to whom to give all orders—this must be an inviolable rule. Every morning the cook reports what is in the larder. Every morning or every night, she comes with her account book. If the family is to be away over the week-end, the big roast will not be ordered on Friday, but on Monday. The baked ham will take its place on Wednesday, rather than later in the week. Chops, small steaks, and other smaller cuts will fill in towards the end. Though this sounds like the most kindergarten dictate of common sense, it is transgressed often and meaninglessly, even in otherwise well-run households."

TWO WAITERS ARE A LUXURY

There were even MENUS FOR LIMITED INCOMES: "Caviare is not a necessity of entertaining, minestrone can be as good as turtle soup, a delicious purée of carrots and beetroot will be as readily devoured as the first green peas at many times the price, and Canterbury lamb will have just as much success as pheasants in the season." There followed "seven menus for lunch and seven for dinner that do not exceed more than three courses, which are compiled of first quality but inexpensive varieties of foodstuffs, and intended for the household of small family and small staff—or no staff at all." LUNCH MENU (1) was Macaroni au gratin . . . Pork Chops. Fried Apples. Mashed Potatoes. Creamed Celery . . . Salad . . . Candied Oranges. DINNER (1) Dressed Crab (or Dublin Prawns). Chicken Cutlets. Creamed Swedes. Scrambled Cheese.

In 1935 June Platt, *Vogue's* first regular cookery contributor since X. Marcel Boulestin, began writing and illustrating "Good Food".

And in 1936, with increasing readership, *Vogue* acknowledged that every one of its readers was not a hostess: "From letters we receive, we gather that among readers of *Vogue* are the young bachelor women who live on their own, or in twos and threes, and do a job of work in the daytime. They lunch in restaurants, but there are many evenings when they prepare their own evening meals, perhaps with limited resources. One such reader asks us to make helpful suggestions." FOOD FOR THE BUSY WOMAN included 10-minute dishes: "QUICK SOUPS can be made by using pea flour, bean flour, or soup squares, which one mixes with cold milk to a paste." 20-MINUTE DISHES: "Hot Sandwich.—Butter two slices of bread. Put a thin slice of cheese on each and a slice of ham between them. Fry the sandwich on both sides in a very hot pan."; and 30-MINUTE DISHES: "*Poireaux en asperges.*—Cook a bunch of spring onions in boiling salted water. Serve with vinaigrette sauce." Luckily June Platt was there to give more helpful recipes.

The Busy Woman was soon forgotten. There followed Lady Morvyth Benson's advice to the FRIDAY-TO-MONDAY HOSTESS: "One delicate matter often worries this particular hostess. Can married couples be relied on to share a double room or not?"

With this problem sorted out (page 96) we find: "Almost as queer as the fact that few sailors can swim is the fact that few English women have a flair for hospitality.

"Sailors, of course, don't care—but to be known as a good hostess is one of the nicest feathers that a woman can wear in her cap, and in this age of informal entertaining it seems a pity that while the caps of our American contemporaries are be-feathered as Hiawatha's own, we, with generations of house-proud women behind us and an inherent knowledge of the art of entertaining to guide us, seem satisfied with not much more upon our heads than shame.

"Why give one of those hectic overcrowded cocktail scrimmages which nobody enjoys? It's just as easy, much nicer and no more expensive to give a series of small and cosy parties with room for all to relax in comfort."

The decade ended on a sombre note. In August 1939: " 'You've got to be Prepared' is a good slogan for shoppers as well as the Services." In September: "The time we spend in the garden and the space we usually devote to flowers can be better occupied by growing vegetables for food and in providing as many as possible with those elements of nutrition which may become scarce. The flower garden, or most of it, must be emptied. The fat, rich soil is the best you will find for vegetables. Much of the lawn, too, will have to go, but the potatoes the ground will produce will compensate for the loss of its cool greenness." In November: "A possible result of bombardment or other war activities is that gas stoves and electric cookers, with some other things, may not function. It is well to cross this particular bridge before you come to it, for an auxiliary source of cooking heat can be easily obtained and kept in reserve. At a pinch one can do wonders with a methylated spirit lamp, with a good supply of spirit. A hot meal may be a life-saver to some exhausted war worker, and though good food can be had straight from the tin, to accept a succession of such meals is depressing and wasteful, for it is not making the best use of the excellent products now available in tinned form.

"All extravagance in cooking must be cut out so that every usable scrap of food is consumed."

Finally, in December 1939: "In Paris—Now—They shelter in the Ritz super-cellars in satin or wool pyjamas, hooded coats, warmly, gaily lined (Molyneux and Piguet). . . . They dine at Maxim's (Albert still presiding) in chic black afternoon clothes—broadcloth and velvet."

Farewell to this Season

by Elsa Maxwell

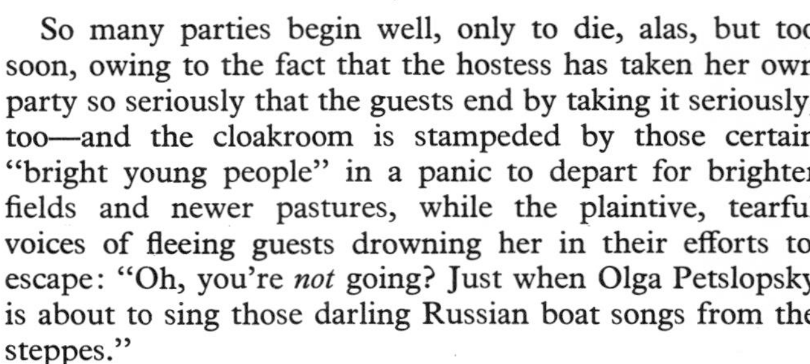

Miss Elsa Maxwell is one of the world's most brilliant party-givers and her murder-dinner-party was a sensation of the London season. In this article, reviewing the season, Miss Maxwell analyses the party of today, and indicates some of its necessary ingredients.

Hoyningen-Huene

Miss Maxwell, mixer of parties

What makes or breaks a party? How often have I been asked this poignant, heartrending question—by sadly disillusioned hostesses of dismal and dreary parties that have been, and by aspiring but fearful hostesses of parties yet to be.

What a delicate analysis is necessary to dissect the different component parts of a really good party! The making of a successful party is like baking of a wonderful soufflé—the ingredients and proportions must be weighed and measured by the hand of an artist—should be taken out of the oven at exactly the psychological moment—and *served hot*.

So many parties begin well, only to die, alas, but too soon, owing to the fact that the hostess has taken her own party so seriously that the guests end by taking it seriously, too—and the cloakroom is stampeded by those certain "bright young people" in a panic to depart for brighter fields and newer pastures, while the plaintive, tearful voices of fleeing guests drowning her in their efforts to escape: "Oh, you're *not* going? Just when Olga Petslopsky is about to sing those darling Russian boat songs from the steppes."

But the brutal, callous guests of the over-serious hostess push her aside, still expostulating, and, with grim determination, leave her special *Pommery* frappéd 1915 champagne—to relax happily in the stuffy, unbelievable atmosphere of a night-club, where a blasé octoroon raucously warbles a hackneyed song, one that has been heard interminably for the last five years, and where the band is bad, the drink undrinkable, the people unthinkable, and everybody completely happy.

"What is the use of entertaining?" sobs the unhappy hostess of a most lamentable soirée. "I sent out invitations a month ago. I have spent weeks in preparation and hundreds of what Daddy makes in the City—and not a cat stayed after twelve." This is the epitaph of most parties, carefully arranged and prepared long in advance—when the edge of spontaneity has been rubbed off and the delicate flower of anticipation has withered with so long an interval between desire and fulfilment.

Carefully studied effects must appear just to happen, and the joy of the hostess in her own party must be the first element encountered by a guest. I have often been moved to sudden inward unholy laughter when, upon entering salon or ballroom, I first catch sight of the harassed and anguished face of an unhappy hostess, so obviously suffering at being trapped by her own party in the doorway, and, as the hordes of that vast vacuity known as the "Visiting List" troop in, her last hope dies, and she knows all is lost.

For the "Visiting List" sounds the death-knell of every party where it is employed. How often I have heard a charming, gay, debonair butterfly anxiously demand from her friend the loan of her visiting list when she is about to issue invitations for a party. Poor butterfly! Little does she know she is thereby placing the noose around her neck with her own hands.

One should never *have* to ask people to a party just because they are on one's list. Guests should be selected with as much care as a new Reboux hat, and should be equally becoming, for a hostess should wear her guests at a party as she wears a hat—with an air! Also, people should not be invited because one dined with them last week—or because you owe them a lunch—or because your father plays backgammon with their father at the club—or because a friend asks to bring a friend—or because you feel sorry for those "poor things "next door: "Let's ask them just this once", and the "poor things" instantly become your deadliest enemies on the spot, murdering your party merely by being there.

Ruthlessness is the first attribute towards the achievement of a perfect party. Also, one should have practically no really established "position"—by that, I mean in the world of finance—religion—or diplomacy. If you are officially associated with any one of these worthy métiers—then give up the idea for ever of achieving a party.

Snobs, also, are curiously incapable of gaiety, perhaps because gaiety comes from the soul, and snobs only take their soul "à la meunière." Also, snobs are so busy nicking notches on each rung of the social ladder as the gangster nicks each kill on his gun.

Wealth does not play a large rôle, either, toward the giving of a good party. Many of the great and glorious artists in that wonderful world of make-believe—without whom no party can be a success—with that true generosity known to them alone, will step immediately into the breach, should a party lag ever so little, and with royal prodigality scatter their genius or their laughter in the face of impending ennui. The party immediately takes on a new lease of life and never ends—that is, if it is the party of a friend. Money cannot buy this—it can only be given.

Then there is the deliberately casual hostess, who prides herself in letting her guests do as they want. This is a great mistake. No guests want to do what they want—everything must be done for them at a successful party.

A good party should occur in one room only, and that room should always be too small for the number of guests invited. The room should be brightly illuminated. It is a mistake to have dim and soothing lights.

One should enter a party to sounds of some kind, for the psychology of sound is an important thing to study in the giving of a successful party. I once gave a party in a room too cold and cavernous, where I knew the band would reverberate in hollow cacophony and smite the ear-drums too unpleasantly upon entering, so I hastily procured some beehives, and, successfully concealing them in the room, the ears of the guests were assailed by a pleasant buzzing during lulls in the music.

Never show the slightest anxiety about the ultimate success of your own party. Show, by your attitude, that you are convinced it will be the best party ever given, and your guests will believe it too, and help to make it so.

Which brings me back to the poignant query: "What makes or breaks a party?"

A new idea, plus a sense of humour, makes a party—and the bores break it.

A party, like a soufflé, must never flop

Won't you come to tea?

BY JUNE PLATT

I do think it's pleasant and restful for a few people to sit round the fire in the living-room, or round the dining-room table and eat paper-thin bread and butter and wild strawberry jam and *cœurs à la crème* and drink cup after cup of hot, fragrant tea—and talk and talk. In case you agree, here are four tea-party menus. I have even brought myself to part with my grandmother's strawberry conserve recipe and the secret of making *pains surprises*. You say you haven't the slightest idea what a *pain surprise* is? Well, if properly made, even to the most observant eye it appears to be just an uncut loaf of sandwich bread tied round the middle with a gay, narrow ribbon and bow. The *surprise* part consists of the fact that the top crust lifts off and the loaf is filled with delectable sandwiches lying face up and neatly fitted in.

For the first party I suggest a *pain surprise* filled with chopped mushroom and mayonnaise sandwiches and tomato sandwiches, a large plate of thin white and brown bread and butter, a *cœur à la crème*, a pot of wild strawberry jam, cocoanut drops and white plum cake.

For the second party prepare a *pain surprise* filled with sweet onion and cucumber sandwiches and chopped nut, watercress and mayonnaise sandwiches. Also a plate of thin white and brown bread and butter and rose-petal jelly, hot Scotch buttered scones and marmalade, strawberry tarts and Devonshire cream, and a plate of cookies.

For the third party a *pain surprise* with ham and horse-radish sandwiches and stuffed olive and chopped, salted almond sandwiches. Hot, toasted marmalade sandwiches, praliné cookies, a luscious chocolate cake, and thin white and brown bread and butter with Cape gooseberry jam.

For the fourth party, a *pain surprise* filled with chopped egg and mayonnaise sandwiches and shrimp and mayonnaise sandwiches. Hot bacon scones, thin white and brown bread and butter, my grandmother's strawberry and pineapple and orange conserve, hot cinnamon toast, and a walnut mocha cake to finish the feast.

And now for the various recipes you need:

Pain surprise

Buy a very fresh loaf of sandwich bread about 14 inches long. With a sharp knife carefully slice off the long top crust in one whole piece. Insert a long pointed knife at one corner between the crust and soft part of the bread until you strike bottom; then carefully saw all round the bread. This will have loosened the block of soft bread except for the bottom. Now, insert the knife not quite at the corner between the lower crust and the side crust and push it in until you hit the back crust; then carefully saw your way across almost to the end. The block of white bread will then easily come out intact leaving a box of crust. Use this bread for making the sandwiches, which if properly cut will fit neatly back in the crust. When the lid is again put on it should look to be in its original state again. Tie a pretty ribbon round it (as in the sketch), wrap in wax paper and keep in the refrigerator until ready for the tea-table.

Chopped mushroom and mayonnaise filling

Wash ½ pound of choice mushrooms, dry well, peel, remove stems and chop very fine. Mix with mayonnaise. Salt and pepper to taste.

Tomato sandwiches

Plunge 2 or 3 ripe tomatoes in boiling water, remove and peel, chill for two hours in refrigerator. Cream some butter thoroughly, then spread lightly on the bread. Cover with thin slices of the tomatoes, sprinkle with salt and freshly ground black pepper. Tomato sandwiches should not be made too long before they are wanted as they get soggy.

Cucumber and chopped sweet onion filling

Peel a young cucumber, slice thin, and soak for half an hour in ice water. Do not salt. Drain well, dry on a napkin and chop with 5 or 6 pickled sweet onions. Spread bread with butter and some of the mixture. Salt and pepper lightly. These, also, should be made as late as possible.

Chopped walnut and watercress

Wash and remove leaves only from a bunch of fresh watercress, dry and chop fine. Add to it 2 tablespoons of finely chopped English walnuts and a very little mayonnaise. Salt to taste.

Ham and horseradish sandwiches

Add 1 tablespoon of pickled horseradish to 3 tablespoons of well-creamed butter. Mix well and spread on bread. Lay thin slivers of cold boiled ham between two slices of the bread.

Rawlings

Mrs Rose Kennedy having tea with Teddy, Bobby, Kathleen and Rosemary at the American Ambassador's residence overlooking Hyde Park

Stuffed olives and salted almond filling
Blend ½ cup of minced, stuffed olives with ¼ pound of finely chopped salted almonds and 3 tablespoons of mayonnaise.

Chopped egg and mayonnaise filling
Hard boil 3 eggs, chop fine, add a tablespoon of chopped watercress and 2 tablespoons of mayonnaise. Salt and pepper.

Shrimp and horseradish filling
Peel and clean ½ pound of freshly cooked shrimps. Run through the medium mincing machine, add ½ teaspoon of French mustard, 1 tablespoon of mayonnaise, 2 teaspoons of pickled horseradish, a few drops of lemon juice, and enough whipped cream to make the right consistency to spread. Salt and pepper to taste.

Thin bread and butter
To make thin bread and butter have a really sharp knife and thoroughly creamed butter. It helps to plunge the knife in boiling water and wipe it before making each slice.

Cœurs à la crème
These may be bought in a few French speciality shops, but a very good imitation can be made at home by working plain cottage cheese through a very fine sieve and putting it into one large or several small-sized heart-shaped aluminium moulds which have had several holes punched in the bottom and which have been lined with a piece of cheese-cloth wrung out in a little cold water. Pack well with the cheese and put in the refrigerator to chill. Turn out on to a plate when ready to use and remove the cheese-cloth. Pour a little thick cream over them. They should be eaten with thin bread and butter and wild strawberry jam.

Cocoanut drops

Mix $\frac{1}{2}$ cup of sweetened condensed milk and 2 cups of moist, shredded tinned cocoanut together. Drop by tiny spoonfuls on a well-buttered pan about an inch apart. Bake in a moderate oven until a delicate brown.

White plum cake

Blanch half a pound of almonds, reserve 1 dozen of them for decoration of the cake and shred the rest with a sharp knife. Scald $\frac{1}{2}$ pound of sultana white raisins and soak them until plump; then dry well. Cream 6 ounces of butter with 1 cup of granulated sugar, add the beaten yolks of 4 eggs and beat well. Sift 2 cups of flour with 1 teaspoon of baking powder, $\frac{1}{2}$ teaspoon of grated nutmeg and $\frac{1}{4}$ teaspoon of salt. Put a teaspoon of vanilla and $\frac{1}{2}$ teaspoon of lemon extract in $\frac{1}{4}$ cup of cold water. Add it alternately with the flour to the butter and egg mixture. When well mixed add the raisins and the almonds, which have been lightly floured, and 1 cup of shredded cocoanut. Now fold in the stiffly beaten egg whites, pour into a well-greased, oblong tin which has been carefully lined with buttered white paper. Bake in a moderate oven for about an hour.

Hot buttered scones

Wash and dry well $\frac{1}{2}$ cup of currants. Mix and sift together 2 cups of pastry flour with 4 teaspoons of baking powder, $\frac{3}{4}$ of a teaspoon of salt and 8 teaspoons of granulated sugar. Work into this 4 tablespoons of salt butter. Add the currants and then mix to a dough with about $\frac{2}{3}$ of a cup of milk. Divide into six parts, toss each piece on to a lightly floured board and pat into a circle 4 inches wide and $\frac{1}{2}$ inch thick. Bake on a hot griddle which has been very well buttered. When delicately brown on one side turn with pancake turner. When cooked through, split and toast under a hot flame, spread with creamed butter and serve on a napkin.

Strawberry tarts

Mix together $1\frac{1}{3}$ cups of flour, 1 level teaspoon of sugar, and $\frac{1}{2}$ teaspoon of salt. Sift several times. Then work in $\frac{1}{2}$ cup of butter with the fingertips. Bind together with 1 beaten egg. Toss on floured board and pat or gently roll out. Spread a tablespoon of thick cream over, roll it up, roll it out, then roll it up again. Put it in the refrigerator for two hours. In the meantime, prepare 2 quarts of strawberries. Pick out 48 of the best, crush the rest and add a cup of granulated sugar. Simmer gently for half an hour. Strain and continue to boil until greatly reduced and very thick. When ready to make the tarts take a little of the paste at a time, roll it out into small circles and line tiny individual tart tins. Crimp the edges and immediately put them back in the refrigerator so that they keep very cold. When all are ready brush the edges with beaten egg and set in a very hot oven. Watch carefully so that they don't burn. When brown remove from oven and place 4 strawberries in each. Then glaze with strawberry juice.

Serve with Devonshire cream made by putting 1 quart of milk and 1 pint of thick cream in a shallow enamel pan. Set in a cool place for twelve hours. When this time is up the cream should have risen to the surface. Now put the pan of milk in another pan of water and place this pan either on top of the oven part of a gas stove or on the very back part of a coal stove, let the milk get gradually warm, not hot. Leave it on the stove until the cream crinkles and pulls away from the edge of the pan. When this happens put the pan of milk in the refrigerator for at least twelve hours. Then carefully skim off cream and put in a glass dish. It should be thick, slightly lumpy or clotted, and have a peculiarly delicious, sweet taste.

Cookies

Cream $\frac{1}{3}$ cup of butter with 1 cup of sugar. Add $\frac{1}{3}$ cup of milk in which has been dissolved $\frac{1}{3}$ of a level teaspoon of baking soda. Add three teaspoons of vanilla and enough flour to make a dough just stiff enough to handle. Toss $\frac{1}{3}$ of it at a time on to a floured board and roll out to $\frac{1}{4}$ inch. Sprinkle well with granulated sugar and cut out. Bake on well-buttered tins in a medium oven until a delicate brown.

Toasted marmalade and butter sandwiches

Make 4 or 5 thin sandwiches well buttered and spread with orange marmalade. Remove the crusts and cut into pieces about 1 inch by 3 inches. These may be made in advance. Cover with a damp cloth till wanted. Then toast quickly on both sides and serve piping hot.

Praliné cookies

First blanch $\frac{1}{4}$ cup of filberts and the same quantity of almonds. Dry them out in a warm oven for a few minutes. Butter a platter. Put $\frac{1}{2}$ cup of sugar in an aluminium saucepan with 6 teaspoons of cold water. Place on fire and watch carefully. When sugar begins to caramelise, remove from fire, add the nuts and pour out immediately on to the buttered platter. The sugar must be a pale golden brown. If it gets too dark it will be bitter. When cold break into pieces and run through the medium mincing machine. Now cream $\frac{1}{2}$ cup of butter with $\frac{1}{3}$ cup sugar, 1 whole egg beaten well and 2 teaspoons of vanilla. Mix well and add $\frac{3}{4}$ cup of flour in which has been sifted a saltspoon of salt. Add three tablespoons of the praliné and bake quickly, but watch carefully as they burn easily. Remove from tins immediately with cake-turner.

Brissaud, May 1933

Chocolate cake

Butter 4 shallow cake tins of the same size and shape. Cream ½ cup of butter with 1¼ cups of powdered sugar. Sift two cups of flour with ¼ teaspoon of salt and 2½ level teaspoons of baking-powder. Add ½ cup of milk to the butter and sugar mixture, then the flour and 2 teaspoons of vanilla. Beat well and fold in the stiffly beaten whites of 5 eggs. Put it into the tins. There should be not more than ½ inch of dough in each. Bake in a quick oven until a fork thrust in comes out clean. When cool put cakes together with frosting made as follows:

Beat the yolks of 4 eggs until light, add 3 cups of granulated sugar and beat well. Add 1 cup milk, 2 tablespoons butter and a tiny pinch of salt. Melt 8 squares of chocolate in a double boiler. Cook the first mixture, stirring well until it boils up hard, then cook 2 minutes. Remove from fire, add the melted chocolate and 2 teaspoons vanilla. Beat until thick enough to spread.

Hot scones with bacon

Sift 1 cup of flour with a rounded teaspoon of baking powder and a level teaspoon of salt. Add a piece of butter the size of an egg. Work it in well with the fingertips. Then bind together with milk into a stiff dough. Toss on to a floured board and roll out to ½ inch thickness. Cut with a cutter 1½ inches in diameter. Bake in very hot oven. Split and butter and put a small piece of freshly fried bacon in each one. Place in folded napkin and serve at once.

Strawberry, pineapple and orange conserve

This recipe makes about 6 pots. Peel, core and shred fine 1 pineapple. Pick over, stem, and wash 1 quart of strawberries. Remove the peel from 3 large navel oranges, keeping it as whole as possible. Remove the pulp from the oranges with a sharp knife, discarding as much of the pith as possible and saving all the juice. Boil the peels in plenty of water until very tender, then remove and with a spoon scoop out the bitter white inside, leaving just the orange outer part. With a sharp knife sliver the skins in tiny thin strips about ½ inch long. Now put the pineapple in a large white enamel pan and add a pint of water. Boil for twenty minutes. In the meantime, put the orange pulp and juice in another enamel pan with 2½ cups of sugar and boil for about fifteen minutes. Then add the rind and continue cooking slowly. When the pineapple is cooked add the strawberries and 4½ cups of sugar. Bring to the boil, then add the orange and let it all boil together for twenty-two minutes, no longer. Skim the jam while cooking and stir carefully to prevent sticking. Put in sterilised jars and seal the next day with wax.

Cinnamon toast

Cut bread in ¼ inch slices and remove crusts. Toast lightly and quickly. Butter well and sprinkle with powdered sugar and cinnamon mixed together. Cut in thirds, place on buttered tin and put under the grill for a moment to melt the sugar slightly. Serve immediately.

Walnut mocha cake

Cream ½ cup of butter with 1 cup of sugar. Add the well-beaten yolks of 2 eggs and ½ cup of milk. Add 1½ cups of flour in which has been sifted 2 teaspoons of baking powder and a pinch of salt. Mix well and add two teaspoons of vanilla and 1 cup of broken and lightly floured walnuts. Fold in carefully the stiffly beaten whites of 2 eggs, pour into a well-buttered loaf tin, bake in moderate oven for about forty minutes or until a fork inserted comes out clean. Ice when cold with frosting made by creaming ¼ cup of butter and gradually adding 1 cup of confectioner's sugar and ¼ cup of cocoa mixed together. Cream well, then soften with hot, very strong, black coffee and vanilla mixed. If it should get too thin, thicken with more sugar and cocoa. Spread unevenly on cake and decorate with unbroken walnut halves.

Before the theatre: Prunier's Snack Bar

Eric

The Well Dressed Salad

The three important requisites for a salad are, first, that the greens must be thoroughly washed and freed from sand (and slugs!); second, they must be shaken completely dry in a wire basket made especially for that purpose, or wiped dry; and, third, they must be crisp and cold. As for French dressing, make it any way you like, but please do mix the oil with the salt and pepper and condiments, and then add the vinegar or wine or lemon juice—not vice versa. The classic recipe for French dressing is one teaspoonful salt, a dash of freshly ground pepper, three tablespoonfuls olive oil, and one tablespoonful vinegar. There are many ways of varying this, however. Some people like to add a pinch or two of sugar—or a dash of Worcestershire sauce, or some ketchup, or a little red wine, or a bit of meat juice, or some pickle juice, or a little horseradish, or what-have-you.

One connoisseur I know, famous for making lettuce salads, paints each leaf with dressing with a broad camel-hair brush so that every little crevice of the lettuce is thoroughly coated—the advantage being that the leaves don't get bruised by tossing. By the way, when anyone says toss the salad, they don't mean have a modified game of football with it—it's more of a folding process. In France they say *fatiguer la salade*. I'm afraid some of us take that too literally. It should be tossed, but it should not be bruised or crushed.

In using garlic, one should never be able to discover even a microscopic piece of it in the salad. The correct system is by use of a *chapon*—a dry heel of bread that is rubbed with a clove of garlic and put in the bowl while the salad is being tossed. This is removed before serving.

If you live in the country, do try to have a little herb garden, for fresh herbs add so infinitely to the glory of a salad, though wonderful results can be achieved with dried ones. The different herbs suitable for a salad are tarragon, chervil, parsley, thyme, chives—and, of course, garlic, onions and shallots or scallions.

We are apt to forget how great a variety of greens can be eaten raw—for instance: watercress, endive, sorrel, dandelion, chicory, escarole, romaine, young spinach, corn salad shaped like daisy leaves, Chinese cabbage, red cabbage, green cabbage—and others I can't remember at the moment.

Condiments for our salad shelf should be mustard—French, English and German—salt, celery salt, black pepper, white pepper, paprika, horseradish, and Worcestershire sauce. Little pepper mills should be bought so that you can grind the pepper fresh each time, for this adds greatly to the success of dressing.

There are many kinds of vinegar which may be used, tarragon, cider, red wine or white wine. Lemon juice may often be substituted for vinegar. French olive oil or Italian olive oil can be used alternatively in making dressings.

The following are some favourite salads, with their accompanying dressings:

Celery salad with mustard dressing

Use a head of celery for each person. Remove all the tough outer stalks—use only tender stalks and take off as many strings as possible. Cut in two-inch pieces and split each piece several times, almost to the end. Curl by putting in ice water for several hours. Shake or wipe thoroughly dry. Then pile in a cold bowl and treat with the following dressing:

Put a small soupspoonful of German mustard in a bowl, add some freshly ground pepper and salt to taste and the juice of a small lemon. Stir well and then add $\frac{3}{4}$ of a cup of thin cream.

Cauliflower salad with French dressing

Boil two cauliflowers until tender but not too soft. Drain well. Pull apart in uniform bunches, then pile in a cold bowl and chill thoroughly. Sprinkle liberally with chopped chervil and finish off with French dressing.

Cucumber, tomato and radish salad

Peel a cucumber and slice fine. Soak in ice water but do not put salt in the water. Peel six ripe, juicy tomatoes and chill them thoroughly. Wash a dozen baby radishes and put them to soak in ice water. Remove cucumber and wipe dry on a linen cloth. Put it in a bowl containing French dressing and mix well. Remove and place in a shallow, cold dish. Slice the tomatoes in thin circles with a sharp knife and arrange them in a wreath round the cucumber. Pour the dressing left from the cucumber over all—then slice the radishes very thin and sprinkle them over the cucumber and tomatoes.

Potato and watercress salad
Boil three pounds of little, new potatoes with skins on in salted water. Peel and slice while still hot. Put in a bowl and marinate them in a cup of dry white wine. Chill, and at the last moment add a bunch of watercress which has been carefully washed, dried and picked over. Then treat with French dressing. Sprinkle the top with two hard-boiled eggs chopped fine and a little chopped chervil.

Hot potato salad
Boil three pounds of new potatoes. Peel and slice while hot. Sprinkle with chopped chives or shallots and finish with French dressing. Place in a bed of fresh lettuce and serve warm.

Chicory and escarole with chicken liver
Wash a head of chicory and a head of escarole, pick over carefully, soak in cold water and dry thoroughly. Make up the following dressing:

Wash two chicken livers and boil until tender with a carrot, an onion, a piece of celery and a bunch of parsley. Remove from juice. Hard boil two eggs. Pass the livers through a very fine sieve. Do likewise with the yolks of the eggs. Put in bowl together with a heaped teaspoonful of French mustard. Mix to a paste—add freshly ground pepper and salt to taste, and pour in, drop by drop, two tablespoonfuls olive oil, stirring always in the same direction. Now thin this by adding a teaspoonful of red wine vinegar and a tablespoonful of red wine. Sprinkle some chopped chervil or chopped tarragon over the escarole and chicory. Pour the liver dressing over all and toss well. Serve this salad very cold.

Romaine salad with hard-boiled egg dressing
Prepare salad in usual manner. Hard boil three eggs. Pass the yolks through a fine sieve and put them in the bottom of a cold salad bowl. Add a teaspoonful of French mustard, freshly ground pepper and salt. Then add three tablespoonfuls of olive oil, and then one tablespoonful of tarragon vinegar. Add romaine or cos lettuce, broken in small pieces, and sprinkle with a teaspoonful of fresh chopped tarragon. Mix well. Sprinkle the top with the whites of eggs which have been chopped up fine.

Wilted salad
Lettuce or sorrel or dandelion may be used for this. Prepare the greens, put in a hot bowl, sprinkle with salt and freshly ground pepper and use this dressing:

Cut six slices of fat bacon in little squares and fry in a hot pan until crisp. Pour the hot fat and the bacon directly on the greens—put a teaspoonful or so of vinegar in the hot pan and then pour it over the salad. Mix well and then eat at once. The salad will wilt slightly, but it is quite delectable for a change.

Vegetable salad
Boil two pounds of new potatoes with their skins on. Cook separately one pound of green peas, ½ pound of string beans, one pound of lima beans, six beets, six carrots cut in cubes, and one bunch of asparagus tips.

Make a boiled dressing for the potatoes in the following manner: Mix two tablespoonfuls of sugar with one level tablespoonful of flour, one level teaspoonful of salt and some freshly ground pepper. Add ¾ of a cup of vinegar and ¼ cup of water. Put this mixture in an enamel double boiler, add a lump of butter the size of an egg, and the yolks of two eggs well beaten. Place on fire and stir constantly until thick. Remove from the fire and chill. When ready to use, add ½ cup of thick cream to dressing. Season again to taste and pour over the potatoes, which have been peeled and sliced thin while still hot, and which have been sprinkled with a teaspoonful of chopped tender chives or chopped onion.

When the rest of the vegetables are thoroughly chilled, marinate them separately with French dressing for half an hour. Arrange the potato salad in a pile on a bed of tender lettuce leaves and place the different vegetables in neat piles round the potato salad.

Spinach salad
Wash three pounds of spinach leaves. Bring quickly to the boil. Then drain well and chill thoroughly.

Put in a salad bowl one teaspoonful of French mustard, some salt, freshly ground pepper, three tablespoonfuls of olive oil and one of vinegar. Mix well, add the spinach and let it soak well, turning it over several times gently so as not to squash the leaves. Serve very cold. This is particularly good with cold roast veal.

Let's Have Some Good Vegetables

There are various reasons for the deplorable condition in which vegetables are often served in this country; foreigners nearly always blame the English cook, but in most cases they should go a little further back and blame the gardener.

The prime cause of the production of so many uneatable vegetables is the annual village flower show. The tremendous tapering turnips, incredible carrots and preposterous parsnips of enormous length that appear there constitute a standard of development from which it is practically impossible to detach the gardener's mind. He is so firmly set upon producing their like that the hostess who wishes to offer her guests those few inches of tender succulence instead of that yard or so of tough and woody fibre had better go and gather the vegetables herself by stealth. They should always be consumed long before they are "ready" according to kitchen garden ideas. Many people who have eaten garden produce all their lives never know how juicy and delicious really young vegetables can be.

The best method of dealing with this matter of youthful garden produce is to insist on frequent sowings throughout the growing season. One can, of course, given the means, raise early vegetables under glass in winter; but these are costly and rather insipid luxuries compared with the same things grown outdoors in their proper season. A little seed of each variety, sown every ten days or fortnight, will keep the house supplied with a succession of tender young carrots, turnips, parsnips, beetroots and spinach. Marrows should be cut when quite tiny, when they have an infinitely preferable flavour to the large ones; and peas and beans should be sown in fairly short rows at short and frequent intervals, instead of in immensely long rows once or twice in the season.

Having grown your vegetables, here are some ways of cooking them that will preserve and enhance their delicate flavour. Each of the dishes described is worthy of being served alone as a separate course. A good deal of patience is required in their preparation—but not more skill than any amateur possesses.

Potatoes panier

Butter a shallow, round copper pan shaped like a pie tin. If you haven't such a thing, a glass cooking dish will do, but it is not quite so satisfactory. Peel 2½ lb of potatoes, the waxy, not the floury kind, wash carefully and leave them soaking in cold milk. Take one potato at a time and cut it very carefully so as to make little slivers of uniform size, 1 inch long by ⅛ inch square—like matchsticks. Put these immediately into the milk. This is to keep them from turning dark. When you have enough prepared, line the bottom of the buttered pan by placing the strips in a basket-weave pattern. The sides of the pan should also be covered. The rest of the potatoes are then cut up in the same way, but just put in as they come until the pan is full to the top. Now melt 1¾ cupfuls of butter and add ½ teaspoonful of salt and a dash of pepper. Pour three-quarters of it over the potatoes so as to cover all of them well. Cover with an inverted pie tin and put into a moderate oven. Bake for half an hour, then add a little more of the butter. Bake fifteen minutes more and add the rest of the butter. Continue baking for another 15 minutes. When ready to serve, empty them on to a hot dish. They should be brown on the top and bottom and soft inside. Whip a quarter of a cup of cream and put on top of the potatoes. Sprinkle with salt, pepper and chopped parsley and serve at once.

Red cabbage

Wash and slice fine 2 tender red cabbages and put them to soak in 2 tablespoons of vinegar and some water. Then chop 1 onion fine and brown it in 2 tablespoons of bacon fat and 2 tablespoons of butter in a frying-pan. Put in the cabbage which has been drained well. Add 1 bay leaf, 3 cloves, 2 peppercorns and 2 tart, juicy apples, sliced fine. Cook slowly until tender, stirring frequently, as red cabbage burns easily when done, melt 1 tablespoon of butter in a saucepan, add 1 teaspoon of flour, stir and put in the cabbage and its juice. Sprinkle with 1 teaspoon of sugar and the juice of ½ lemon. Simmer for a minute or two and serve.

Baked beets in cream

Wash 10 beets of uniform size thoroughly and put them into a hot oven. Bake for one hour, until they become soft, then peel and slice thin. Pour half a cup of thick cream over them and heat the beets in it. Salt and pepper to taste, and just before serving add the juice of one lemon.

French beans, cream and egg sauce
With a very sharp knife, carefully cut off the ends from 2 lb of young French beans. Wash carefully and tie in little individual bunches, as you would asparagus. Put the bunches into furiously boiling salted water; cook until tender but not floppy. Place the bunches carefully on a hot dish, removing strings but still keeping in bunches. Pour over them a sauce made as follows: heat $1\frac{1}{2}$ cups of thick cream in a double-boiler—and when it is very hot, pour it slowly on to the beaten yolks of 3 eggs. Salt and pepper to taste, put back in double-boiler and stir a few seconds until thickened, stir in a small lump of butter, then pour over the beans and serve at once.

Provincial potatoes
Wash and boil in their skins 3 lb of new potatoes. Put 2 oz of butter in a saucepan. Cut it up and pour over it 3 dessertspoons of olive oil, and grate into this the rind of half a lemon. Add some chopped parsley and chopped chives, a little freshly grated nutmeg, a pinch of flour and some salt and pepper. When the potatoes are cooked, peel and cut into quarters or eighths and put them into the butter mixture. Heat but without letting the butter boil. When ready to serve, add the juice of 1 lemon.

Parsnip fritters
Wash and boil 4 or 5 parsnips. When tender, take off the skins and mash them fine. Add a teaspoon of flour, 1 beaten egg and a little salt and pepper. Have some whole shelled walnuts ready and form the parsnip mixture into little balls with 1 walnut in each. Fry to a golden brown in butter in a frying-pan. Decorate with parsley.

Can du Jour

While reading recently an old book by the famous Carême, dated 1858, I was delighted to find the answer to a question which has been in my mind for a long time: how long have we known the art of preserving and tinning? Carême tells us that "the art of treating plants, their flowers, roots, and fruits to preserve them and to extract from them their elements, sugars, liqueurs, oils and perfumes dates back to the very cradle of Civilisation". And then he goes on to tell us that Pliny, in his book of Natural History, gives a veritable maze of processes for conserving fruits and their perfumes.

The ancients went on the principle that water and humidity were the principal causes of decomposition of matter, so they dried or salted their provisions, or enveloped them in sugar, or immersed them in vinegar or alcohol to keep them. Then along came Nicolas Appert, born in 1750, who revolutionised the canning business by "le Système Calorique" which means, I think, to subject to great heat. Anyway, now that we have our modern chemists and inventors and machinery there is practically nothing that grows on earth that can't be found in dried, bottled, or tinned form on the grocers' shelves.

Now, it does seem to me that with everything at our disposal, we ought to do a little more than just buy a tin, open it up, heat it up, and eat it up. The purpose of this article is to stimulate the cook into getting the very best results from that formidable array of tinned goods. Try working out your favourite plat-du-jour, using tinned foods wherever possible; then, if you don't like yours, please try mine.

Tomato soup à la crème dorée
Open 4 tins of concentrated tomato soup and heat in a double boiler. Peel 1 onion and cut it in half. Stick 2 cloves in each half. Put the onion in a large double boiler and pour over it a quart of rich milk. Scald, but don't let the milk boil. Beat 1 cup of cream until almost stiff. Now add $\frac{1}{2}$ level teaspoon of bicarbonate of soda to the tomato soup and stir well. Also add 1 teaspoon of sugar and a little salt, then add gradually the hot milk from which you have removed the onion. When smooth and well mixed pour into individual little earthenware casseroles. Now put 1 tablespoon of the whipped cream in each dish and spread it so as to cover the whole surface of the soup, put the dishes immediately under a very hot grill and watch carefully. As soon as the cream is lightly browned serve at once.

Hot chicken broth
The next time you serve hot tinned chicken broth try adding just before serving a few very thinly sliced spring onions and some very thin slices of tinned Chinese water chestnuts.

Tongue au gratin
Open and slice very thin a 27-ounce jar of ox tongue. Open 1 tin of clear beef broth and empty it into an oblong shallow Pyrex dish. Sprinkle into this a few drops of vinegar. Peel and chop very fine 6 shallots with a little parsley. Add 2 tablespoons or more of India relish or finely chopped sweet pickle, salt and freshly ground pepper. Prepare $1\frac{1}{2}$ cups of grated breadcrumbs. Sprinkle the bottom of the baking dish with half of the shallots and parsley and pickle and half of the crumbs. Lay on this bed the sliced tongue, and sprinkle the rest of the ingredients over the top ending with the breadcrumbs. Dot with 2 tablespoons of butter and bake in a good oven until brown. In the meantime reduce by simmering another 13-ounce tin of beef broth until it is almost a glaze. When ready to serve the tongue, pour the glaze over all and serve at once with some fluffy mashed potatoes.

A modified cassoulet
I don't dare call this cassoulet because my French friends would object strenuously, but it is a very good bean dish just the same. Order a little shoulder of lamb weighing about $2\frac{1}{2}$ pounds and ask the butcher to bone and roll it. Peel and chop fine 2 or 3 little white onions and 2 or 3 shallots with 1 clove of garlic. Tuck another piece of garlic into the lamb. Brown the lamb in a little butter or, better still, chicken fat, in an iron cocotte on top of the stove, and don't let it burn. Add the chopped onions, shallots and garlic, and salt and pepper the meat, and add the bones from the roast. Cover and put the cocotte in a moderate oven to continue cooking for about an hour and a half. Then, at this stage, add a tin of purée of tomato, $\frac{1}{2}$ cup of tomato ketchup and half a cup of consommé. Cover and put back in oven for half an hour longer. In the meantime open a 12-ounce tin of cooked ham. Put it in an enamel pan with 1 cup of consommé and 1 bay leaf and simmer gently. Now remove the lamb from the cocotte and put the gravy through a fine sieve. Remove string from lamb and slice it. Pour the remaining juice from the ham into the strained gravy and slice the ham. Now open an 8-ounce tin of little cocktail sausages and brown them lightly in butter. You are now ready to assemble the so-called cassoulet. Open 4 large tins of oven-baked beans with pork and tomato sauce. Put the contents of one in the bottom of a large earthenware casserole and add a layer of lamb, add another tin of beans and then the ham, more beans and then the sausages, and last of all the last tin of beans. Now add enough tomato juice to the sauce to make 1 pint in all and pour it over the beans. Cover the top with a few strips of bacon and bake with a cover for half an hour, then remove the cover and bake slowly half an hour longer or until brown on top. Serve directly from the casserole.

Ham and sausage polenta
First make the polenta. Into 6 cups of actively boiling salted water pour slowly $1\frac{1}{2}$ cups of yellow cornmeal. Cook in double boiler for half an hour. It should be very thick. When done stir into it 1 cup of freshly grated Parmesan cheese and pour it out on to a buttered square dish so that it will be about 1 inch thick. When cold cut in squares.

So we decided to go all Gipsy and take a caravan holiday. Last night we parked within a stone's throw of the sea and I've had some extra-nice bathes today – the heat's been tropical! So that lovely 'Tosca' perfumed Eau de Cologne has come in extra useful. It's so heavenly

Advertisement

Now open 1 8-ounce jar or tin of boiled ham and cut it in $\frac{1}{2}$ inch squares. Brown these together with 2 5-ounce tins of little cocktail sausages in a little butter until a golden brown, but not dry. Pour off all the fat, put the sausages and ham in an enamel pan and add 2 grated onions, an 8-ounce tin of tomatoes, and, for flavouring, a small bouquet of parsley, a small piece of bay leaf and the tiniest pinch of thyme. Also add 1 tin of clear beef broth. Reduce well by simmering. When done, remove the bouquet garni. Cover the bottom of a buttered baking dish with half of the polenta. Pour over it half of the sauce and sausages and ham. Dot with butter, sprinkle with more cheese, and repeat the process. Place the dish in a hot oven and bake until browned slightly. Serve at once.

Cocktail sausages in wine on croûtons
Open 2 5-ounce tins of cocktail sausages and fry them in a little butter until brown all over but not dry. Pour off all the fat and put the sausages in a little enamel pan. Pour over them $1\frac{1}{2}$ cups of good dry white wine and simmer gently until the wine has reduced two-thirds. Prepare 8 fried croûtons about $2\frac{1}{2}$ inches square and keep them hot. Dissolve 2 teaspoons of beef extract in 3 tablespoons of boiling water. Add a few drops of lemon juice and 3 tablespoons of melted butter and the reduced wine from the sausages. Place the hot drained sausages on the hot croûtons on a hot platter and put the platter in the oven to keep hot while you finish the sauce. Beat the yolks of 2 eggs well and put them in the top of a small double boiler and add gradually the meat sauce, and cook slowly, stirring all the while until thick. Add a little salt and some freshly ground black pepper, and pour over the sausages. Serve at once.

Brunswick stew

Ask the butcher to bone and cut up 2 4-pound roasting chickens. Put the bones in a pot and just cover them with cold water. Place on fire and bring slowly to a boil. Skim carefully and add 4 peeled carrots, 3 pieces of celery and 5 or 6 little white onions. Simmer for 2 hours, adding 1 teaspoon of salt fifteen minutes before the soup is cooked. Strain and cool. Then put the pieces of chicken, which have been wiped clean with a damp cloth, in a deep enamel pot. Pour over them the broth and place on fire to come slowly to a simmer. Skim, reduce the heat and cook until just tender. Now add a tin of peeled tomatoes from which you have drained the juice, the same size tin of lima beans minus their juice and which you have washed off in cold water, the same size tin of sweet corn and its juice, and 1 heaped cup of celery scraped, washed and cut in one-inch pieces. Simmer twenty minutes longer, stirring frequently. Season to taste with salt, freshly ground black pepper, a dash of cayenne and a heaped teaspoon of granulated sugar. When ready to serve add 2 cups of cream and when it is hot serve in a soup tureen to be eaten from soup plates.

Chicken stuffed with macaroni in cheese sauce

Clean 2 young chickens weighing from three to four pounds. Wipe them inside and out with a damp cloth and salt and pepper them inside. Open two 16-ounce tins of cooked macaroni in a creamy cheese sauce and stuff the birds with it. Sew and truss securely. Put $\frac{1}{4}$ pound of butter in an iron cocotte and when it is hot brown the chickens on top of the stove, turning them over and over. Slice 1 carrot and 1 onion and add them to the chicken. Salt and pepper well and pour over them $\frac{1}{2}$ cup of consommé. Cover and cook slowly on top of the stove for about an hour and a half, basting from time to time and adding a little more consommé if necessary. Keep the birds breast side down as much as possible. At the end of an hour and a half remove the cover and put the birds into a hot oven to brown and crisp a little, having first poured off most of their juice. Strain the juice, remove the fat and reduce to almost a glaze. Place the birds on a hot platter, remove the strings, carve, garnish and pour the juice over all and serve.

Ragoût of olives

Chop very fine 3 peeled shallots and let them simmer till they are a golden brown in about 2 tablespoons of butter in an enamel pan. Add 2 8-ounce tins tomatoes, 1 cup of good dry white wine, and 2 teaspoons of beef extract dissolved in 1 tablespoon of boiling water. Reduce by simmering until quite thick. In the meantime open and drain a 13-ounce bottle of olives stuffed with pimento. Pour boiling water over them and let them stand a few minutes, drain again and scald once more and drain well. Now heat 2 good tablespoons of olive oil in a little pan and add the olives and 2 tablespoons of capers. When they have heated through, add them with the oil to the sauce and continue to simmer gently. When ready to serve, make some crisp toast, the crusts removed, and butter lightly. Put the ragoût in a hot small earthenware casserole and serve at once, accompanied by the hot toast. This is delicious served with roast duck, and in this case add a little of the meat juice from the duck and a few drops of lemon juice.

Chilled mould of fruit

You will need for this an oblong quart-and-a-half mould measuring about three-and-a-half inches deep by four inches wide by nine and a half inches long, which has a tight fitting cover. Open and empty into separate bowls a 1-pound 14-ounce tin of halved and pitted apricots, the same sized tin of fresh prunes, which must be pitted carefully so as not to spoil their shape, 2 8-ounce tins of halved pears, and a 1-pound 5-ounce tin of pitted red pie cherries. You will also need 3 ripe but perfect bananas. Line the mould with heavy waxed paper, leaving enough extra on the sides to fold over and cover the fruit when you have packed it into the mould in the following manner. Start by putting a layer of apricots cut side up in the bottom of the mould. Place a red cherry in between each apricot. Next put a layer of pears cut side up, tuck more cherries in the crevices and then add a layer of prunes and a layer of cherries. Now peel the bananas, split them down the middle and cut in one-and-a-half inch lengths. Stand them up round the mould side by side, cut side in, and fill in the rest of the mould with more fruit, leaving the apricots to cover the top: but this time put them cut side down. Fold the waxed paper over, butter the edges of the mould, cover with another piece of paper and place the cover on securely. In packing the fruit, enough of their juice should cling to them so that they are surrounded with juice when packed, but if you find this is not the case then add a little of each juice before sealing. Spill a little water on the bottom of the ice compartment and place the tray on it, or pack in ice with a little rock salt for about four hours. The fruit should be very cold, but it does not freeze stiff. Now put $\frac{1}{2}$ cup of each fruit juice in a jug, mix together and chill well. When ready to serve the fruit, put 2 generous tablespoons of red raspberry or currant jelly in a bowl, break it up lightly with a fork and pour over it 2 tablespoons of Framboise liqueur or Kirsch and add the chilled juice. Unpack the fruit, turn it out carefully on to a cold platter and serve at once accompanied by the sauce and a plate of lady fingers.

Francis Marshall

Happy Birthday

There are two ways of decorating a cake, one is to do so free-hand with the help of pastry bags, and the other is to stick sugar ornaments symmetrically and decoratively on the iced cake with a dab of icing to secure them.

Remember not to put a heavy icing on a delicate cake or to use ornamental icing on too soft a surface, and avoid putting heavy ornaments on a thick icing unless it has a firm crust or the ornaments will sink.

And now directions for making ornamental icing, otherwise known as royal icing. There are numerous books procurable which give excellent detailed instructions, including a variety of designs to follow. You will also need one or two good pastry bags with standard coupling attached and a reasonable variety of tubes. A revolving cake-decorating stand is useful; a good little whisk broom for brushing excess crumbs off the cake before icing; and a large and a small flexible palate knife are a big help. A wooden spoon is essential. When the icing is made keep it constantly covered with a heavy damp cloth. If this is done it will keep moist for even a day or two, but leave it exposed to the air and it will dry out almost immediately. Never allow icing to dry or harden in tubes.

The following recipe will make enough ornamental icing to decorate a big cake. It is best to separate the whites of eggs twelve hours before using them, keeping them in the refrigerator until ready for use. All utensils must be perfectly clean and free from grease or oil. Use a china, glass or porcelain round-bottomed bowl and a wooden spoon to beat the icing with.

Sift 1 pound of confectioner's sugar through a fine sieve or sifter kept especially for the purpose. Don't use the flour sifter. Put 3 unbeaten egg whites in a big bowl and add one third of the sugar and beat until smooth and creamy, then add about 1 dessertspoon of strained lemon juice or ½ teaspoon of cream of tartar. Now add a drop of ultramarine blue if no other colour is to be used. Keep on beating, adding all the rest of the sugar gradually. Continue beating until the mixture is so thick and firm that when the spoon is drawn up and out of the mixture it will leave a peak in the centre of the icing that doesn't settle back nor topple over. When made, cover at once with a damp cloth.

When ready to decorate a birthday cake the first thing is to find the exact centre and mark it with a pin prick. Next measure the circumference with a tape measure and divide the edge into equal sections. Mark with more pin pricks. Be sure to leave enough room in the centre of the cake if there is to be an inscription. Plan where the candles are to go and be sure that they will be evenly spaced. Start decorating the centre of the cake and work towards the edge, then down the sides. If separate silver balls or ornaments are to be added to the design, place a tiny dab of white icing on the object and place on the cake. Don't poke the object down into the icing. If you are using candles, place them, if possible, in their holders before putting them on the cake. Don't hurry. If you keep the bowl of icing covered you may take as long as you like.

A baby's first birthday cake

First grate the rind of 1 lemon. Next squeeze and strain the juice of 1½ lemons. Add the rind to the juice and add ½ cup of cold water. Now separate the whites from 6 cold eggs. Beat the yolks until light and creamy. Add ¾ cup of granulated sugar and continue beating until very light. Now take another beater and beat the whites, to which you have added a pinch of salt, until quite stiff. Fold in ¾ cup of granulated sugar, add the lemon juice and water and beat with the rotary beater for 5 minutes. Fold the whites and yolks together, then fold in lightly 1½ cups of sifted cake flour. Pour into a large ungreased round cake tin. Bake in a slow oven (about 300° F.) for fifty or sixty minutes. Invert the cake tin when done on to a cake rack so that air may pass under it, while cooling.

Ice with twice-cooked icing tinted a very pale pink. Boil 1½ cups of granulated sugar moistened with ½ cup of water, until it forms a soft ball in cold water. In the meantime beat the whites of 2 eggs until stiff but not dry. Add the cooked syrup slowly to the whites, beating with a rotary beater, then add ⅛ teaspoon of cream of tartar, 1 teaspoon of vanilla and a drop or two of red colouring and beat with a spoon until smooth and thick. Put the bowl over boiling water and stir until the spoon makes a grating noise on the bottom of the bowl. Remove from fire and pour it on to the sponge cake, letting it run over the sides and smoothing it on with a silver knife. When it has dried enough to form a light crust, decorate it with one pink candle in the centre, in a little blue rose. Put a delicate border of white ornamental icing round the top edge and a heavier one round the bottom. Polka dot the top of the cake with tiny pink rose-buds, and the sides with forget-me-nots, made by squeezing five little dots of pale blue icing out in a circle touching each other just slightly, leaving a little hole in the centre into which a dot of yellow is dropped.

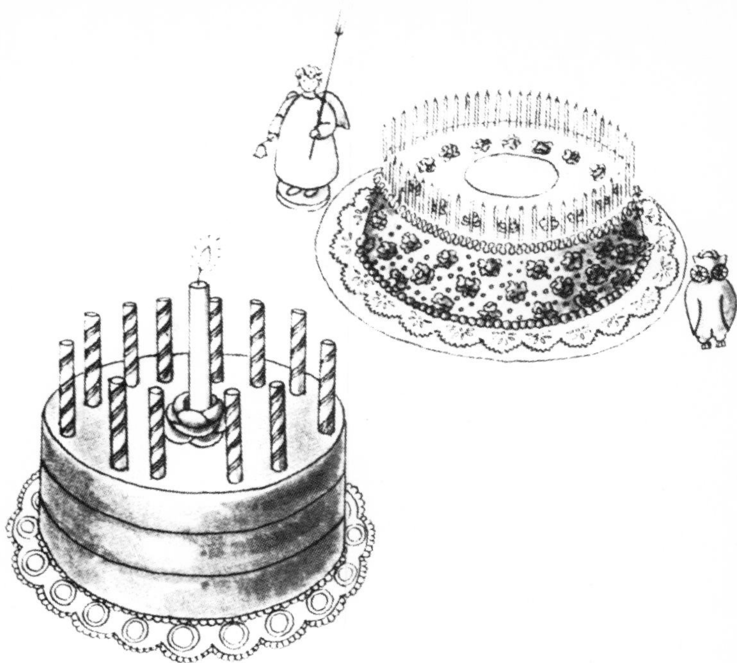

A cake for a girl

Butter 3 layer cake tins well. Cream one cup of butter and add gradually 2 cups of powdered sugar until light and fluffy. Add the grated rind of 1 orange and 1 teaspoon of orange extract. Sift 4 cups of flour with 6 level teaspoons of baking powder. Separate the yolks from the whites of 5 eggs. Add a pinch of salt to the whites and beat until stiff. Then beat the yolks until light and creamy. Add yolks to butter and sugar and beat well. Add the sifted flour, alternating with 1 cup of milk. Lastly, fold in the whites and pour into the tins. Bake in a medium oven about 20 minutes or until a straw comes out clean. Fill with the following:

Beat the yolks of 2 eggs until creamy and add 1 cup of sugar (granulated). Grate the rind of 1 orange and add it to the strained juice of 1 orange. Add the juice to the sugar and egg and add 2 tablespoons of butter. Cook in double boiler, stirring constantly until thick. Cool before using it to fill the cake.

Ice with the following: beat yolks of 4 eggs until very light and creamy. Moisten $1\frac{3}{4}$ cups of granulated sugar with $\frac{1}{2}$ cup of water and boil until it forms a soft ball in cold water. Pour gradually into the egg yolks, beating constantly with the rotary beater until all the syrup has been added. Add 1 teaspoon of lemon extract and 1 teaspoon of orange extract and continue beating with a silver spoon until it begins to grate slightly. Pour over the cake and spread over sides and top with a silver knife. Put fifteen candles into holders and arrange them so as to form a one and a six, making sixteen, written in candles. Decorate the edges and sides with white ornamental icing. Put sugar cupids round the edge.

A cake for a boy

Cream $\frac{1}{2}$ cup of fresh butter with two cups of light brown sugar, free from lumps until light and fluffy. Beat into this, one at a time, 3 whole unbeaten eggs. Melt 4 bars of vanilla chocolate in a double boiler, moistening it with a few drops of water and 2 teaspoons of vanilla. As soon as it is soft, stir it into the egg, sugar and butter mixture, and beat well. Sift 2 cups of cake flour with $\frac{1}{2}$ teaspoon of salt and 1 level teaspoon bicarbonate of soda. Add alternately to batter with 1 cup of buttermilk, beating well with each addition. Pour into 2 well-buttered large layer cake tins and bake in a moderate oven for 30 minutes or until an inserted straw comes out clean. Fill with the following:

Beat the yolk of 1 egg until very light. Add $\frac{3}{4}$ cup of granulated sugar and beat until light. Add $\frac{1}{4}$ cup of milk and $\frac{1}{2}$ tablespoon of butter and a pinch of salt. Melt 2 squares of unsweetened chocolate in a double boiler. Put the egg and sugar mixture in a deep enamel pan and cook, stirring furiously until it boils up hard. Cook a minute or two, then remove from fire and stir in the melted chocolate, and 1 teaspoon of vanilla. Beat until thick and smooth, then spread over one layer and place the other layer on the first one, being sure that they are squared at the edges. Now make this twice-cooked icing, to cover the cake:

Boil $1\frac{1}{2}$ cups of granulated sugar, moistened with $\frac{1}{2}$ cup of water, until it forms a soft ball in cold water. In the meantime beat the whites of 2 eggs until stiff but not dry. Add the cooked syrup slowly to the whites, beating with a rotary beater, then add $\frac{1}{8}$ teaspoon of cream of tartar and 1 teaspoon of vanilla and continue beating with a spoon until smooth and thick. Put over boiling water and stir until the spoon grates slightly on the bottom of the bowl. Pour over the top, letting it run over the edge. Smooth with a silver knife to cover the sides completely, and pour what is left over the top so that the top will have a thick coating. Let the icing dry until it has a thin crust before decorating. Find the centre of the cake and plant a little rose tree of candles there. Count the candles on the tree and plan to put more around the edge of the cake to make the required number. Decorate the remaining space with dots and scrolls.

Famous Hostesses

Their recipes and table settings

Lady Portarlington

It is the habit of every good hostess to keep a recipe book and to record there not only dishes well known of old in her family but also to receive for it as gifts recipes from houses where she has stayed or dined, and, chief of favours, words of wisdom from the chefs of her favourite restaurants. The former, the very English kinds of recipe, however, are at the moment the most desired. The menu is written in English, the food is English or Scottish, and French dishes and translations of names give way to readily understandable words. This is because of a change in our habits. The English breakfast is no more for most women. Their menfolk may stroll beside sideboards covered with heaters on which lie creamed eggs, sausages and mushrooms, haddock, eggs and bacon, game pie, picking this and that, but the women have toast and tea for their figures, good—unless it is a hunting day. But miss all these admirable and very English dishes they will not. One therefore sees them transferred to the lunch table, and even at dinner time they can replace the lighter but more complex French fare.

Certain hostesses are always being asked for their recipes. Of such are Lady Portarlington, Mrs Syrie Maugham, Lady Juliet Duff and Lady Colefax, and with generosity they have handed on to *Vogue* the secrets of their households.

Before you read their recipes, consider certain personal ideas of theirs, tricks of presentation. One of the most valued possessions of a house is its silver. Silver is still very much in evidence, but not always, as formerly, employed in the actual serving of food. It still adorns the table; in fact tables may be laden with it, for it forms the chief decoration as do the rare porcelains in France, but the dishes out of which one is served are now of glazed earthenware or wood—that is what has now come to pass. It is the newest whim of fashion. And very chic it is too, when one's table is covered with the best Queen Anne or Georgian silver, for the salad to be served in a wooden chopping bowl, accompanied by a wooden fork and spoon. Baked potatoes are served in a shallow walnut dish; salad in a white pine bowl; cheese on a wooden slab, with a wooden-handled knife to match, potatoes and green vegetables in the earthenware dishes in which they are baked; casseroles in the vessels in which they are cooked. This form of "rustic" presentation of food conjures up visions of the kitchens in which they are made—and kitchens nowadays are very handsome affairs, almost as picturesque as those perpetuated by the Dutch masters. Also, food to be good must be hot, and in transferring food from one dish to another—very often in the butler's pantry—this end is defeated. So, up from the kitchen comes the kitchen ware. It is the fashion of the hour.

Now first for some recipes of LADY PORTARLINGTON:

Ox-tail ragoût
Cut into sections ox-tail that has been well washed, fry it in butter, then add small carrots, small turnips and onions, and fry again. Season with pepper, salt, one section of garlic, a bouquet of thyme, parsley and bay leaf. Add enough water to cover, and braise for three hours. Take out ox-tail and vegetables, strain the stock to remove herbs, and return the meat and vegetables to a pan. Bring to a boil and serve in a casserole.

Scotch callops
Pass through a mincing machine two pounds of fillet of beef with no fat. Chop an onion very finely, fry it in butter, and then add the beef, allowing it to simmer for half an hour. Place it in an *au gratin* dish and serve with poached eggs on top.

Pulled and grilled turkey
After the bird has been jointed, remove the meat from the breast and cut it into small dice. Fry an onion, finely chopped, in butter, add the diced turkey, and sauté one minute. Joint the thighs into two or three pieces, roll in cream and breadcrumbs, and brown in oven. Serve the browned and diced turkey in a dish with cakes of stuffing, small sausages and strips of crisp bacon.

Devonshire pâté
Make a puff paste, line a tin with it, and put in layers of chicken, sliced egg, and sliced ham, seasoned to taste. Sprinkle with parsley, finely chopped, one-fourth teaspoonful of thyme and one teaspoonful of chopped onion. Cover with pastry, brush over with a beaten egg, and bake for one hour. Turn out and serve hot or cold.

Pork pie
One pound of pork, salt and pepper, one pound of flour, six ounces of lard, one egg and one gill of cold water are required. Cut the pork into small dice, put it into a cooking pan, add water, and let it come to a boil. Pour boiling water and lard into the flour until a dough has been formed. Allow it to cool, then turn it on to a board and knead well. Cut off one-fourth of the paste and keep warm. With the remainder, line a pie mould well greased. Dip the pork in cold water, season, and fill the mould with it. Roll out the remaining pastry, cover the mould with it, and press the edges. Decorate with small pieces of paste cut in leaves and arranged in a circle around a hole in the centre. Brush well with egg and bake for two hours.

Apple tart
Make a short crust, line a pan with it, and fill in the usual way with cut apple, adding sugar and a rind of lemon. Cover with a short crust, bake, and allow it to become cold. Before serving, remove the upper crust and fill with whipped or Devonshire cream. The pie should be put on ice before serving. The cream filling under the crust adds a pleasant "*en surprise*" element to a dish that too often lacks any element of the unexpected.

LADY JULIET DUFF sent us the following:

York ham
A York ham weighing about sixteen pounds is required. Soak it for twelve hours and boil it for three hours. Then remove the skin, cover well with Demerara sugar and put in a slow oven from one and a half to two hours. When the sugar starts to glaze, baste the ham well with a pint of champagne.

Syrie Maugham's country dining-room, with plaster palm tree decorations

MRS SYRIE MAUGHAM's gifts are not only for decoration. She is a highly successful hostess and here are two of her favourite recipes:

Pancake with haddock

Four ounces of flour, a half pint of milk, two eggs, and a pinch of salt are required. Remove the skin and bone of a highly cured Finnan haddock, chop finely, cook in cream and butter, and have ready before making the pancakes, so that they may be stuffed immediately after they are cooked, and served piping hot.

Burnt cream

One pint of cream, five whole eggs, five yolks of eggs, one ounce of sugar. Beat together till boiling point is reached, then pour into a fireproof dish, and, when cold, put a thick layer of castor sugar on top and brown under grill until hard. Serve with cream.

LADY COLEFAX gave us the recipe for this pudding:

Gentleman's pudding

This pudding requires the following ingredients: butter and flour in an amount that equals the weight of two eggs, castor sugar in an amount about equal to the weight of one egg; three tablespoonfuls of raspberry jam; and a half teaspoonful of bicarbonate of soda. Beat the butter and sugar to a cream, add the flour and eggs, one at a time (three eggs in all), beat well, then add the jam and bicarbonate of soda. Butter a pan and steam the mixture for two hours. Serve with a sauce made in the following manner. Take two yolks of eggs, one tablespoonful of sugar, and one glass of sherry. Whip these ingredients to a froth over hot water, add a quantity of raspberry jam, and serve hot around the pudding. Any jam may be used, and cream may also be served with it.

American hostesses are famous for their ideas. What do they serve at their London tables? Here are one or two answers:

Fish soufflé or mousse

From MRS REED VREELAND.

Two whitings, two whites of eggs, two ounces of butter, one tablespoonful of flour, one teaspoonful of anchovy essence, and a half cupful of milk. Melt the butter, add flour and milk, making a stiff sauce. Add the finely broken fish, flavour with salt, pepper, and anchovies. Then, beat the whites of eggs stiffly, mix well into the fish, and steam for twenty minutes. Serve with mushroom sauce in a sauce boat.

Jugged hare

From MRS CHARLES CARTWRIGHT.

Skin, clean, and cut a hare in neat pieces not larger than an egg, season with pepper and salt, and fry over the fire with two ounces of butter, and two ounces of chopped bacon. When it is a good brown colour, remove, and put it into a wide-mouthed jar with four good wineglassfuls of port wine or claret. Cover the jar and put it in the oven for twenty or thirty minutes. Remove and add a pint of strong game stock, a tablespoonful of strained lemon juice, and a herb bag composed of the following: a piece of cinnamon, four cloves, four bay leaves, a blade of mace, a sprig of thyme, twelve peppercorns, two Jamaica peppers, a sprig of marjoram, and parsley. Cover the jar and put it in the oven again for three hours—the jar should be placed in a pan containing boiling water. When the meat is cooked, strain off the gravy and thicken with one and a half tablespoonfuls of flour and butter mixed together. Boil this and pour it back on the meat, heat again, and serve with forcemeat balls around the base of the dish. This is excellent for lunch or dinner. Forcemeat balls are made with equal quantities of breadcrumbs, and suet and chopped parsley—all mixed well and rolled into round balls, dusted with egg and breadcrumbs, and fried in deep fat.

Chippenham cheese savoury

(A favourite of King Edward.) From MRS ASPINALL-OGLANDER.

For this you will require six ounces of grated Parmesan, a wineglassful of cream, two tablespoonfuls of milk, and two eggs. Beat the eggs, less one white, with cream and milk in a saucepan. Add cheese and keep stirring on a slow fire until the mixture is thick and creamy. Serve if possible in the vessel in which it has been cooked, handing hot toast first to each guest and allowing him to pour over it a spoonful of cheese.

MADAME TRIES HER HAND

in her Paris kitchen

Maybe Colette started it. She is an enviable sight, apron tied round her waist and contentment on her face, as she prepares the *galettes* and *vin chaud* for her tea-parties. Or perhaps it's just the periodic yearning of complex minds for simple pleasures. At any rate, cooking has become the new social accomplishment of Paris. The great national talent is replacing politics, the ballet and even the *vie intérieure* as a dinner-table subject.

"I made the whole dinner last night without getting a single spot on my apron." . . . "I hear that Marie-Blanche has a new electric refrigerator." . . . "You sée, I always use just a drop of Madeira in the sauce, and my professor agrees with me that it is much better than lemon."

These new enthusiasts trek over to the Sorbonne for lessons. There is no room for amateurs in such an important matter. Matutinal discussions with her chef have always been a vital part of the day of a French hostess, and she must know what she is talking about. Now it is only one step further to take a hand herself, perfect one or two *spécialités*, and gather a small but admiring audience for her new talent.

Some of the most unlikely people are cooking. The Hon. Mrs Reginald Fellowes has had a perfect little kitchen built in next to her sitting-room and, if you think this is an idle gesture, consult some gourmet who has exclaimed his way through a dinner prepared by her own white hands. André Dubonnet's new super-kitchen is the pride of the household, and nightly it is invaded by guests inspecting gadgets and begging to help.

Photographs by Schall

Comtesse Charles de Polignac stirs them up • Colette watches the pot • Comtesse Alexandre de Castéja handles a crisis

Colette's truffes au champagne

Take good-sized truffles* for this dish (a little over a pound of truffles to half a bottle of champagne). Clean them well and then peel them. Season the truffles with pepper and salt and cook them in the champagne in a covered saucepan, together with a quantity of *mirepoix* sauce. (The *mirepoix* sauce is composed of one carrot, one onion, one stem of parsley, a tiny bit of thyme, and one bay leaf cooked together with a very small amount of water.) Cook the mixture twenty minutes, keeping the saucepan carefully covered. Then remove the truffles, keeping them covered and hot, and cook the sauce and champagne mixture again to reduce it to a quarter of its original quantity. Drain the juice and pour it over the truffles just before they are served.

Comtesse Charles de Polignac's spaghetti à la napolitaine

Cook about nine ounces of spaghetti (sufficient for five helpings) in salted water for twenty minutes. Then carefully drain the spaghetti. Dice eight ounces of *jambon de Paris* very fine and add a jar of pimentos cut in very thin slices and nine ounces of sliced mushrooms. Cook all these ingredients together in butter. About ten minutes before serving mix together the spaghetti, peppers, ham and mushrooms; add a very little ground pepper and place the mixture at the back of the stove. Immediately before serving add enough veal gravy to moisten.

Comtesse Jean de Vogüé's lobster à l'armoricaine

This dish is Comtesse Jean de Vogüé's speciality, and

Comtesse Jean de Vogüé in an act of valour

to make it you take a few carrots, onions, thyme and laurel leaves and parboil them in butter. Then cut lobster meat into slices and add to the above ingredients. Add salt, white pepper and cayenne pepper. Flame the lobster with a glassful of brandy, add the necessary quantity of white wine and cook the whole mixture over a quick fire. Next, take out each piece of lobster very carefully, pressing it gently to drain off the sauce. Put the drained sauce into a saucepan with a large piece of butter and a spoonful of tomato sauce and cook slowly for a short while to reduce the mixture to a thicker consistency. Then add the lobster pieces to the sauce and serve very hot.

Comtesse de Castéja's œuf en camisole

Two favourites of the Comtesse de Castéja are *œuf en camisole* and a special salad dressing. For the *œufs en camisole*, eggs are poached in the usual way. Then each egg is enveloped in a light French pancake, rolled up and placed on a piece of thin toast, and served.

The salad dressing is made by mixing together milk and vinegar (the milk replacing oil) in the usual proportions for salad dressing, and then adding to this mixture a little tomato juice and pepper to taste.

Comtesse de Maille's cream-and-fruit tart

Make a short paste as follows: mix together four ounces of flour, one and one-half ounces of butter, the yolk of one egg, water, salt and pepper and allow the resulting paste to stand for about one hour. With this paste, trim the bottom and sides of a pastry mould and bake until partly done. During the baking process, pour one pint of boiled milk on about four ounces of sugar that have been mixed with four egg yolks, the white of one egg, and one tablespoonful of flour. Pass this mixture through a sieve; then place it in the paste shell and bake the whole tart in a moderately hot oven for about thirty minutes. When the tart is cold, add fruit from which the stones have been removed. If the fruit is white, cover it with apricot jam. If it is red, cover the fruit with currant jam.

* If fresh truffles are not obtainable, truffles packed in glass jars may be substituted for the fresh variety, in the proportions given in the recipe.

Vogue's enquiring gourmet interviews

Madame Helena Rubinstein

At lunch with Madame Rubinstein, you might begin with a clear bouillon, then progress to a divine entrée of spinach purée rolled up in little crêpes. Then, a fish curry (with tiny mushrooms and lobster claws and baby scallops) served with rice and chutney, followed by fresh pineapple or strawberries with Kirsch. The coffee is black as the ace of spades, in bright red cups.

The spinach in crêpes is easy enough, if you can catch the trick of making the batter very thin and cooking the pancakes just long enough. To make the purée, you cook a pound of spinach, chop it, and put it through a strainer. To this, you add six tablespoonfuls of cream (enough to make a thin paste), salt and pepper to taste, six tablespoonfuls of grated cheese, and a pound of small white mushrooms, which have previously been cooked in butter and chopped fine. When this is thoroughly mixed in a paste, a tablespoonful is allowed for each pancake. The pancake batter consists of two tablespoonfuls of flour for each person, one egg for every two or three persons, a pinch of salt, and just enough half-and-half water and milk to make a very thin batter. The pancakes should be very thin and very lightly done, and they should be stuffed the minute they are taken from the pan. When stuffed, they are placed in a baking dish, bits of butter are dropped on them, and the tops are sprinkled with grated cheese. They are baked only long enough in the oven to melt the cheese. Here, again, the practical viewpoint emerges. If you have some liver or kidneys or little slivers of chicken and haven't any mushrooms, then chop these up instead.

This is the *sauce indienne* that will transform any boiled or broiled fish into a *specialité*. A medium-sized onion is fried, chopped fine, and put to boil for about ten minutes with a heaped teaspoonful of curry-powder which has been dissolved in a cupful of fish stock (or water, if you haven't any fish stock) with salt and pepper to taste. Just before serving, the sauce is thickened with cornflour, then two tablespoonfuls of chutney, two or three drops of lemon juice, and two or three drops of Worcestershire sauce are added, and the final mixture is allowed to boil for two or three minutes.

Here is a favourite fish recipe, which often appears on Rubinstein menus amidst the plaudits of guests:

1½ *pounds of halibut or fillet of sole*
½ *pound of shrimps*
½ *pound of scallops*
a few teaspoonfuls of good oil
1 *teaspoonful of anchovy paste*
2 *tablespoonfuls of grated Parmesan*
½ *pound of small white mushrooms*
½ *pint of fresh cream*
1 *tablespoonful of butter*
1 *teaspoonful of cornflour*
salt, pepper, cayenne pepper
paprika

The halibut or sole is washed, dried in a towel and sprinkled with salt, pepper, and paprika. A few spoonfuls of good oil are poured on it, and it is covered and allowed to stand for two hours, after which it is grilled. The scallops are fried very lightly in a few tablespoonfuls of butter with a little oil, and the shrimps are boiled. The mushrooms, which have been peeled and scraped, but not washed, are fried in a tablespoonful of melted butter and two teaspoonfuls of cream, well seasoned with salt and pepper. The cream is brought to a boil in a pan, then a teaspoonful of cornflour, dissolved in water, is added and stirred in for about a moment until the mixture thickens, when a teaspoonful of anchovy paste, mixed in a little cold water, is added. Last, the cheese, mushrooms, salt, pepper, and cayenne pepper to taste are put in. The fish is arranged in a flat baking dish, surrounded by the scallops and shrimps, the sauce is poured over the fish, the top is sprinkled with grated cheese and a dusting of paprika, and the pan is placed for one moment under the grill.

One favourite entrée at lunch is individual cheese soufflés, and they are a happy inspiration, too, as an accompaniment to a green salad, especially when they are served in the little individual baking dishes with handles. To make these, a heaped tablespoonful of flour and a heaped tablespoonful of butter are combined with enough milk to make a fairly thick sauce. Next, ten tablespoonfuls of grated cheese, the yolks of three eggs, and salt, pepper, and cayenne pepper to taste are added to the sauce and mixed well. The whites of the eggs are beaten stiff and turned into the mixture very lightly and quickly. The individual soufflé dishes are filled three-quarters full, placed in a pan of boiling water, and baked in a slow oven. As the soufflés begin to rise, the heat is gradually increased, until the soufflés have been in the oven for about fifteen minutes, when they should be delicately browned.

Here is a delicious curry combination:

4 *large onions*
3 *large tomatoes*
1 *large acid cooking apple*
1 *banana*
3 *teaspoonfuls of raisins*
3 *pounds of fish halibut, shrimps, lobster, or scallops*
1 *cupful of rice*
½ *cupful of chutney*
2 to 3 *heaped teaspoonfuls of curry-powder*
6 *cupfuls of fish stock or water*

The onions are first fried in slices and then chopped. (Incidentally, here is a point of great significance. If you fry your onions *before* you chop them, you retain all their flavour, and there isn't any danger of their burning up in little pieces.) The tomatoes are peeled and the seeds are removed, the apple is fried and chopped, and a banana is fried and mashed. These, together with the raisins, are placed in an aluminium or enamel pot. The fish stock (or water) is added, and the mixture is simmered for three hours or until it thickens, when the chutney and curry-powder are added, and it is allowed to simmer for ten minutes longer. In the meantime, the fish has been cooked (the halibut fried, and the shrimps or lobster boiled), and it is added to the curry mixture and allowed to simmer for a few minutes. The fish curry is served in the middle of the dish with the rice surrounding it.

Chicken curry is made in this same fashion, substituting chicken for fish, and chicken stock for fish stock. The pieces of chicken are fried to a nice brown, but not thoroughly cooked, and are added to the curry after it has been simmering for two hours, and allowed to simmer for the third hour in the mixture.

As in the case of every epicure the world over, Madame Rubinstein feels strongly about the vital matter of mixing a French dressing. This dressing will go over any green things, or mixture of them. A tablespoonful of wine vinegar, three tablespoonfuls of the finest olive oil, salt, pepper, French mustard, chopped chervil, and tarragon to taste are mixed together. A very small stale crust of bread is rubbed with garlic on both sides, finely diced and added.

If you want a delicious, light cake to be made in a hurry for tea-time, try crispets. One egg is beaten to a foam and mixed with a half-cupful of sugar. Two tablespoonfuls of sifted flour, mixed with half a teaspoonful of baking powder, are added slowly, with constant beating. Flavouring to taste is added, and teaspoonfuls of the mixture are dripped on a greased pan three or four inches apart and baked in a slow oven.

Another tea-time or cocktail tit-bit that is easy and ingenious and good is made by melting butter to a creamy consistency and mixing a few drops of Worcestershire sauce with it. This is spread on oblongs of toast, which are covered with cheese, then placed under the grill till the cheese is melted, when it is sprinkled with a dash of cayenne pepper and salt. Use Gruyère or sharp Cheddar cheese, or a combination of the first two, for these. If you put two little squares of cheese on each bit of toast, and allow for their spreading, you provide two convenient bites, avoiding the necessity of having to put the whole thing in your mouth at once because the cheese refuses to "bite."

And now, since, after all, this is an interview with a world-famous beauty specialist, here is a bona fide beauty recipe—a vegetable bouillon, which does wonderful things for your system. Take a "cure" with it, drinking all you want of this for one day of each week, and eating nothing else, and see your beauty increase a hundred fold. Besides, it's good!

To make two quarts of the bouillon, you use eight and a half ounces of carrots, four ounces of potatoes, three and a half ounces of turnips, two to three ounces of leeks or small white onions, two-thirds of an ounce of dried white beans, two-thirds of an ounce of split peas, two-thirds of an ounce of lentils, coarse salt to taste, and four quarts of water. The vegetables are cut in small pieces, the water is added, and the bouillon allowed to simmer for three and a half to four hours.

Food on the Way

by Cecil Beaton

The grapes had been forgotten and so had the chicken sandwiches, but among the debris of suitcases and tweed overcoats in the back of the car the six peach-fed ham sandwiches were discovered and eaten with relish at the hour when most people are sitting down to their midday meal.

The skies were grey, blustering winds. One quaked at the idea of a Channel crossing, and while the car was being put aboard at Folkestone it was decided to go to the nearest hotel for a solid meal. The weather report was bad, and it is said to be easier to ward off sea-sickness on a full stomach. The lunch menu was proffered by an unnecessarily proud waiter who had nothing but the interminable English hostelry fare to offer. Who can eat soup at midday? The thought of the lukewarm cod did not whet the appetite, nor did the four different ways of cooking potatoes surprise us. We ignored the inevitable mutton, the trifle, the prunes and the flake-dry Cheddar cheese, and chose a cutlet, for safety's sake, immersed in Worcestershire sauce and salad. Really the tyranny of English hotel dining-rooms is appalling!

Perhaps many English do not mind what they eat? The scene in the dining-room is a typical one—small cowed groups are chewing uninterestedly in silence—the only sounds are a staccato tapping on plate of knife and fork, an occasional gently clearing of the throat, a deep gulp and the hoarse whisper, "Would you mind passing the salt?" What a difference from the animated gaiety in any French, American or Spanish restaurant, where the waiters seem to enjoy themselves, or especially in Germany, where before each course they wish one "Guten appetit".

Now, gourmand, expect no technical treatise, no learned discourse on epicurean delights. Expect no strange recipes or information of undiscovered haunts where the fare should be heavily starred in Baedeker. You are being written to by a food novice on holiday. One who, like most children, was brought up to consider eating as a means of warding off starvation rather than an elegant enjoyment. One who was for ever being told to "Tidy up your plate", to "Waste not, want not". That there were so many beggars longing for the discarded crust that not to eat it was a sin. Until recently I ate automatically the heaped platefuls in front of me. But to-day, though disapproving of those that peck and leave the bulk, I respect my appetite and do not use my stomach as a refuse bin; and, since I am more conscious of what I eat, I find so much less is necessary to satisfy.

And now I am going to tell you, in terms of food, of my most recent journeys.

What do I remember? Let us make a chronological list—Cahors, Perpignan. The *foie gras* and truffle country. We climbed through the blue-shuttered window of the pompously-named Hotel des Ambassadeurs, and in the tiny dining-room received a meal to satisfy the most discriminating palate.

Oh, the delight of the *foie gras*, pink and juicy, dappled with black truffles! And the truffle omelet to follow was milkily wet, yet stringy, just as an omelet should be, and, without exception, never is in England. The delicious purple wine that we drank out of a carafe stained the teeth, gums and tongue as though we had been gathering blackberries and had surreptitiously eaten as many as were put into the baskets.

The best things in Spain were the *Ensamaidas*, huge pastry puffs astonishingly lighter than foam, that if squashed, could be packed in a thimble. And with what surprise did one find in Barcelona raspberries, which, spelling English summeryness, one had said *au revoir* to for another year in July. But it was nice to take a lingering farewell, in this tropic atmosphere, to the English summers of tennis under the tall trees, standard roses and hammocks—and the fruit was particularly good.

What else do I remember? The hors d'œuvres at the Hotel Jules César, Aix-en-Provence, were unforgettable. No sign of a sardine, Russian salad, cold egg or anchovy. Here the hors d'œuvres were composed of foodstuffs so far completely unknown to me, and were such a boon after the inevitable hotel array. Here it seemed that twigs of heather and thyme were mixed with the persimmons and the onions were emasculated and treated to taste as gingerbread smells.

At Cannes the hors d'œuvres are lush and luxurious, with leeks and a dozen different salami slices and the best corn on the cob to be found outside California. But what is not already related of the food on the French Riviera? You know so well about the Colombe d'Or at St Paul, and the bouillabaisse at the Lucullus restaurant at Marseilles; but a confession, a disappointment. The night we dined the food was coarse, the iodiney bouillabaisse lobsterless, and the begging street performers were hideously obscene.

They tell so many stories about food in Italy, about lasagne verdi alla Bolognese (green noodles made of spinach purée served with meat sauce). They whisper of white truffles grown artificially with serums in the roots of old oak trees, they report that once one has tasted them one willingly ignores their smell, and it is said that a fonduta, which is a dish of white truffles sliced and grated on melted cheese, is the supreme achievement. But in Italy I have but little appetite. In Venice especially I am hungerless, deterred by the canals smelling of not fresh hard-boiled eggs, the damp table napkins, the knowledge that the macaroni is ever ready. And the food seems almost as intolerably lacking in variety as in English inns. In Italy one eats melon and raw ham and scampi and pasta until one tires of the taste, and wherever one goes, the menu consists of the interminable minestrone, spaghetti, entrecôte, cheese and fruit, and it seems odd that the hotter the sun shines the sourer the wine should be.

Having lived on Florian's sherbet and water-ices, it was with base thoughts that I left for Germany, where food plays so vast a part in one's existence. The bread is no longer of chalk and water and does not smell of a laundry, soup is sweet, there are innumerable varieties of trout and little birds to make any mouth water. At Innsbruck the appetite knows no bounds. *Wienerschnitzel* and *sauerkraut* and beer are never better than at the old Golden Adler here, and those cakes that look so old-fashioned that they must have been made in the eighties are delicious if you try their frothy sweetness, and that wafer is in itself a poem. Why not more often a wafer? There could be so many varieties. It is astonishing how limited one's choice of food is made for one. Why, for instance, only hot cross buns, if one likes their spiciness, at Easter? Why only wedding cake, if one likes its richness and china exterior, at wedding nuptials, when the buffet is already groaning beneath the conventional array of viands? Why not Christmas pudding any time of the year? It is so enjoyable when cut in slices, fried and served with cubes of brandy butter. And why not brandy butter served with wafers as a sweet?

No food article is complete without a visit to Munich to the Hotel Vier Jahreszeiten. Run from a communal kitchen is the hotel restaurant! The Keller restaurant is downstairs with extraordinarily good food, and upstairs,

Cecil Beaton

Lunch at the Waltherspiel, Munich

Lunch at the Lido

in the sombre dining-room, the courteous Mr Waltherspiel supervises the serving of—may we say it?—the best food in the whole world. Here, everything tastes as though, until this moment, one had lost one's sense of taste. The toast is a dream and smells as good as it tastes, butter is as butter should be, and when it comes to being served with fish one knows one had never lived fully before. How can one tell of the delicate crayfish, surrounded by such a subtle sauce? What can one say of the roebuck, of the slice of peculiarly treated ham served on a wooden plate? How can one be believed when relating of the richness of duck cooked in a cantaloup melon? "Duck in a melon? Who ever heard of such a thing?" But I know. I lick my lips, wink slyly and rub my tummy. Who cares if my top trouser button must be undone and, to show the way I feel about it and because they are particularly good here, I shall finish with raspberries and cream.

Meanwhile at home, so many pages have been torn off the calendar, the heat of the sun becomes weaker, and it is time to be returning.

On the way back, I lunch off moules at Prunier's and stop at Le Touquet, where my hostess served vast quantities of Irish stew, cooked by a very French chef, and the result was delicious. We ate *crême de fromage* with sugar and redcurrants and drank champagne with peaches mashed in it, and one afternoon, as we were about to start for a walk, our discussion on Chinese tortures was disturbed by a giant-woman with the enquiry, "Aimez-vous les petits canetons?" And on our hostess replying "Nous adorons les petits canetons," the giant rushed to a cart of quacking ducks and with a dull thud had cut off the heads of three hysterically fluttering birds before our astonished eyes. But there was no opportunity to savour the slaughterer's livestock, for next day I returned home to be confronted by glowing fires, game, honey-dew melons, mushrooms and Laver, a delicious caviare-coloured and oyster-tasting brand of seaweed from Cornwall. It is no use clinging sentimentally to the dregs of a dead summer. Autumn is here and now is the time to enjoy the cracking and crunching of filberts and a glass of Madeira.

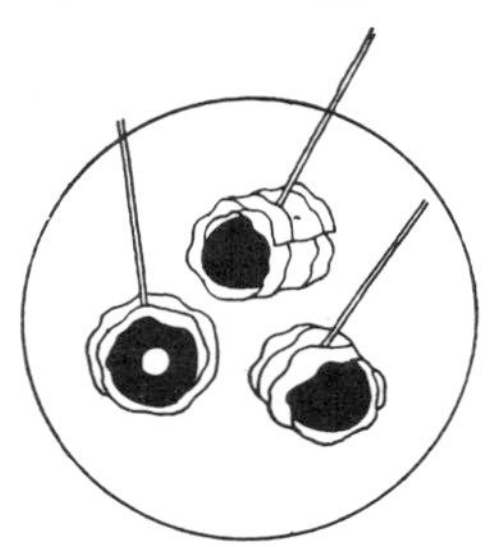

Cocktails and Canapés

by A. H. Adair

Norman Parkinson

Plus ça change, they say, *plus c'est la même chose*! In which "they" are not altogether right. Luncheons and dinners, served later, have become shorter, finer; supper plays an important role and now breakfast even must be thought of, for how can we hope to keep our young friends on the dance floor until the morning without injury to their health if we don't give the poor sweets some food before they rush off to ride, skate, play golf or run down to the sea for a "dip" before luncheon?

So the catering departments in our homes have had to be reorganised and some sacrifices made. The most significant change is undoubtedly the fading popularity of tea as a meal. And who can regret that monument of Victorian wastefulness? The rows of tiers of cakes, buns, scones, bread and butter of all hues, sandwiches, and even eggs, radishes and watercress, which ruined the already sluggish appetites of our parents . . . and to think that they then dined at seven and devoured ten courses!

No, decidedly, *ce n'est plus la même chose*. We are much more sensible, and from six to eight in the evening we add zest to our modern appetites with that perfect symbol of modern life, the cocktail. The reason that cocktails exist is that they play their part in the general readjustment of habit and thought to modern conditions. And so, the tea parties of *autrefois* give place to the cheerful gatherings at cocktail time, and the teacups which we vainly tried to support with a rocky bun, or against which sagged a limp sandwich, have acquired the dignity of antiques, leaving us our two hands free to talk with.

And here we must be practical, for we cannot leave things vaguely to chance, gin and Vermouth if we are to make our cocktail parties successful. The cocktail drinkers of to-day are as discriminating about their *apéritifs* as their fathers were about their port, and they have discovered the subtle charms of a well-balanced cocktail set off, so to speak, by a *bouchée* of just the right flavour.

Here, then, are suggestions for cocktails. In giving the following recipes, those have been chosen which require as a basis only rum, gin or whisky, for until the bar is well equipped it is better to start with simple ingredients which are always to hand. The quantities given are for six people and can be increased or decreased proportionately.

Rum cocktail I
Put two and a half glasses of Jamaica rum into the shaker with half a glass of Italian and one glass of French Vermouth. Add two glasses of strained orange juice, a pinch of powdered cinnamon, and crushed ice. Shake well.

Rum cocktail II
Put into the shaker three glasses of Jamaica rum, one glass of French Vermouth, one of Dubonnet and one of grenadine syrup. Add crushed ice and shake well.

Bacardi
Put three glasses of Bacardi rum into the shaker with three glasses of fresh lime juice (or a mixture of lemon and grapefruit juice in equal proportions), sweeten to taste with soft sugar; add crushed ice, shake well and serve.

Guinet
Take three glasses of Gordon's gin, two of Dubonnet and one of dry sherry. Put these into the shaker with a dash of Angostura bitters. Add crushed ice, shake, let the shaker stand for a minute, shake again and pour out. Squeeze a piece of lemon peel over each glass.

Strong gin cocktail
Four glasses of gin, one of French Vermouth and one of orange juice. Add a few drops of orange bitters, crushed ice, and shake well.

Mild gin cocktail
Put into the shaker two glasses of gin, two glasses of orange juice, one of French Vermouth and one of Italian; add crushed ice, shake and serve.

Duppy
For this cocktail put a few cloves in a jug three-quarters full of Canadian Club whisky, three or four drops of orange bitters and fill up with any strongly flavoured sweet liqueur—Grand Marnier, Cointreau, or Curaçao, then proceed with the shaker as usual.

Here, too, are some suggestions for various Zakuski suitable for serving with cocktails:

Croûtons of fried bread, drained well and cut into fingers, spread with mashed sardines mixed with butter, a little of the oil from the tin, and pepper.

Brown bread made into sandwiches, filled with Roquefort cheese and butter mashed together.

Sticks of celery cleaned and stuffed with a mixture of Roquefort cheese and butter and cut into pieces.

Fried bread spread with a mixture of fillets of anchovies in oil chopped and pounded into a paste with chopped parsley, chervil and tarragon (these should be kept warm—a new use for the muffin dish).

Buttered dry biscuits or Swedish bread spread with a little mayonnaise sauce to which you have added a few drops of Worcester sauce and some pickled walnuts finely chopped.

Cold sausages (which have been very crisply grilled), cut into small pieces.

To this list one can add an endless collection of similar concoctions: in fact, in the larder alone one should be able to find all the principal ingredients among the "left-overs" which, with a little ingenuity, can be made into the most successful kind of "amusing" hors d'œuvre. One should also have little dishes of olives (a profusion of olives of all kinds—stuffed, black small Provençal and large Spanish olives—is good) and some good English Cheddar cheese cut into cubes. Chipped potatoes and salted almonds are always a success as additional items, though they have become slightly banal.

Dinner hour at the Savoy

HOW ONE LIVES

from day to day

Surveying the kitchens of the Ivy

Supper at Rules

The Jardin des Gourmets has a delightful atmosphere of French rusticity

Entering the Spanish Grill at the Dorchester

Week-end Guests

A London Hostess to her Country Housekeeper

Dear Mrs Simpkins,

I want you to prepare the green room for one married couple and the garden suite for another. Also the newly decorated room for one man. They will all arrive in time for dinner on Friday, but not in time for tea. Tell Simpkins to mix cocktails (equal quantities Dubonnet and brandy and a half quantity of Cointreau, well shaken and iced) and prepare cheese balls, also celery stuffed with cream cheese, paprika dusted. Sherry as well. The master will be down in time to go over the wine question with him.

Will you yourself please see to details in the rooms? Padded hangers in more than plenty in all cupboards. A Thermos of iced water in each room as well as Malvern water and glasses. Both Turkish and Virginian cigarettes (Player's No. 3). Biscuits at each bedside also and see that the tin lids are replaced to be airtight. I will do the books and flowers for each room myself when I arrive.

Be sure to tell Emma when she unpacks to take away each lady's night things and press before she lays them out for the night. Also dresses and underwear.

In the lounge fill the flowery china bowl three-quarters full with the boiled sweets, fondants and caramels I am sending down, just putting them all in together. Be sure that the writing tables in each room have clean blotting-paper and pads, fresh ink, pens, the house stationery, and stamps laid out.

Lay out the correct colour of linen for the bath towels, mats, and bed linen for each room. Put the flowered sheets and pillowcases on the beds in the green room. Be positive that the hot water supply is more than adequate all day, early and late, that the electric bulbs and switches are in order and electric heaters in each room. Put rubber wedges for every window, and see that the curtains run well and meet adequately.

Warn Emma that she must help to pack, as well as unpack, and therefore have in a big supply of tissue paper.

Lastly and most important, here are the menus for the two main meals a day. I am sending the recipes I want used for each so that you can order in supplies in time. Mr and Mrs Mainwaring leave after dinner on Sunday, Mr Graham probably also. Col and Mrs Cust stay until Monday after an early breakfast.

For cheeses your master is sending back a Stilton in a pot, also some Brie. (He may change his mind to Double Gloucester or Wensleydale.) Get out the green tomato chutney and the spiced peaches and plums to serve with the cold meats on Saturday. For the sirloin choose a fine piece with a deep undercut. Remove this and cook the upper part in the usual way, reserving the more delicate portions for Saturday night. The ham chosen should be the wide end of the gammon, not the knuckle end, and it should weigh about seven or eight pounds.

FRIDAY DINNER

Tomato soup.
Sole à l'indienne.
Ham baked in cider. Spinach purée.
Roast potatoes.
Glacé suisse.

SATURDAY LUNCHEON

Haddock custard.
Cold sirloin of beef. Mixed salad.
Cold ham. Devonshire potatoes.
Apricot tart and cream.
Cheese and celery.

SATURDAY DINNER

Scotch broth.
Whitings écossaise.
Roast fillet of beef and mushrooms.
Sprouts and sauté potatoes.
Cold baked pears. Riz Chantilly.

SUNDAY LUNCHEON

Stuffed sardines. Tomato salad.
Black olives and brown bread and butter.
Lancashire hot pot. Carrots and turnips.
Apples in a syrup.
Junket.
Cold beef, ham and salad on the side.

SUNDAY DINNER

Fish soufflé.
Chicken pasty. Vegetable salad.
Potatoes in jackets.
Caramel oranges and sponge fingers.
Ham toasts.

Sole à l'indienne
Fillets of sole, poached and folded, and then placed on a bed of curried rice, to which some almonds, peeled and shredded have been added. Mask all this with a good curry cream sauce.

Ham baked in cider
Soak the ham overnight in cold water; then wash well and trim off any hard skin. Place it in a large vessel with some sliced onion and carrot, parsley, bay leaf, four cloves and peppercorns; add cold water to cover, bring to boiling point and simmer for about three hours. When it has been cooking for $1\frac{1}{2}$ hours, add a good pint of cider. Let ham cool in this liquor; lift out, remove skin and sprinkle with brown sugar and breadcrumbs and paprika and insert a few cloves. Bake for an hour in a slow oven. Serve with a sauce made of the liquor with more cider added and very slightly thickened. This is delicious next day cold for luncheon.

Glacé suisse
Slice a Swiss roll, then put it together again with vanilla ice cream and decorate it with whipped cream.

Haddock custard
Boil your Finnan haddock in milk; when cooked, flake it gently and place it in a fireproof dish, a soufflé dish is best. With the milk it was cooked in make a custard with some eggs, adding more milk if required and seasoning. Pour on to the fish and stand the soufflé dish in another dish containing water; put it in the oven and bake till it sets and is brown on top.

Apricot tart
Apricot tart is made of dried fruit steeped and cooked in a crock in the oven till fat and juicy, with some lemon juice added. Then a crust is put over them in a pie dish and baked in the usual way.

Whitings écossaise
Rub some fillets of whitings in flour till it adheres, then put them in a frying-pan with a good piece of butter; they must be slowly fried and not allowed to colour or to be dry. Mix some minced parsley and green onions, also minced, with a little stock and two tablespoons of cream. Pour this over the fish just a little before that are cooked. You must be sure to move the fish about carefully or they will break. Serve in a very hot dish.

Baked pears
Use large dessert pears, fully ripe; do not core them and bake in sugar and water, basting frequently, and serve in their syrup.

Stuffed sardines
Take some good sardines in olive oil and split them lengthways down the middle with a sharp pointed knife. Remove carefully the bone and stuff with the following mixture: the yolk of a hard-boiled egg, salt, pepper and grated cheese, worked together and moistened with a little cream.

Lancashire hot pot
First of all it is essential to have a deep fireproof dish with a lid to it; place at the bottom a layer of small mutton cutlets, or lamb, trimmed neatly and most of the fat removed; sprinkle these with flour, pepper and salt . . . small pieces of kidney may be added if liked. Next, a generous layer of sliced Spanish onion, then a layer of peeled and sliced potato, pepper and salt. Begin again with cutlets and repeat these layers till dish is full, finishing with potato. Lastly pour stock into the dish until dish is three-quarters full; put on lid and cook slowly in oven for about two hours, removing lid at the end to allow potatoes to brown and become crisp. Tie a napkin around dish and send to table. When properly cooked the hot pot should be pleasantly moist without much liquid, and the meat and potato well blended.

Boil equal quantities of carrot and turnip: when cooked, turn into a colander and chop very finely, add butter, pepper and salt, and serve with the hot pot. They should be a golden pyramid, and are the correct accompaniment of Lancashire hot pot.

Apples in a syrup
Peel and core some fine cooking apples, and cut them in halves or quarters. Put about half a pound of golden syrup in a saucepan with half its quantity of water and some lemon juice, and a few drops of cochineal. Drop in the pieces of apple when the syrup is boiling, and stew gently for half an hour or until the apple is quite soft. They must remain whole and be transparent. To be served cold.

Chicken pie or pasty
Boil a young fowl till tender adding to the water in which it is cooked a small onion and a sprig of lemon thyme. When done, remove the meat from the bones and cut it in pieces; strain some of the liquor and season to taste.

Fill a pie dish with layers of chicken and three hard-boiled eggs cut in slices; pour over some of the seasoned liquor, also some cream and cover with crust, leaving a hole on the centre. Brush over with beaten egg and bake till well browned, and pour in some more of the liquor and cream, through the hole in the crust. Serve either hot or cold, but, if cold, add a little gelatine to the gravy.

Caramel oranges
Peel about six good oranges and cut them into sections without any skin or pith, using a very sharp knife. When the oranges are ready, make a caramel with a quarter of a pint of water and four ounces of loaf sugar. If more oranges are used, more caramel will be needed. Arrange the oranges in a glass bowl in layers, sprinkling each layer with castor sugar, and a thin layer of caramel, which should be a pale golden colour. Continue with each layer until the dish is full. Then pile whipped cream on top of all and decorate with chopped nuts.

VOGUE'S SNACK BAR

Patterns for pimentos

Exciting as the colours of their jackets, are ways of using pimentos. Their queer metallic taste puts a lovely kick into a dish. Try them in salads as the French do—cut in strips and seasoned with oil, vinegar and a touch of garlic, or mixed with skinned and sliced tomatoes, green and black olives: the same dressing. Or this way, which is Spanish and sheer heaven—mixed with tomatoes, aubergines, and onions, flavoured with garlic, cooked for an hour in oil, served with eggs crisp-fried in oil. Used as cups, stuffed with minced chicken, herbs and onions, and heated in the oven for 30 minutes with the Regulo set at 3 they are grand.

Hot crisp buns

If you've a cook who's good at making breads, consult her quickly about what to put inside the napkins on your luncheon table. To the guest who's bored to tears with unvaried racks of toast or wheaten biscuits, no more enjoyable surprise than to unfold the serviette on some hot and most divinely crisp example of fresh baking, such as small French croissants, light as air, or baby brioches that taste of butter. Small spicy buns, or caraway-seeded rolls that look like plaits. Toasted brown or white scones, ready split for buttering. Scotch oatmeal biscuits, or miniature bread loaves, madly crusty on the top. Think up some more ideas and vary them from day to day.

Edwardian recipe

Mutton pies. Make some half-puff paste and line some cases about the size of a small saucer. Cut some mutton into small dice, add some chopped onion and season highly with pepper and salt, also some chopped mushroom and a little parsley. Use some very good brown essence mixed with a little Harvey sauce. Cook all together. When cold fill your pastry cases and place a cover of the paste over each, fluting round with a knife, and with a paste brush egg over with one beaten egg. Bake a nice brown (Regulo number 6) and serve hot, for a shooting or golf lunch.

Summer drinks

Peppery Colonels way out East, and sleepy Colonels way down South, most certainly thought up some lovely things to drink. On long hot days which call for long tall glasses in the hand, one can be thankful and wax lyrical about their masterpieces. There's coolness in the very names Mint Julep, Orange Blossom—and magic in the mixing. Herewith a list of recipes from one who's learnt the art. Serve them instead of cocktails, and don't forget to have lots of ice on hand so people can renew the coolness of their drink.

Mint Julep. Place some fresh mint leaves (chopped up) in a tall glass, a teaspoonful of sugar, and a squirt of soda. Mash this mixture well until it is very pulpy. Then fill the glass with very finely chopped ice: top up with rye whisky.

"Old-Fashioned." One teaspoonful of sugar in a heavy glass tumbler: add a few drops of Angostura bitters and a slight squirt of soda: stir round with a spoon. Add the juice and the peel of half a slice of orange and half a slice of lemon. Again stir around with spoon. Next add a double rye whisky, and fill the glass with small pieces of ice, another squirt from the siphon, and place on top a maraschino cherry and a sprig of mint. (If desired a piece of pineapple or a strawberry may be added.)

Orange Blossom. Pour one bottle of gin into a large bowl or pitcher. Add the juice and peel of five oranges and one lemon, sugar to taste. Then add about four bottles of dry ginger ale and plenty of ice.

Gin Rickey. Squeeze the juice of half a fresh lime into a tumbler, add sugar to taste, a double gin, small pieces of ice, and stir round. Fill tumbler to the top with soda.

Nan Paterson. Into a tumbler put a slice of lemon peel, a double gin, and ice. Fill to the top with dry ginger ale.

Irish soda loaf

They have a way with bread in Ireland that is akin to genius. Here is the recipe, bribed from an Irish "Nanny," for the making of a good-sized loaf. Try it for tea some day to prove we haven't kissed the Blarney Stone. Put 1 lb of flour in a bowl; add a large pinch of salt, one teaspoonful of cream of tartar and a quarter teaspoonful of bicarbonate of soda. Mix well and rub through sieve, then add sufficient milk to make a little dough. Knead quickly, form into a long flat cake, and bake in a moderate oven for 40 minutes (no peeping for the first 35 or your bread may turn to bitter disappointment).

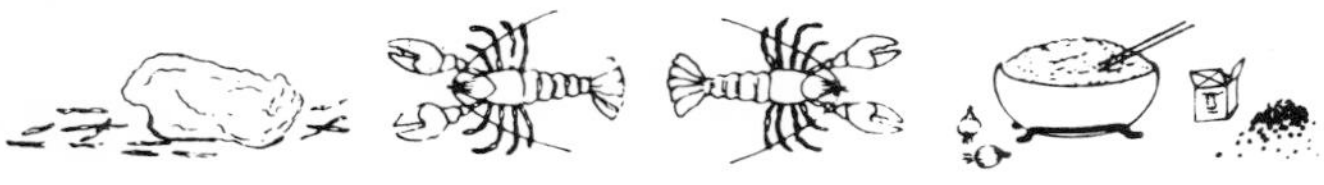

A curry that's cold

Run the risk of startling your Anglo-Indian friends by persuading them that an ice-cold curry can have just as much charm as its "hot-cha" prototype. Here's an old family recipe for a cold lobster Madras curry that even the Boxiest Wallah will be forced to admit is a Good Thing All Through. To make it, you want two tablespoonfuls of best curry powder, two peeled onions, two or three apples, a handful of sultanas and a lobster. (Two lobsters if there are more than four people.) Fry the onions and the curry powder in a large lump of butter. When brown, turn into a deepish saucepan, add the lobster in small pieces, the cut-up apples and the sultanas. Stir steadily and often at first, never allowing it to boil. Five hours, no less, is the right time for it to simmer.

Bring out your soup tureens

At the sort of meals where people walk about and help themselves to sandwiches and snacks, no better main hot dish than a delicious soup. No prettier way to serve it than in an old-fashioned soup tureen (deep as the ocean to hold the heat), with little cups beside it and the biggest thing in ladles you can find. Here are two good soups:

Rice soup. Chop the meat of a lobster and some chicken livers, add a handful each of French beans, carrots, mushrooms, celery root, green peas and a chopped onion. Cover with water. Add a large cupful of rice, a few peppercorns, chopped parsley, cayenne pepper. Simmer until the rice and vegetables are done, then add $\frac{1}{4}$ lb of ground almonds and two tablespoonfuls of fresh cream.

Thin pea soup. Shell 2 lb of fresh green peas. Slice four onions very thin, and put them into boiling water with a pinch of salt. Boil until tender. Drain and keep the juice. Keep out two tablespoons of peas and keep them warm in juice, pass the rest through a medium sieve, then again through a finer sieve. Make a sauce by melting two tablespoonfuls of butter, adding 2 teaspoonfuls of flour and half a pint of heated thin cream. Mix sauce with purée and keep warm. Season well, add juice and whole peas.

Vegetable interests

These days, everybody's keen on vegetables, nobody's keen on too many complicated dishes.

Therefore to serve a vegetable course as an alternative to fish or savoury or both, makes increasing sense at dinner parties.

What nicer, for instance, than to start with soup, go on to chicken or game (with not much more accompaniment than an exquisite salad) and present, before the sweet, something as full of charm as a mushroom or tomato soufflé, a dish of cauliflower very much *au gratin*—or either sweetcorn or small *fonds d'artichauts*, cooked in cream and flanked in the dish with bacon, ultra-thin and wavy as a corrugated roof.

Here are some recipes for more of these vegetable dishes—we've assembled them with greedy interest from recent house-to house "collecting."

Choux à l'allemande. Shred the leaves of a savoy cabbage. Then blanch in boiling water for one minute and strain. Boil until tender, strain and add a tablespoonful of béchamel sauce, a pinch of pepper and salt, a pinch of Parmesan cheese. Dish up with small croûtes of puff paste round the cabbage.

Soufflé of cauliflower à la Baronne. Trim a cauliflower, blanch and rinse it, put it in boiling water with a little salt and let it cook until tender.

Then drain and cut in pieces. Place them in a buttered soufflé dish with alternate layers of raw sliced tomatoes, season with salt and pepper and fill up the dish with a mixture prepared thus:

Make a white sauce (with 2 oz of butter, 2 oz of flour, $\frac{1}{2}$ a pint of milk). Add the raw yolks of 2 eggs, a dust of cayenne pepper and a pinch of salt; stir until it boils. Add 3 oz of grated Parmesan and 3 egg whites whipped stiff. Mix all together and pour over the vegetables in the soufflé dish. Bake 25 minutes (Regulo 6).

Petits pois a l'oignon. Take a quart of small green peas (and of the bottled or tinned variety when you can't get fresh ones). Put in a saucepan with 2 lettuces chopped very fine, a piece of fresh butter the size of an egg, a little salt, pepper and grated nutmeg, one piece of lump sugar, one whole onion and a little very good consommé. Boil together for an hour, remove the onion and just before serving, mix in a teaspoonful of flour and a little fresh butter.

Game pie

"Sing a song of sixpence . . ." but you don't need four and twenty blackbirds to make this "pretty dish". Only two pheasants or four partridges plus a few simple ingredients. The result—seasonable excitement on your "cold" sideboard, or reserve strength on your pantry emergency shelf. Here's the formula: 2 lb calves' liver, 1 lb fat bacon cut in pieces, the legs of two pheasants (or four partridges), pepper, salt, mixed spice, chopped parsley and shallots, a little thyme and bay leaf.

Fry all these together in butter, not too much. Then grind all through a mince machine twice. Line a deep pie dish with fat bacon, set fillets of game (pheasant or partridge) on top. Then add alternate layers of forcemeat, fillets and sliced truffles until the dish is full. Top with slices of fat bacon and a layer of water paste. Cook in a tin of water in the oven for two hours (Regulo 5). When cold, remove the paste and brush over with glaze.

Satai for supper

Not only a good new dish but a good new dish for "dunking" is the following. It hails from Java, was taught us by a reader, and makes a "satai-sfying" change from the usual kedgeree and eggs and bacon line of thought at supper-cum-breakfast parties. This is what you do. Make a thick curry sauce, using one finely chopped onion and a chili fried in butter. Add a little sugar, vinegar and chutney, a generous helping of curry-powder, a bay leaf and plenty of milk or cream. Cook gently and reduce all to a thick sauce. String cubes of beef, mutton, pork or veal on wooden skewers and lay these in the sauce until thoroughly impregnated. Take out and grill quickly. Serve heaped in a large platter, with a bowl of the same sauce as accompaniment. (No need for rice with this dish—the meat is dipped in the sauce and eaten off the skewer.)

Savoury oatcakes

Soak four ounces of Scotch oatmeal in half a pint of milk. Add two tablespoons of flour, three ounces of chopped beef suet, a little black pepper and salt. Shape into small round flat cakes, and fry for a few minutes on both sides in hot bacon fat.

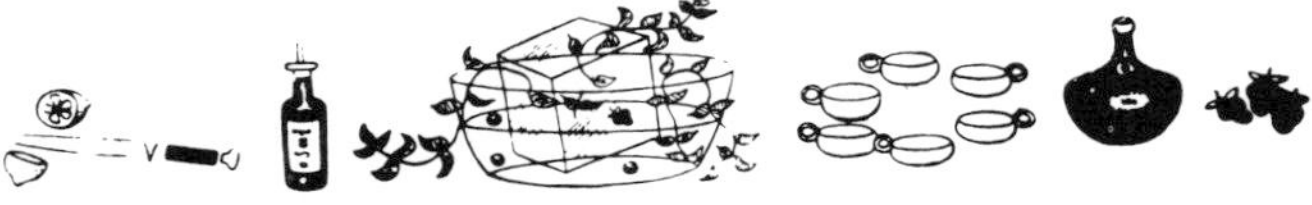

Jellies and jams

In September jam-brewing is very literally in the air, making itself smelt in nice, hot, sugary wafts from almost every kitchen. While the creative mood is on her give these divine old-fashioned recipes to your cook, and look forward to your teas accordingly for months ahead.

Green gooseberry jam. Take 7 lb of gooseberries, 8 lb of sugar, 2 pints of redcurrant juice. (Make this by stewing 4 lb of redcurrants in a pint and a half of water.) Strain it through a sieve, add the gooseberries and sugar and boil for 1 hour, stirring well.

Hip jam. Take some hips, split them and remove all seeds, wash and drain them on a sieve. Take ½ lb of apple jelly and boil it until it dissolves, then add 1 lb of hips to 1 lb of sugar. (If you have 10 lb of jelly in your pan, add 5 lb of hips, ditto of sugar.) Boil for ten minutes then pot.

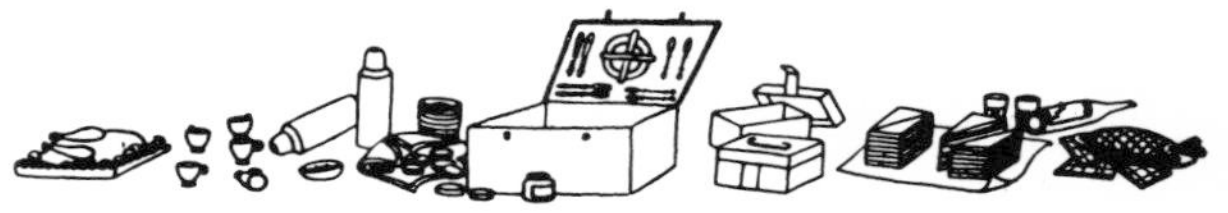

Apple jelly. Pare and core a bushel of good-looking apples. Cover them with water, let simmer until cooked. Pass through a jelly-bag and to each pint of juice allow ¾ lb of crushed white sugar. Cook them gently for three hours until the fruit is very soft, then squeeze first through a colander and then through a sieve. Put away in air-tight jars.

For youthful appetites

When in the holidays your house is swarming with perpetually hungry boys and girls, and your cook is being driven dotty by constant raids upon the kitchen, meet the crisis with a constant stock of simple "eats" placed somewhere handy in the house. So that en route for those exhaustive expeditions of the young, pockets may be filled with something "for the road," such as wheaten biscuits sandwiched with cream cheese (some chopped-up ginger is a good addition) or buttered water biscuits with a good thick layer of Gruyère cheese between them. Chocolate bars of the plain, sustaining sort, or lovely crunchy ginger nuts will meet with warm approval—here's an excellent recipe for the making of the latter.

Ginger nuts. 1 lb of flour, ½ lb of butter, 1 oz of ground ginger, ½ lb sugar. Mix together into a paste with ¾ lb of golden syrup. Roll into biscuits and bake in a moderate oven (Regulo 4).

Edwardian recipes

This time it's not for food. Just a heavenly way of utilising snippets from your garden in a manner that will scent your house and linen cupboards.

Pot-pourri. In a sunny room, dry some rose-leaves, lavender, lemon verbena and any kind of sweet-smelling leaf at hand. Add ½ lb of powdered orris-root, ¼ lb cloves, 2 sticks of cinnamon, 2 oz of allspice, 1 lb of bergamotte, 1 dram of musk. The spice should all be powdered and mixed in with the leaves, and only sweet-smelling roses should be used.

Sugar and spice

The season of nursery parties being thoroughly upon us, here are a few Southern specialities that hail from "ole Virginny", and have made many a "young Massa" and "lil Missy" clap their hands with joy.

Strawberry shortcake

(Any good brand of bottled strawberries may be used for this recipe.)

2 *lb flour, sifted*
1½ *large tablespoons butter*
2 *teaspoons sugar*
2 *teaspoons baking powder*
¾ *cup milk*

Mix dry ingredients together and sift them, then work in butter with tips of fingers; add milk, making a soft dough. Bake quickly in a moderately fast oven (Regulo 6) from twelve to fifteen minutes in two well-greased sandwich or layer cake tins. When cool (not cold) butter each layer and put strawberries, previously crushed and sugared, between them; press down well to allow juice to soak into both layers. Place whole strawberries close together on top. With this serve a sauce made of crushed strawberries and sugar, and also serve fresh rich cream.

Washington cream pie

½ *cup butter*
½ *cup milk*
½ *teaspoon salt*
½ *cup sugar*
1¾ *cups flour*
2 *eggs*

Cream butter and sugar, then add eggs well beaten, sift flour and add alternately with milk to mixture. Bake in two shallow tins in a moderately quick oven (Regulo 5) for thirty minutes. When cool, place the following filling between the layers of cake, and dust with sugar on top.

Filling

Take one teacup of flour, two eggs, one cup of sugar and one pint of boiling milk. Mix and heat gently in a saucepan, stirring constantly until it thickens, and add a half teaspoonful of vanilla or lemon extract.

Cinnamon sweet toast

Slice white bread in pieces about half an inch thick, dip in milk after edges have been cut off. Then dip in egg and breadcrumb, and next in brown sugar, well mixed with ground cinnamon. Be generous with the sugar and cinnamon. Fry in very hot fresh lard until slices are a light brown. Serve very hot, well sprinkled with a mixture of half cinnamon and half sugar.

Francis Marshall

"Lobster mayonnaise twice, and step on it"

Dining-rooms of Distinction

A Dramatic Dining Room

This black and white room shows the new type
of dining-room that modern life is evolving.
It is in no sense a sitting-room, but the dramatic effect
of the decoration makes a complete harmony
of the few essentials, and there is no feeling of bareness

Modernism Goes Romantic

This romantic modern living-room is in the Paris flat which M. Marc de Nicolas de Plantier has decorated for himself. The tables in glass and metal, the divan and chairs in white lacquer with coral-coloured upholstery, the pale beige walls and blue ceiling make a perfect setting for the landscape panel by Raymond Faucher which decorates the dining recess

Did this glass age make Lalique; or did Lalique make the glass age? In any case, this French designer has done more than anyone to make glass chic and beautiful. This glass table with luminous fine ware to match it would adorn any modern dining-room. It is from Breves' Lalique Galleries

A very distinguished dining-room designed by Raval and Bertrand for M. André Durst's house in Paris. The glass-and-metal table is very simply decorated with a restrained arrangement of flowers between a pair of magnificently simple rock-crystal obelisks, which are mysteriously and effectively lighted

Friday-to-Monday Hostess

by Lady Morvyth Benson

Here now is a hostess, invited to express her views, reactions and so forth, upon the subject of week-end entertaining in the country.

Incidentally, should you consult the Arlen Mayfairites, they will tell you never to speak of week-ends, always of Fridays to Mondays. No one knows why. It's just one of those things—like children they'd say, talking of bathing costumes instead of bathing dresses. But that's neither here nor there.

This hostess, however, invited to express her views, does so with alacrity, finding it an absorbing subject, and her favourite one, if it comes to that. Firstly though, she intends to touch lightly on a thing which has always puzzled her.

Just what constitutes the word "hostess", and to attain it, what qualifications are required? Surely, any man or woman, having once dispensed a glass of sherry to friends in a back mews, has as much right to the title as Mrs Corrigan or Mrs Ronnie Greville. Assuming this is so, this lady having but a small house and accommodation will continue to call herself hostess, without a blush.

Some years ago in New York, before America discovered England, she was asked—"Is it true of English country parties, that, before going to bed, male guests are discreetly informed as to the identity of female occupants of rooms adjoining?" Like little Audrey, she laughed and laughed, knowing it to be true enough, but with a difference.

The male guest will undoubtedly have taken a look at the name next door before ever he goes down to dinner. Also, the good hostess will have thought all this out long before the guests arrive, it being, in her opinion, neither unmoral nor immoral to conclude the following.

Two people, knowing each other well, invited to stay together, feel more fortified to face best or worst in a house, maybe full of strangers, can they but shout encouragement through half-closed doors, meet on the way to the bath, share the same moment of trepidation descending to dinner, or enjoy a word in the mornings snitching a bite off each other's breakfast trays.

And that almost, though not quite, disposes of the allocation of rooms.

One other delicate matter often worries this particular hostess. Can married couples be relied on to share a double room or no?

Say there be but two suites of double and single rooms. The dressing-room of one is so tiny as to necessitate anyone sleeping in the bed having to get out to turn over. The other is fair-sized. How to ascertain that the couple sharing a double room are allocated the small dressing-room and vice versa? Hardly a question that can, even after the third glass of wine at dinner, be put to the most intimate friends, and then it would be too late. Nothing to be done, therefore, but take a chance, and hope that a good night or two will be had by all.

Prospective hostesses who fail to awake with a thrill on Fridays, and a sense of loss on Mondays, miss a lot.

Many there are who have gardeners and flunkeys to arrange both flowers and house.

But it's a hundred per cent more fun to do it personally.

First there's the cook to interview, with a thought to the favourite food of these particular guests.

Then the housemaid to see, a tour of the rooms, a peering at sheets, a feeling of disappointment that the old faded French ones should not have been replaced by the new Madeira linen.

Are the Thermos flasks filled with iced water, boxes with biscuits, Turkish and Virginian cigarettes to hand?

Should the novels be renewed? Has the writing table and the little square tray for writing in bed been got ready?

Do these flowers match that chintz? Why oh! why must the housemaid always leave the hearthrug rucked up and a little crooked. A race alas! with no eye for symmetry.

Now there's the flowers to do for the downstairs sitting-rooms.

In summer, mixed bowls, à la Fresh Flowers decoration, always lovely, if a trifle over-done.

An expensive essentiality is that drinks should be available almost all day. Nothing can be more uncongenial, from a

Mr Cecil Beaton and his friends picnicking in truly rustic fashion in the garden of his house at Ashcombe

guest's point of view, than to want a drink madly, however unreasonably, at 11.30 a.m., and to feel too embarrassed to ring and ask for it.

Rare wines and liqueurs with meals are not nearly so appreciated to-day as a steady supply of "Gin and Tonic", Beer and Cider.

And so they arrive. The question being what to do with them? The answer "Nothing". Let them relax, let them make their own arrangements.

There are things to do. A swimming pool, squash court, garden, horses, dry fly river, speed boat, and good neighbouring golf course.

Many may prefer, and often do, to remain in bed, or sleep stretched on sofas for practically the whole forty-eight hours they are with you.

That being their whim, you must accept it, as must you also when they order six caddies on Saturday evening and change their minds about golf on Sunday.

Booked caddies at half a crown a piece are quite a liability for the host.

Final problem: games of chance. This too has to be thought out with care, so that no strain shall be put upon the modest purse.

Those who are bored, unless enriching themselves at the expense of fellow guests, and who sit all day and night in exclusive heaps commercialising the house, are unlikely to be asked twice.

Bridge, Backgammon, Bezique, Poker, Chemin de fer, Spillikens and Shovehalfpenny, all are safe to play if house stakes are accepted; a limit to the pool and division by four at the end. No one in consequence has, as yet, turned the children's pea-shooter upon themselves, or been found drowned in the pool.

And that's enough about entertaining, but for the old story of the man who, upon entering his club, found a friend absorbed behind a newspaper.

After several abortive attempts at conversation, he remarked "and has your wife been entertaining this summer"? Glancing up, the man with the newspaper replied absently, "Not very."

Raw

On leave, he likes to dine against the sophisticated decor of La Popote du Ritz. You in his favourite black, his favourite lace, feminine to the last flounce

40s

"Rations for one—dinner for two" . . . "A new taste thrill—shredded raw cabbage in salads" . . . "Spreading out your points is as important as spreading out your clothes coupons" . . . "Stretching the joint" . . . "Instead of a turkey, stuffed goose necks" . . . "Special treats. An Orange. An Egg. A Kidney. Peanut Butter" . . . "Two courses can make a sturdy meal."

This was the beginning of the forties in *Vogue*. Rationing, which began in 1940, continued until July 1954. Meat, the first food to be rationed and the last to end, was the major difficulty. At its worst, in March 1949 and February 1951, the ration was 10*d*. a week and consisted of 8*d*. "carcass meat" and 2*d*. of "canned corned meat". Tea, sugar, cheese, bacon, cooking fats, butter and margarine, chocolate and sweets were all rationed. At least you always got your ration; sometimes you didn't have an egg for months. Occasionally there were special rations; sugar for jam-making, an extra 4oz butter for the Coronation in May 1953, extra margarine for Christmas. Almost all tinned foods came under a complicated system of "points" which were interchangeable with bread "units". For the whole of the forties this was the basic week's ration:

TEA 2–3 oz
SUGAR 8 oz–1 lb
CHEESE 1 oz–8 oz
BACON 2–8 oz
COOKING FAT 1–3 oz
BUTTER AND MARGARINE 4–8 oz
MEAT 10*d*.–2*s*. 2*d*.

In spite of this, the average diet throughout the country during the war was actually better than it had been before because the overall quantity of food was closely controlled.

The maximum charge for food in restaurants was 5*s*. for a meal restricted to three courses, two if bread were served. Thus many people were eating in restaurants for the first time.

A house charge of up to 7*s*. 6*d*. was allowed if entertainment or some other

Home-guards of health

Of course you don't want to be a food crank. But it is useful to know that there are certain homely foods that can do a marvellous job of protecting you and your family against illness.

Enlist these "home guards" in your diet, and keep them regularly on duty!

Here are a few simple exercises:

1 Serve a good big helping of any green vegetables every day. Greens should be cooked quickly; served at once; keeping hot or warming up lessens their value.

2 Serve, also, a good portion of root vegetables. Be sure that carrots are served several times a week. When cooking potatoes, boil or steam them in their skins for utmost health value.

3 Give something raw and green every day. Sometimes it may be a salad of shredded cabbage heart or other tender greenstuff; or watercress or mustard and cress for tea; or plenty of chopped parsley in a sauce, on potatoes, or in a salad.

4 This health "exercise" now looks after itself; eat national bread and dishes made with national flour!

5 Every member of the family should have his or her full ration of butter, margarine, and milk and cheese.

DRIED EGG RECIPE LEAFLET *FREE*

Save your shell eggs for the children and for boiling and poaching. Use Dried Egg for all your cooking. Dried Egg is very easy to use and makes the most delicious scrambled egg, omelettes, Yorkshire pudding, pancakes, boiled or baked custard, cakes and puddings.

A sheet of 12 Ministry of Food tested recipes using Dried Egg will be sent free to all who ask. Please send postcards only, asking for Cookery Leaflet No. 11, and address, The Ministry of Food, Room 629 U, London, W.1.

ISSUED BY THE
MINISTRY OF FOOD

Photographs: Cecil Beaton, Rawlings, Parkinson

Miss Scott-Ellis and Miss Stanley pick dwarf runners

Lady Diana Cooper feeds the pigs

Mrs Henry Hopkinson at her station canteen

extra was provided, and the price of wines rocketed. There were plenty of experiments: omelettes made with powdered eggs; pigeon, guinea fowl, venison on the menus—even owls it was suggested. Whale meat was tried but dropped for lack of interest.

One night in cabaret at the Savoy Vic Oliver said: "We are employing extra small waiters tonight in order to make the sandwiches look bigger."

The famous hostesses were all digging for victory, working in canteens and feeding evacuees. Mrs John Betjeman was photographed milking her own goat, Lady Anglesey feeding her hens, Miss Mary Churchill gathering the greens, Miss Katheryn Stanley collecting the windfalls and Miss Scott-Ellis picking the beans. Mrs Henry Hopkinson ran a station canteen, Norman Parkinson ran his "Parks" Pig Food Service and Lady Diana Cooper tended three acres and a cow. Lady Spencer-Nairn "supplemented the home farm and kitchen garden by growing vegetables in the formal flower beds", and Margaret, Lady Grant, said: "Remember that a bowl of good soup, with grated cheese and a roll, makes a meal."

Larder Data . . . on the theme of self-sufficiency

This was an article in August 1940: "A well-stocked store cupboard is one of the best contributions you can make towards national defence. It means your family can be adequately fed in emergencies without the risk of going out of doors. If air-raids dislocate supplies, it means that you can leave local food stocks to be drawn on by people who cannot afford to store and that the food queues will be the shorter by your absence. It means that you are a small self-reliant fortress within the great fortress that is Britain. The Minister of Food has asked everyone to store at least a week's food supply. Here are some suggestions on the subject.

Think in terms of meals when you store

"It isn't a matter of isolated tins, bottle and packets, but the meals they can produce. Unrelieved sardines or tongue will soon pall, and with such a variety of tinned food on the market, there's no excuse for boredom. Reading along the grocer's shelf nowadays is as interesting as reading the menu in a restaurant—Irish stew, Lancashire hot pot, boiled beef and carrots, tripe and onions, curried mutton, steak and kidney pudding, Melton Mowbray pie. The name of Maconachie is one to look for.

"Unusual tinned fish meals are Clam chowder, Shad roe and Kedgeree made from fresh English fish.

Plan for a balanced diet

"You need fruit and vegetables to keep in good health, but their perishable quality makes them the first to disappear in emergencies. It's fortunate for us that such as Smedley's have developed the British canning industry in recent years. As the

Mrs John Betjeman milks Snowdrop, her prize goat

Norman Parkinson collects pig swill

Miss Mary Churchill shoulders a stook

seasons come round and the crops come to harvest, Smedley's alone store them away to the tune of a hundred million cans a year.

Bread and butter foods are easily forgotten

"The staple things you eat at every meal but it doesn't occur to you to store. One feels lost without bread; lay in the tinned date-and-nut variety. Biscuits, too, help to take the edge off the over-richness of some tinned foods. Have you thought of water—poured out *like* water in peaceful times; treasured beyond price the moment it gets scarce? Keep a supply of bottled water—boiled, then sealed in scrupulously clean bottles. Apparently so innocent, water is dangerous stuff if not treated properly, so buy it professionally bottled if you are in any doubt about it. Then milk. How many would enjoy their tea and coffee without milk? Yet the milk supply is obviously among the most vulnerable. Libby's condensed milk fills this bill; or Lingfo-milk—a powder which simply needs water added.

"Butter and margarine can be had tinned; and some kind of spread, such as Honeycream in cartons, is a good stand-by.

"If you haven't laid down all the eggs you should, fill the gap with Eggo—dried eggs in packets."

Meals without cooking

"Provide for the times when people may want hurried meals at queer hours; when gas may be cut off; when the fuel for your portable stove fails ('Primus' is the first name that comes to mind, but they are scarce now, being Swedish. Coleman stoves, at the Army and Navy stores, do the job well). For uncooked meals, provide tinned cooked sausages, tinned Kraft cheese, spiced ham, turkey and ham, or veal and ham roll—all tinned.

Little luxuries

"Keep a mildly gourmet flag flying with a few delicacies to be brought out on special occasions to astonish and cheer your friends. Pâté de venaison aux truffes, roast grouse in gravy, and other innocent diversions. Fortnum and Mason hum with ideas.

Do your own preserving

"Besides the ordinary jam-making and fruit-bottling, here are two tips that reached us recently. One concerns rhubarb—which should be bought when it is plentiful and cheap; the coarse outer skin peeled off and the inner stalk cut into inch cubes, packed in glass jars, and covered in water under a screw-on lid. It keeps at least a year and tastes like fresh-picked fruit if it is cooked as soon as opened.

"The other notion is pure squirrel stuff. Towards the end of September, buy the last of the new potatoes; pack them in tins with close-fitting lids, and bury them under six inches of earth (marking the spot, unlike the squirrel). By this means you can eat new potatoes with your Christmas dinner.

"Ancestral home or no, the terrace must have more manure"

Miscellany

"Did you know sardines actually improved with keeping, as the olive oil matures? Lay down a sardine cellar now and serve vintage specimens in years to come. Olive oil, of course, is superbly nourishing: buy while you may as supplies are bound to become scarce. In the last war (1914–18) a small bottle cost as much as 17*s.* 6*d.*

"Did you know that Selfridges had got a candle to end all candles—a solid square pillar which burns 112 hours and ingeniously consumes its own drippings instead of letting them pour down?

"Did you know that lumps of sugar were the best restorative for strained nerves? Keep some in the basket that should stand ready to be carried to the air-raid shelter when the warning sounds; complete with brandy, bottled water and a little food.

"Have you got a tin opener?"

The Ministry of Food took advertising pages to explain that a batter was actually better AND EASIER TO MAKE! when you used dried eggs, *and put them in dry*. Save Bread: Save Ships—4 things you can do—followed by four recipes for using up STALE BREAD. And TRY THIS SALAD DRESSING (no milk required). Fray Bentos advertised NEW WAYS OF SERVING CORNED BEEF—using 3 rations of corned beef (6*d.* worth).

By 1943 it was realized that "things would never be the same again". And *Vogue* was saying "The post-war servant problem is attracting attention. Here is a suggested solution." The solution, by Frances Howell, was "the establishment of a domestic service corps". "The machinery for such a corps is already largely in existence. It only needs adapting. In the Women's Services there are thousands of young women who are performing nothing but domestic duties. Built all over the country are hundreds of hostels in which the members of such a corps could be housed if they did not want to live at home. Each member would work an eight-hour day, say, either from 6 a.m. to 2 p.m., or from 2 p.m. to 10 p.m. In that way each girl would have proper leisure time and privacy, and the employer's demands should be fulfilled more efficiently and expeditiously.

"Up till now there have been very few specialists for domestic work. A small house relies on one servant who is expected—presumably by the light of nature—to be able to do everything, and of course can't. A large house has a multitude of servants who, performing their special functions at rare intervals, spend the rest of their time waiting on one another: a monstrously uneconomic system. How much better it would be to have a source from which one could draw a laundress, for example, or a cook to do a slap-up dinner, with a waitress to serve it.

"This is not to say that you might awake to see a strange face above your breakfast tray every morning. Obviously it would be a bad thing to have an ever-changing staff, since so much of housekeeping is a thing of personal taste and individual order. It should be an easy matter for the service corps to record that XY is engaged permanently by Mrs Z when both employer and the employed are satisfied.

"And the governing word is *both*."

That brainwave never materialized, so *Vogue* came up with another useful suggestion: "If you have space for a goat you need not be short of milk this winter, for the 'poor man's cow' will supply you with all you need. A goat is a tie; she must be milked regularly twice a day, or she will drop her yield; but you can arrange the times to suit your own convenience. . . . It is unwise to consider keeping a goat if you have only a tennis lawn for pasture. The grass may be excellent and the goat may enjoy it, but soon the animal has to be tethered over grass she was eating only a few weeks back, and her health suffers. For special rations, you should apply at the beginning of every month to your Feeding Stuffs Officer at your War Executive Committee. Remember: 'Any person making any statement which he knows to be false in a material particular shall be guilty of an offence against that Regulation.' Inspectors are unlikely to visit you, but they have the power to do so."

The conservation of food, fuel and time continued to be everyone's problem. "As we all know, one of the easiest ways to accomplish these economies is to pop everything into one pot."

Perhaps this was taken too literally because it was followed by "BETTER COOKING—Suggestions and recipes from W. Bronson, Manager of the Maison Basque restaurant: 'C'est la guerre!' This is the parrot cry which covers a multitude of sins of omission. And at home the same cry arises too often—a cry this time, of patient martyrdom from the innocents forced to swallow bad cooking 'because food is rationed . . . because there's a war on.'

"This is no excuse. Somehow, in spite of fabric rationing and labour shortage, couturiers have maintained the traditions of high fashion. And what goes for the *haute couture*, goes equally for the *haute cuisine*. Only the flash-in-the-pan amateur is dependent on quantities of exotic food, defeated by the lack of this or that in a recipe. To the true cook, the artist in his profession, present conditions present a challenge; spurring him on to devise substitutes for vanished dainties, to make succulent the starchiest standbys.

"Nor is the wartime cook so impoverished. The gardens of England, dug-for-victory, are full of delicious vegetables; woods and fields abound with titillating herbs. . . . Remembering what any French peasant can do with a few pea-pods in a pot-au-feu, we should be ashamed that, over here, so much should go to make so little." And he gave two excellent menus (see page 133) 'which can be produced

Dodie Masterman

from unrationed ingredients, and at a cost of about 12*s.* for six people.'

By 1945 a favourite occupation of the Forces, sick of dehydrated carrot, dehydrated meat, dehydrated eggs and longing for a good thick steak, was planning the meals they would have when rationing ended and "the lights came on again all over the world". *Vogue* played this game too (page 120).

Vogue's "Portfolios of Wartime Economies", begun in 1943, came to an end in 1945. But the seven- and eight-course meal had disappeared for ever except for very grand occasions. Doris Lytton Toye wrote a cookery page for *Vogue* from 1945 until the end of the decade, with excellent recipes and simple menus and she reported the important changes in cooking: "The new look has spread to the larder, insomuch that 'quick-freeze' methods have come to stay, turning our bill of winter fare topsy-turvy." She wrote in 1948: "Having just visited a bewildering display of frozen food in a glass case somehow reminiscent of an aquarium, I know how many varieties of fruit and vegetables can be frozen. Expensive? Not if we offset the roundabout price with the gain on the swings of waste, trouble and time: peas, indeed, seem cheaper than when bought in the pod. The quality of some of the British packs is, in my opinion, superlative, superior both in grading and in preparation to the Continental."

And later in the year: "The pressure cooker opens up a whole new outlook on cooking and adds new zest to the kitchen. The cooker's compactness and cleanliness are excellent points, and it has a wonderful way of cooking a variety of food at the same time (disposed on racks) without losing or mixing any of the flavours. To the late homecomer with little time to cook, a pressure cooker is just manna from heaven.

"The technique is very simple and you have only to read and absorb the perfectly clear instructions to realise that the cooker, correctly handled, is positively foolproof. You couldn't blow yourself up if you tried."

The career girl now was not only acknowledged but actively encouraged: "Did you know that, for 2*s.*, you can have a neat carton containing brown or white bread and butter, a hard-boiled egg, a meat sandwich, a Kunzle cake, a tangerine and a paper napkin? Alternatively, you can have ham and tongue sandwiches or cheese or sardine-filled rolls, a home-made jam tart and an apple. Ring the Gordon-Johns Service to call at your office every day in case you want to buy from him."

The first pictures of liberated Paris appeared in 1944 and by the end of the decade people were flocking to France again. *Vogue* devoted eight pages to A GUIDE TO PARIS EATING by Alexander Watt, with a gastronomic map "intended to be the constant companion of the visitor to Paris". "Contrary to what might be expected, there exists today a greater number of restaurants in Paris than before the war. The telephone book lists no less that 2,727."

In London, "Peace is here, but not yet plenty". The Modern Hostess "quite often doubled with the cook. And often from choice, for once having experienced the compensations of the staffless home, and the ease with which last-minute guests can be invited, she is unwilling to relinquish the freedom of the kitchen."

Paper, as well as food, was rationed but, with a substantial increase, before the forties faded *Vogue* was able to announce a circulation of OVER 100 000 "the largest ever achieved in Great Britain by a class magazine." Now every issue would include a cookery article: "We hope the bill of fare will prove satisfying—and will at the same time whet your appetite for more."

New ways of Serving
CORNED BEEF
FRAY BENTOS BRAND
OXO
All supplies of Corned Beef including FRAY BENTOS are now distributed by the Ministry of Food.
CORNED BEEF PIE
3 rations of corned beef (6d. worth).
1 cup finely shredded raw vegetables (carrot, potato, leek, swede, etc.)
1 Oxo Cube.
1 teaspoon chopped parsley.
Small piece fat.
Short crust pastry (6 ozs. flour, 3 ozs. fat).
1 dessertspoon flour.
Melt the fat in a small pan and lightly fry the vegetable. Stir in the flour and cook a few minutes. Add 1 cup of cold water and the crumbled OXO cube. Stir until thickened. Draw off the heat, add cubed meat, parsley and seasoning to taste. Line a small plate with pastry and spread it with the meat mixture. Cover with pastry, seal the edges and decorate with pastry leaves. Bake in a moderate oven 30 minutes. 4 servings.
CORNED BEEF CAKES
8 ozs. Corned beef.
1 small cupful browned crumbs.
1 dessertspoon flour.
1 teaspoon chopped parsley
8 ozs. mashed potato.
1 Oxo Cube.
Small piece fat.
Dissolve the OXO in a cupful of hot water and let it cool. Flake the meat, mix it with the parsley, potato and half the crumbs. Melt the fat, blend the flour with it, cook a few minutes and then stir in the OXO stock. Cook until it thickens stirring all the time. Bind the meat mixture with this sauce and seasoning if necessary. Form into flat cakes, roll in crumbs and press them on. Heat in a well-greased frying pan or baking tin. About 8 small Cakes.
OXO

Wartime Entertaining

Note: *When these recipes were written cream was non-existent, meat and butter in short supply and eggs rare. So when it says cream substitute, use fresh cream—it will be better; use butter instead of margarine if you prefer and of course fresh eggs instead of dried ones.*

Cecil Beaton

Wrens dining at Greenwich, 1941

Menus Without Meat

Barbara Jones

Frisons
Pull apart the leaves of a cabbage. Blanch them in boiling salted water, adding a small piece of bread tied in muslin, to make the cabbage more digestible and to prevent the strong smell. Drain it, and chop it coarsely. Put in a pan a little fat, half a glass of water; add the cabbage, salt and pepper, two or three spoonfuls of rice, cover and let it cook for twenty minutes. Remove the lid and sprinkle with grated cheese, let it brown for a few minutes in the oven. Regulo 8.

Vermicelli à la mexicaine
Slice an onion very thin; cook it lightly in fat. Add some raw vermicelli and let it, too, turn golden brown. Add little by little enough warm broth to cover the vermicelli; season and let it swell gently. For a winter dish, prepare tomato sauce with purée of tomatoes; in the summer, use fresh sliced tomatoes. Put in a greased bowl, sprinkle with grated cheese: a layer of cooked vermicelli, a layer of grated cheese, a layer of tomatoes, etc. Heat in the oven. Regulo 5.

Oatmeal steaks
These steaks have a great resemblance to brains. The night before, put ½ lb of oatmeal to soak in a mixture half milk, half water. The next day add two spoonfuls of flour, salt, pepper, chopped parsley, an onion finely chopped and lightly cooked in margarine, one yolk of egg, and one beaten white. Stir all together until thoroughly mixed; then drop it spoonful by spoonful into boiling fat. Drain and serve immediately. These quantities will serve six people.

Herring and potato salad
Boil two large potatoes, skin and slice them. Remove the head of a smoked herring; cut it in two lengthways, brush over with oil and grill it. Take out skin and bones, put the fish in a salad dish with two spoonfuls of chopped parsley and onion (optional), two spoonfuls of mustard, two spoonfuls of vinegar, four spoonfuls of oil and some pepper. Add the potatoes, a soupspoonful of warm water, and stir gently. This salad should be prepared the previous day.

Macaroni salad Lucullus
Cook some macaroni in salted water, take it off while the macaroni is still firm; drain and keep warm. Prepare some highly seasoned mayonnaise. Mix in a salad dish the macaroni, mayonnaise, some very thick tomato purée, and, in season, some cooked *fonds d'artichauts,* very finely chopped. Add, if you wish, a chopped hard-boiled egg and a little lean ham cut in thin slivers: finish off with a sprinkling of chopped parsley.

Potato purée with breadcrumbs
This dish can be prepared with left-over potatoes. Grease a pie dish; fill with alternate layers of the following: potato purée, thick béchamel sauce, grated cheese; top with a sprinkling of bread raspings, dotted with margarine. Put in a hot oven until a fine golden-brown crust forms. Regulo 7. Raspings are obtained by drying scraps of bread in a slow oven, and pounding them fine.

Tunny fish loaf
Peel and boil six medium-sized potatoes; break them up with a fork; add a fist-size lump of bread that has been soaked in milk and squeezed out. Pass it all through a mincing machine, with the contents of a ¼ lb tin of tunny fish. Next dip rather a tall mould into water. Fill it with the mixture, packing it in closely. Put a plate over it, pressed down by a weight, and leave to cool till next day. Turn it out and serve with mayonnaise.

Potatoes à la crème
Take some potatoes. Cut them in quarters, cover with water and cook gently, not allowing them to fall to pieces. Drain; place in a hot serving dish. Melt a little butter or margarine, without cooking it. Boil a cup of cream for two minutes. Pour over the potatoes, first the butter, then the cream. Serve immediately.

Endives provençales
Cook endives in boiling salted water; drain them very thoroughly, wringing them out in a cloth, if necessary, to squeeze out all moisture. Dip them in salad oil. Arrange the

whole endives on a dish in alternate layers with rather thick tomato sauce, to which you have added grated Parmesan and garlic (optional). Top with grated Parmesan and brown in the oven. Regulo 7.

Kedgeree
For this you want $\frac{1}{2}$ lb of rice and 1 lb of haddock. Cook the haddock in court-bouillon; drain it and crumble it. Cook the rice in boiling salted water until each grain is separated (about 15 to 20 minutes). Gently mix the rice and the fish, add a little butter, some chopped parsley, a chopped hard-boiled egg and a spoonful of Worcester sauce or ketchup. Re-heat and serve.

Endives Albert
Blanch the endives in boiling water; drain them and fry them a golden brown in margarine. Roll each one in grated cheese and wrap in a thin slice of ham. Put them on a dish on which you have put a light covering of béchamel sauce, and pour a little béchamel over them. Sprinkle with grated cheese and some knobs of butter. Brown in the oven and serve very hot.

Pudding à la reine
Over 5 oz of breadcrumbs, 3 oz of sugar and the juice of one lemon, pour a pint of boiling milk. Add four beaten egg yolks and a spoonful of very finely powdered coffee. Put the mixture in a well-buttered dish and bake for 25 minutes. Regulo 5. Now cover it with currant jelly and the beaten white of four eggs, whipped stiff with some sugar. Replace in oven to brown.

Polenta
Put a $\frac{1}{2}$ lb of maize flour into $1\frac{3}{4}$ pints of boiling salted water; let it boil for about 20 minutes, taking care to stir it all the time. Add $2\frac{1}{2}$ oz of grated cheese and the same weight of butter. Place the mixture in a moistened dish, and leave to cool. When cold, cut it into squares or diamonds and fry in butter or oil. Place on a very hot dish, powder with grated cheese and pour over some melted butter.

Shelter dinner: "The Clicquot '23, sir, and cook reports an incendiary bomb in the area, sir"

Christmas goose
1 goose
6 apples
water or stock
Rub salt over the goose outside and inside; stuff with the peeled whole apples. Make the roasting pan very hot and fill it with an inch of water. Put in the goose, breast down, and roast for two to two and half hours, basting frequently with its own gravy and, if that is not enough, with water or stock also. Quarter of an hour before serving baste it well and brown in a very hot oven for fifteen minutes. Garnish with paper frills round the neck and legs and with fresh parsley round the dish. Serve with the baked apples from the inside, and chestnut purée. (An alternative stuffing is chestnuts; if you use these, serve the goose with apple purée.) A tip worth knowing: If the goose is old, put it in the pan with the lid on first and leave it in the oven for one and a half hours, then finish off without the lid.

On page 110 we give another recipe for Roast Goose, stuffed with sage and onion, and some Czech specialities that make delicious dishes of goose neck, feet and giblets.

Sauces for goose and guinea fowl
Cranberry Jelly.—Boil a pint of cranberries quickly in a very little water. When they have popped, add sugar and simmer for about 15 minutes. Sieve it for appearance's sake and serve cold. A variation of this sauce can be made by stirring in a head of shredded celery while the jelly is still hot.
Gooseberry Sauce.—Cook some green bottled gooseberries in just enough water to prevent them from burning. Drain and rub through a sieve; add a few small pieces of butter (or margarine), a dusting of sugar and a spoonful of stock.

Dovetailed dish
Take a brandied orange and place it inside a boned pigeon. Grill slightly. Wrap in a simple stuffing and place it inside a boned chicken. Grill this slightly, wrap it again in stuffing and put it inside a boned duck. Roast for about three hours.

Stuffed duck
The classic sage and onion stuffing can be varied at Christmas dinner by one of the following new festive stuffings:

Two slices of fat bacon chopped and made hot; to which are added a similar quantity of chopped calves' liver, the liver of the duck, a little grated onion, herbs, pepper and salt. When well cooked add breadcrumbs, put through a sieve, bind with egg yolk and stuff the duck with the mixture.

Or simmer the duck's liver in a little white wine; sieve, and add several cooked chestnuts. Mix well and stuff the duck, proceeding to roast it in the usual way.

Roast duck with sauce rouennaise
2 Aylesbury ducks
2 teaspoons chopped shallots
2 cups red wine
pinch of thyme
½ bay leaf
parsley
½ cup tomato sauce
1 tablespoon butter
1 teaspoon brandy
cayenne

Roast the ducks in the usual manner, but keep the livers uncooked. In the meantime prepare the sauce: cook the chopped shallots in the wine with the thyme and bay leaf and simmer till reduced to half cup. Add half cup tomato sauce, heat gently, and strain through a fine sieve. Drain all the gravy from the ducks and skim off the fat from this, then add the juice to the sauce. Now rub the two duck livers raw through a sieve. Put the liver in an enamel saucepan and add little by little the hot sauce, stirring all the time. The heat of the sauce should be sufficient to cook the liver. Pass the whole through a sieve again and heat very cautiously on a very low flame. Season to taste, add the brandy, a dash of cayenne, and a tablespoon of butter stirred in bit by bit. Carve the ducks and garnish with parsley. Serve with the sauce in a separate boat.

Stuffed pheasant

Stuff a pheasant with this mixture: Pork sausage meat, chicken livers, chopped parsley seasoned and bound with yolk of egg. Protect the breast with a thin slice of fat bacon. After roasting in a moderate oven for about 35 minutes, remove the bacon so that the breast may brown, add a claret glassful of sherry, a spoonful of tomato purée, and grated nutmeg if you like it. Roast for another 20 minutes, basting frequently. Serve garnished with croûtons of fried bread spread with *foie gras*.

The same stuffing and method of cooking can be applied to guinea fowl.

Pheasants with gin and juniper

2 *pheasants*
3 *oz fat salt pork*
4 *oz bacon*
4 *oz butter (or margarine)*
6 *juniper berries*
1 *wineglass gin*
For sauce: *One 6-oz pot redcurrant jelly*
2 *oranges*
cayenne
mustard

Lard the birds with a little fat salt pork, and truss. Line the bottom of the roasting-pan with the strips of bacon, some butter, and pepper and salt. Rub each bird with butter, salt and pepper them and put three juniper berries inside each. Put them into a hot oven for 15 minutes, then pour over them the gin mixed with a little hot water. Moderate the heat of the oven and continue to cook for another three-quarters of an hour or until brown. Serve on a hot dish with the strained juice over them. Send them to table with the following sauce: put the jelly into a bowl and break it up well with a silver fork. Add the grated rind of one orange, a pinch of salt, and a dash of cayenne, then the juice of two oranges into which you have mixed a tablespoon of mustard.

Roast goose

Goose
1 *lb gravy beef*
1 *thin slice pork*
7 *large onions*
6 *fresh sage leaves*
1 *teaspoon salt*
1 *teaspoon sugar*
mustard
1 *large apple chopped fine*
2 *cups breadcrumbs*
2 *tablespoons butter (or margarine)*
nutmeg
parsley
cayenne
small lemon
flour and butter for cooking
3 *tablespoons port*

This is the classic goose with sage and onion stuffing. Choose your goose with great care; the best are young birds from ten to twelve pounds.

To make the stuffing, boil six large onions until tender. Drain and chop fine. Add the chopped sage leaves, one teaspoon salt, one teaspoon sugar, one teaspoon mixed mustard, a little pepper, the chopped apple, a dash of nutmeg, the breadcrumbs, and two tablespoons melted butter. Mix all lightly and put into the stomach of the bird. Now peel lemon, keeping the peel in one strip if you can, place the lemon peel in the centre of the stuffing, sew up the bird, and truss well. Place in roasting-pan, cover the breast with the pork and put into hot oven for 45 minutes. Remove from oven, pour out all the fat, sprinkle the bird with salt and pepper, dredge with flour, and return to oven. Reduce the heat, and when the flour has browned, add a cup of hot water, and baste the goose often. It should cook at least three hours. When ready, mix a teaspoon of mustard with water, add a pinch of cayenne and the port wine. Heat gently. Make a slit in the apron of the goose, remove the lemon and pour into the body the hot port. Garnish and serve immediately with the gravy made as follows: Slice a large onion and fry it in butter with the pound of beef cut into little cubes, until slightly browned. Then pour over it one pint of boiling water. Skim and add a little parsley, a sprig of thyme, one clove, and three peppercorns. Simmer until well reduced. Strain and add the drippings from the goose. Skim off fat. Make a roux of one teaspoon of butter and one of flour, cook together for five minutes, add the gravy, simmer till it thickens, and serve with the goose.

Here are three recipes for using all those parts of a goose which cannot be roasted:

Goose giblets

Besides the giblets themselves, the Czechs use the head, wings and claws of the goose, in this dish. Clean and singe all the parts and put in a pan with onion, carrot, celery, parsley; peppercorns, spice, salt to taste; cover with water. Cook gently until tender. In a separate pan, melt margarine to absorb three tablespoons of flour. Add the liquid from the giblets to this, stirring well. When thoroughly mixed, put over a gentle heat and leave to simmer for one hour. Chop the giblets and the other parts and add to the liquid. Heat through and serve with boiled potatoes or rice.

Stewed goose liver with onions

Clean the goose liver thoroughly and make a few light cuts in the surface. Brown the onions in fat and add the liver with caraway seeds, salt and pepper to taste. Leave it to stew gently in its own juice, turning when one side is done. When cooked through, add a little flour and water. Let it simmer until thickened. This dish is served either hot with its own gravy, or cold with fried potatoes.

Stuffed goose necks

Carefully peel the skin from the goose necks. Clean thoroughly and sew up one end. To make the stuffing take one part veal and two parts pork, and mince together. Add some rolls soaked in water. Put the mixture in a pan and add a beaten egg and salt and pepper, and ground ginger to taste. Cook for half an hour, stirring well. Stuff the necks not too tightly, otherwise the skin will burst, and sew up the other end. Cook them in hot fat together with some bacon, onion and a few whole peppercorns. When done remove from the pan and make a gravy by browning some flour in the fat, adding a little water and leaving to cook through. Strain over the necks when ready to serve. This dish may also be served cold. It is excellent cut as a sausage.

Stretching the Joint

by Beatrice Dawson

A joint remains the manner in which most people prefer to take their meat ration. Here are some recipes that will stretch it so that one small joint makes three meals; and incidentally avoid the monotonous alteration of hot and cold roasts.

All the dishes, except "Mutton Charlotte," can be made from any joint of beef, mutton or veal. Amounts of rice, vegetables, etc., vary according to the quantity of meat you have and the number of people you have to feed with what is left over after each meal.

Get every ounce of goodness from your ration; use any bones there are for stock for gravy. Make plenty with this and the juices of the meat; it's a good standby when making dishes from left-overs. Add stuffings to make your ration go further. Or cook it with vegetables; try sieving them to make a rich—and filling—sauce. Left-over meat needs unusual but definite flavours to make it more palatable. Add apple and onion to cold mutton, tomato to chutney and curry sauce, even the humble Worcester sauce adds flavour to tasteless mince.

JOINT NO. 1

Pot roast: First day

Cover the bottom of a casserole with sliced carrots, onions or leeks and celery; add a bouquet of herbs, a little grated nutmeg, Worcester sauce and one or two tablespoonfuls of golden syrup according to the size of the joint. Dot with small pieces of fat. Lay the meat on top of this and add one or two cups of stock or water. Cover tightly and cook slowly in the oven for three hours, turning meat two or three times. Bake the potatoes at the same time, taking care to break the skin with a fork 10 minutes before serving, to let out the steam and dry them.

Indian timbale: Second day

Boil some rice in weak Bovril, dry slightly, and with it thickly line a well-greased mould. Fill the centre with layers of roughly chopped meat, tomatoes if you have them, and chutney. Make enough thick curry sauce to cover the meat and tomatoes, and bake or steam for three-quarters of an hour to one hour. Turn out. If baked it should be crisp and brown on the outside.

Scotch rissoles: Third day

Mince the remainder of the meat. Mix with half the quantity of fine oatmeal and a very little flour, mixed herbs, chopped parsley, pepper and salt. Lightly fry a little onion or leek; add meat and oatmeal mixture moistened with a little stock or water, stirring until the mixture thickens and the oatmeal is cooked. Let get cool and form into rissoles. Make some mashed potatoes into the same shapes. Roll both in oatmeal and fry.

JOINT NO. 2

Roast mutton: First day

Bone the joint, cut off most of the fat. Make a good deal of stuffing by mixing breadcrumbs, a little onion, a little suet, paprika and mixed herbs. Moisten with milk. Fill the joint; and tie up. Melt some dripping in a casserole and put in as many slices of onion or leek as you can manage. Rub the joint with salt and pepper and brown on all sides in the fat. Add the bone to the casserole *but no liquid whatsoever*. Cover, and cook very slowly for two and a half to three hours on top of the stove. A quarter of an hour before serving, add enough cooked rice to absorb most of the gravy that will have appeared in the dish. Slice the meat and serve surrounded by rich brown rice.

Mutton Charlotte: Second day

Well grease a round cake tin and sprinkle with sugar. Line with slices of bread and margarine. Melt a little margarine in a saucepan and cook a small quantity of grated onion and two or three coarsely chopped apples until golden brown. Fill the mould with layers of sliced cold mutton and stuffing and apples. Put a layer of dry bread in the middle. When filled, cover with slices of bread and margarine and bake in a moderate oven three-quarters of an hour to an hour. Turn out and serve.

Pancake sandwich: Third day

Make some potato pancake by mashing cooked potatoes with a little margarine and adding flour until they have a dough-like consistency. Roll out, cut in rounds and fry on both sides. Arrange half of them on a dish. Pour over them the remains of the meat which has been minced and well heated in a thick well-seasoned brown gravy. Cover with the remaining pancakes so as to make a sandwich. Serve very hot. Put a spoonful of chutney or tomato sauce on top of each sandwich if you have any to spare.

.... there's nothing like a nice cup of tea

Cecil Beaton

Dodie Masterman

The hostess who realises the great charm that the tea-hour holds is accustomed to follow with as much fidelity as possible the established manner of serving afternoon tea. A well-brewed cup of tea—brewed by the hostess herself and never entrusted to the disinterested hands of servants—hot toasted muffins, crumpets, or scones, with marmalade or jam, not too sweet—this has been the tradition of the tea hour

Lee Miller

Top On service: a sit-down tea in quarters

Centre On leave: at the nurses' club

Bottom Mr Condé Nast, proprietor of *Vogue*, at a New York benefit to raise money for Britain

Opposite Mrs Winston Churchill likes to have tea in her private sitting room at 10 Downing Street, where hangs Orpen's portrait of the Prime Minister

The Hon. Mrs Peter Rodd (Nancy Mitford) at her tea-table

Francis Marshall

"Come When You Can" Cooking

"Come when you can," is the way most invitations are, of necessity, phrased nowadays. It's a phrase that gives the guests freedom but puts the hostess on her mettle. She can cope in any of three ways: by serving a dish that can be tossed up quickly, after her guests have arrived; by preparing beforehand a dish that only needs heating; by choosing something slow-cooking, that doesn't spoil with being kept on the hob. Here, then, are some recipes in these three categories, chosen with an eye on rationed foods and those in short supply.

First, those which take the shortest time to prepare and cook.

Epicurean kidneys
Take one sheep's kidney for each person and cut them nearly through from the round or outer part. Spread margarine over them and grill. Fill the hollow part with tartar sauce and serve on toast. Pour the following sauce over them: 1 tablespoonful of Colman's mustard, 2 tablespoonfuls of melted margarine, 3 tablespoonfuls of malt vinegar, 1 tablespoonful of tarragon vinegar, ½ pint cream substitute. First mix mustard, margarine, malt vinegar together, add tarragon vinegar and bring to boil without burning. Take off stove before serving and add cream, which should be slightly warmed. This sauce is also good on grilled meat or fish.

When mackerel are in season here is a simple way to serve them. Allow one for each person.

Grilled mackerel
Wash them and sprinkle with pepper and salt. Place a small piece of margarine on the top. Grill seven minutes on one side, five on the other. Serve with green salad.

Mackerel in oatmeal
Wash and split them. Roll in oatmeal and sprinkle with pepper and salt. Fry them in hot oil. Herrings are good cooked this way also.

Mutton chops with pineapple
Allow one chop and one slice of pineapple per person. Roast or fry the chops. Season with salt, pepper and paprika. Dip slices of pineapple into flour and fry in margarine to a golden brown. Top each slice with chop sprinkled with parsley and paprika.

Potato Platski
Allow two medium-sized potatoes, peeled and finely grated, per person. Strain away some of the liquor, then add flour to the potato pulp until you have a fairly stiff batter. Season with salt and pepper. Have plenty of fat very hot in a frying-pan, and drop in enough of the mixture to form pancakes a little larger than a fried egg and ¼ inch thick. Fry until brown and crisp, then turn and brown on the other side—3–5 minutes altogether. Top with a mixture of minced meat or creamed fish and serve.

Sweet croûtons
Allow one piece of bread per person. Soak them in egg and milk and fry light brown in margarine. Melt some chocolate in a little water and pour over each portion. You can serve jam if you have no chocolate. Another more unusual way to serve these croûtons is to dip them in a little sherry or Madeira after you have soaked them in the egg and milk. After frying, sprinkle with sugar mixed with grated nutmeg and cinnamon. Drain the croûtons well before and after frying.

Dishes which can be prepared beforehand and cooked or finished off when your guests have all arrived.

Potato layer pie
Take four large potatoes and boil them in their skins. Grease a pie dish; cut the potatoes in thin slices and make a layer at the bottom of the dish. Sprinkle with pepper and salt and add another layer of potato. Now add a layer of sliced hard-boiled eggs (two cooking eggs do very well). Chop ¼ lb of ham, tongue, or any left-over meat for the fourth layer. Finish with a layer of sliced potatoes and cover with a thin cheese sauce. Sprinkle with breadcrumbs. Bake for 25 minutes. Enough for four people.

Fried scallops with tartar sauce

1 pint of scallops
3 tablespoons olive oil
1 lemon
1 egg
milk, breadcrumbs
lard for frying

Marinate the scallops in a mixture of olive oil, lemon juice salt and pepper, for one hour. Prepare some breadcrumbs. Beat the egg with a little milk. Heat the lard in a deep pan with a wire basket. Roll each scallop in egg and breadcrumbs. When the fat is just below smoking point, cook the scallops but do not allow them to touch. They should be a light golden colour and take about two minutes. Serve with tartar sauce. Allow two scallops for each person.

The lemon is not essential, but its inclusion greatly improves this dish.

Southern stewed apples

1 large apple per person, brown sugar if you have it, otherwise granulated will do, 1 orange, 1 teaspoon ground cinnamon.

Peel, core and quarter the apples and put them into an enamel pan with ½ cup water and some sugar. Simmer for ½ an hour, then add the pulp of half the orange and the thinly peeled rind of the whole orange, together with the cinnamon. Continue simmering until a rich tender compote is formed.

Pilaff

Pilaff is one of the nicest ways of using up cold left-overs. Cook your rice according to your own idea of how to do it best. Remember that ½ lb rice serves six people. When the rice is cooked, melt some margarine in a frying-pan, put in your rice, salt and pepper, a pinch of saffron, teaspoon of curry-powder, one sweet red pepper cut in small pieces, a handful of raisins (stoned and previously soaked) and whatever you have in the way of left-over fish, meat or chicken, sprinkled with paprika. Add some stock and cook until the stock has disappeared.

Recipes for dishes that need slow cooking, and so are ideal for meals that are liable to be late.

Hare à la crème

1 hare
2 oz margarine
1 carrot
1 turnip
1 onion
3 slices of bacon
1 teacup vinegar (not malt vinegar)
10 peppercorns
5 bay leaves
1 tablespoon flour
2 oz cream substitute

Do not buy the hare cut, just have the skin taken off and the inside removed. Cut the hare into pieces over a basin, remove the ribs and abdominal skin. Take care that all the blood is dropping into the basin. Place the pieces of meat in the basin and add water to cover. Pour all the liquid into a saucepan; add the vinegar and the vegetables

Honeyman

cut into slices and the spices, and bring to the boil, slowly. When boiling, pour it over the hare, cover the basin and leave for one or two days. When ready to cook, dissolve the margarine in a large baking tin, salt the meat well and put it into the tin; cover it with the bacon. Roast for ¾ hour in a hot oven and then add as much of the stock as possible with all the vegetables and spices, and roast for another hour, replacing the evaporated gravy with the remaining stock. When the hare is tender, arrange the meat on a hot dish. Strain the gravy into a saucepan, pressing the vegetables through the strainer, add the cream and the flour, dissolved in half a cup of water, bring to the boil. Season to taste and pour over the hare. Serve with dumplings (recipe below) and cranberries. The number this will serve depends on the size of the hare.

Czech dumplings

1 lb plain flour
1 pint tepid water
1 egg
1 extra yolk
½ teaspoon salt
2 oz margarine
6 stale rolls or adequate quantity of stale bread

Beat the eggs, salt and water together. Put the flour into a deep bowl, add the mixture gradually to the flour whilst stirring it thoroughly. Beat the dough well till bubbles form. Cut the rolls into half-inch squares, and brown them in the oven with the margarine. Add the browned squares to the dough, mix well and allow to stand for one hour. Tie the mixture in a wet pudding cloth and place in a saucepan containing enough boiling water to cover and boil for one hour. Cut into slices and serve with boiled beef, goulash, hare, roast pork, etc.

Chicken à la paprika
1 boiling fowl
1 large onion
1 dessertspoon paprika
2 tablespoons flour
margarine
3 oz cream substitute

Joint the chicken. Then fry it and the onion separately, remove from the frying-pan and turn into a saucepan, add the paprika and enough water to cover it. Simmer gently for 2 to 3 hours, or until the meat is tender. Add the cream and the flour, dissolved in water, stir and bring to the boil and serve at once.

Pork goulash
2 lb pork shoulder
1 onion
1 lb sauerkraut
2 tablespoons flour
½ tablespoon paprika
fat
3 oz cream substitute

Fry the sliced onion, place in a saucepan; cut the meat into squares, sprinkle with salt, fry and add to the onion. Add cold water, paprika, and bring to the boil. After stewing for half an hour, add the sauerkraut, which must be washed first. Simmer gently for two hours, replacing the evaporated water; season to taste. Then add the cream and the flour, dissolved in water, stir well; bring to the boil and serve with boiled potatoes. Will serve six or eight.

Spiced beef
Fry one small onion in a little margarine golden brown. Trim fat off 1 lb beef; cut the meat in two-inch lengths and fry brown. Put 4 cloves and 2 chopped walnuts in the bottom of a casserole, add steak and onion and just cover with water. Cook slowly until done and then thicken with Bisto. Leave to simmer until required. Enough for three or four.

Lee Miller

Rabbit en casserole
Cut the rabbit into joints. Heat some margarine and put the pieces of rabbit perfectly flat in the pan and let them cook slowly for ten minutes, turning once. Be careful not to let them colour. Then add enough milk to cover the meat, and a liqueur glass of white wine. Cover the pan closely and simmer very gently for an hour. Remove the rabbit and keep it hot. Strain the liquid into a saucepan. Add the yolks of two eggs which have been thinned with a little milk. Stir continually with a wooden spoon, and when it begins to thicken add a little margarine cut into small pieces and a tablespoon of grated cheese. Beat the sauce until it is frothy. One small rabbit serves four.

Stuffed cabbage
1 lb minced beef, 4 thick slices of bread, 1 egg, 2 lb cabbage (either a large one or two small ones), ½ pint milk, a little finely minced onion or leek, salt and pepper. Cut the crusts from the bread and soak it in the milk, add the meat, salt and pepper (or teaspoon of paprika), onion and the beaten egg.

Mix well. Separate the leaves of the cabbage carefully and put into boiling salted water. Cook for 5 minutes and drain. Fill each leaf with a tablespoon of the mixture, roll over and fill a fireproof dish, so that the rolls are tightly pressed together. Add a little water and 2 oz fat. Bake in a slow oven for an hour. Make a sauce by thickening the liquid in the pan—add more water if it has lessened in cooking—and flavour with tomato sauce. Pour this over the rolls and bake for another ten minutes. Serve with boiled potatoes. Enough for six. If using left-over meat, cooked rice is better than the soaked bread. Regulo 6.

Vegetable pie
2 lb mixed vegetables—potatoes, spinach, cauliflower, carrots, beans, and anything else in season—stock, a little cream, 2 eggs, 2 oz grated Parmesan cheese.

Prepare the vegetables, parboil them and strain. Cut them up fine, cover with stock and bring to the boil, stirring in the cream. Allow to get cool. Separate the eggs and beat the whites to a stiff froth. Add the yolks, the whites and the cheese to the vegetables, mix well and put into a buttered dish. Cover with breadcrumbs and bake slowly. Serve six.

Steamed fruit pudding
4 oz of breadcrumbs, 4 oz currants, cleaned and picked, 4 oz apples, which have been weighed after they have been pared and cored, 2 oz of sugar, 2 eggs, the grated rind of ½ lemon, 1 small teaspoon of baking powder, nutmeg and salt.

Chop the apples coarsely, add the breadcrumbs, currants, sugar, lemon rind, a good pinch of nutmeg and salt. Mix all together and then add the eggs, which have been well beaten. Let the mixture stand for half an hour. Then stir in the baking powder. Add milk if the mixture is too stiff. Steam for about 3 hours and serve with sweet white sauce. Sufficient for five or six.

Precious

No scrap of bread is too small to save — it means saving valuable shipping space. Of course your best and most direct way of helping, is to take less bread into the house. Most households find they can do nicely with three-quarters of the bread they used to buy and yet can give every member of the family all the bread he or she individually needs.

The secret is in eating up every scrap of bread that comes in. Don't forget the end of the loaf. It's the bit that's apt to get left over. You always intended to do something with it. But how often was it thrown out, after all!

Half a slice of stale bread saved by everyone in this country every day, means a convoy of 30 ships a year freed to take munitions or men to our fighting fronts. If you explain this to your family you'll find them eager enough to help you save on bread!

Save Bread: Save Ships

4 things you can do

1 **Cut down your purchase (or making) of bread.** Most households find they can do nicely with three-quarters of the bread they used to buy.

2 Put the loaf on the dresser or side table. Cut only as required.

3 Use every crumb.

4 Don't eat bread whilst potatoes are on the table.

Some ways of using up STALE BREAD

CRISPY PIE-CRUST. Cut bread into dice ¼ in. thick. Cover a savoury pie with them, setting the dice closely together. Pour over them a little thin custard (salted) taking care that every piece of bread is moistened. Bake in a brisk oven.

SOAKED BREAD. This is the foundation of a countless number of puddings and cakes. No bread is too stale for it, and there is no need to remove any crust. Break into small pieces, put into bowl, cover completely with cold water and soak thoroughly. If the bread is to be used for a savoury, use vegetable boilings instead of water. Then squeeze the bread *hard*, put back in the bowl and beat with a fork until quite free from lumps and pieces of crust. The beating is most important and makes all the difference between a dull heavy pudding and a smooth, spongy texture.

MINCE SLICES. Mix 8 ozs. mince with 4 ozs. cooked mashed potatoes and 4 ozs. fine crumbs. Season to taste. Roll out on a floured board into an oblong ½ in. thick. Cut into slices and fry in a very little hot fat or grill for 5 to 7 minutes. Serve with leek sauce.

MAKING RUSKS. Cut bread into neat figures, or fancy shapes, about ½ in. thick. Bake in a warm oven until crisp and golden brown. Pack in an air-tight tin. This is a valuable emergency store which will keep good for months.

TURN WASTE INTO DELICACIES!

ISSUED BY THE MINISTRY OF FOOD (S61)

A new taste-thrill!

Yes; here it is: clean-tasting, nutty, with a hint of "pep" to liven up war-jaded palates. Anyone who has not yet tasted a salad containing shredded raw cabbage is missing a real taste-treat.

Then, too, first class as are properly cooked greens and fresh fruits for giving you that feeling of well-being, for clearing the skin, for rosy cheeks, good teeth, and glossy hair, *uncooked* cabbage and other green-leaved vegetables are even better still. So why not brighten up your menus and do yourself and family good at the same time! Eat "something green and raw every day" as the Radio Doctor says. Just try these three ways of enjoying salads :—

Pilchard Salad

4 pilchards, ½ lb. cold cooked potatoes, cubed; 1 doz. radishes; 2 tablespoons chopped parsley; 1 finely chopped leek; 2 tablespoons salad dressing; ½ lb. shredded cabbage or other greens; watercress.

Flake the fish and mix with the other ingredients except the cabbage and 1 tablespoon parsley. Add sufficient salad dressing to moisten well. Pile on the shredded greens and decorate with parsley, watercress and radishes. *To make the "flowers" if you wish, split long-shaped radishes nearly to base several times with sharp knife. Put into cold water and they will open out.* (Instead of the pilchards, sometimes have cheese, hard-boiled dried egg, small pieces of meat, bacon, or other fish. With bread and butter or margarine and a milky drink any one of these salad combinations makes a complete meal.)

Palette Salad

For eye appeal and encouragement to appetite this salad takes some beating. Serve as a "side-dish" or as a separate course. *3 oz. shredded cabbage, 4 oz. grated beetroot, 2 oz. grated parsnip, 1 oz. chopped leek, 2 oz. carrot cut in strips. All the vegetables are used raw.* Lay shredded cabbage in oblong dish. Arrange a border of grated beetroot round edge of dish, and other vegetables as desired.

Salad Sandwiches

These are an excellent way to introduce salad-eating to young children, who sometimes "can't get through" a plateful of salad. Ring the changes by mixing with the shredded cabbage some watercress, mustard and cress, parsley or any other vegetables, chopped or shredded. Sprinkle with a little seasoning if liked. If you are making salad sandwiches for packed main meals, mix with the vegetables some body-builder such as hard boiled dried egg, grated cheese, chopped meat or bacon, or some fish. Mix with salad dressing.

ISSUED BY THE MINISTRY OF FOOD (S91)

Clubs and Pubs

Pubs provide anything from the
quick impersonal drink dear to men,
to the personal atmosphere of a club.
From no food at all
to some of the best cooking in London.
El Vino in Fleet Street, (*right*)
with its marble-topped tables
and hurried drinking, is a favourite
with Fleet Street men.
Mooney's, Soho, (*left*) *is less hectic*
but always crowded.
The Antelope, off Sloane Square,(*below*) *is*
known for its food, leisurely drinking,
and atmosphere of smart well-being

R. Bouché

Clubs—to drink and eat in with atmosphere as varied as their licensing hours (some open afternoons—most keep pub time). Dignified, informal, sporting, modernistic, there is no limit to their decoration. Some, small poky rooms; others more inspiring—like the Belfry (below, right), high-ceilinged and believed haunted—it was once a church and is now one of the most popular and select of clubs. The Pheasantry (below, left) in Chelsea, is cosmopolitan—dress ranges from evening dress to corduroy slacks

Let's face it men sometimes want to be alone, to relax far from sound or sight of women. Men's clubs are part of London's tradition, some to live in, some to eat, drink and talk in many historic, all for men only. The Garrick Club, famous meeting-place of actors, has a fine collection of Zoffanys. Sketched here, right, Gray Wornum, architect responsible for the interior decoration of the "Queen Elizabeth," with playwright-barrister Gordon King

Courses in the air

You know how it's been these last years—however the talk started, it always drifted round to food. One hostess decided to sublimate this, by keeping a visitors' food book. Each guest wrote down his ideal post-war meal. No limitation as to price, season, climate or drinks, but not more than five courses—not to please the Ministry of Food, but on account of the paper shortage. Here's a selection from this gastronomic post-war planning (for which Vogue accepts no editorial responsibility) with a blank for your own fancy

CHOSEN BY A DUTCH PARATROOP LIEUTENANT

Gin and Dubonnet
••
Grape Fruit (without sugar)
••
Grilled Dover Sole with butter, slice of lemon and parsley
••
Lettuce and French Dressing
••
Edam Cheese
Chambertin
••
Coffee
Vieille Cure with whipped sweetened cream

CHOSEN BY A POLISH SQUADRON-LEADER

Smoked Salmon
Polish Vodka
••
Lobster Salad
Chablis
••
Roast Chicken
Baby Potatoes, Tomatoes and Watercress
Ch. Pontet Canet
••
Artichokes à la Reine
••
Pêche Melba
••
Coffee
Liqueurs

CHOSEN BY AN AMERICAN GIRL

Rum Collins
••
Shad Roe on Toast
••
Chateaubriand Steak (underdone)
Mushrooms, Wild Rice
Lattice Potatoes
Coco Cola
••
Strawberry Shortcake
Vanilla Malted Milk Shake
••
Coffee
Mint Julep

CHOSEN BY A SLOVAK ARCHITECT

Pointes d'Asperges Vinaigrette
Corton Blanc
••
Steak Grillé Béarnaise
Pommes Frites
Ch. Mouton-Rothschild
••
Tranche d'Anana Nature au Marasquin
Asti Spumante
••
Coffee
Armagnac

CHOSEN BY AN ENGLISH PUBLISHER

White Lady
••
Caviare de Beluga
Fresh Lemon, Chopped Spring Onions
Vodka
••
Chateaubriand (plutôt rouge)
Corn (not on the cob) with Butter Sauce
Pommes Soufflées, Petits Pois
Clicquot 1926
••
Asperges Fraiches Maitre d'Hotel
••
Fresh Peach Slices with Devonshire Cream and an Alexander Cocktail served as sauce
Imperial Tokay
••
Café
Hennessy 1812
Notes.—Nautch girls with the Peaches. Mint Juleps at 10.15. Ambulances at 12.45.

CHOSEN BY AN OLD-FASHIONED ENGLISHMAN

A large plate of Eggs and Bacon (2 eggs, and more if I want 'em, and plenty of crisp rashers)
••
Entrecôte Minute (with a large piece of yellow fat at the side)
French Fried Potatoes (cooked in deep butter)
••
A Creamy Rice Pudding
Pre-1914 Liqueur Whisky and Apollinaris throughout

CHOSEN BY A FRENCH-SWISS ARTIST

Pernod
••
Bouillabaisse
Sauterne
••
Café
Bénédictine

CHOSEN BY THE HOST

Tio Pepe
••
Pink Texas Grapefruit
••
Grilled Dover Sole Maitre d'Hotel
Montrachet
••
Saddle of Baby Welsh Lamb
Pommes Anna Petit Pois
Ch. Léoville-Poyferré
••
Brie
Romanée Conti
••
Strawberries with Devonshire Cream
Ch. d'Yquem
••
Coffee
Hine's 1878

CHOSEN BY YOU

Recipes 1945-1949

by Doris Lytton Toye

An enthusiastic amateur cook, Mrs Lytton Toye decided to take her Cordon Bleu in 1935 and studied in Paris, Brussels and Vienna and, until war broke out, she ran a cookery school with Marcel Boulestin.

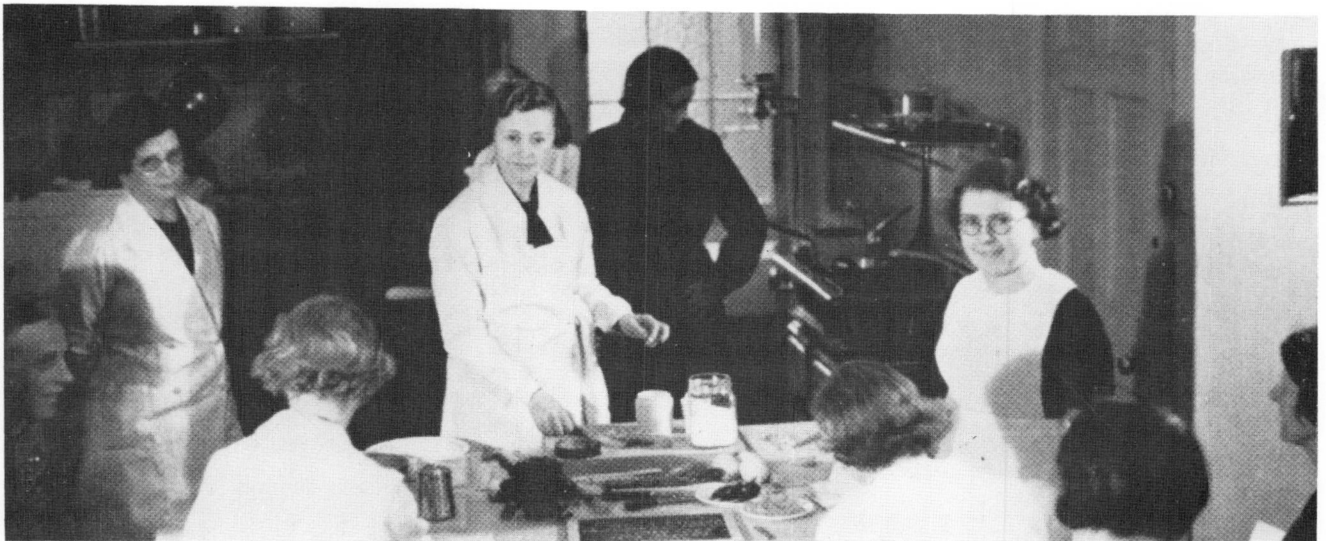

Doris Lytton Toye in her cookery school

Soup

Celery and almond soup
Wash and clean a head of celery and two large leeks. Chop them. Melt a generous nut of magarine in a pan, add the vegetables, and cook them gently over a very low flame with the lid on for 10 minutes. Shake the pan occasionally. Pour in 1 pint of water, bring to the boil and continue cooking slowly till celery and leeks are tender. Mash them into the soup with a potato masher, then pass through a strainer. Return to pan, bring once more to the boil; thicken the soup with a level tablespoon of barley flour diluted in a little milk. Add a heaped tablespoon of ground almonds, stir in well and simmer altogether for 15 minutes. Season to taste. Serve in cups with fried croûtons.

Clear vegetable soup
Wash 1 average carrot, 1 small turnip, half a parsnip, a small leek, 2 finger-lengths of celery. Peel carrot, turnip, parsnip; chop leek and celery finely; shred the root vegetables on a medium grater.

Melt $\frac{1}{2}$ oz margarine in a pan, add vegetables, and place lid on firmly. Cook on very low flame for 10 minutes. Shake occasionally. Pour on $1\frac{1}{2}$ pints boiling water with coffeespoon salt, dash of pepper and of sugar. Bring to the boil and simmer for 15–20 minutes.

Fish soup from Norway
Cut 2 lb of cod, hake or fresh haddock into pieces. Place in a pan with $3\frac{1}{2}$ pints water, little salt, few peppercorns, a bay leaf. Bring to the boil, then simmer, covered, for $1–1\frac{1}{2}$ hours. Strain. Melt $1\frac{1}{2}$ oz margarine in a pan, add $1\frac{1}{2}$ oz flour and cook few minutes. Add fish liquor gradually, when boiling, season and flavour to taste with little sherry or Marsala. Some of the fish, sieved, can be put in to

thicken the soup to a cream or merely flaked fish may be added. Left-over fish utilised for croquettes, etc.

Potage aux lentilles printanier

Steep ¾ lb lentils, well washed, for ½ hour. Melt, in a soup pan, 1 oz dripping; put in an onion, shredded, set the lid on the pan and cook over a low light for 15 minutes. Shake the pan from time to time. Add the drained lentils, 2 bacon rinds, a crushed tomato, 3 pints boiling water, salt and pepper. Simmer for about 2 hours. Pass soup through a sieve. Return to pan with some shredded carrot and turnip; cook slowly until the vegetable is soft. To finish, make the soup smooth with a spoonful or so of top of the milk, rectify the seasoning if necessary, add some chopped parsley and a few cooked green peas in order to brighten the proceedings.

Potage aux betteraves

Chop a small onion finely, cook it gently in bacon fat or margarine. Grate 3 small cooked beetroots, add to the pan with ¾ pint vegetable stock or water and a pea of Marmite, also several bacon rinds tied in a knot. Boil, then simmer for ½ hour with pepper and salt, and a *bouquet*. Slake a dessert-spoon of barley flour with 1 gill milk; stir into soup. Cook together for ten minutes. Take out *bouquet* and bacon rinds. Press through fine strainer or sieve. Reheat, and finish with teaspoon or so of vinegar and pinch of sugar. Sprinkle the pink potage with freshly chopped parsley, chervil or chive. Call it conceit, but should you possess green and white Rockingham cups, serve this soup in them, the colour scheme is quite ravishing.

Potage Monte Carlo

Cut 8 small dice of bread and sauté them in butter till crisp. Place four in each soup-bowl and sprinkle with sugar.

While the bread is frying, heat ½ pt of milk in saucepan to boiling point with pinch salt: mix 1 tablespoon dried egg and an eggspoon curry-powder with 1½ tablespoons water. Blend with the milk, then stir over fire till thickened, but not boiling. When very hot, correct seasoning, little pepper and salt, and pour over the croûtons of bread. On top, cast a pinch of any chopped herb you care for.

Potage printemps

Peel and cut in quarters two large potatoes. Clean and chop one medium leek. Remove the leaves from a bunch of water-cress; wash the stalks and tie in a bundle.

In a large pan, put the potatoes, leek and watercress stalks, then cover them to twice their depth with water. Boil it fast, uncovered, until the potato begins to drop into the liquid. With a potato masher, crush it into the soup; and cook till you have a sort of rough purée. Watercress leaves, pepper, salt and a nut of margarine go in at this moment, and you bring the potage up to desired consistency with milk, fresh or household. After the milk addition it should not boil, but do see that it is piping hot and sufficiently seasoned.

Note. When reducing a liquid it is wiser to add salt at the end—remembering that you can always add but you cannot take away.

Potage rubis

Chop finely one small onion; cook gently in a covered pan with ½ oz margarine. When onion is translucent, add 3 small cooked beetroot, grated, and sauté these together for a minute. Put in a piece of bay leaf, a sprig of thyme, salt and pepper, 1½ pints of boiling water, 2 or 3 bacon rinds, a pea of Marmite. Bring to boil, simmer 15 minutes. Slake a level tablespoon of arrowroot in a little water, pour into soup and cook till clear. Strain soup into bowl, and stir in vinegar or lemon juice to sharpen delicately, also a pinch of sugar. Cool soup, then remove any fat. Freshen up the colour by addition of some extra beetroot juice. Chill well.

Iced cream soups, such as green pea or tomato, are made by adding the cooked purée to a béchamel sauce. This type of soup should just veil the back of the spoon at boiling point: they thicken up as they cool.

Soupe à l'oignon gratinée

A brown onion soup that one devoured gleefully about 2 a.m. in Montmartre. Peel and slice thinly 3 medium onions. In a large pan, melt some clarified fat. Fry the onions gently, stirring so that they acquire an even golden tint; if they burn, the soup tastes bitter. Next, throw in several slices of toasted French bread, permitting this to brown a bit with the onions. Moisten with enough boiling water and clear stock to make 1½ pints of liquid. Add salt, plenty of fresh ground pepper, pinch of sugar. Simmer for 15 minutes. Ladle the soup into small brown fireproof bowls, or "terrines", a slice of bread in each one (this will float to the surface). Scatter grated cheese all over the toasts liberally, set a fragment of margarine on top. Place high up in a hot oven until the cheese begins to melt and colour.

Vichyssoise

This is best as a very cold summer soup, but it is also excellent hot. Cut away the green part from 3 large leeks, trim and wash them upside down under the cold tap. Splitting them lengthwise, but not quite through, helps to extract any lurking grit. Slice them finely. Slice also one medium onion and a stalk of celery. Melt 1 oz margarine in a large pan, put in the leeks, onion and celery, cover the pan and permit them to become tender over a flame. Shake the pan occasionally. Add 3 large peeled potatoes, finely sliced, 1 pint of boiling water and a pinch of salt. Simmer covered until the vegetables are perfectly soft. Sieve or pass soup through a fine strainer. Return to pan, thin out with ¾ pint of light stock, preferably chicken, then simmer a while and skim well. Season to your liking; finish soup with a breakfast cup of evaporated milk and some chopped chives or watercress.

White mulligatawny

Slice a medium onion; fry in margarine till golden. Stir into this a dessertspoon of patent barley flour and one of curry-paste or powder. Cook 5 minutes. Pour in gradually, stirring, 1 pint white stock or vegetable stock, 1 tablespoon ground almonds if possible. Simmer for two hours. Add 1 dessertspoon redcurrant jelly and a squeeze of lemon juice. Pass through a fine strainer. Put back in saucepan, season and boil up. Before serving, pour on to a liaison of 1 dried egg mixed with a little top of milk.

Pâtés

Terrine de lapin

Terrines are similar to pâtés in their make-up, the only difference being that a terrine consists of alternate layers of stuffing and thin slices of meat. Both can be made from any game, from veal and ham, or chicken; rabbit, also, is excellent "en terrine". Don't be alarmed if the method sounds complicated, for it's worth the labour.

Choose a large, fat rabbit, or hare. Cut the flesh from the bones into thin slices of meat, removing all nerves and skin, season with salt and black pepper. Then marinate in a little dry white wine for several hours. Take equal quantities of minced fresh pork and veal, the two together should be the same volume as the rabbit meat. Season it well, adding a little spice. Line a terrine with thin strips of larding bacon. Place a layer of the veal and pork "farce" at the bottom, dipping your fingers in the marinade of the meat as you press it down. Next a layer of the rabbit meat. Fill up with alternate layers of rabbit meat and "farce", the last layer should be "farce". Pour over the marinade, place more strips of bacon on top with a bay leaf and a sprig of thyme. Set lid on the terrine, then "seal" the rim of the terrine with a water and flour paste. Put terrine in a baking dish surrounded by an inch or so of water; bring to the boil on top of stove then cook in an oven hot enough to keep water bubbling. About an hour should suffice, but your terrine will be cooked when the fat rendered on top is clear. To be quite sure, run a skewer through to know if meat is tender. Cool with a weight placed on top.

A terrine has a very finished appearance when roofed with jelly, but the jelly should only be poured in when the terrine is perfectly cold. The jelly itself should be cold, though not setting.

Potted cheese

Pound equal quantities of Roquefort and grated cheddar with a good knob of butter or margarine, as much as you can spare; adding, as you go, a little dry white wine or a thimbleful of cognac. Season with screw pepper, salt to taste and a tiny pinch of sugar. When all is smooth and luscious, press into a small earthenware pâté pot. Cover with silver paper and the lid, and store in a very cool place. Serve as a *bonne bouche* on a special occasion.

Fish

Denton Welch

Colin niçoise

Remove skin and bones from two steaks of cod. Wash and dry them. Put in a buttered dish; pour over ½ gill white wine, ½ gill water, adding a slice of onion, few peppercorns, *bouquet* and crushed clove of garlic. Cover with greased paper. Bring to boil on top of stove and poach in the oven 15 minutes. Drain liquor; keep fish hot. *Sauce.*—Melt ¾ oz margarine, add ¾ oz flour; add ¼ fish liquor. When sauce thickens add ¼ pint milk, a tablespoon cream. Cook few minutes. Finish sauce with little shredded tomato and chopped green olives or green pepper when in season. Mask your cod steaks with this sauce and serve with purée of potato.

Brown nut fish

Will turn the plebeian cutlet of cod or hake to a succulent morsel. Procure even-sized cutlets. Wipe them and remove skin and centre bone. Place them in a well-buttered dish, sprinkle with a little curry-powder, chopped capers (if possible) and chopped blanched almonds. Season them and put small pieces of butter on them; lay tiny shreds of bacon on top. Pour a few tablespoons of stock into dish. Bake at moderate oven for about 20 minutes, basting occasionally. Now sprinkle with breadcrumbs; return to oven to crisp the crumbs, five minutes or so. Serve in their hot dish with slices of lemon.

Coquilles St Jacques

Choose fine fat scallops. Free them from their shells, take away the darkish yellow beard that lies between the raised white centre and the flat surround. Wash and drain them, then place in a pan with a little salt and bring to the boil over a moderate fire. Keep the liquid, and chop the scallops into small cubes. Melt a nut of margarine in a pan, add a finely chopped onion, and cook, covered, so that the onion does not take colour. When the onion is transparent, put in chopped fish, good pinch of curry-powder, chopped parsley, and enough breadcrumbs to make a consistent mixture. If too stiff, then add a little of the liquor reserved. Simmer for a quarter of an hour, then fill the shells, smoothing the top with a knife. Sprinkle more breadcrumbs and place a nut of butter on each. Brown them in a hot oven. Sliced mushrooms harmonise well with these fish.

Jugged haddock
Soak the haddock or smoked fillets in cold water several hours, to eliminate the saltpetre. Drain. Place fish in a jug sufficiently large to accommodate it. Cover with milk and water at boiling point, adding few peppercorns and a bay leaf. Set a plate on top and a folded cloth to keep in the heat. Stand jug on an asbestos mat over tiny flame. Allow to poach for 25–30 minutes. Slip fish into bowl, then with a fish slice arrange gently on hot dish; sprinkle with bright chopped parsley. Serve with mustard butter balls, made from softened margarine and French mustard in even quantities. Thicken up some of liquid for a sauce if you like, or use the liquor for fish soup, or fish risotto with shrimps and bacon.

Halibut and lobster maison
Cook the halibut in milk and water, drain it and cut into chunks. Lay it with pieces of lobster in a buttered dish; also as much cooked macaroni as you desire. Season well. Pour over a creamy sauce made from the fish liquor. Sprinkle generously with cheese and heat in oven until nicely brown.

Stuffed herrings
Herrings stuffed with their own roes, mashed, breadcrumb, onion, seasoning and herb; laid in folded, greased papers and baked, are delicious. Try this papillote cookery for cutlets of fish or finger trout, too; the fish juices provide sauce enough. Besides, the twisted paper boats, brown at the edges, look attractive and there's all the fun of undoing them at table and tipping the juice on to one's plate.

Harengs normande
Decapitate 6 fresh herrings, clean them, keeping the roes. Dry in a cloth. Roll in seasoned flour, then fry in hot fat till golden. Grill them if need be. Place in hot dish. Melt some margarine in a pan, throw in 4 onions finely chopped. When they start to colour slightly, add half a glass of water in which you have mixed 2 good spoonfuls of vinegar. With salt and pepper to taste, permit to cook and reduce for several minutes. When liquid is almost absorbed, mix in a good tablespoonful of French mustard. Stir in rapidly. Serve herrings hot, completely masked with this "hachis" of onion.

Maquereaux Quimper (cold)
Take mackerel of even size, clean, then cook very gently in fish stock. When tender, lift them out and cool. Gently remove fillets from the bone. Blend a tablespoon of French mustard with two egg yolks (dried eggs reconstituted somewhat thickly). Stirring, add little vinegar, salt and pepper, chopped parsley, tarragon and chervil. Just melt a nut of butter without being liquid; mix delicately into the sauce when lukewarm. The finished sauce should have the consistency of mayonnaise. Dispose your mackerel fillets around the dish and the sauce in the middle. Decorate with parsley.

Rougets en papillote
Take an oblong of greased greaseproof paper for each fish. Lay the fish in it, season with mill pepper, salt, a dash of lemon juice or sherry, and add a nut of butter. Fold the lengthwise edges of the paper once or twice to seal firmly. Then twist the ends so that you have a sort of paper boat. Place on a baking tin and bake in a moderate oven about 25 minutes. Send to table in their boats, and don't waste a drop of the precious liquid inside, it gives all the sauce needed.

When there's an R in the month and oysters, if ever, are cheap, an oyster tucked in each fish is a revelation.

Rougets à la meunière
Choose small and very fresh fish. Wash, clean and dry them. Fry them gently in melted margarine (a mixture of oil and butter or margarine is best) until tender, but not broken. Arrange them on a hot dish. Melt a morsel of margarine in the pan, throw in a dessertspoon of finely chopped onion and a good pinch of chopped parsley, tarragon, and chervil, salt and pepper. Cook a few minutes, stirring, then pour the contents of the pan over the mullet. Serve at once.

Sole or merlan dieppoise
Poach four fillets of sole or whiting in buttered dish, with a gill of fish stock, few tablespoonfuls mussel liquor, little white wine, about 10–15 minutes in moderate oven. Drain off liquid, keeping fish hot. Make your sauce in the usual way using these proportions: $\frac{3}{4}$ oz butter, $\frac{3}{4}$ oz flour to $\frac{1}{2}$ pint liquid. Simmer the sauce till thoroughly cooked, skim it. Rectify the seasoning. Add any essence that may have drained from the fish. Garnish the soles with mussels and shrimps and pour over the sauce.

Sole Trouville
Cut fair-sized sole into three pieces, diagonally. Butter a fireproof dish, sprinkle with grated breadcrumbs and finely chopped onion. Brown the crumbs in the oven. Pour over them a glass of boiling cider. Lay pieces of fish in the dish; bake them for ten minutes. Meanwhile work a knob of margarine with a little flour and chopped parsley. Season the soles and spread them with the flour mixture. Continue baking till fish are cooked. Serve them in their own dish.

Sole meunière à l'orange
Cut off the heads, obliquely, from two small soles. Remove the black skin, scrape the white skin; snip away the side bones. Wash and dry the fish, season with salt and pepper, roll in flour. Melt some margarine or clarified fat in a flat pan. When fat is hot, lay in the fish. Cook slowly 6 minutes, turn and cook the other sides. Meanwhile prepare an orange as for orange salad. Warm the sections in a pan. Dress the soles in a hot dish, sprinkle each with a good pinch of chopped parsley and some lemon juice. Dispose the sections of orange down the centre of the soles. Melt a piece of butter in the fish saucepan; when it begins to froth and turn golden brown, pour it over the fish and serve immediately.

Iced salmon kedgeree
Poach ¾ lb salmon in water with a little vinegar and butter; that is, bring it very gently to the boil, then let the water just move. Vigorous boiling toughens the flesh. When tender allow to cool in the liquor. Boil 3 tablespoons of rice as for curry. Cool. Flake the fish and mix with the rice, lightly using a fork. Make a thin béchamel sauce with ½ oz margarine, ½ oz flour (level tablespoon) and rather more than ½ pint of milk, including some of the fish liquid. Flavour with anchovy and finish with some cream from the top of the milk. Season highly and stir till cold. Fold sauce into fish mixture. The result should be loose, like creamed rice. Chill thoroughly. Hand rolls of brown bread and butter, stuffed with mustard and cress.

Meat and Poultry

Denton Welch

Poulet portugaise
Joint a young bird, separating it into eight portions. Sauté them in hot fat in a flat pan till nicely coloured. Remove from pan. Reheat fat: fry in it a finely chopped onion, add a few sliced tomatoes, a crushed clove of garlic and some sliced mushrooms. Simmer all together a few minutes. Season, then lay the pieces of bird on top. Cover with a lid and simmer gently till tender. Put in a little stock or water if it shows signs of becoming dry.

Petites saucisses à l'orange
Shred the rind of an orange very thinly, the zest only. Cook in very little water till tender. Melt 1 dessertspoon butter or margarine; mix in same quantity of flour, and cook 2 minutes over flame. Add, away from fire, teacup of stock, bit by bit. Cook this sauce, and simmer well. Add the orange, cayenne, season and the rind. Cook for a few minutes. Broil 8–10 Parisian sausages, or 20 chipolata. Arrange these on slices of toasted French roll, and pour over the sauce. Scatter with finely chopped parsley. Serve a good potato purée with it.

Polish tripe
For four persons, blanch 1½ lb of fresh tripe (see note). Drain: and run cold water over. Cut into fine strips about 1½ inches long. Replace in clean pan, cover with warm water and bring to the boil. Simmer for about 1 hour. Peel 3 large onions, cut them in halves. Add them to the pan with a *bouquet*, 6 peppercorns, 2 cloves and little salt. Cook very gently for another hour. Remove *bouquet*. Blend a level tablespoon of barley flour with 1 gill milk smoothly, pour into pan, stirring. Cook for ten minutes. Finally put in a liaison of 2 dried eggs mixed with milk plus 2 teaspoons vinegar. Stir as you add this, but do not let it boil. Correct seasoning, and serve in hot soup plates with grated cheese in a bowl, apart.

Note. Blanching means covering with cold water and bringing rapidly to boiling point. A *bouquet* is a bay leaf, sprig of thyme and some parsley stalks tied together. For those who dislike peeling onions because they leave such a persistent odour on the fingers, rub your fingers, and the knife, immediately afterwards with raw mustard and rinse under cold tap. No trace of onion will remain. Do they make you weep? I'm told that a match held between the teeth renders onion-peeling painless.

Rolled beefsteak
Have a slice of stewing steak or flank cut ¾ inch thick; about 1½ lb. Lay it on a board, beat with a rolling pin. Season the meat; spread over it the following mixture; ¾ large cup fresh crumbs, a tablespoon chopped and sautéd onion, ½ cup chopped celery (or mushrooms, if cheap), a morsel of bacon, chopped; tablespoon of mushroom ketchup, seasoning, little powdered egg to bind with not quite ¼ cup stock. Roll up meat and secure with strings. Dust with seasoned flour. Melt some fat in a deep strong pan, put in the roll, turn until browned. Pour in boiling water to come half-way up, adding a carrot and turnip cut in half lengthwise. With lid on the pan, simmer as slowly as you can, about 3 hours. Remove the strings, strain off the gravy thicken lightly and pour over the meat. More exciting when a jar of bottled tomatoes is poured over the roll instead of all water. Put them in half-way, also a bay leaf and a pinch of basil. No need to sieve this sauce unles you prefer to do so; but take out the carrot and turnip.

Corned beef hash
Chop 2 slices of bully beef. Allow twice the volume of cooked diced potato. Then chop a little onion. Melt about 1 tablespoon of margarine or bacon fat in a frying-pan. Cook onion slowly, add meat and potatoes, continue cooking just a second; sprinkle with salt and pepper and moisten with milk to barely cover. When the liquid boils press contents of pan down evenly, reduce heat and cover with a pan lid. Simmer gently till it forms a nice brown crust on the bottom. Fold over like an omelette, using a flat knife to scrape up any crisp morsels. Turn into a very hot dish, garnished with parsley. A creamy white sauce, laced with grated horseradish, seasoned with salt, pepper, a pinch of sugar, and a touch of mustard, gives a final filip.

Bœuf en gelée
Place 1½ lb of stewing beef and 1 rasher of bacon in stewpan. Cover well with water; bring slowly to the boil, then skim. Stew gently for 1 hour. Next, put in 1 onion stuck with 4 cloves, 1 sliced carrot, a *bouquet,* 6 peppercorns, level teaspoon ginger powder, same of cinnamon, pinch salt, and, if available, some red wine. Simmer gently till meat is absolutely tender. Cool; strain off liquid through a muslin. Cut up meat and arrange in casserole. Heat 1 pint of the liquor; dissolve in it 5 level teaspoons gelatine and be sure it is sufficiently seasoned. Pour cooling jelly over the meat. When set, place in refrigerator for a couple of hours.

Loin of pork with prunes
Rub a loin of pork with a lemon until juice is exhausted. Half cook a handful of prunes, stone them and cut in quarters. With a sharp knife slit the rind of the meat here and there and stuff with the prunes. Grease a baking tin, lay in the joint and pour over the prune juice. Place in hot oven and baste frequently. When crackling has ceased, lower heat and continue cooking till tender. Add some stock to pan if needed. Dust with salt just before taking the joint out of the oven.

Denton Welch

Sauce bâtarde
This resembles the above, but is very quick and economical these fatless days. . . . With a wooden spoon, cream ½ oz margarine or butter and ½ oz flour (1 level tablespoon) in a small pan. Add ½ pint milk. Place over fire; bring to boil without stirring. When it boils, remove from heat, whisk briskly—no, there won't be any lumps—and season to taste. Simmer 5 minutes.

Sauce provençale
Admirable partner to grilled or fried fish, to chop or cutlet. Take 1 lb tomatoes, skinned and pipped, ½ gill oil, crushed clove garlic, salt, pepper, and pinch of sugar, the same of basil (king herb or *herbe royale,* why don't we use it more? It is most subtle with fish or tomatoes). Heat the oil and other ingredients, then simmer gently for ½ hour, strain.

Simple white sauce
To 1 pint liquid, milk or milk and water, 1½ oz margarine, 1½ oz flour. Melt fat in saucepan; add flour; stir over flame for few seconds till mixture looks honeycombed. Away from fire, add liquid gradually till smooth. Stir briskly over fire till boiling: simmer 5 minutes gently. Season salt and pepper. Use as a base for parsley, shrimp, anchovy sauce.

Flora's sauce
(Made hot for grills.) This sauce is an emergency idea for your store cupboard and is made in the following proportions.

Take a bottle of any good spiced brown sauce, breakfast cup of Ideal milk, a little made mustard, dash of Worcester sauce. Let it boil up and thicken a little. Half this quantity may be plenty for a small household.

Richer béchamel
This is a foundation to a good cream sauce, *Mornay*, for instance, with egg yolk, cheese and cream for finishing. Heat 1 pint milk in a pan with a bit of onion, or shallot, a small sliced carrot, a bay leaf, a few parsley stalks, 5 peppercorns. Heat slowly to extract the flavour of the vegetables. Melt 1½ oz margarine in another pan, add 1½ oz flour, away from fire: blend well. Cook this roux till it whitens, stirring. Pour on the strained milk, little by little, till even in consistency. Bring to boil, stirring. Simmer for 15 minutes; remove any scum, strain through fine strainer. Reheat and season to taste.

Salt is best added at end of cooking process when sauces are cooked for some time. Dried milk may supplant cow's milk, evaporated milk replace cream.

White devil
For *réchauffé* of cold chicken or game. Place any remains of game, cut into neat portions in fireproof dish. Mix together 1 cup of Ideal milk, 1 teaspoon each of Harvey and Worcester sauce, little French mustard, salt and pepper. Pour over the meat. Bake in hottish oven, standing the dish in tin of hot water, for about 15–20 minutes. Garnish with sprigs of watercress.

Sauce piquante
For grills, croquettes, etc. Chop finely 1 small onion or 2 shallots; put in a pan with 2 tablespoons meat stock and 1 gill good vinegar. Cook over a fast flame till reduced by half. Season and finish the sauce with some finely chopped gherkin.

Beurre noir
For fish. Melt 1 oz margarine or butter in a pan. Allow to cook till it turns brown, then pour on a few drops of vinegar, shaking the pan. Pour over the fish, grilled or baked, and serve immediately, sprinkled with parsley. Capers may be added if liked.

Beurre maître d'hôtel
Cream 1 oz butter on a plate, work into it a little lemon juice, teaspoon chopped parsley. Season. Form into pats and set in cool place. Use with any fish or meat grill.

Vegetables

French beans, Hungarian style
String the amount of beans you intend to use and cook them in the usual manner. Then, just melt a thimbleful of chopped onion in some hot margarine. Put in the drained beans and enough tomato sauce (see below) to bind the whole together. Simmer for 10 minutes or more. Send to table piping hot. Crisp bits of bacon give substance to this and blend well.

Salsa di pomidoro
Cut 1 lb or more of tomatoes, ripe ones, in quarters. Reduce them to a mush over fast flame, then sieve. Melt knob of margarine in a pan, add a little chopped onion, cook gently a few minutes. Add the tomato purée, half a bay leaf, spring of thyme, salt, pepper and a pinch of sugar, also a small bead of garlic, crushed. Cook till the tomato becomes thick. Pass through a strainer.

Carrots Vichy
Scrub some young carrots well, then slice across finely. Place in a pan with water to barely cover; also a nut of margarine, ½ teaspoon sugar, a good pinch of salt, a little pepper. Bring to the boil, then cover and simmer till the carrots are tender and the liquid is syrupy. Shake them to give them a shiny coat, without breaking. Turn into a hot dish and sprinkle with chopped parsley or mint.

Beignets de chou-fleur
Boil the buds of cauliflower in salted water, but do not let them get too soft. Drain very well. Prepare a batter with 4½ oz flour, 1 egg yolk, a cup of milk and a little salt. Beat smooth, lastly add the whipped white. Dip the sprigs of cauliflower in this and fry in boiling fat till golden. Drain on fine paper, then keep hot in warm oven. Pile on a hot dish, garnish with parsley *bouquet* and hand a tomato or cheese sauce with it.

Creamed new potatoes with lemon
Peel and boil very small new potatoes in salted water. Scald sufficient evaporated milk to cover the potatoes in a saucepan with a good pinch of salt; when nearly boiling, drop in the potatoes, turn the flame low and cook for 15 minutes. Finish with the juice of 1 lemon, pepper, and extra salt if needed. Sprinkle freshly chopped parsley on dishing up, or feathery green dill if available.

Lancashire potato cakes
We loved these as children, eating them straight from the oven. My mother had a rough and ready way something like this: Sift 2 tablespoons flour with ½ teaspoon salt, then work it into ½ lb mashed potato. Melt ½ oz fat and

add it with a little beaten egg to bind to a stiff dough. Roll out, fairly thinly, cut into rounds or quadrants. Cook on a griddle for 3 minutes on either side, or in a brisk oven for about eight minutes. Eat that day as they discolour when kept.

Oven creamed potatoes
Pare and slice 4 medium potatoes very thinly. Butter a baking dish, and dispose half the potatoes in it. Dust with pepper, salt and flour. Repeat this operation. Heat 2 small cups of milk with piece of butter, pour over potatoes. Cover dish and bake in moderate oven half an hour. Remove cover and permit top to become delicately browned. Maybe you like onions; if you do, then infuse a slice of onion stuck with a clove in the milk.

As I write I am reminded constantly of Budapest. I wonder does the house still stand where I met the second cousin to the foregoing recipe? Though pre-war, if evaporated milk is employed instead of cream, with extra salt, it will adapt well. This is the original form.

Poireaux au gratin
Have ready some boiled and well-drained leeks and potatoes steamed in their jackets. Line a gratin dish with the leeks cut small. When the dish is nearly full, cover with a layer of potatoes, peeled and sliced thickly. Season as you go. Make a cheese sauce from: 1 oz margarine, 1 oz flour (heaped tablespoon), $\frac{3}{4}$ pint milk. When the sauce is well-cooked, season to taste with salt, pepper from the mill and a little mixed mustard; fold in 2 oz grated cheese. Pour sauce over to mask the potatoes and bake in a moderate oven until brown. This supper or luncheon dish can be made from sea kale or celery instead of leeks.

Pommes de terre au fromage
Butter or grease a soufflé dish; almost fill it with a good purée of potatoes. Smooth the surface and then pour on some salted evaporated milk. Sprinkle thickly with grated cheese, season with pepper and dust with paprika. Set in a tin of hot water in a hot oven for about 15 minutes. If the top is not sufficiently browned, then place under the grill for a few minutes.

Pommes nouvelles rissolées
Cook even-sized new potatoes in their jackets. Peel them when cool, then sauté in hot fat, shaking pan from time to time till they become golden. Drain, sprinkle with salt and scatter with chopped parsley. Best as a garnish to cutlets, but pleasant eaten with a green salad.

Pommes parmentier
Peel and cut potatoes into dice, wash them; drop them into salted, boiling water. Bring the water to the boil again. Drain and dry the potato cubes. Heat some clear fat in a frying-pan, put in enough potatoes to cover the bottom of the pan. Toss, or turn, from time to time to insure that they colour evenly. When ready, transfer to hot dish, season and keep warm. Continue frying until all potatoes have been used. Scatter chopped parsley over them. Make POMME FOURCHETTE like this but sprinkle them with cheese and finish under the grill.

Potato rolls
Sift 2 lb self-raising flour with one teaspoon salt. Rub in 1–2 oz fat. Have ready $\frac{3}{4}$ lb mashed potato (1 lb of unpeeled potato will yield about $\frac{3}{4}$ lb). Beat 1 pint of milk and water or milk into the potato. Make a well in the centre of the flour and pour in the milk-potato mixture. Work all together quickly till smooth. Turn on to floured board and knead a little. With floured fingers, shape into a roll and cut into pieces. Form into oval rolls and bake in moderate oven about 15 minutes. Makes about 32 small rolls. Cheese and black pepper may be added, or chopped herbs to the basic recipe. Powdered celery gives a piquancy for eating with cheese.

Red cabbage from Denmark
Shred cabbage finely. Melt a little margarine in a strong saucepan; add a cup of water, a tablespoon or two of vinegar, salt and a little sugar. When this boils, put in the shredded cabbage, cover with lid and cook gently till tender over low heat, about 2 hours. Redcurrant juice is added when the vegetable is finished. (Plum jam juice would serve instead.) Very suitable for cooking in a haybox in fuelless days.

Spinach
Spinach is sometimes prepared in Italy as a steamed pudding simply bound with thick white sauce and yolk of egg. Turned out on a hot dish and topped by sautéed liver in a brown sauce. If you like spinach, you should like it this way. Much more unusual is spinach, chopped and sautéed with some sultanas and anchovies. Perhaps not to everyone's taste; still, out of the common, and for the adventurous.

Denton Welch

Puddings

Iced bread and butter pudding
Prepare two wafer slices of bread and butter. Cut them into squares and spread with marmalade. Dispose them, overlapping, in a buttered soufflé dish. Scald 1 pint of milk with a pinch of salt: meanwhile beat up three eggs, or two if needs be, and a tablespoon of sugar. Add hot milk to eggs, whisking, then pour the whole over the bread. Stand the dish in a tin of hot water in a moderate oven and cook for about 35 minutes or till custard is set. Half way through, scatter a little sugar over the top. Allow to go cold, then place in refrigerator.

Iced summer pudding
Make warm a pint of thick fruit syrup, blackcurrant, raspberry and redcurrant or red plum. Add a little lemon juice, dissolve in it 5 teaspoons, level, of softened gelatine. Strain and cool. As it thickens, fold in $\frac{1}{2}$ gill of evaporated milk. Set a layer of the fruit jelly in a basin. Place a layer of sponge cake on top, cover with jelly: and so on till basin is full. Set overnight in the refrigerator. Turn into glass dish and surround with a chilled compôte of the same fruit.

Celebrity pudding
A steamed pudding with a central layer, to be varied according to our particular whim. Sift 4 oz flour (4 heaped tablespoons) with 2 level teaspoons baking powder, pinch of salt. Rub in 2 oz margarine (or margarine and fat) till fine and sandy. Add a level tablespoon sieved dried egg (2 whole eggs) and one of sugar. Moisten with about 4 tablespoons liquid, half milk, half water, till you have a smooth paste. Divide in two, grease a basin: put a good tablespoon of golden syrup in the bottom, press in half the paste. Next a layer of cooked stoned and sliced prunes; or apricots; or thick marmalade. Press remaining paste on top. Cover with a greased paper. Steam for 2 hours. Turn out. Hand with it treacle sauce, marmalade sauce, or lemon-flavoured custard in a sauce boat. An ounce of semolina instead of one of flour makes a light pudding, but a little more liquid will be necessary to allow the semolina room for expansion. Steamed puddings when allowed to stand in a warm oven before turning out develop a pleasant crust.

Orange and lemon cloudy jelly
Grate the rind from an orange and a lemon. Squeeze out the juice, add up enough water to make up 1 pint. Add 2–3 oz sugar and the grated rinds. Allow to steep for an hour or so. Dissolve 5 level teaspoonfuls gelatine in a little of this liquid, put in the remainder and heat all till just tepid and stir well. Colour with a drop or two of cochineal—children are fond of pink jellies. Strain into a wetted mould and allow to set.

Caramel oranges
Prepare 5 oranges as if for a salad, place them in a crystal dish with their juice. Make a dark caramel from $\frac{1}{4}$ lb sugar and a little water. Very, very slowly dissolve the sugar and water over a minute flame in a clean aluminium pan without stirring. As soon as every particle of sugar is dissolved, turn up the light and boil until it becomes a good golden brown. Pour out immediately on to an oiled slab. When cold, crush the caramel toffee with a rolling pin and scatter over the oranges. Leave awhile in a cool place. Should the oranges not be sweet enough, sprinkle a little sugar between each layer.

Glace à la russe
This is made with blackcurrant leaves. If you live in a town, ask your country friends to pick some for you. Bring $\frac{1}{4}$ lb sugar and $\frac{1}{2}$ pint water to the boil. Infuse a small handful of young blackcurrant leaves in this syrup, for 2 hours. Strain, add juice of 3 lemons and freeze as you would for a water ice.

Poires belle dijonnaise
Ripe Comice or William pears figure in one of the freshest sweets imaginable (peaches are equally good). Peel, halve and poach the pears in a light syrup for a few minutes to preserve their whiteness. Four large pears will suffice. Fill pear halves with the following blackcurrant ice and mask with a thin raspberry sauce, from fresh fruit.

Blackcurrant ice
Take $\frac{1}{2}$ pint blackcurrant purée not too liquid. Sweeten to taste. Dissolve $1\frac{1}{2}$ level teaspoonfuls gelatine in 1 tablespoonful warm water. Strain into the cold purée. Freeze to a mush in refrigerator tray then stir in 1 gill whipped evaporated milk (the milk should be scalded and chilled before whipping). Put in tray and freeze.

London night life: the Orchid Room
R. Bouché, February 1947

Frosted currants
Stewed red or white currants seem to be all pips and one rarely eats them raw. Choose some firm ripe bunches of either and frost them. Dry the clusters in a clean cloth. Beat up an egg white on a plate, just breaking it without making it too frothy. Flavour with a drop of rum. Dip each bunch in egg white and then in powdered sugar. Leave on the dish with the sugar near stove in gentle heat to dry. Turn occasionally.

Flummery aux fruits
Here is a simple dessert to be made with any fresh fruit you please, strawberries, apples, pears, Victoria plums, peaches, pineapple, etc. Prepare fruit, cut it up fairly small; sugar it and leave in the refrigerator for an hour, covered. Whip up the white of an egg, add a teaspoonful of sugar, set in refrigerator also. Heat ½ pint milk with a pinch of salt; put 2 level tablespoonfuls semolina in a folded paper. When milk boils, scatter in the cereal, stirring to avoid lumps. Cook, a few minutes, till it becomes thick. Remove from flame and sweeten with tablespoonful sugar; fold in fruit and whipped white of egg. Set in a soufflé dish rinsed in cold water. Chill. Turn out and mask with a custard made from the yolk and ¼ pint milk.

Cerises jubilee
Stone large black cherries; cook gently in light syrup, keeping them firm. Drain fruit and place in tiny ramekin dishes. Keep hot. Reduce the syrup, then thicken with arrowroot, allowing 1 tablespoonful to each half pint of syrup. Cover cherries with the thickened syrup. Heat some rum, about a coffeespoonful to each serving. Set alight as they are handed round.

Kaltschale
Austrians like to drink Kaltschale, fruit soup, on hot summer days, using raspberries, strawberries, red or black currants. The currants would have to be cooked till just tender. Pass 1 lb berries through a sieve; whisk the purée with 4–5 oz sugar till light and frothy. Mix into it gradually 1½ pints of scalded and chilled milk. Serve cold.

Pêches Madeleine
Pêches Melba we all know, Pêches Madeleine may be a novelty. Skin ripe fruit, halve them and remove kernels. Fill with skinned and pipped grapes and chopped walnuts. Chill them. Serve with a raspberry sauce, hot.

Hot raspberry sauce
Made either from a purée of sieved fresh berries, sweetened; or 2 tablespoonfuls of jam melted in a little water, thickened lightly with arrowroot then strained, a squeeze of lemon juice added with a touch of carmine to revive the colour.

Ananas en surprise
Cut a slice from the top of a ripe pineapple. Scoop out the centre and remove any woody parts. Cut flesh into small pieces. Prepare a thick custard, enrich with a few tablespoonfuls of evaporated milk, scalded and cooled; fold in the fruit; fill the case. Set on ice. Place on a dish with a napkin around to hold it steady. Cover with the tufted top.

Use canteloupe melon in the same way, mingling strawberries or raspberries with the melon flesh. Fill the case and ice as for the pineapple, omitting the custard, of course.

Pommes paillard
Cut some firm, peeled, eating apples in thin slices, arrange them overlapping in buttered dish. Make a syrup of sugar and water, add little white wine, or cider, and pour over the apples. Sprinkle sugar over and cook in top of oven till apples look transparent. Sugar again and place under grill to caramelise the top. Chill well.

Savouries

John Minton

Gnocchi alla Romana
Gnocchi alla Romana belongs rightfully to luncheon, yet it makes a cheerful course for a supper. Boil ½ pint of milk and one of water with a pinch of salt. At boiling point, scatter in 5 level tablespoons of semolina, stirring. Cook about 7 minutes. Add a good knob of butter, pepper, and French mustard; then 2 eggs, fresh or powdered (re-made). Cook a second or so. Away from fire, fold in 2 oz grated cheese. Spread this mixture, half-inch thick, on a buttered slab. Let cool. With a 2-inch cutter, cut rounds of the gnocchi. Arrange these overlapping around a greased dish, piling the remnants in the middle. Sprinkle with cheese and paprika. Place in hot oven for 15 minutes till souffléd.

Gaufrettes fromages
This is a savoury that is always appreciated—the only trouble is that there's never enough! Cream some margarine. Work into it the same amount of grated cheese. Spread the paste liberally on unsweetened ice wafers. Place them in a hot oven till just browned and crisp. A little anchovy essence

in the mixture varies the taste. Allow at least three for each person. To serve with cocktails, cut wafers in half.

Fromage à la mystique
Butter a shallow fireproof dish. Pour in a layer of salted evaporated milk; sprinkle with cheese. Cut some fresh toast into fingers, having removed the crust. Arrange on the dish. Season with salt and pepper from the mill. Pour over more evaporated milk and strew thickly with more cheese. Bake in a fairly quick oven. Like all savouries, it must be served piping hot.

Aigrettes
Beat 2 egg whites to a stiff froth—you could perhaps use egg whites left over from making mayonnaise. Fold in 2 oz grated cheese, adding salt and cayenne as desired. Shape into balls the size of marbles. Fry in smoking hot fat till golden brown; they swell as they cook. Drain, sprinkle with grated cheese. These puff balls are delicious. A useful tip when beating up egg whites is to add a tiny pinch of cream of tartar, they stand better and do not break at the edges.

Malaxé
Pound together 6 oz Danish blue cheese and half its quantity of softened margarine. Season with salt, milled pepper, and a suspicion of cayenne. Beat in a tablespoon of cognac or white wine. Press the mixture into an earthenware pot; a pâté de foie gras terrine with a hole in the lid is best. It will keep good 2–3 weeks in a cool spot.

Camembert frit
Take a moderately ripe, not too runny cheese. Pare away the excess outer coating but without taking away all the rind. Cut it into wedged-shape pieces, 8–10 portions. Season sparingly with cayenne pepper. Dip the sections into egg-wash, then in fresh breadcrumbs; shake off any superfluous crumbs. Repeat the egg and crumb process in order to give as thick a coating as possible. Fry the portions in smoking hot fat or oil until they are a pale golden brown. Drain on white paper. Serve immediately, piled on a napkin and garnished with tufts of parsley. Served with French mustard, this makes an unusual savoury.

Camembert en aspic
Choose a cheese in good condition. Scrape it gently with a silver knife, but do not remove all the rind. Run a layer of cooling aspic into a clean cake tin: when the jelly sets, place the Camembert upon it, then pour cold but still liquid aspic round the sides and over the top. Let it set firmly. Dip the cake tin in warm water for a few seconds to loosen the jelly; reverse on to a cheese board. Have either hot salted crackers or croissants, split and toasted, to eat with it. Accompanied by a fresh salad, dressed with French dressing, this makes a pleasant luncheon dish.

Jams, Jellies and Pickles

John Minton

Zest of China oranges
(An 18th century recipe.) Pare off the outside rind of oranges, or lemons, very thin. Strew with powdered sugar, as much as their moisture will take. Dry in a hot stove. Store in corked bottles.

Apple jellies, unless made from fine crab apple, taste sweet and have no flavour. Here are two subtly flavoured jellies.

Apple and elderberry
Cook 3 lb tart apples and 3 of ripe elderberries separately, in enough water just to cover. When reduced to a mush, strain off juices. Allow 3 lb sugar for each pint of juice. Then continue as for any other jelly.

Pure elderberry juice is worth processing to serve with apples or bottled gooseberries in January.

Apple jelly with geranium
Make an apple jelly. For the last 5 minutes of boiling throw in a spray of sweet-scented geranium. Remove geranium as jelly is cooling.

Mint jelly for winter use
Remove stem and blossom ends from 3 lb tart apples, cut them in quarters, put into a pan, preferably an enamel one, just cover with cold water. Bring to boil covered and simmer till apples are soft. Mash the fruit in the pan with a wooden spoon, allow the juice to drip through a clean cloth placed on sieve, or through a jelly bag. Measure the juice. Allow 1 cup of sugar to each cup of juice, boil the juice in preserving pan for 20 minutes, add the sugar, heated; bring to boiling point and boil 5 minutes, during the last 3 minutes pass a bunch of fresh mint through the jelly, bruising it slightly in the fingers, till the required flavour is obtained. Finish with 1 tablespoon of lemon juice or vinegar and tint a pale green with vegetable colouring. Finely chopped mint may be added if liked.

Lemon or orange cheese
Grate rind and squeeze juice from 3 lemons. Melt 3 oz margarine in double saucepan; add juice and rind with 6 oz sugar. Beat up 2 eggs, either fresh or reconstituted ones. When mixture is dissolved, add eggs, stir till thickened. Pour hot into clean warm jars. Seal when cool.

Pickles and spices

For all pickles use an enamel rather than an aluminium pan. Malt vinegar is used in the following recipes:

Pickled peaches in syrup

Skin 2 lb small peaches. Boil ½ pint vinegar, 1 lb sugar, small piece of cinnamon stick, and 6 cloves for 10 minutes. Drop in peaches a few at a time and poach until tender. Lift them out into hot jars: cover with hot syrup. Seal at once.

To spice plums

Wipe 2½ lb firm plums. Prick them with a needle. Boil together 1 pint vinegar with 1½ lb sugar and a muslin bag containing a piece of cinnamon stick, few allspice berries, teaspoon cloves, blade of mace. Pour this over the plums and stand all night. Drain off the syrup, boil it 10 minutes; pour over fruit again. Leave several hours. Then bring the whole again to the boil. Remove spice bag and pack plums into hot jars; cover with syrup. Seal.

A chutney

Chop ¾ lb apples, ½ lb shallots and ¾ lb tomatoes; add to them ¾ lb sultanas. Put them in an enamel pan with ½ lb Demerara sugar, ¾ teaspoon cayenne, 4 chillies, 6 cloves, 1 teaspoon salt. Cook for 30 minutes, add 1 pint of malt vinegar, and simmer for 3 hours, stirring occasionally. Almost cover the pan with a large china plate (not a metal lid) to keep the flavour in. While chutney is still hot pour into dry, warm bottles. Place a piece of greaseproof paper over the pickle before you seal it. Store in a dry place.

Green tomato chutney

Slice 5 lb tomatoes and 1 lb onions. Simmer them gently till soft. Add 1 lb sugar with 1 teaspoon salt, 1 of spice and pinch mustard seed; also 1½ pints vinegar. Cook together, stirring, lest the pickle catch, till of the right consistency—not too stiff or too liquid.

Piccalilli

Wash, prepare and cut up a mixture of vegetables—marrow, cucumber, cauliflower, French beans, cabbage, green tomatoes, small whole onions. Cover with 1 quart of water mixed with ½ lb salt for 1½ lb vegetables. Leave till next day. Boil vegetables, drained, with 1 pint of vinegar for 12 minutes. Mix ½ oz dry mustard, level teaspoon turmeric, and 1 teaspoon flour with little vinegar; add to pan. Boil together stirring about 3 minutes. Pour into hot jars and seal.

Have-your-cake-and-eat-it marmalade

Shred 1 grapefruit skin, 1 orange skin. Squeeze the juice from a lemon, cut up the skin. Place skins and juice in a bowl with 2 quarts of water. Next day, simmer till peel is quite tender. Add 2 lb sugar, with 2 tablespoons black treacle. Boil about 1 hour.

Boxford marmalade

Cut up the pulp and peel of 10 Seville oranges and 1 lemon. Soak them all night in 6 quarts of water. Reserve pips. Next morning boil the fruit and water for about 2½ hours, fairly fast, and for about another half hour, very fast, to reduce the liquid to half (if necessary it can be boiled longer, it depends on the natural juice in the fruit). Pour 1 pint of boiling water on to the pips; leave for 3 hours, stir well and pour the strained liquor on to the fruit, add 8 lb preserving sugar and boil fast another hour. When once the sugar is added do not boil for more than an hour or the colour will spoil.

Peel for cakes

Remove some of the white pith from orange or lemon skins: grind them through the mincer. Put into jars and cover with boiling golden syrup. Tie down and store in dry place.

Drying herbs

Wash them and pick them free of stalks, then dry thoroughly in clean cloth keeping them, of course, separate. Place on wire trays covered with paper and dry in linen cupboard, on top of the refrigerator or in any moderately warm place. When quite dry and crisp rub through the fingers and push through a fine strainer with a wooden spoon. Store in glass bottles and keep them tightly corked. Dried this way, parsley, mint, tarragon, chervil, etc., keep their colour and flavour. Do not forget during the winter season to dry the little green celery tips, they are most useful in the summer for salads and flavouring when there is no fresh celery.

Denton Welch

Better Cooking

Suggestions and recipes from W. Bronson, manager of the Maison Basque restaurant

MENU I
Potage poireaux pommes
Râble de lièvre
Sauce piquante
Crêpes normande

Potage
Take $1\frac{1}{2}$ lb potatoes, cut into small dice; 3 leeks, thinly sliced; and a nut of margarine. Put into a fairly large saucepan, season well with rough salt and a pepper-mill, cover with stock and $\frac{1}{2}$ pint milk (dried milk will do), bring slowly to the boil and simmer gently for at least 20 minutes.

Râble de lièvre
Take the saddles of two hares and marinade them overnight in a little vinegar and a *bouquet garni*—made by tying a sprig of thyme, a bay leaf, a bit of garlic, inside the leaves of a celery head. When you are ready to cook them, put them into a heated pan with a little hot fat and roast them for 12 minutes only in a very hot oven. Take them out and cut into slices the thickness of a half-crown. (The remaining carcases can be used later in a delicious game soup.)

Sauce piquante
Take 3 shallots, 1 pickled cucumber, and some tarragon, and chop them up finely. Add a few peppercorns; cover with a wineglassful of wine vinegar and a little thick brown stock. Cook very slowly for 10 minutes, pour over the sliced hare, and serve hot with a purée of potatoes.

Crêpes normande
Take 8 oz flour, powder equal to 2 eggs, add a pinch of salt, pour over $\frac{1}{2}$ pint milk or water, and mix into a smooth batter. Pour into a frying-pan containing hot fat, enough for one pancake at a time, spreading thinly, and cook until slightly brown. Spread these with apple purée and make them into little rolls. To make the purée, take 2 lb good-sized apples, quarter them and stew in a saucepan to which enough water has been added to prevent them burning. Make into a purée by rubbing through a sieve and add sugar when cool. A thin sauce of home-made raspberry jam improves these pancakes.

MENU 2
Moules marinières
Sauté de foie de veau paysanne
Corn on the cob

Moules marinières
Take two quarts of mussels. Clean them well with a scrubbing brush, in several changes of water. Then put them in a large saucepan with one pint of dry cider, a lavish handful of finely chopped parsley, chervil, tarragon and six chopped shallots, season with pepper-mill and boil until mussels open.

Sauté de foie de veau paysanne
Take 1 lb liver, cut into strips, dip in seasoned flour and brown them in a frying-pan for 7 or 8 minutes. Whilst they are frying, get ready another pan with a little hot fat, and in this fry one rasher of bacon, sliced; two shallots, sliced; four tomatoes, quartered; and two slices of marrow, cut and cubed. Sauté together slowly until nicely brown, add to your awaiting liver, sprinkle with finely chopped parsley and serve with pommes purées.

Corn on the cob
These must be taken out of their husks and cooked in boiling water from 15 to 20 minutes. Take out and cover with *beurre noisette* (melted margarine flavoured with salt and pepper).

where to go and what to wear when DINING OUT

DINNER AFTER THE PLAY

THE CAPRICE

Plum walls of silk, silver candlesticks, and Mario, the presiding genius . . . For dining, a brown velvet suit with the new dropped shoulder-line; by Brenner, at Meda Sports: Samuels, Manchester; Greensmith Downes, Edinburgh. Brown velours hat: Agmar

BOULESTIN

Small, quiet, for the gourmet rather than the "good-time-girl."

Be advised on dining by Jean Brun, the manager, and advised on wining by Maurice Richier (he who knows to a nicety which year is best); wear this black velvet suit, again with the dropped shoulder line, this time by Marcus; at Galeries Lafayette: Vincent Williams, Chester; Griffin & Spalding, Nottingham. Black velours toque by Agmar

Country Ways for the Cook

Nell Heaton chooses beer and cider to spice these easy dishes of the countryside

Norman Parkinson

Cider biscuits

You need 2 oz fat, 4 oz flour, 1 reconstituted dried egg, 2 tablespoonfuls cider, 2 tablespoonfuls jam. Rub the fat into the flour till it is the consistency of breadcrumbs. Mix in the egg, cider and jam, and knead well together. Roll out very thinly, cut into rounds, and bake in a moderate oven for about 15 minutes.

The flavour may be varied by adding lemon essence or grated rind of lemon or orange. Another method is to use a sprinkling of rolled oats as a garnish.

Cider cakes

You need 1½ lb self-raising flour, a pinch of salt, 1 teaspoonful each of baking powder and mixed spice, ¼ lb margarine. Cut the margarine into lumps and rub into the flour. Add the other ingredients and moisten with enough warm cider to make a stiff dough. If desired, add a reconstituted dried egg and some chopped dried fruit. Place in small tins and bake in a quick oven for about 30 minutes.

Beer caudle

A grand drink for a cold day. Use 2 tablespoons fine oatmeal to 1 pint beer and make in the same way as gruel. Sweeten with sugar and add flavour with ¼ teaspoonful each of mixed spice and ground ginger. Cook the caudle till thick, stirring all the time. Serve in individual bowls.

Fish baked in cider

You can use any kind of white fish. For stuffing: oatmeal as required, pepper, salt, parsley, a knob of margarine, and 1 tablespoonful chopped onion. For sauce: ¾ pint cider, pepper, salt, parsley, cornflour, margarine, nutmeg.

Soak the oatmeal for 30 minutes in a little cold water with salt, pepper, and a good chopping of parsley. Drain, knead with the margarine and onion (or chives), and use to stuff the fish. Place in a well-greased fireproof dish, add salt, pepper, and chopped parsley to taste. Moisten with ½ pint cider, cover with a lid and bake in a moderate oven for 30 to 45 minutes. Add extra cider if the fish becomes too dry. When it is almost cooked, strain off the liquor to make sauce as follows: For each ½ pint of liquid, blend 1 dessertspoonful of cornflour with a little cider and a grating of nutmeg. Pour on the liquid, bring to the boil, and add a small knob of margarine. Pour over the fish and simmer for 15 minutes before serving. Garnish with watercress.

Cider jelly and cream

For the jelly, you need ½ lb cherries or 2 large apples, 1 pint cider, cinnamon, gelatine and sugar or golden syrup. Wash and pick over the fruit, removing cherry pips, or peeling and cutting up the apples. From a packet of gelatine, take the amount required to set 1 pint of jelly (see instructions on packet), soak in a little of the cider, add the fruit, rest of the cider, and a little cinnamon. Bring to the boil, add sweetening, and pour into a well-moistened mould or individual glasses to set. Serve with **Mock Cream** made as follows:

Blend 1 tablespoonful cornflour with a little milk. Bring a cupful of milk to the boil, add a few drops of vanilla essence and pour on to the cornflour. Re-boil and beat till cold. Beat together 1 oz unsalted margarine and 2 oz sugar till creamy, add the sauce gradually till all is well blended and creamy.

Stewed sausages with beer

You need 6 small sausages, about 1 pint beer, 1 teacup of brown sugar, some salt, pepper, vinegar, caraway or dill, 2 rashers of bacon (optional). Put the sausages into a saucepan, cover with beer, and simmer gently for 40 minutes. Remove the sausages. To the liquid, add a wineglassful of vinegar, the brown sugar, ½ teaspoonful caraway or dill seeds, a grating of lemon rind or a dessertspoonful of lemon squash, salt and pepper. Stirring all the while, boil till the sauce thickens. Add the sausages and simmer for 15 minutes; or place the sausages in a casserole, cover with sauce, add the bacon and place in a hot oven till the bacon is browned.

Cider soufflé

You need ½ lb prunes with orange or lemon flavouring, or the same amount of cherries with cinnamon flavouring, 2 oz margarine, 2 oz flour, ½ pint cider, and 2 fresh eggs. Wash and steep the prunes, cook and stone them and rub through a sieve. (Treat cherries in same way, but do not steep.) Make a roux with the margarine and flour, in a double pan if possible. Stir well, but do not allow the flour to brown. Add gradually the cider and flavouring, and cook all together till thickened.

Beat separately the whites and yolks of the eggs. Stir the yolks into the fruit, fold in the stiffly whisked whites and place the mixture in a well-greased soufflé case. Sprinkle on a little castor sugar and bake in a moderately hot oven (about 375°) for 25 to 30 minutes. Serve with **Honey Sauce** made as follows:

Mix together ¼ pint of cider, and 2 tablespoonfuls honey and bring to the boil. Add a teaspoonful of cornflour or arrowroot blended with a little warmed honey, return to the pan and re-boil. Serve hot.

Beer soup

You need 1 quart of beer, flour, margarine, sugar, cinnamon, ginger, lemon rind or lemon essence, 3 reconstituted eggs, parsley and ½ wineglassful of rum, sherry or Madeira. In a medium-sized saucepan, make a roux from 1 oz of flour and 1 oz margarine. Cook for a few minutes but do not brown. Pour in the beer and stir well till the liquid boils. Remove from heat and leave for the time being. In a double saucepan, infuse together the rum or wine, a small piece of the ginger, ½ teaspoonful cinnamon, 1 oz sugar and lemon flavouring. Leave for a while and go back to the soup-pan. Add 3 well-beaten eggs to the soup, return to heat but do not boil. Add 1 oz margarine to the infusion in the double pan, stir into the soup and serve with bread sippets and chopped parsley.

Sauces, Sweets and Savouries

Damson cheese
To each pound of fruit, allow ¼ lb sugar. Place the fruit in a pan and reduce it to pulp over a low heat. Remove the stones, add the sugar and stir in well, then boil quickly for 20–30 minutes till the mixture thickens. Pour into small pots and seal. Apricots make good cheese, too.

Rosepetal jam
Prepare the petals by cutting off the white tip at the base of the petal with scissors. You will need the petals of about 30 sweet-scented roses. (Deep red roses make the best jam.) Place them when freshly pulled into a dry pan and rub them in 2 lb of sugar. Then add 2 pints of water, bring very slowly to the boil to extract the rose flavour, and boil for about 20 minutes, stirring frequently. The petals should then be transparent. Add a level teaspoonful of citric acid and boil for about 10–15 minutes. While hot, pour into jars, seal and store in a cool, dry, dark place to keep the rich colour.

Tomato sauce
Take about 20 ripe tomatoes, blanch them by plunging into hot water for 2 minutes and then into cold, and then skin them. Place them in a saucepan with 3 large finely grated onions, 1 celery stalk and a muslin bag containing 2 bay leaves, about 14 mixed peppercorns and 4 cloves. Simmer together till pulped then add ¼ teaspoonful pepper, 2 tablespoonfuls salt, 1 teaspoonful paprika, ½ lb grated apple, 1 lb sugar and 1½ pints of vinegar. Boil all together till the mixture thickens. Pour into hot jars and seal. If a seedless sauce is preferred, pass the tomatoes through a sieve after pulping.

Herb jellies
MINT—for cold lamb or tongue. Wash, dry and chop the mint and place it in a pan. To each 2 heaped tablespoonfuls of mint, add a small pinch of salt, ½ pint of apple pulp and 6 oz sugar. Boil all together for about 5 minutes, then pour into jars and seal. Green colouring may be added if desired. SAGE—good with cold pork. Use powdered sage instead of mint in the above recipe. ROSEMARY—for use with rabbit dishes. Use freshly chopped rosemary leaves instead of mint. THYME—with cold veal. Use 1 tablespoonful of freshly chopped thyme in place of 2 tablespoons of mint. TARRAGON—for cold fish. Substitute 1 tablespoonful of freshly chopped tarragon for 2 tablespoonfuls of mint. PICKLED NASTURTIUM SEEDS—for Caper and Tartare Sauces. Pick the seeds before they are too old and put into a basin with a covering of salt. Leave for 24 hours, wash well in cold water and dry in a clean cloth. Pack into small bottles. Bring to the boil enough vinegar to fill the bottles, with a few peppercorns added. Cool, strain, then pour over seeds.

Parsley honey
To each pound of parsley, allow 1½ pints of water. Take freshly pulled parsley, wash thoroughly and simmer in a covered casserole or pan for about 2 hours. Strain through muslin and measure. Put the liquid into a clean pan and allow 1 lb of sugar and a small pinch of citric acid to each pint of liquid. Bring the mixture slowly to the boil, then boil quickly for about 20–25 minutes. When it becomes syrupy and thickens, bottle in hot jars. Leave for 2–3 months to mellow. Add a few heather bells or scented rose leaves to give a specially good flavour.

Red cabbage and celery chutney or sauce
Take 1 lb each of shredded heart of red cabbage, diced celery, apples and sliced green tomatoes, and 3 bay leaves. Place in a pan with just enough water (about ½ cupful) to start them cooking. Allow to boil quickly for about 10 minutes with the lid on tightly; add 4 cloves, ½ oz each of mixed ground spice and ginger, a saltspoonful of curry powder, ½ lb of sugar and 1 pint of vinegar. Boil all together till reduced to two-thirds the quantity, then bottle in hot jars.

To make sauce, rub the pulped ingredients through a hair sieve, add spices, vinegar and sugar and return to the pan. Add ½ lb extra grated apple and 1 pint of vinegar. Boil quickly till the liquid thickens and then pour it into hot bottles.

Pickled peaches, pears, and plums
PEACHES—Remove the skins from 2 lb peaches. Boil together for about 15 minutes a cupful of vinegar, 2 cupfuls of sugar, ¼ teaspoonful cinnamon and 4 cloves. Drop in the peaches and cook till just tender. Pack carefully in jars, fill up with the hot syrup and seal immediately. PEARS—Parboil the peeled pears before plunging them into the syrup as above, and then cook them till they are transparent, adding a small piece of rock ginger, a blade of mace and 2 bay leaves to the syrup, as well as the other spices. Pack in hot jars and seal immediately. PLUMS—Wash and wipe the plums and dry with a cloth. Prick the skins in several places with a sterilised darning needle. Make the syrup as for peaches and pour it over the plums. Leave them for 2 hours to marinade, then drain off the syrup. Bring to the boil, drop in the plums and boil for 2 minutes. Then pack them in hot jars immediately.

Horseradish
Grate, dry and bottle to use for flavouring. It gives added zest to fish as well as to beef. The grated horseradish can be mixed with mayonnaise, added to whipped cream with a pinch of mustard and a little vinegar, or stirred into brown gravy.

But Irish Bread...

by Maura Laverty

John Minton

I hate to admit it, but there is no denying that Irishwomen were behind the door when the culinary gifts were being given out. In the matter of soups, sauces, soufflés, and sweets, we are only trotting after the women of other countries. The only plea I can advance to excuse our ways with fish is that the people from whom we inherited those ways possibly felt it would have been an irreligious thing to have tried to lessen the rigours of Friday's fast. We know so little of meat cookery that we'd probably have become a nation of vegetarians were it not that our Irish meat is so good that it can withstand the worst punishments devised by the most sadistic cook.

Those are our culinary shortcomings. We have one kitchen virtue: we make grand bread.

We have a reverence for bread. As children, we are taught that to waste food of any kind is a sin which must be told in Confession, but that to waste bread is a crime which even the bishop himself hasn't enough power to absolve. Should a child be so depraved as to throw a crust of bread into the ashes, he is warned that before he dies retributive hunger will make him follow a crow seven miles across hill and dale in the hope that it will drop just such a crust. Our memories of the Great Hunger of 1847 may have something to do with our respect for bread and the importance which we attach to being able to make it properly. And we *can* make it. But our bread is not the porous yeast bread of other countries. It is bread leavened with bicarbonate of soda and buttermilk—something as peculiar to ourselves as pig's cheek and the Abbey Theatre.

Every time Ireland is put in the dock, I feel our diplomatists are sadly lacking as counsel for the defence that they don't bring forward in mitigation of our crimes the fact that we have given a four-leaved shamrock to the world. One leaf is W. B. Yeats, another is boiled potatoes in their jackets, another Barry Fitzgerald. The fourth leaf is soda bread. And the greatest of these is soda bread. Spongy white soda bread with floury, brown-crossed crust . . . flat sweet griddle bread with an inch-and-a-half of tender, well-baked dough sandwiched between thin crisp crusts . . . wholesome brown bread with growth and health and energy in its pleasantly rough nuttiness . . . dark spicy treacle bread that has been left for twenty-four hours to become firm and mellow, and is then sliced thinly and spread with good country butter . . . currant bread and buns, Indian meal bread, "spotted dog" rich with raisins, seedy bread . . . there seems to be no end at all to our ways with soda bread.

The queer thing is that in its native habitat soda bread is never so called. We call it "cake" or "cake bread". A loaf of bread comes out of the baker's van, but a cake of bread comes out of the oven in the kitchen.

The secret of good cake bread is three-day-old buttermilk, a light hand for mixing and kneading, and a brisk oven. Thick milk, i.e., new milk which has gone sour, isn't nearly as good as buttermilk for bread-making. But buttermilk is not always easy to come by. In the winter, when the cows go dry, some of us use a very effective substitute which we call "winter buttermilk" or "barm," and this is how it is made:

Mix a quarter of a pound of flour to a smooth paste with one cupful of cold water. Put this in the bottom of a large jug or crock. Add two grated raw potatoes and two mashed cooked potatoes. Now mix in seven cupfuls of cold water. Cover and leave on the kitchen mantelpiece or in some such warm place for at least two days. When you are baking, pour off carefully, and without disturbing the sediment, as much liquid as you require. This liquid may be used in exactly the same way as buttermilk, and will give you lovely light bread. Add fresh water to make up for what you have used. Stir up the contents of the vessel, cover it and put it by for the next baking. The one lot of potatoes and flour will give you a fortnight's supply of winter buttermilk.

There is another way of making sure of a constant supply of buttermilk when you haven't a cow in the paddock at the back of the house. You can start a buttermilk plant with yeast, sugar, and skim milk, or milk-and-water. The buttermilk plant is a kind of fungus like the vinegar plant. After a few weeks, it will grow and grow, and you'll be able to supply all your friends with a cutting. The milk it produces is very good for the blood, particularly in rheumatic cases. It is pleasant to drink, too.

To start the plant, you'll need:
1 oz sugar
1 quart tepid milk and water mixed
1 oz yeast

Cream the yeast with the sugar, gradually add the tepid milk and water. Put the mixture in some vessel that may easily be washed and scalded, cover it and leave it in a warm place for a few days, or until the milk smells and tastes like buttermilk. When you want to use the buttermilk, put a piece of muslin in the bottom of a strainer and strain the milk through this. The funny looking substance like lumpy cornflour which remains will be the buttermilk plant. Rinse every drop of milk off it by pouring a cupful of tepid water over it. Let the water run through the strainer into the buttermilk—it will all make excellent liquid for mixing cake bread. To start a new lot of buttermilk, scrape the plant off the muslin and put it back into the scalded and well-rinsed vessel. Add another quart of tepid milk-and-water, cover it and leave it as before to increase and multiply.

The first ounce of yeast will go on growing, giving you buttermilk until the end of time. But the plant needs a certain amount of care.

1. It must be strained at least every five days. If you don't want the milk for baking, you can always drink it. I knew a woman so crippled with rheumatics that she couldn't kneel down to say the Rosary. After six months of drinking this buttermilk she was able to do the Lough Derg Pilgrimage on her knees.

2. Make sure the milk and water is never more than lukewarm. Strong heat kills yeast.

3. Cleanliness is very important. That careful rinsing after straining and the scalding of the container must be done religiously if the plant is to live.

Basic recipe for soda bread:
1 lb flour
1 teaspoonful salt
1 teaspoonful sugar
1 teaspoonful bread soda
buttermilk to mix

Sift the dry ingredients several times. Make a well in the centre. Pour in the buttermilk gradually, mixing in the flour from the sides. The amount of buttermilk needed will depend to a great extent on the quality of the flour. In any case, it's a good rule to make the dough rather wet than dry. A dry ragged dough gives a tough cake. The dough should be of such a consistency that it does not leave the sides of the bowl clean when turned on to a floured board. Knead it lightly for a few minutes, turning the sides of the dough in towards the centre, and working it round and round while doing so. Now turn it upside down so that the smooth side is on top, pat it to a round, brush it with milk, and cut a cross on it to keep it from cracking in the baking. Let the cuts go down over the side of the cake to make sure of this. Bake it for 45 minutes in a hot oven (450°).

Brown bread
Use half wheatenmeal (whole wheat flour) and half white flour. Increase the sugar to 1 dessertspoonful and rub in, if you like, 1 dessertspoonful of dripping (bacon fat). I always add as well a fist of flakemeal (oatmeal). It gives a lovely, nutty texture.

Griddle bread
The mixture as for soda bread. Roll out the dough 1 inch thick. Cut in four farls (cakes). Cook them on a griddle or on a heavy iron frying-pan over a medium heat. If the heat is too strong the undercrust will get thick and brown before the heat has a chance to penetrate and this will result in a sodden streak in the middle of the bread which is the sure sign of bad griddle bread. When they have been cooking for about 12 minutes, and a thin skin has formed on top, turn them and give them another 12 minutes.

Treacle bread
Increase the sugar to 1 tablespoonful and add to the buttermilk a half cupful of warmed treacle. A beaten egg may be added as well, in which case you may as well go the whole hog and rub 2 ounces of butter into the flour. Raisins, currants, and chopped nuts make this party bread. Give it an hour in a greased tin in a moderate oven.

Seedy bread
Increase the sugar to 1 tablespoonful. Rub 2 ounces of lard into the flour, and add 1 dessertspoonful of carraway seeds.

Indian meal bread
We call this "Yalla Male" bread. Use half and half Indian meal and flour. This bread is grand for breakfast. It gives a certain extra something to bacon and eggs.

Tea scones
Use white or any mixture of flour. Increase the sugar to 2 tablespoonfuls. Rub 3 ounces of fat into the flour. Add half a pound of fruit. Add a beaten egg to the buttermilk if you'd like extra-nice scones. Roll half-inch thick, cut in rounds, and bake 20 minutes in a hot oven.

One last word about soda bread. Never mix it to a firm dough. I find my bread is lightest and spongiest when the dough is not too firm and not too sticky. I like it to be at that stage of softness when to lift it safely from table to oven constitutes a feat of manual dexterity.

"Bread", by Salvador Dali. Collection of the artist © *A.D.A.G.P. Paris 1976*

The loaf—threatened stronghold against starvation

50s

"Frozen food has opened a new era of cookery and leisure. . . ." "The brown paper bag method of cooking can be a tremendous timesaver. . . ." "The women who continues her career after her marriage should invest in a pressure cooker; a *moulin de légumes*; a chafing-dish and a Swedish cocotte. . . ." "One of the smaller, but currently most effective, marks of science on our lives is that the hostess need never again bend alone over a kitchen stove hearing laughter (or worse, silence) from her guests in another room. There is growing both a sale and a need for—and production of—the type of cooking appliance in and on which she can cook in front of their eyes."

Guille

In the fifties everything was being done to make life easier for people who had "to housekeep without a cook". THE ART OF ENTERTAINING series began with a do-it-yourself dinner party: "The one essential thing is that your guests shall find a relaxed hostess. They must never know that you have been home a bare half-hour, that the daily woman failed to arrive, that the oven failed to regulate. Get your husband or a man friend you know and trust to deal with ice and mix drinks. Save your strength with the bits you provide with the drinks. Nuts, *good* biscuits and olives are enough if dinner is not to be late. Allow a good half-hour for drinks, to cover lateness and proper introductions."

There was still rationing (until July 1954) although the 5*s*. limit on meal prices was lifted, but with the Festival of Britain in 1951 *Vogue* readers were told to "go frankly native giving only dishes that are typically British, the things our grandsires relished and that our countryfolk still delight in. We may not be able to provide sirloins of Scotch beef, or regale visitors with saddles of Welsh lamb, still there remains much that we can do on our slender meat ration (10*d*. a week in February 1951) and the fish that swim about these shores are second to none."

The "Bounty of Britain" included recipes for native delicacies such as Isle of Wight Crab, Scotch Barley Broth, Sussex Game Pudding (rich and rare), Oxford Hare (stuffed shoulder of mutton) and Lancashire Hot Pot (see pages 178–9).

The hostess had become the International Hostess, "from France, England, Italy, America" and favourite recipes included Homard frappé from Loelia, Duchess of Westminster (Surrey), Truites Denise from Christian Dior

Antony Armstrong-Jones

(France), Kidneys sautéed in white wine from Mrs David Bruce (Paris), and Fritto misto from Countess Roberti (Rome).

BEFORE THE THEATRE "Mrs Diana Daly serves cheese on hot biscuits and Lady Mildred Lamington has a variety of fillings for double-decker toast sandwiches —ham, cheese and walnuts, or demi-sel cheese mashed up with goat's cream and chives."

AFTER THE THEATRE "Lady Mildred Lamington advises firmly against lobster, crab or cucumber late at night . . . and has a recipe for *Poule au Pot*, chicken boiled with celery, turnip, onion, carrots and herbs and served in a casserole with the vegetables and stock—this could be simmering during the play".

André François

Food as well as Hostesses became more international. "Eat your holiday souvenirs!" said Robin McDouall: "When you dine out and the soup, the fish, the meat and the salad are all heavily laced with garlic, you can be pretty sure your hosts are just back from Provence. If there is grated Parmesan with the soup and with the risotto, and the *suprême* of chicken is served under a cheese sauce, your hosts are just back from Italy. Not that everything is drenched with garlic in Provence or mobled with cheese in Italy; it is just that your hosts' nostalgia has run away with them."

Nell Heaton, just back from Austria in 1953, supplied recipes for Schnitzels and Sacher Torte and warned: "Never order extra butter because that will cost you just about a shilling (the English shilling is equivalent to approximately three Austrian schillings)."

"Holiday-makers in search of the Caribbean sun may have the opportunity of trying some of the food described here in its native surroundings" introduced a page on Creole Cooking by Sheila de Burlet, and Beryl Gould Marks wrote about a "Feast from Spain". In 1955: "Indian food is becoming more and more popular and grocers in and out of Soho are stocking more and more of the ingredients. Here, Mrs Savitri Chowdhary explains the drill for an Indian dinner-party menu." Her first piece of advice—"Never, never use curry-powder". She adds that with 'bought' curry-powder one may make a palatable dish, but not really an Indian one (see pages 151–9 for recipes).

Eating out was an essential part of food in the fifties and *Vogue* published three gastronomic maps. The first, in Festival year 1951, was a "detached cosmopolitan view" by New Yorkers Oden and Olivia Meeker who reported: "We have consumed everything but the maître d'hôtel impaled on a flaming sword. And with the assistance of *Vogue* staff we have listed a hundred and fifty restaurants we feel we can recommend:

"SUPPLY: No matter what our relatives in Chicago think, hunger-pinched Britons are not fainting in platoons in Trafalgar Square. Almost everything is available in good supply now, though napkins are still not as plentiful as they should be, and meat and eggs are still short.

"PRICE: drink is disproportionately high contrasted to any Latin country: A good, cool lager can be had almost anywhere, however, and the few places which won't carry anything so *déclassé* as beer deserve to lose their more judicious customers.

"PUBS: These oases of cut glass and mahogany, so intensely respectable and intensely British, full of snug cheer and quiet talk, offer some of the best food in the country.

"SEAFOOD: A dozen oysters and a pint of this or that mellows the soul, banishes melancholy and wards off beriberi.

"ON BEING KNOWN: For some unfathomable reason, certain restaurateurs serve good food to people they know and indifferent food to people they don't know.

Plate by Picasso © *S.P.A.D.E.M. Paris 1976*

November 1950

It's a help to make a reservation, and an authoritative voice can be a help, too. Whatever the techniques, we strongly urge that customers refuse to be quelled by haughty waiters."

By the time the third map was published in June 1959: "You can eat really well in London if you know where to go. . . . It is time we began to be proud of the fact that one can eat cheaply in London better than anywhere else in the world, and that our expensive restaurants like the Mirabelle, the Caprice or La Réserve can produce a meal as fine as anything to be had in Paris.

"What London used to lack as little as six years ago was the cosy, intimate 'neighbourhood' restaurant, the little place round the corner where the local inhabitants could get a good dinner without having to go as far as the West End. Now there are dozens of them, all over Chelsea, Knightsbridge and Kensington, scattered through Marylebone, Bayswater and Hampstead. Often they are run in a deceptively casual way with ballet students for waiters and strings of onions looped from the ceiling, but the food is far from amateur and usually extremely good.

"Another development is the growing popularity of all things Oriental, including food. There have always been good Chinese and Indian restaurants in London and today they are flourishing as never before. London now also boasts the only Siamese restaurant in Europe and the only Japanese restaurant in England.

"Indeed, one of the advantages of a cosmopolitan capital is the opportunity it offers to slip away in imagination to another country—to lunch in Russia or Portugal, dine in Italy or Greece, return home, perhaps, to America or Australia—all within no more than a sixpenny bus-ride of Piccadilly Circus.

"Oddly enough, perhaps the most difficult thing to find in London, gastronomically speaking, is good English food.

"English cooking, at its best, is essentially *home* cooking, as good as its materials and excellent when relying on the farm and the kitchen garden. The tradition is a country one, based on the farmhouse and the country house in its hey-day, and it adapts none too happily to urbanity. Consider the following good English gastronomic day: breakfast—porridge, kippers, bacon and egg, toast and Oxford marmalade. Lunch (in a City chop-house)—steak, Stilton and a glass of port. Tea—anchovy toast, crumpets, cake. Dinner at, say, Simpson's—turtle soup, saddle of mutton and apple pie."

In July 1956 a new word appeared in *Vogue*—Motel. . . . "This slick, gadgety little word means hotels for motorists. They are at the same time something to which we have a perfect right—a natural appendage to motoring—and a possible menace that may threaten the few bits of countryside we have left. At present we have only one chain of motels and a few individual concerns, but these must be regarded as the thin edge of the wedge. We had better not simply acclaim them as a novelty, but take them seriously and judge them with discrimination.

"To English motorists, broken to the drill of waiting for the office staff to arrive before a bill can be produced, and the further frustration of finding their car neatly hemmed in by seven others, the idea of simply opening garage doors and driving away into the freshness of the morning is so Arcadian that its reality can hardly be grasped. And this is sure enough the snag that has withheld motels from us

LONDÔN

Marc

Penn, August 1951

Plate designed by Terence Conran for the *Chanterelle* restaurant

hitherto. What a motorist regards as heavenly privacy, local authorities and guardians of our morals see as an invitation to vice."

Doris Lytton Toye contributed regularly during 1951 and spasmodically later, and other cookery writers included Peter Pirbright and Gretel Beer, Iris Syrett, Lily McLeod, Rosemary Kornfeld, Alexander Watt, Georgina Masson and Mary Bromfield, wife of the author Louis Bromfield. There was no permanent cookery writer until 1956, a Red Letter Year for food in *Vogue*–Elizabeth David started her Food at its Best series, followed by French Regional Cooking.

Her influence was felt not only in kitchens throughout the country but in the many restaurants of a completely new type which had sprung up all over London. Her dishes found their way onto the menus of Dr Hilary James's *Le Matelot* in Elizabeth Street and Walter Baxter's *Chanterelle* in the Old Brompton Road where things like taramasalata and garlic bread which we take for granted now were amazing then. For the rest of the fifties Elizabeth David contributed brilliant articles under titles such as The Tools of the Trade, Menu Mishaps, Untraditional Food. On pages 165–174 are her Cooking Hazards—making soufflés and cream sauces, cooking rice and roasting joints can be as hazardous now as it was in the fifties. Elizabeth David points out the "reasons for some culinary failure and provides solutions to the hoodoos that on occasion seem to beset even the most professional of cooks".

Anthony Gross

VIPs in Paris Restaurants

Summer 1955: who eats what and how to cook it by Alexander Watt

EDGAR FAURE, France's Premier, dines often at the excellent Italian restaurant Le San Francisco. He usually chooses *osso buco* for the main course. Another habitué is the novelist and Nobel prizewinner François Mauriac, who prefers an exciting dish made of chicken breasts, sliced ham, and Gruyère cheese, with a rich Madeira sauce: this is on the menu as *cotes de volaille à la bolognaise.*

For *osso buco,* first cut in fine julienne strips a few leeks, carrots, onions, and a little celery: brown in olive oil in a casserole, along with ½ cupful chopped bacon. Meanwhile dredge in flour 6 shanks of veal, each a good inch thick; brown in a frying-pan and transfer to the casserole. Add salt, pepper, ½ cupful dry white wine. Cook until liquid is slightly reduced. Then add 2 tablespoonfuls tomato purée, 1 cupful chicken broth and simmer for about an hour and a half. Transfer the veal to another pan, keep hot in oven. Strain the juices from the casserole through a fine sieve; then cook gently until the quantity is again slightly reduced. Sprinkle finely chopped parsley, garlic, lemon peel over the shanks of veal; pour the sauce over them, and simmer for a few minutes more. Serve very hot.

ALEC GUINNESS apparently has a taste for the grand manner, revealed in his preference for Le Grand Véfour, a *luxe* "three-star" restaurant at the end of the Palais Royal Gardens. Napoleon went there often as a young general, and it was in the coffee-house, next door, that he first met Joséphine de Beauharnais. The interior of Véfour is genuine Directoire, with beautifully carved and painted panelling and handsome furniture; and the cellar, happily, has one of the best stocks of Bordeaux in Paris. Among the specialities is a rich little fantasy called *croûte landaise,* for which Guinness reportedly has *une petite faiblesse.*

For *croûte landaise,* heat gently under the grill sufficie n *foie gras* to spread ¼-inch thick over a slice of bread previously fried in butter for each person. Pour over this *sauce Mornay* (which is really *sauce béchamel* with a little added cream and grated cheese). Sprinkle on top mixed grated Parmesan and Gruyère cheese. Glaze under a hot grill and serve the *croûte* instantly.

CHRISTIAN DIOR takes very little time off for lunch, but now and then when he feels the need of being truly restored he walks over to the Plaza-Athénée. There Monsieur Diat, who controls the huge staff of the hotel's kitchens, concentrates principally on simple superlative food, the fare of harried businessmen and, of course, of dieters. Dior particularly enjoys his *poularde grillée Plaza-Athénée.*

This consists quite simply of a tender young chicken boned from the back (this is a tricky operation, so ask your poulterer to do it for you), and browned quickly in butter in a pan. After 10 minutes remove, place in oven and sprinkle with plenty of chopped, raw mushrooms. Season with salt and pepper and pour on ⅓ cupful melted butter. Place in a 400° oven and cook for 10 to 12 minutes basting frequently. Remove and sprinkle finely chopped *fines herbes* over the chicken. Serve with potato straws and melted butter.

If you are not on a diet, then serve with potatoes and a

rich *sauce Périgueux*. Cut into thin strips enough potatoes and fresh (or tinned) truffles for four persons. Sauté them—don't fry them—in butter, in a small *sauteuse*. When cooked, press them down flat to make a round wad. Turn carefully upside down on a hot serving dish and place the chicken on top.

To make the sauce: Take ¾ cupful *demi-glace* (a composition of *sauce espagnole* and *fonds de veau*, which is a concentrated veal stock), add 2 tablespoonfuls of essence of truffles and simmer over a low flame until reduced by one-third. Strain through a fine sieve. Reheat but do not allow to boil. Remove from fire and add 2 tablespoonfuls chopped truffles. Serve in a separate dish.

GRAHAM GREENE likes Le Berkeley. He goes there primarily for the *steak au poivre*.

To achieve *steak au poivre* for four, first trim all the excess fat from 4 good-sized sirloin steaks. With the heel of the hand, press into each one freshly ground coarse black pepper. Add a pinch of salt. Melt 4 tablespoonfuls of butter and 2 of olive oil in a heavy copper frying-pan; sear the steaks quickly on both sides. Then pour over them 2 oz cognac and ignite. When the steaks are cooked—and they should not be cooked too much—remove from pan and keep hot. Pour into the pan ¼ cupful dry white wine, ½ cupful heavy veal stock. Cook until the quantity is reduced by one-third. Correct seasoning, and pour over steaks.

JEAN COCTEAU can sometimes be seen eating *rognons de Cadiz* at Le Catalan, a small convivial restaurant on the Left Bank. The atmosphere and food are essentially Spanish, with guitarists and gipsy dancing from nine to eleven o'clock every evening.

For *rognons de Cadiz*, begin by scrubbing well 24 medium-to-small mushrooms caps. Fry these in butter for 7 or 8 minutes; remove and keep hot. Pour into the pan ½ glassful of port, and cook until slightly reduced. Add 3 dessertspoonfuls of fresh cream and stir constantly for three or four minutes over a low flame. Add 2 dessertspoonfuls of *demi-glace* (a composition of *sauce espagnole* and *fonds de veau*, which is concentrated veal stock). Then add a dozen drops of Worcester sauce and a pinch of cayenne. Continue stirring and allow mixture to reduce slowly until the sauce is thick and shiny. Remove pan from fire, add a few small chunks of butter; stir well, and keep hot in a double boiler.

Meanwhile cook enough rice for four people, split, scrub and grill 12 lamb kidneys; grilling takes about 5 or 6 minutes. Put a mound of rice in the middle of a large serving dish, and surround it with the mushroom caps. Place half a kidney on each mushroom cap. Pour the sauce over the rice. Then complete the decoration by deftly spearing each kidney-mushroom with a toothpick on which you have first impaled an olive and a cube of ham.

JEAN GABIN, the delightfully durable star of more French movies than anybody can remember just off-hand, eats at Chez Monteil, an engaging *bistro* in Les Halles, the central markets of Paris. He can often be found there sitting down with *le patron* to a hearty lunch of *canard à l'estragon*.

To cook this at home for four people, prepare a good-sized duck as you would for roasting. Make the stuffing: First chop the duck liver very fine; sauté in 2 tablespoonfuls butter. To this add ½ lb pork sausage meat, 2 tablespoonfuls *foie gras* (or *paté de foie gras*), a dessertspoonful of fresh tarragon, and salt and pepper to taste. Mix well, add a little cognac, first pouring off excess fat if there is any. Stuff the duck, salt and pepper it, and roast for 15 minutes in a 400° oven. Then reduce heat to 300° and roast for 40 minutes more. Remove from roasting pan and keep hot. Put into the pan ½ cupful dry white wine, and ½ cupful water; bring gently to boiling point. Remove and thicken with a mixture of butter and flour. Correct seasoning, and serve with the duck.

SIR LAURENCE OLIVIER, when he eats at the famous Parisian restaurant, Maxim's, usually has *sole Albert*: a variation, called after the director of Maxim's, of the classic sole *au Vermouth*. Vivien Leigh often orders *frivolités de langoustine*.

The *frivolités* present one difficulty; you must make first of all a very light puff paste. Shape this into small canoe-like pastries. Fill with shrimp—ideally they should be Dublin Bay prawns—which have been cooked first in a court bouillon, and, of course, shelled. Mask with luke-warm *sauce béarnaise*. This is how to make the sauce. Stir together with a wooden spoon the yolks of 5 fresh eggs, 2 tablespoonfuls butter, salt, pepper. Cook gently until eggs thicken; be sure to remove from fire, and add 2 more tablespoonfuls of butter, ½ teaspoonful of vinegar, a little freshly chopped tarragon. This sauce should have the consistency of mayonnaise.

André Malraux, novelist and art critic, is one of the members of the *Club de la Casserole,* which meets regularly at Lasserre, a fashionable restaurant in the Champs-Elysées quarter. The atmosphere here is one of velvety calm, and on summer nights the roof slides back so that late diners can enjoy the night air and the stars along with their cognac. The chef, a winner of the culinary *Prix Prosper Montagné,* prepares a special *pannequet soufflé et flambé* which is sometimes the choice of Malraux when he dines at Lasserre.

This *pannequet* consists of a soufflé which is wrapped in a thin pancake. First make the pancakes, using any standard receipt for thin dessert pancakes. Then make a *crème pâtissière:* Beat together until very thick and lemon-coloured $\frac{3}{4}$ cupful sugar and 6 egg yolks. Mix lightly $\frac{1}{3}$ cupful flour. Gradually add 2 cupfuls hot milk, heated with one vanilla bean, stir constantly with a wire whisk. Place over hot water or over a very low flame and keep stirring until it just reaches the boiling point. Cool.

To prepare enough soufflé for 6 pancakes, beat into 6 tablespoonfuls of the warm *crème pâtissière* with a wooden spatula, 1 egg, 2 egg yolks, and 2 tablespoonfuls of Grand Marnier or Cointreau. Next beat 6 egg whites until very stiff; fold these in slowly and carefully. Then place an equal portion of this mixture on each of the pancakes, and roll them, allowing some of the soufflé to run out at the ends. Heat on a hot, buttered silver dish in a 250° oven for 3 or 4 minutes. Remove, sprinkle with powdered sugar, and instantly rush the platter to the table. Flame the pancakes with a little of the same liqueur used in the soufflé.

Dr Charles Paul, doctor and gourmet, dines whenever he can at Lapérouse, where the *poulet docteur* was created in his honour. A superb old-fashioned restaurant, Lapérouse is managed by Monsieur Topolinski, whose family have been in charge there for more than fifty years. The *canard de Colette,* called after the author of Gigi, is another Lapérouse speciality.

For *poulet docteur* clean and truss a 3 lb roasting chicken. Salt and pepper it; brown quickly in 4 tablespoonfuls of butter heated in a copper casserole. Cover, reduce heat, and allow to cook, basting frequently for about 45 minutes. Then add a large glass of port. Leave the cover off and allow liquid to reduce by one-third. Next add $1\frac{1}{2}$ cupfuls heavy veal stock. Continue cooking gently until the chicken is tender, remembering to baste frequently. Meanwhile, cut 2 chicken livers in half, and sauté them lightly in butter along with $\frac{1}{4}$ lb of tender veal cut in very thin strips. To this add a little freshly chopped tarragon. When the livers and veal are done, place them on a hot platter, and top with chicken, cut up for serving. Cook the juices in the casserole until slightly reduced; then pour over the chicken.

Pablo Picasso, when he comes to Paris from the Midi, sometimes goes to Chez Camille Renault in Puteaux, just across the Seine at Neuilly. A shuttered *bistro,* it looks from the outside fairly dull. Inside, the atmosphere is comfortable and friendly. Camille Renault, a big open-hearted man, besides being an expert chef has a great feeling for art and for astrology. On the walls hangs a mixed collection of paintings, and a number of dishes are called after artists—*poulet Gauguin, retour de Tahiti,* for example, and, of course, *poulet Picasso.*

To make this chicken dish at home for four people, select a tender young chicken and get your poulterer to split it up the back and to flatten it. Place it in an oven dish. Pour over 2 tablespoonfuls pure olive oil and cook uncovered in a hot oven (450°) for 25 minutes. Then remove from the oven, place on a serving dish and pour $\frac{1}{4}$ cupful slightly melted butter over the chicken. Keep hot. Next peel, quarter and seed 4 large ripe tomatoes and place in the juice in the pan in the oven along with 20 large green olives and 20 large black olives which have been pitted. When the olives are hot and the tomatoes start to get soft (3 or 4 minutes will suffice), remove, season with salt and pepper and pour over the chicken.

Culinary hats by Picasso © *S.P.A.D.E.M. Paris 1976*

"Paella

Feast from Spain

by Beryl Gould-Marks

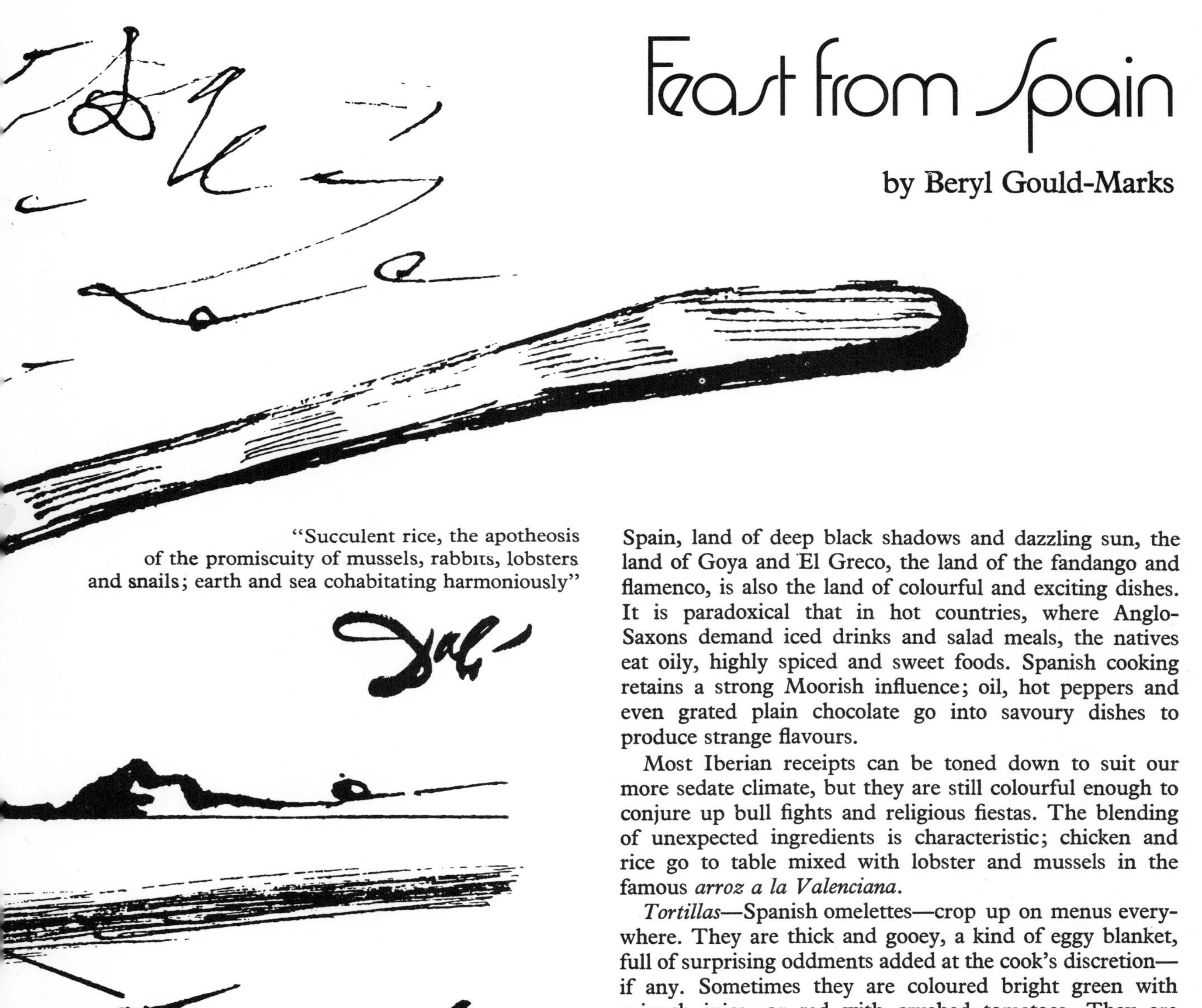

"Succulent rice, the apotheosis of the promiscuity of mussels, rabbits, lobsters and snails; earth and sea cohabitating harmoniously"

Dalí

© A.D.A.G.P. Paris 1976

Spain, land of deep black shadows and dazzling sun, the land of Goya and El Greco, the land of the fandango and flamenco, is also the land of colourful and exciting dishes. It is paradoxical that in hot countries, where Anglo-Saxons demand iced drinks and salad meals, the natives eat oily, highly spiced and sweet foods. Spanish cooking retains a strong Moorish influence; oil, hot peppers and even grated plain chocolate go into savoury dishes to produce strange flavours.

Most Iberian receipts can be toned down to suit our more sedate climate, but they are still colourful enough to conjure up bull fights and religious fiestas. The blending of unexpected ingredients is characteristic; chicken and rice go to table mixed with lobster and mussels in the famous *arroz a la Valenciana.*

Tortillas—Spanish omelettes—crop up on menus everywhere. They are thick and gooey, a kind of eggy blanket, full of surprising oddments added at the cook's discretion—if any. Sometimes they are coloured bright green with spinach juice, or red with crushed tomatoes. They are made like ordinary omelettes, but the chopped additions, such as ham or diced potato, are mixed in, and the omelettes are well cooked on both sides.

Breakfast chocolate

For breakfast, Spaniards drink a small cup of thick syrupy chocolate made with water and sipped alternately with creamy cold milk. It is wonderful for elevenses, too. Take 1 oz plain chocolate to a breakfast cup hot water, a pinch of cinnamon, a very little vanilla (I keep a vanilla pod in a jar of sugar and use the sugar when I want a subtle vanilla flavouring), and sugar to taste (roughly a dessertspoon to a cup). Melt the chocolate in some of the hot water, then add the rest and simmer slowly for 10 minutes. Add the cinnamon, vanilla and sugar. Beat with a fork till it is frothy.

Castilian bean casserole

A cheap and sustaining peasant-dish, this is used in Mexico as well as in Spain. Take 2 cups cooked butter beans or lima beans, 4 oz diced salt pork, 1 large onion, and a clove of garlic chopped, ½ lb skinned and chopped tomatoes, 1 tablespoon black treacle, 1 dessertspoon brown sugar, plenty of red pepper or crushed chillies, salt, and a small wineglass of sherry. Mix all the ingredients in a casserole, and season as highly as your taste can take. Cook in a moderate oven for an hour.

Chuletas de ternera a la Catalonia

This is an unusual veal dish. Take 4 thinly cut fillets of veal, 2 large sliced onions, a chopped clove of garlic, 2 oz grated cheese, 3 tablespoons chilli sauce (or 1 tablespoon Worcestershire sauce and 2 of tomato sauce), boiling water, flour, salt, pepper, chopped parsley and olive oil. Season the fillets highly and dredge with flour. Fry till light brown in 2 tablespoons very hot olive oil. Spread the onions and garlic over the veal. Pour in the sauce and just cover with boiling water. Cover closely and simmer for half-an-hour. Sprinkle in the grated cheese, and cook gently until it melts. Serve with chopped parsley on top.

Red pimentos stuffed with ham and spinach

Cut the top off each pimento and carefully remove the seeds. Poach the pimentos in boiling salted water until they are just soft. Cook the spinach separately till it is tender. Drain and press out as much water as possible. Melt a little butter in a pan, put in a tablespoon of chopped ham to each pimento, a crushed clove of garlic and the spinach. Season highly, stir well and cook for about 6 minutes. Stuff the pimentos, arrange them in a fireproof dish with a little strong stock, and cook in a moderate oven for 15 minutes.

Tomato jam

A rare and unusual offering for a special guest, this is very good with scones. Take 3 lb firm ripe tomatoes and reduce them to a purée by chopping them and cooking them without water until they are absolutely soft. Press with a wooden spoon and cook a little longer. Pass through a sieve. Add an equal quantity of sugar by bulk, a good pinch of cinnamon and a grating of nutmeg. Simmer for half-an-hour and then add a tablespoon of rum for each pint of jam. Continue cooking until it forms a jelly. Put it into small jars and tie down.

Black beans with sausages

Take ½ lb black beans (brown beans, haricot beans or lentils are all equally good, in different ways), ½ lb salami or similar dried sausage cut into ¼-inch cubes, 1 chopped onion, 1 chopped clove of garlic, ½ lb skinned tomatoes, 1 thinly sliced red pimento, 1 tablespoon chopped parsley, salt and pepper, a glass of red wine, 2 tablespoons olive oil.

Soak the beans overnight, then cook them in salted water till they are tender; drain well. Fry the onion and garlic in the oil till light brown. Add the skinned tomatoes and the pimento, crush the tomatoes with a wooden spoon as they are cooking. Add beans, sausage, parsley, and wine. Season highly, stir thoroughly, cover closely and simmer for half-an-hour.

Spanish salad

Mix together slivered raw pimento, chopped green and black olives, finely sliced tomatoes, cooked rice, and garlic pounded with an anchovy fillet. Season and sprinkle with chopped parsley. Toss in a dressing of olive oil and wine vinegar.

Arroz a la Valenciana

To me this is the supreme example of Spanish gastronomy. Take the diced meat of a young chicken or rabbit, 1 quart stock (made from the bones and giblets, cooked with a bay leaf, salt and pepper), 1 pint large heavy mussels, a dozen or more shelled prawns or a small lobster, 2 chopped cloves of garlic, 2 sliced onions, ½ lb cooked French beans, ½ lb cooked peas, a good pinch of saffron, 3 cups rice, salt, pepper, 3 tablespoons olive oil, a small glass of dry sherry.

Put the cleaned mussels into the simmering stock. As soon as they open, take them out of their shells and put them on one side. Strain the stock carefully. Fry the chicken or rabbit in the oil until golden. Add the garlic, onion and saffron. One minute later put in the rice. Stir vigorously until the rice is coated and coloured. Season very highly. Pour in the stock and cook slowly without stirring until the stock is nearly absorbed. Test the rice, and if it is still hard, add more stock. When the rice is done, add the diced shellfish, the cooked beans and peas. Pour in the sherry; stir, but do not disturb the bottom. When quite dry, serve and give a little of the slightly burnt bottom crust to everyone.

Artichoke bottoms with chestnuts

Though this is extravagant, it is rewardingly delicious. Take tinned or fresh artichoke bottoms, stuff them with a mixture of chestnut purée, chopped bacon and cooked mushrooms. Put them in an oven-proof dish, top with grated cheese, pour a few drops of sherry over each artichoke, season, and cook slowly in the oven for half-an-hour.

Indian Dinner-party

by Savitri Chowdhary

Michael Wickham

An Indian meal has its own pattern. First, a *juicy* curry of fish or vegetables (though here Mrs Chowdhary suggests a soup-like dish), served with rice *pulao*; then a more substantial meat or chicken curry, with plain rice, a milk curd dish, perhaps a lentil dish, a *dry* vegetable curry, and a green salad; then a small helping of one of the delicious, rich Indian sweets; then coffee and fresh fruit. If you want to drink (Indians, of course, usually don't), a white wine is best.

The flavouring often used in her receipts, *garam-masala*, is a mixture of ground spices (use a small coffee mill); 2 oz black peppercorns, 2 oz coriander seeds, 1½ oz caraway seeds, ½ oz ground cinnamon, 20 or more large cardamons. Here is Mrs Chowdhary's menu for a dinner party for six:

1st course

Dahi carhi (Similar to soup)

1 oz ghee
2 tablespoons besan (split pea flour) or 1½ tablespoons cornflour
2 teacups stale curd or yoghurt
2½ teacups milk and water
2 medium-sized onions
1 medium-sized potato or a few pieces of cauliflower
1 medium-sized capsicum (sweet pepper) (optional)
1½ teaspoons salt
1 teaspoon garam-masala
1 teaspoon turmeric
½ teaspoon chilli-powder or ¼ teaspoon cayenne pepper (optional)
a small amount of fresh dhania (coriander) or any other fresh herbs

Using a heavy saucepan, fry gently in *ghee* for a few minutes the sliced onions, sweet pepper and pieces of potato or cauliflower. Add tumeric, salt and the chilli-powder. Mix well and cover the saucepan until vegetables are tender.

Sieve the *besan* or cornflour into a mixing bowl and gradually mix in it the milk and water and the curd (or yoghurt). Pour this over the sizzling and tender vegetables. Bring to the boil and keep stirring until the *carhi* thickens slightly. After that it can either be cooked, well-covered, on low heat for 30 minutes, or in the oven (Regulo 5) for the same length of time. Mix in the *garam-masala* and the broken-up herbs and simmer for another 10 minutes. *Dahi carhi* should be served in soup-bowls whilst piping hot.

Rice pulao with mushrooms

¼ lb small white mushrooms
1 teacup best rice
1 oz ghee
1 teaspoon salt
6 cloves
¼ teaspoon turmeric (optional)
a few small pieces of cinnamon
a few cardamoms
2–2½ teacups hot water

Soak the rice for about half an hour. Fry gently, in *ghee*, the cloves, cinnamon, cardamoms and the turmeric for 1–2 minutes. Add well washed and lightly scraped mushrooms, and salt. Allow to sizzle for 5 minutes, then add rice. Fry gently and stir continuously for another few minutes. Add hot water. Bring to boil, then cover with a tight lid. Cook very slowly for 30 minutes; or after covering, the rice can be cooked in the oven (Regulo 4) for the same length of time.

2nd course

Pork or lamb curry

1½ lb lean meat (pork or lamb), cut in desired sized cubes
1 oz ghee
2 medium-sized onions
4 flakes of garlic
4 medium-sized tomatoes
1 teaspoon garam-masala
2 teaspoons salt
a small amount of fresh or dried Fenugreek or other desired herbs
1 full teaspoon turmeric
½ teaspoon or more chilli-powder or ½ teaspoon cayenne pepper (optional)
1–1½ teacups hot water

Fry gently the sliced onions and the minced garlic in the

ghee. Add the turmeric, salt, chilli-powder and the *garam-masala*. Allow to sizzle a little longer. Add the well-washed cubes of meat and fry gently for another 5 minutes. Cover the saucepan and cook on low heat for 45 minutes. Add sliced tomatoes and the hot water. Cover and cook slowly for 40 minutes more. Add the chopped herbs 10 minutes before removing from heat. If there is too much gravy, simmer it away a little, uncovered.

Potatoes and peas

12 *small new potatoes*
1 *oz ghee*
2 *medium-sized onions*
2 *teacups fresh or frozen peas*
4 *tomatoes (medium sized)*
a small amount of fresh dhania (coriander) or any other fresh herbs
2½ *teaspoons salt*
1 *teaspoons turmeric*
1 *teaspoons garam-masala*
½ *teaspoon chilli-powder or* ¼ *teaspoon cayenne pepper (optional)*
1 *tablespoon lemon juice*
1–2 *teacups hot water*

Fry sliced onion gently in a saucepan for a few minutes. Add turmeric, *garam-masala*, salt and the chilli-powder. Mix well, and then add sliced tomatoes, and potatoes (scraped, not peeled). Let these sizzle for 10 minutes, stirring frequently. Add peas, and after a few minutes pour in the hot water. Bring to the boil and then turn heat low. Cover and cook until peas and potatoes are tender (not broken), then add lemon juice. Simmer another 10 minutes. The tomato skins float and can be removed. Mix up in broken-up herbs just before finishing off.

Curried cauliflower

2 *lb cauliflower, weighed after the outside leaves have been removed*
1½ *oz ghee*
1 *medium-sized onion*
1 *medium-sized potato*
¼ *oz fresh or well-soaked root ginger*
1½ *teaspoons turmeric*
2 *teaspoons salt*
1 *teaspoon garam-masala*
½ *teaspoon or more chilli-powder or* ¼ *teaspoon cayenne pepper (optional)*

Using a large heavy frying-pan, fry gently the sliced onion and ginger in the *ghee* for 3–4 minutes. Add turmeric and chilli-powder and let it sizzle for a little while. Cut the cauliflower into thin 2-inch long pieces, keeping some of the stalk with the flower. Wash, drain and put the pieces in the sizzling mixture along with the cubes of potato, which should be scraped, not peeled.

Stir with a slice to avoid crushing. Cook gently, uncovered, for 10 minutes. Then add salt. Mix and cook for a little while longer, then cover with a loose lid and cook gently until the cauliflower is tender (not broken). Mix in the *garam-masala* and, if the curry is not dry enough, remove the lid and turn heat a little higher.

Puris (Indian fried bread)

This mixture will make 18 *puris*
3½ *teacups wholemeal flour*
½ *oz ghee*
1 *teaspoon salt*
a little more than a teacup of warm water
½ *lb fat, or its equivalent in oil, for frying*

Prepare the dough by mixing the hot *ghee* in the sieved flour, and after adding salt, gradually mixing it with warm water. The dough for *puris* should be fairly stiff and well-kneaded.

To shape the *puri*, take a little of the dough, make into a ball, then with the help of a little dry flour roll it out round and fairly thin. Repeat until all the *puris* are rolled; keep them separate from each other.

Using a deep chip-pan, heat the oil or fat nearly to smoking point and fry each *puri* separately, fairly quickly, on medium heat. Encourage it to rise by slightly pressing the sides with a slicer or turner after the *puri* is partially cooked, and splashing some of the hot fat from the pan on top of it. When the *puri* has risen (some only rise slightly), and is golden brown on both sides, it is ready. Drain well and place on a warm, shallow dish. After they have been fried, the *puris* can be kept warm in a very low oven for a little while.

3rd course

Rasgullas (syrupy sweetmeat)

2 *teacups sugar*
4 *teacups water*
3 *pints milk*
3 *tablespoons lemon juice*
1 *dessertspoon very fine semolina*
12 *small pieces broken-up lump sugar*
1½ *tablespoons rosewater or a few drops of other sweet flavouring*

To make soft milk cheese, boil the milk in a heavy aluminium saucepan and, when it comes to the top, pour in the lemon juice. Bring to boil once again and, when solid lumps have formed, strain them through a muslin bag, which should then be placed on a clean board. Keep the bag pressed with a heavy weight to get rid of all liquid. Then place the cheese on another board. Add the fine semolina, and pound and knead until it starts to become greasy. From this, form 12 round balls. Break each ball in half and place a small piece of sugar between, then press and shape together again.

Make the syrup by mixing sugar and water together, and boiling for 7 minutes on medium heat. Take out 1½ teacups of this thin syrup and keep it by you.

Place the *Rasgullas* in the syrup remaining in the saucepan. Bring to boil, then turn the heat low and keep boiling gently (uncovered), shaking saucepan frequently. Gradually add the syrup previously taken out, so that the *Rasgullas* are being cooked in thin syrup all the time. This will take about an hour and a quarter. Remove from heat and, when cool, add the flavouring. The *Rasgullas* are served warm or cold, with a little of the syrup. They can be prepared in advance.

Ranch Recipes

from Malabar Farm, Ohio by Mrs Louis Bromfield

Emergency lunches

These were born in days of acute distress, days such as happen to every one of us: the day when the husband announces blithely over the breakfast table, or calls gaily from the office. "There will be three or four or five extra for lunch today." Or when a distant cousin writes she will be there that day and hopes that it won't be an imposition on you if she brings the relatives with whom she is staying—aunts, uncles, cousins, and children: or when a friend passing through on his way here or there telephones that unfortunately he is travelling with friends, may he bring them?

The first of these recipes was given to us by a French friend who was visiting us, though it is of English origin. It is very easy and quick to do, and looks and tastes as if a world of gourmet cooking had gone into it.

Œufs Schenfield

4 hard-boiled eggs
1 pint cream
6 tablespoonfuls meat jelly (warmed until liquid)
Worcester sauce
anchovy paste
tarragon leaves

Chop the whites of the eggs very fine. Add to the yolks, anchovy paste and Worcester sauce to taste, and half the jelly, and mix well. Then add the whites, and the cream, which must be whipped lightly. Season with salt and pepper to taste. When this is well mixed, cover with the remainder of the jelly and tarragon leaves, place in a mould or bowl, and chill in the refrigerator. Serve cold.

With this we serve—and it is a very good combination—a green or mixed salad, with a salad dressing invented by one of us.

Salad dressing Malabar

15 tablespoonfuls olive oil
5 tablespoonfuls vinegar
1 sliver garlic
1 teaspoonful Worcester sauce
½ teaspoonful salt
½ teaspoonful pepper
2 teaspoonfuls mustard
1 pinch cayenne

Chill and shake well before using. The dressing can be kept in the refrigerator for future emergencies, so make as much as you like at a time.

For dessert we serve compote of fruit, or raw fruit, such as strawberries or raspberries and cream depending on the season or the supply on hand.

If this does not measure up to a full meal—and if there are members of the male sex about, it most probably won't—I suggest starting with a good substantial soup. Here is my husband's special recipe for potato soup and Vichyssoise (in one).

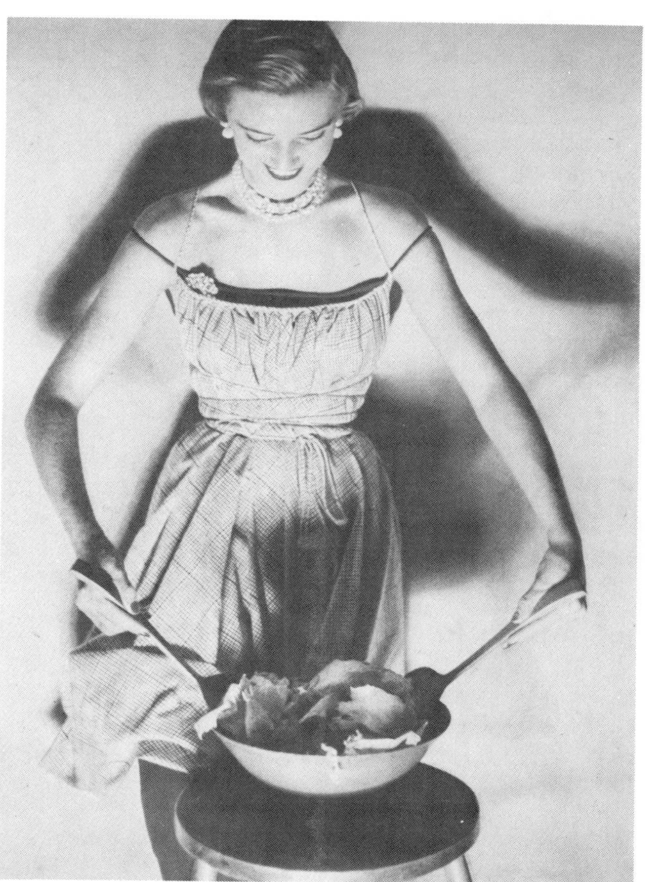

Norman Parkinson

Potato soup Malabar
Vichyssoise Malabar

8 medium-sized potatoes
3 medium-sized onions
1¼ cupfuls chopped celery
2 tablespoonfuls chopped parsley
2 tablespoonfuls chopped chives
2 tablespoonfuls chopped dill
2 quarts water

Boil together until the potatoes are cooked to pieces. Add a bay leaf for taste the last fifteen minutes of cooking. Before serving, add plenty of cream and butter. Season to taste. Top each serving with chopped chives and parsley.

To turn it into Vichyssoise, put through a sieve and cool in the refrigerator.

While still on quick and easy luncheons, I suggest a recipe we received from France a few weeks ago, which can be used as an entrée, and which looks and tastes like something worked and brooded over for days.

Cold fish soufflé

1 lb tomatoes
1 lb white fish (cooked)
½ pint cream
3 tablespoonfuls aspic in liquid form

Pound the fish and add the aspic. Season to taste, then whip in the cream. Place in mould on ice till frozen. When the soufflé is set, add tomatoes on top.

We like to serve asparagus or broccoli with this, with a sauce mousseline, the recipe for which also comes from France.

Sauce mousseline

2 eggs
4 oz butter
a dash of lemon
½ pint cream

Put the yolks of the eggs in a double saucepan, stirring over a low fire. Add little by little the butter, cream, lemon, and seasoning. If the sauce appears to be turning into oil (and there is danger of this), add a little cold water and stir briskly. At the last moment, add chopped parsley and the whites of the eggs, which must be beaten solid. Sauce mousseline is also very good on poached eggs, or fish—other easy entrées.

A good salad which is also a dessert is this cherry salad, with a fruit-salad dressing concocted by our cook Reba, who has a talent for such things.

Cherry salad

tin of cherries
roasted almonds

Drain and pit cherries, stuff them with almonds. Serve on crisp lettuce leaves with fruit-salad dressing. (Other nuts may be used in place of almonds.)

Fruit-salad dressing

2 eggs beaten well
½ cupful cherry juice
½ cupful lemon juice
½ cupful sugar
a pinch of salt

Cook the above ingredients in a double saucepan until thick. When ready to serve, add 1 cupful whipped cream. (The first four ingredients may be cooked and kept several days, and the cream added when used.) Orange juice or any other juice may be substituted for the cherry juice.

Quick Welsh rarebit

Place in a frying-pan a good-sized lump of butter and melt until brown. Then stir in, slowly, grated or finely cut cheese, stirring constantly with a fork. When cheese is melted, stir in cream until texture of mixture is about right to spread on toast. The cream should be heated before adding in order to prevent the cheese from separating. Then add pepper, Worcester sauce, and any other flavouring ingredients, and serve on very dry toast.

The whole trick of the dish is the speed and dexterity with which it is made. It should be ready within two or three minutes, after the cheese is added. If a Golden Buck is preferred, stir in a well-beaten egg. This does away with the hocus-pocus of double saucepan and chafing-dish. Rarebit for four persons is nearly the limit. In the case of a larger quantity, speed and dexterity lose out and the cheese may separate.

Keith Vaughan

Creole Cooking

by Sheila de Burlet

West Indian pastures do not produce the prime beef of Britain, so Creole meat dishes are usually lavishly seasoned with the pepper, aromatic barks, roots and herbs which grow in the estates and gardens of the West Indies. There is Pepper Pot, for instance, a combination of sucking pig, chicken, veal, goat and agouti, and indeed any flesh or fowl, but no fish. Pepper Pots improve with age, and the oldest known Pepper Pot is said to be rising seventy-five years old. It simmers succulently in the kitchen of a men's club in Trinidad. The essential ingredient which preserves the meat is cassareep, the concentrated juice extract of the cassava. Don't miss the chance to sample a Pepper Pot if you are lucky enough to discover one.

The best cooking is usually found in private houses—from local recipes devised by cooks of Spanish, French, Indian, African and British origin; but ask any local cook the exact amounts used and the answer will be: "I doesn't rightly know."

Rice is always served as a vegetable. Boiled in plenty of salted water, it should be turned out into a colander or sieve, and well washed under the kitchen tap (hot or cold, it does not matter which). Allow the rice to dry in a warm oven, still in the sieve. Even if the rice is going to be fried later, I always boil and dry it first to get every grain separate.

Rum is drunk extensively throughout the islands, and it varies enormously in taste and colour, from island to island, even from estate to estate. The finest rum is always bottled in the island of its origin.

Rum and soda or rum and ginger ale are both good drinks. A very dry rum or gin cocktail is the usual aperitif served before lunch or dinner, and should be drunk in one gulp while it has a good head of froth on it. It is simply a cocktail glass of dry rum or gin (no sugar whatever) with a dash of Angostura bitters, shaken with ice in a cocktail shaker, poured and drunk immediately. The following recipe is, however, for a traditional morning drink.

Rum punch

Mix, in the following proportions: One measure of sour (juice from fresh limes or lemons), two of sweet (a light syrup of sugar boiled with water, kept ready chilled for use; 4–6 oz sugar to 1 quart water), three of strong (rum), four of weak (crushed ice and water).

Add Angostura bitters, lime peel, a dusting of grated nutmeg, and a glacé cherry. Serve very cold in tall glasses. Another very good punch can be made using tinned Trinidad orange or grapefuit juice, which needs to be sweetened and diluted with water. Mix three-quarters of juice to one-quarter of rum.

Here is a menu for a typical West Indian meal:

Pumpkin Soup
Chicken Pelau
Citrus Salad or Fruit
Jamaican Blue Mountain Coffee

Pumpkin soup

2 lb pumpkin
2 tomatoes
1 onion
2 pints milk, or good stock
butter, pepper, salt

Peel the pumpkin, and cut up small, with the tomatoes and onion, in large saucepan. Do not add any liquid at all. Cook in a very slow oven for about two hours. When cooked, sieve the vegetables, add the hot milk or stock, a knob of butter, pepper and salt to taste.

Serve with small croûtons of fried bread.

Chicken pelau

1 roasting chicken
1 lb Patna rice
1 red pepper (or tinned red pimento)
green peas (1 lb cooked garden peas, or a packet of cooked frozen ones, or a small tin French petits pois)
a handful each of seedless raisins and sultanas
1 tablespoonful sugar
salt and cayenne pepper
butter

Boil the rice, rinse, and keep warm. Cook the chicken, whole or cut in pieces, in the butter and sugar. Remove the chicken when cooked, and keep it warm. Into the hot sweet butter stir the cooked rice, which should absorb all the fat. Add cayenne pepper to get the contrasting hot and sweet taste. Mix in the raisins, sultanas, pimento and peas, salt to taste. Bed the chicken on the dish of rice, or cut it up and mix in the pieces with the rice mixture.

Boiled chicken pelau
Using the same ingredients as above, except for the sugar, simmer the chicken in water until cooked. Boil the rice in the chicken stock, drain well, then add the other ingredients.

Citrus salad
A huge bowl of chilled grapefruit is excellent after pelau (elaborate puddings do not mix well with rum punch). Allow at least two grapefruit per person, choosing firm, fresh ones tinged, if possible, with green; avoid buying the tired flabby ones.

Cut in half, scoop out all the fruit, removing pips and pith, and sprinkle it with sugar. If fresh grapefruit are not available, do not despise the excellent tinned grapefruit imported from the West Indies, to which you can add tinned mandarins.

Tinned guavas, mangoes, and paw-paw each in a separate bowl would be a genuine island offering.

Now here are some other West Indian dishes that are family favourites with us.

Water melon salad
Cut the melon in half, and remove all the black seeds. Scoop out the pink inside, cut up roughly, sprinkle with sugar, and return to the green shell, or just serve the cut up fruit slightly chilled in a glass dish.

Pineapple
Choose one or more ripe pineapples. Cut off the top complete with leaves. Scoop out the fruit, chop it up, sprinkle with a little dry wine or sherry, and then mix it into ¼ pint whipped cream. Return to the pineapple shell, put the top back. Chill.

Stuffed avocado pears
Cut in half, remove stone, fill with shrimps, cover shrimps only with real mayonnaise, serve cold.

Stuffed crab backs
English sea crabs have to be used in lieu of the large local land crabs. Allowing one crab for each person, remove all the meat. Soften 2–4 oz butter, add a teaspoonful or more Worcester sauce, salt, cayenne pepper, and toasted crumbs. Mix, then add the crab meat. Stuff the shells. Bake for a few minutes, serve very hot. A minute quantity of minced pimento can be added if liked. Alternatively, this whole mixture can be heated in an already-baked pastry flan.

Salt fish pie
1½ lb salt fish (dried salt cod, or smoked haddock mixed with the cod)
2 lb cooked potatoes
4 hard-boiled eggs
1 lb each onions (optional) and tomatoes
¼ pint (or less) good olive oil
milk
Cook, bone and flake the fish. Cover the bottom of a deep, well-greased pie dish with sliced potatoes, then successive layers of fish, raw onion rings, hard-boiled eggs sliced, and tomatoes sliced. Repeat layers until dish is three-quarters full. Pour in olive oil and a little milk. Cover pie with soft mashed potatoes. Bake about twenty minutes and serve sizzling hot.

Aubergine pie
1 or 2 egg plants
1 lb minced beef or veal
1 small onion chopped up finely
1 pint thick tomato purée
salt and pepper
Cut the egg plant in slices about ¼ inch thick. Fry in a little olive oil, and then put the pieces at the bottom of a fireproof dish. Fry the onion until golden brown, and add the mince, stirring the two together. When the meat is cooked, put it on top of the egg plant. Add the tomato purée. Bake in a hot oven for about fifteen minutes. Grated cheese can be added if liked.

To make the tomato purée, cook (without any water at all) a pound of ripe tomatoes, sprinkled with a little sugar, salt and pepper, a bay leaf, and a bruised clove of garlic which should be removed when the tomatoes are sieved. Tinned tomato purée can be used instead of fresh purée.

Mocca cream pudding
This is very rich and requires no cooking at all. It must, however, be put in a refrigerator or a very cold larder for a couple of hours before it is required.
4 oz castor sugar
4 oz butter
2 eggs
strong coffee (about 2 tablespoons)
sponge fingers
sherry
¼ pint pouring cream
Line a pudding basin with sponge fingers, and sprinkle with sherry. Cream the sugar and butter very well, add the lightly beaten eggs one at a time, always beating well, add the coffee slowly, beating until the mixture is soft. Pour into the lined basin and top with more sponge cake. Press down with a plate. Chill until required, when it should be turned out and covered with cream. Grate some chocolate over top.

Bananes au fromage
Make a white sauce, add plenty of grated cheese, bake whole bananas covered with sauce.

Guava jelly
This can be bought in tins, and is delicious on hot buttered toast, and also with biscuits and cheese. Guava cheese is not a cheese at all, but a sweet rather like fudge.

Don't Be Frightened of the Snails

by John Coates

Marc

Abroad is different. That is its charm. The sun and the snow are different: the beds and the by-laws: the drink and the food . . .

My favourite part of abroad is France. It is also the nearest and easiest to get to. Having filled in a form for your passport, another for your money, another for your foreign touring documents, another for your insurance, and another for vouchers in case your car breaks down abroad, all you have to do is drive to Dover and wait. Sooner or later you will get to France. The French, in their infinite willingness to make the English feel at home, have invented a special form for cross-channel passengers. It is made of thin cardboard, and it is quite easy to fill in, as the information required—except for the date—is already in your passport. You just have to copy it out. Either pencil or ink is accepted. A similar form—again you have to be careful of the date—permits you to leave France on your way back.

Perhaps you think I have invented the fact that this form is supplied solely to make the English feel at home. Perhaps you think that the French, being notoriously a logical race, wish to keep a check on their tourists, and that in some dim Ministry in Paris a man in a black apron is noting down in a ledger when you arrived in France and when you left. Please don't delude yourself. What they do with the forms I don't know; but if you arrive in Dunkirk at dawn you will be asked to complete one. If you drive into Belgium an hour later there is no form for you. If you return to France from Luxembourg at lunchtime there is still no form. If you leave by Basle at midnight and return via Strasbourg, the next day there is no record on thin cardboard of your exit and entry. The forms are kept solely at cross-channel ports. For in their willingness to make the English feel at home the French are amending their by-laws. This is but one example. There are others. The English passion for undressing on the beach instead of in a *cabine* is already catered for. It is only a matter of time before something is done about the sale of alcohol.

All this I can accept without complaint. But when it comes to food, the matter is too serious to be passed over in silence. Abroad, the food is different—*was* different anyway. At my lycée I was a *demi-pensionnaire*. The *pensionnaires* slept at school: the *externes* went home for lunch. The *demi-pensionnaires* were in between. They slept at home, but had lunch at school. Quite a different lunch from the one I used to get at my English prep school. To start with, it was palatable. First we had soup in a soup-plate. (In five years at an English prep school I never had soup for lunch.) Then we had what has recently come to be known as a main dish on a dinner-plate. Then we turned over the dinner-plate and had a pudding on its reverse. Perhaps I should explain that the tables were scrubbed. But in any case the food was so good that the plates were clean and the sauces mopped up with bread by the time we turned them over. With this went a glass of red wine. For my first few days as a *demi-pensionnaire* I swopped my wine for a second helping of pudding. Then I learnt better; and, fortunately or unfortunately, I have had a taste for wine ever since.

In France, then, I learnt as a schoolboy that the food was different and palatable. Later I learnt that it was cheap and frequently exquisite. As an impecunious undergraduate I could afford to eat in the Pyramide et Point at Vienne. On my first visit there I ate—as everyone should—*gratin de queues d'écrevisses*, and my enjoyment was only marred by my English companion's inability to finish up his sauce. He had been at school in England, poor man, and had been taught that it was impolite to clean his plate. He had kindly driven me from Calais, so I had to sit in silence—or almost in silence—while his share of the most delicious part of one of the most delicious meals I have ever had was sent back to the kitchen as inedible.

In the years of freedom allowed me—they were all too few, now I come to add them up—I ate in many parts of France. For value there was the Hotel Fourcade at Castelnaudry where the meal cost 18 francs, *boisson comprise*. (The franc was about 120 to the pound in those days.) Towards

the end of the meal a *foie gras truffé* about the size of a two-pound loaf was put on the table. . . . Perhaps the host reckoned that we had eaten so much by then that we couldn't still be hungry. . . . Perhaps we even paid a small supplement for what we could eat of the loaf. For a sort of rococo Edwardian elegance lingering on into the thirties, there was the Chapon Fin at Bordeaux. For private hospitality on the supreme scale there was the lunch I ate during the vintage at a small château in the Medoc country. It began at one o'clock and it ended at half past six. At about two, one of our party began to express his thanks for the excellent meal he had received, only to be told that till then we had been sampling what the vintagers were eating outside. We drank eleven clarets and—to show there was no narrow sectarianism—five or six burgundies. We drank them from the same glass. Wine growers aren't fussy about glasses; they merely appreciate wine.

The food I ate in France during these years was French food, different from English food. In the words of my Yorkshire nanny who kept house in France, and who taught a succession of French cooks to speak English, it was messed-up food. She meant it was cooked with sauces; and nanny didn't approve of mopping up sauces with bits of bread. Nanny, like a number of pipe-smoking Englishmen, didn't approve of sauces at all—except mint sauce. She liked to see what she was eating. If what she was eating happened to be dull, there was to her something slightly immoral in trying to disguise that dullness with a sauce. A number of pipe-smoking Englishmen have an oddly similar view about a woman's face and make-up. Nanny even went so far as to prophesy that sauces would do me no good. But apart from the time I ate a surfeit of lampreys in sauce and had to go without lunch the next day, they have never done me any harm. Perhaps it was lampreys rather than the sauce, and perhaps people called John should be careful of lampreys.

All this was in the old days. Those cooks to whom nanny made her meaning unmistakably clear in louder and louder English have passed on the news. Those waiters and waitresses who have watched pained, pipe-smoking Englishmen fumbling with their forks in the sauce for something recognizable and solid, have helped to spread it. The English don't like sauces. To an Englishman, food with a sauce is messed-up food. It isn't healthy. It is quite possibly poisoned. So the French, in their determination to make the English feel at home at all costs, have—almost—banished the sauce. I admit it still exists. They still serve *gratin de queues d'écrevisses* at Vienne. But without wine, coffee or a tip the meal cost two thousand eight hundred francs the last time I passed through; and now that I am a modestly successful writer on a travel allowance instead of an impecunious undergraduate, I can't afford to eat there. However, at Sept-Saulx, the other side of Reims (and away from the main road with GB cars passing up and down, of course), you can eat chicken with a sauce made of tarragon, champagne and cream at a price even Englishmen can afford. But don't tell too many people.

Sauces, then, aren't banned by law. They are still made at places difficult of access to Englishmen for one reason or another. But all over France, in the districts Englishmen frequent—and, alas, they frequent most districts—sauces are discreetly hidden away. One can't blame the French. The Englishman comes in such numbers that even with his meagre travel allowance he is a valuable industry. Twin beds have been imported for him. Indoor sanitation has been installed for him. A rather better whisky than he gets at home has been brought specially from Scotland for him. And now at last, with ruthless logic, large slabs of ungarnished meat are available for him in the restaurants all over France. Beef, veal and pork; steaks, chops and cutlets; *entrecôtes, filets* and *escalopes*; irrespective of the animal and irrespective of the language, it is always meat, visibly meat. Grilled or fried. Sauceless. Healthy in English eyes. Not messed-up. Stark. Bare. Plain. Meat. With a few fried potatoes to make it and you thoroughly at home.

I have tried complaining about it. I have read through a list of twenty different slabs of meat, with hors d'œuvres on top and ice cream below, and asked for the menu French people get. I have offered to teach the chef how to make a sauce. I have asked for what the owner is going to eat. Waiters have looked at me with incomprehension. I am an Englishman. One of those slabs of meat must surely be to my taste.

And so sadly I say to you: don't be frightened of the snails. Go to France and feel perfectly at home. The chances are that snails won't be on the menu at all. And if they are the chances are you could have bought the same tin yourself at your local grocers. They have to come out of a tin, of course; the new chef doesn't know how to cook snails. Abroad in France—the food is no longer different.

L'Art d'Accommoder les Restes

by Yvonne Arnaud

This phrase—in a letter in 1955 from Yvonne Arnaud the famous French actress—sums up an important part of her views on cooking. Her own translation?

"Well, you know, it is sort of . . . sort of . . . well, you put something you 'ave with something else and make something different *entirely*. But (voice rising triumphantly) much *more* so you understand"

Eric

Miss Yvonne Arnaud, Frenchwoman to the last meticulous syllable of the most complicated phrase, has a natural preference for the calm order and sequence of the French meal. For her, if she could choose, would be the *sole Mornay—escalope de veau—haricots verts—salade—fromage—dessert* kind of meal, served with wine and without haste.

But with an English husband, forty years in this country behind her, and a busy life in the theatre, she has adopted—with Gallic reservations—our native liking for something less formal. "You know," she said, "a lot of English food is terrible, but some have the talent for what you call the pot luck. A lot of Englishwomen serve a better meal when fifteen people arrive suddenly than they do for a dinner party they worry about for weeks."

Miss Arnaud, at the Surrey farmhouse where she lives with her husband, likes to be ready for any culinary emergency, using frig and larder not merely as repositories for left-overs, but as store-cupboards for providing the ingredients for the after-theatre meal, or the Sunday when friends call unexpectedly.

Making a good start

Among things she usually has handy, for instance, is a good *pâté maison*. This will keep for a week or more. Here is a good standard recipe, though she may vary it by using chicken livers, rabbit or game, whatever she has by her—as well as, or instead of, calves' livers.

Wash, dry and remove veins from 1 lb calves' livers: then cut in thick slices. Put them in a dish and sprinkle with salt, fresh ground pepper, a little rubbed thyme, a bay leaf. Pour over a small glass of sherry and leave to marinade for an hour, turning occasionally. Fry 1 tablespoon of finely chopped onion in bacon fat without browning. Drain liver and add to pan, and "seal" quickly. Put all through the mincer when it is cool. Rub an earthenware dish with garlic, pack in the liver and pour in the strained marinade mixture. Cover with greaseproof paper, put lid on closely, and cook for 30–40 minutes. When cold, cover with a layer of melted bacon fat or aspic jelly.

"This," says Miss Arnaud, "is a delicious start to a meal but make sure you take the *pâté* from the frig at least an hour before you are going to eat it and be certain the toast you serve with it is thin, crisp and piping hot."

Fish dishes

A tin of tunny-fish is a standby always in the cupboard. For a hungry party, she flakes a couple of tins of the fish into a bowl, adds chopped celery and apples, cubed cooked potato, sprigs of cold cooked cauliflower, a tin of red Spanish pimentos, slices of skinned tomato—in fact anything to hand—and mixes all with mayonnaise.

Another item always in the store cupboard is a tin or two of crawfish or lobster. These she uses to make a hot tart which can be eaten either as a beginning to a meal, or as a main dish if a good *pâté* is eaten first and a salad after. First you line a pie tin with rich, short pastry and then warm the pounded crawfish in butter, seasoned with a little cayenne and a drop of lemon juice. Fill the case, make a pastry lid, and bake as for any tart.

She also uses tunny-fish (one of the few tinned foods she approves of), with some radishes and curls of crisp butter, to make an excellent hors d'œuvre.

Ways with eggs

Unlike most Frenchwomen she says she *loathes* soup in any form, she makes it most reluctantly for her English husband, and refuses to suggest any recipes for this "disgusting abomination".

Eggs however, are another matter, and cause great animation in discussion. To make one of her favourite quick supper dishes she always has on hand (a) *œufs mollets,* and (b) a tin of artichoke bottoms.

Put the eggs in cold water, bring to boil and boil briskly for five minutes. Plunge into cold water for 20 minutes, (or longer, as suits you), then shell. They are firm outside, but soft inside. Put an artichoke bottom in a buttered little fireproof dish. Add another shaving of butter and a thin slice of *pâté de foie gras*. Put on top an *œuf mollet* and pour on a little cheese sauce. Warm in oven, then put under grill for two minutes.

Two-day vegetables

Miss Arnaud halves labour and *ennui* with vegetables by cooking enough to have deliberate left-overs for the next day. She has many winning ways with such remains: she may, for instance, turn them into exciting little pancakes to serve with a rather plain meat dish, or, in the French way, as a course in themselves.

Use sliced parsnips, carrots, vegetable marrow, celery, onion, sprigs of cauliflower; dip the pieces in good white sauce (always a small jar in the frig), then in breadcrumbs, then in beaten egg, mixed with one teaspoon of water, then in more breadcrumbs. Fry quickly in deep hot fat and serve at once.

In winter, she is fond of white endive, poached, wrapped in slices of ham, garnished with cheese sauce and eaten as a main dish. Having left several ungarnished she produces them in a moment next day as an extra vegetable, warmed in a fireproof dish, dotted with shavings of butter and breadcrumbs, and browned under the grill at the last moment.

If a variety of vegetables is left over, Miss Arnaud makes a mixed dish this way:

First fry a little onion in butter, then add a couple of skinned, sliced tomatoes. When they are soft, add the chopped, lightly cooked vegetables, and put all together in a casserole and mix gently over a low flame. Season carefully. You can also add a little macaroni and chopped cold meat if you have them among the left-overs.

Filling salads

Miss Arnaud is full of resource concerning cold dishes—perhaps for Sunday night supper when the others have had soup (not Miss Arnaud), or a hot egg dish. Cold meat or chicken or game she likes with coleslaw (she calls it cold slaw). To make it, she cuts a fresh savoy cabbage into long fine shreds and mixes it with mayonnaise (ready in the larder). On top she puts some finely grated carrot and quite a lot of chopped nuts, usually almonds. She adds: "I also can make it with cut celery or a little beetroot or finely chopped green peppers."

Another of her salad ideas is stuffed apples. She cores some fine big well-flavoured specimens and fills the centre with a mixture of finely chopped celery, beetroot, torn lettuce mixed with mayonnaise. Sometimes she adds a little chopped chicken if there is any.

Cooking Hazards

by Elizabeth David

Rice

Every amateur cook, however gifted and diligent, has some weak spot, some gap in her knowledge or experience which to anyone critical of her own achievements can be annoying and humiliating. To some it may be a question of not being able to get a roast precisely right; to others, a cream sauce which only spasmodically comes off; and even to those who admit to having little talent for pastry or cakes, it is irritating to be defeated by a process which to others appears so effortless. Some regard the confection of a mayonnaise as the easiest thing in the world, some with terror and despair. There are those who have a talent for perfect rice dishes, while for others the stuff invariably turns to a mush. And it is no coincidence that when dishes go wrong, it nearly always happens when they are cooked for guests, and consequently in larger quantities than those with which one is accustomed to dealing.

Sometimes this is due to something so obvious as cooking for eight in the same utensils as those normally used for four, or to the cook having overlooked the fact that even a good-tempered dish like a meat and wine stew may disloyally change its character and appearance, losing all its professional-looking finish, if kept waiting too long in the oven. Or perhaps the joint, twice as large as usual, has been cooked twice as long, whereas what should really have been taken into consideration was not the weight but the shape and thickness of the joint.

Sometimes, of course, the trouble is more psychological than technical. Take rice, for example. Because a rice dish has gone wrong once, no doubt because the cook had no experience of cooking the particular rice she was using, she will ever after be scared stiff of making it. There *is* something rather specifically dismal about a failed rice dish. And I would never advise anybody to cook a risotto for a dinner party which had to be managed single-handed, because it is a bad dish to keep waiting. But there are so many other ways of cooking rice and some of them appear to be specially designed for the kind of meals we all cook these days—meals consisting of dishes which simply must not be of the kind requiring split-second timing. Good quality rice is essential, though. The two kinds to look for are the long-grained Patna type and the round-grained Piedmontese rice called Avorio or Arborio, which has a hard core in the centre of the grain so that it is almost impossible to ruin by overcooking. The flavour of this Piedmontese rice is also much more pronounced than that of the Patna type, which makes it a good one to use when the rice itself, rather than any flavouring or sauce, is the main point of the dish.

All the following recipes are ones in which the rice can be kept waiting, not indefinitely it is true, but long enough to give you a chance to have a drink before your meal, without keeping an eye on the stove.

A good point to remember about the boiling of rice is that ten times the volume of water to that of rice is an ample quantity to calculate. So measure the rice in a cup or glass, and then reckon the amount of water accordingly.

Chicken pilau (1)

For four to six people the ingredients are two scant teacups (8 to 9 oz) of Patna long-grain rice; 3 teacups of chicken stock from which the fat should not be removed, since it helps to lubricate the rice; salt, pepper, about a teaspoon of mixed spices (cardamon seeds, a scrap of grated green ginger root, allspice, mace, pepper, cumin seeds or whatever mixture happens to suit your taste); approximately a cupful of meat from a cooked chicken cut from the bone into neat little strips.

Two-thirds fill with water a very large saucepan of about a gallon capacity. Bring it to the boil and throw in a heaped tablespoon of salt, then the rice. Boil it steadily for exactly 7 minutes after the water has come back to the boil. Drain the rice into a small mesh sieve or colander in which the holes are not so large as to let through the grains of rice, for being only partly cooked, they are not yet swollen. Hold the colander under the cold tap and rinse until the water runs clear. Turn the rice into an earthenware pot or other fairly deep fireproof dish, of about 3-pint capacity. Stir in the spices all pounded together—the quantity can be increased if you like—and add the chicken meat and the hot stock. Bring just to simmering point on top of the stove. Have ready a clean, dry, folded linen teacloth and put this over the rice. Cover with the lid of the pot. Put in the centre of a low oven, preheated to Gas No. 3, 330° F. In just 20 minutes' time the rice should be swollen and tender,

Elizabeth David in her kitchen
John Ward

all the liquid absorbed. The rice is ready to serve on a heated shallow dish with, if you like, a few slivers of almonds or some pine nuts lightly browned in the oven on the top, and some chutney and lemon separately. It will, or should, serve six people as a first course, four if it is the chief dish.

Be sure that your teacloth is one which has been properly rinsed when it was washed and does not smell of soap powder or detergent, for there is a risk of this communicating itself to the rice.

If the dish has to be kept waiting, take it from the oven once it is ready, but leave it covered with its cloth and its lid. For 10 minutes at least it will keep hot without spoiling. But do not attempt this system of cooking with poor quality, small grain pudding rice, nor with any of the American patent rices for which the amounts of liquid to rice and the cooking times are given on the packets.

Chicken pilau (2)

Supposing that your oven is occupied by another dish cooking at a temperature much higher or lower than the one at which the pilau is to cook, here is another method, using the same ingredients.

Boil your rice for ten minutes instead of seven, rinse and drain it. Heat an ounce of butter, or a tablespoon of oil, in a pot or bowl or saucepan which will stand inside another one. Put in the pieces of chicken and, on top, the rice into which you have stirred the seasoning and spices. Pour in, for 2 cups of rice measured before cooking, one cup of hot stock, and another tablespoon of butter or oil. Cover with a folded teacloth and a lid. Steam in your improvised *bain marie* for about half an hour.

This is also an excellent method for cooking moist rice to serve with a meat or chicken dish.

If you want your rice coloured and spiced with saffron, pound up about half a dozen of the little filaments, pour the warmed stock over them before you start cooking the rice, and strain them off when you add the stock to the rice.

Lobster with cream sauce and rice

Here is a lovely dish for a dinner party, for which all the main preparations can be made in advance.

For a first course dish for four people allow 1 large cooked lobster or crawfish, a hen one if possible, for the coral improves the flavour of the sauce; 2 oz of long-grain Patna rice; and, for the sauce, 3 oz of butter, 2 level tablespoons of flour, ½ pint of milk, 4 tablespoons of white wine or dry Vermouth, ¼ pint of cream, seasonings, breadcrumbs.

Melt 1½ oz of the butter in a thick saucepan, stir in the flour off the fire; when smooth add the heated wine or Vermouth and then a little of the milk, also heated. Return to the fire, gradually adding the rest of the milk, stirring all the time. Season with a little salt, freshly milled pepper, nutmeg and a scrap of cayenne. Turn the flame very low and leave the sauce cooking over an asbestos mat.

If you have a hen lobster, extract the coral and the creamy parts from the shell and pound them up with another ounce of the butter. Cut all the white flesh of the lobster into small neat pieces.

When the sauce has been gently cooking for about 10 to 15 minutes add the cream and let it cook another 5 minutes. Now stir in the butter and coral mixture. After another couple of minutes press the sauce through a sieve. Return it to a clean saucepan and, if it is being made in advance, cover the sauce with a film of melted butter, which will prevent the formation of a skin on the top.

Cook your rice in plenty of boiling salted water for 7 minutes only, rinse and strain it quite dry.

When the time comes to finish cooking the dish, allow 10 to 15 minutes for heating the sauce and 20 minutes for the dish to bake in the oven. The sauce should be re-heated with the pan standing in another one containing hot water. When it is hot, stir in the lobster flesh. Taste for seasoning.

Have a shallow buttered *gratin* dish ready. Spread the rice at the bottom. On top pour the lobster mixture, without disturbing the layer of rice. As with all *gratin* dishes, the dish itself should be quite full to the top. Strew fine, pale golden breadcrumbs over the mixture; add the remaining half ounce or so of the butter in little knobs. Heat in a low oven, Gas No. 2, 310° F., for 15 to 20 minutes. At the end of this time the rice will be quite tender, and because it has been so slowly heated in the cream sauce the lobster will not have toughened and dried as it does when re-heated too abruptly; but do not be tempted to put more rice or to make a thicker sauce—you will get a stodgy dish.

To get a good glazed surface on the top of the dish, it can be put under a hot grill for a minute or so until it is blistering and bubbling. If you are going to make this dish in larger quantities, make sure you have the appropriate size of dish, or do it in two dishes rather than cram it into one which is too deep.

Rice with cheese sauce

This is a first course adapted from an Italian one—one in which the sauce, being a *fondue* of cheese and eggs, is just the kind of thing which turns malicious when you do it for guests, either refusing to thicken, or curdling when you try to hurry it up. So instead of this unreliable mixture, make a cream sauce strongly flavoured with Gruyère or Parmesan cheese. The rice is cooked *in bianco*—in other words, plainly boiled.

Ingredients for four good helpings are: 10 oz of round grain Piedmontese Avorio rice and, for the sauce, 1½ oz butter, 1 level tablespoon of flour, ½ pint of milk, ¼ pint single cream, 3 oz of coarsely grated Gruyère cheese or 2 oz of grated Parmesan, salt, pepper and nutmeg.

The cream sauce can be made in advance in the way described for the lobster recipe above, and left until it is needed, with a film of butter over the top. It must be re-heated in a *bain marie*, and the cheese added and stirred smooth when the sauce is hot. See that it is rather highly seasoned, and leave it with the water simmering very gently underneath until you are ready for it.

The rice is cooked in approximately 10 times its volume of water, with 1½ tablespoons of salt. Avorio rice takes longer to boil than Patna—about 18 minutes. Rinse under the tap and drain in a colander. Have ready a lightly buttered soufflé dish, cake tin, or fireproof bowl. Put your cooked rice into this; on the top put a folded teacloth. Put it in the oven, turned right down to its lowest temperature. There you can safely leave it for 15 to 20 minutes, before turning it out on a shallow and well heated dish and pouring the sauce over and round it.

Rice with prawns and cream sauce

This is a little dish which can be cooked even in the most minuscule kitchenette, for the initial preparation of the ingredients requires no space, and the prawn sauce is made in less time than it takes to describe it.

Suppose the dish is for just two people as a main course, to be followed by a salad and a sweet: measure out a full teacup, about 6 oz, of Patna rice, and throw it into a saucepan containing 10 cups of boiling water to which you have added 1 tablespoon of salt and, after the water comes back to the boil, a tablespoon of olive oil, which helps to disperse the scum and prevent the water from boiling over. Boil for 13 to 15 minutes. Rinse and strain as usual in a colander. Turn into a lightly oiled or buttered tin or small soufflé dish, cover with a folded cloth and leave in the lowest possible oven, as described in the recipe above, while you attend to the prawn mixture.

For this you need about 6 oz of peeled prawns (you can buy 4 oz and 2 oz packets of frozen prawns which usually have a better flavour than the ubiquitous scampi). Preferably they should be thawed out by the time you start to cook them, and sprinkled with lemon juice, pepper and nutmeg. Probably no salt will be needed.

Heat $1\frac{1}{2}$ oz of butter in a small, thick frying-pan. In this cook the prawns, very gently, for a minute or so. Pour a small glass of brandy, 4 to 6 tablespoons, into a soup ladle or little saucepan. Warm it over a low flame. Catch light to it. Pour it flaming over the prawns. Shake and rotate the pan so that the flames spread, and when they go out, turn the heat low and let the mixture simmer a couple of minutes so that the brandy loses its crude taste. Increase the heat again, pour in a scant quarter pint of thick cream, let it bubble until it starts to thicken, again shaking the pan and spooning the cream up and round. Stir in a little chopped parsley. Turn your prepared rice out on to a hot dish and pour the prawn mixture over and round it.

Roasting

You know that old saying about people being born roasting cooks. Personally, I don't believe a word of it. Brillat-Savarin, who was responsible for spreading this and a good many other arbitrary maxims (the one about a meal without cheese being like a beautiful woman with one eye has been a splendid gift to the cheese manufacturers, but could it have a rest now?), was a superb and original writer about culinary matters, but was no practising cook. As a matter of fact he never pretended to be. And in one of Carême's books published a few years after Brillat-Savarin's celebrated *Physiologie du Goût* there is a reference to the fallacy contained in the statement that one is *né rôtisseur*. Carême, the greatest professional cook of his time, considered that a good roasting cook was only produced by a combination of great practical experience and the most profound study of the subject.

In England, a vast deal of moonshine is talked and written about this branch of cookery. Englishwomen are brought up to believe that an instinctive knowledge of the art of roasting is part of their birthright; to produce an unsuccessfully roasted joint means disgrace, followed by a sad case of guilt and the future avoidance, whenever possible, of the performance of this English rite. Before us rise shades of our grandmothers and their faithful cooks who, so we are always being told, set superbly roasted joints upon the table twice a day for seven days a week. So one would hope, with all that experience. But, in fact, did they? Have the people who write so nostalgically of the food of a past age ever had any experience of the rigours of English country house cookery or first-hand knowledge of the conditions prevailing in the basement kitchens of a Victorian town house? Have they read the cookery books of the period and, if so, how do they explain the suspiciously large number of recipes for dealing with the remains of undercooked roast mutton and overcooked roast beef?

In any case, well or badly cooked, we must remember that these were joints on a large scale such as few families nowadays need or can afford. Little bits of rolled beef ribs and half legs of lamb now constitute the Sunday joint in thousands of households; fast roasting is unsuitable to these small pieces and even the most experienced carver is hard put to it to make anything of them. No wonder we are obliged to torment ourselves preparing mountains of vegetables and filling puddings to make up for the inadequacy of the meat.

The fact is that the number of *small* joints which make presentable roasts *on the bone* is pretty limited. Birds, being as it were complete in themselves, are another matter. Even so, a well roasted chicken or duck with a crisp golden skin and moist, juicy flesh are not so common as one might expect they would be. But this is because so often they are either kept waiting or warmed up, and although we may think ourselves a nation of born roasters we do not yet appear to have got round to understanding that, of all forms of cookery, a roast is least suited to these treatments.

One day I was lunching unusually early in one of our London restaurants well known for its fine roast meats. I ate some most perfectly cooked saddle of lamb. A few weeks later, having arrived at the same restaurant for lunch at 1.30 instead of 12.30, I ordered the same dish. It was lifeless, flabby, insipid. What else can you expect when a joint is kept in a warming dish for an hour or two?

As for the vegetables which usually accompany a roast, the potatoes can nearly always be flavoured in some way with the lovely fat and juices which come from the meat itself, and this is when potatoes really do come into their own. Green vegetables I rarely serve with a roast. They are not relevant.

Roast wing rib of beef

Having bought, say, a 5 to $5\frac{1}{2}$ lb piece of wing rib on the bone (much less than this does not make a successful roast), place it on a grid standing in a roomy baking tin. The grid is important, for it keeps the meat from stewing in its own fat; it is also important to remove the joint from the refrigerator, if you have been obliged to keep it there overnight, several hours before cooking time. Preheat the oven to a moderate heat, Gas no. 4, 355° F. Brush the top surface of the meat with olive oil. No other fat is necessary. Above all, no mixed-up fat saved from the past seventeen years of roasting. Place the meat in the centre of the oven and leave it completely alone for a whole hour. Then turn it over. Cook another one and a quarter hours if you like the beef *very* underdone all through, one and a half hours if you like it well done on the outside and red in the centre and one and three-quarters if you want it well done, and red only in a small patch right in the middle of each slice. Remove the beef to the hot serving dish and let it stand for a few minutes before starting on the carving.

Potatoes boiled in their skins and already all but cooked, then peeled and halved lengthways, can be nicely roasted in the fat underneath the meat during the last 1¼ hours of cooking. They will emerge pale golden, soft inside and just crisp on the outside.

I cannot see myself that any sauce, other than the lovely and plentiful juice which comes from the meat as you carve it, can be needed, but if you feel you must have one, probably the nicest is the traditional horseradish—a very mild and creamy one rather than the more usual ferociously hot concoction. The comparatively slow roasting, no basting method of this recipe is unorthodox by cookery school rules. That it is the method which ensures the retention of the maximum of natural juice in the meat you can see for yourself by the very small amount which has run into the roasting tin by the end of the cooking time.

Roast loin of pork with wine and herbs

Pork being, like duck, a fat meat, is best moistened with stock or wine rather than any extra fat, and should preferably be slow roasted. It is an easy meat to cook, for it is not spoilt if left a little longer than the specified time.

For a small pork roast, the neck end of the loin, comprising seven or eight cutlets, is admirable. It is excellent cold if it is not all eaten at one meal. Get the butcher to pare off the rind, without removing any of the fat unless the joint happens to be a very fat one, and to chine the bones.

Rub the meat well with salt, pour a glass (4 to 6 oz) of red or white wine over it, strew it with a little thyme or marjoram and a few slivers of garlic, and leave to steep for a minimum of two hours.

Put the meat fat side up, and covered with oiled paper or foil, into a baking tin with the rind underneath and the marinade poured over. Cook it in a preheated moderate oven, Gas no. 4, 355° F., simply checking from time to time that the liquid is not drying up. If it is, add a little warm stock or water. After an hour's cooking, remove the paper and have ready 2 tablespoons of chopped parsley mixed with 2 tablespoons of fine breadcrumbs. Spread this mixture over the fat side of the pork, pressing it gently down with a knife. Lower the oven to Gas no. 2, 310° F., and cook for another 40 minutes, basting it now and again with its own liquid. The breadcrumbs and parsley will form a nice golden coating.

The best potato dish to serve with this is a very smooth purée, rather runny, which you put into a deepish dish, pouring all round the edges a ring of the delicious wine and herb-scented juices from the pork. In France a dish of this potato purée and meat gravy is sometimes served as a separate course, the meat itself coming afterwards, either hot or cold, with a green salad. As a matter of fact roast pork is, I think, much better when cold than it is hot.

Roast duck

A plain roast duck is one of the most excellent of dishes but one of the most difficult of all roasts to get quite right; for if the breast is properly cooked and still just pink inside, the legs are almost bound to be uneatably underdone. If the bird is only for rather small helpings for three or four people this doesn't matter, for only the breast and wings are served, carved into elegant long pieces, the legs being kept and re-cooked for a second dish next day. But if the whole duck is to be eaten at one meal then the legs must be properly cooked as well. In either case it seems preferable to me to roast the bird slowly, and during the process to get rid of at least some of the excess fat.

Suppose you have bought a full grown 5 lb duck which, when drawn and dressed, will weigh about 3 lb, start off by making a stock as follows: put the giblets (but not the liver) in a small saucepan with, if possible, 2 or 3 tablespoons of white wine or Vermouth; a small sliced onion, a little piece of carrot and a chopped, unpeeled tomato. Let the wine bubble and reduce for a couple of minutes. Add a little salt and a bouquet of herbs including parsley, thyme and celery leaves. Cover with three-quarters of a pint of water and allow it to simmer gently for an hour or so.

To cook the duck, turn on the oven low, to Gas no. 3, 330° F. If the duck has been trussed with a wooden skewer thrust through the legs and its tail and rearing up in the air, remove the skewer so that the duck lies flat. Rub it all over with olive oil. Put it *on its side* in the roasting tin, and leave it to cook, uncovered, for 30 minutes.

Now pour from the tin all the fat which has run out. Turn the bird over on to its other side. Over it pour half a pint of the strained stock, hot. Leave it for another 30 minutes.

Turn it breast upwards and cook another 10 minutes, for the skin of the breast to brown, and pour off the stock to make a sauce as follows: in a wide shallow pan melt a finely chopped shallot in half an ounce of butter; chop the liver, which should have been steeping in warm, salted water for half an hour, and mix it with a tablespoon of chopped parsley, and a little salt and pepper; add this mixture to the shallot in the saucepan. As soon as the mixture stiffens, pour in two tablespoons of white wine. Let it bubble. Add the stock from the bird (from which you pour as much as possible of the excess fat, but there should not be very much because the main part of it has already been poured off), and heat it just to simmering point.

Now, with the duck ready for carving on its hot serving dish, take the pan of sauce from the fire and into it put 1½ oz of butter cut into little pieces. Shake and rotate the pan until the butter has amalgamated with the sauce and thickened it, but do not put the sauce back on the fire again or the butter will overheat and turn it oily. This makes an excellent little sauce which is a welcome change from the more usual orange-flavoured one.

Anthony Denney

A duck of this size should just about serve six people; but it must, although fully grown, still be a young bird, not an elderly one suitable only for braising or stewing; and a duckling proper, which weighs only about 2 lb when plucked and drawn, will need only about 45 minutes cooking by the slow roasting method.

Instead of potatoes as an accompanying vegetable, try celery stewed in butter, or Jerusalem artichokes boiled and then sauté with a tomato or two and some chopped parsley; these are both vegetables which go wonderfully well with duck.

If the roast duck is to be eaten cold, don't bother with the sauce, which is only suitable for serving hot. Simply have a green salad and perhaps an orange salad, or, as an alternative a bowl of little cubes of crisp honeydew melon, which really does not need any dressing at all.

Pot-roasted chicken with olive stuffing

Pot-roasting is a very easy way of cooking a chicken, provided you have a suitable utensil. It should be deep enough to contain the bird, lying on its side, with the lid fitting tightly over the top; it should also be rather narrow, so that it is all but filled by the bird; for if it is too big the butter or other fat in which the bird is cooking will be spread over too large an area and will dry up or burn. Also, of course, the pot must be a thick heavy one in which the contents will not stick and in which an even temperature will be maintained throughout the cooking. All this sounds painfully obvious but, all the same, the importance of these points is not always understood until it is too late.

To make an olive stuffing for a roasting chicken weighing $2\frac{1}{4}$ to $2\frac{1}{2}$ lb when drawn and dressed, stone and chop 20 black olives (about $2\frac{1}{2}$ oz) with 2 oz of stale white bread (weighed without the crust) soaked in cold water and squeezed dry, a little piece of onion or garlic, a sprig or two of parsley; bind with a beaten egg and season with a little pepper and nutmeg, but no salt. Stuff the bird, and, if you have it ready in advance, keep it *out* of the refrigerator.

Heat 3 tablespoons of olive oil in the pot or saucepan, but don't let it get to the sizzling stage. Put in the chicken on its side. Leave it five minutes over gentle heat. Turn it over on to the other side, so that both the thigh and one side of the breast of the bird are in contact with the oil. Cover the pan, and cook for one and a half hours altogether, at a very low but steady pace, and turning the bird over twice more during the process. You have to do this with your hands and an oven cloth, as it is easy to damage the skin of the bird if you use a fork.

At the end of the cooking time the skin of the chicken is beautifully golden and crisp, and for once the legs will be cooked through as well as the breast. Remove it to the heated serving dish.

Have ready half a dozen medium-sized potatoes, boiled in their skins but kept slightly undercooked, then peeled and cut into squares (or, when obtainable, whole small new potatoes). In the oil left from cooking the chicken, and in the same pan, with the heat increased, brown the potatoes, turning them round and round with a fork; in five minutes at the most they will be ready. Lift them out with a draining spoon, put them at one end of the dish with the chicken, sprinkle them with salt and parsley, and at the other end put a little bunch of watercress. The dish is ready. You have a complete and delicious main course—and only one pan to wash up.

I should add perhaps that the olive stuffing, although so good, is definitely rather odd. If the chicken is for guests with conventional tastes then it might be better to substitute a routine pork or herb stuffing.

Cream Sauces

A harrowing cooking story was recently told me by a friend. She was preparing a chicken with a cream, tarragon and egg sauce for a dinner party. Outside a fog was thickening. The guests were late. The waiting sauce curdled. She stirred another egg into the sauce and added a little more cream and poured another drink and when she returned to her sauce it was no less curdled than before. The cycle was repeated until she had used a dozen eggs and an extra pint of cream and what the now half-tipsy company had for dinner was chicken with an immense quantity of scrambled eggs and cream. During dinner the guest of honour revealed that she was on an eggless diet (she might perhaps have indicated this beforehand). By midnight the fog was impenetrable. To allow her guests to drive back across country would have been tantamount to attempted manslaughter on the part of the hostess. The story is quite sufficiently sad without the details of the night of suffering for one and all which ensued. But it provides a warning. For in the ordinary way this perfectly competent and sensible cook would have stopped to think that a cooked egg sauce is a very different affair from an uncooked one like a mayonnaise or a Hollandaise and is unlikely to be brought back to life, once curdled, by the addition of more eggs and more cream. What to do then? Start all over again, with a new batch of ingredients? Heaven forbid, after all those martinis.

Serve the chicken totally without sauce? A bit bleak for what was intended as a celebration dinner. Quickly beat up some butter with any tarragon which may happen to have been left over and serve it as a separate sauce without revealing that it is an improvisation? Possibly, if one had that much presence of mind. Better, though, to have planned a meal which didn't need any last-minute tricky manipulations. Or to have cooked the dish in the morning or the day before and served it cold, after a hot consommé or some other non-creamy soup. As a matter of fact this particular dish of chicken with cream sauce is at its best cold.

Here is the detailed recipe for it, followed by three other dishes with cream sauces which are quicker and less complicated to make.

Chicken with cream and tarragon sauce

For a roasting chicken, weighing about 3 lb when plucked and drawn, the other ingredients are onions, carrots, butter, a lemon, four tablespoons of white wine or Vermouth, a bouquet of herbs, seasonings and tarragon (fresh whenever possible) and, for the sauce, about a third of a pint of thick cream and the yolks of 4 large or 6 small eggs and more tarragon, plus a pint of the broth from the chicken.

Work a lump of butter, about 1 oz, with a few leaves of fresh or dried tarragon, salt, pepper and a squeeze of lemon juice and put this inside the bird. Rub it on the outside with the cut lemon.

Three-quarters fill a heavy saucepan or braising pot, in which your chicken will just fit nicely and be completely covered with liquid, with water (or if you should have it, stock from a previous chicken) into which you put the giblets of the bird, an onion and a couple of carrots, a bouquet of parsley, tarragon and a crushed clove of garlic all tied with a thread, a dessertspoon of salt and about 4 tablespoons of white wine or Vermouth. Bring to simmering point. Put in your chicken. Cover the pot. Simmer very gently, for an hour at the most. Remove the chicken to a dish. Strain the stock into a bowl. Measure out a pint of it. Put this in a saucepan with the very well beaten yolks of eggs. Cook very gently, stirring the whole time until the sauce starts to thicken like a custard: add the cream and about a tablespoon of very finely chopped tarragon. Go on stirring until the sauce is once more the consistency of thick cream. Take from the fire and continue stirring until it has partially cooled, tasting also for seasoning, and adding more tarragon if the flavour is not sufficiently pronounced.

To serve the chicken, carve it when cold, preferably removing the skin (although with a young bird this is not absolutely necessary) and arrange it on a shallow round or oval dish—if you like, with a little well-seasoned plain boiled rice underneath and round it. Only shortly before serving pour over your sauce.

Now many people find it difficult to get the cream and egg sauce to the right consistency, even when they are making it calmly and with plenty of time to spare. First, remember that the more thoroughly the egg yolks are beaten to start with, the less chance there is of them curdling; the electric blender is of great help in this matter, but if you haven't one, beat and beat with a whisk until the yolks are foaming. Second, start your sauce off straight over the flame, but a gentle one, and in a roomy saucepan. Stir it so that your spoon reaches every part of it, not just the surface. When it shows signs of starting to thicken, put the saucepan into another much larger one, containing water, and preferably sufficiently shallow for the handle of the pan containing the sauce to come above the edge of the second one. The water in the underneath pan can just be brought barely to simmering point, and then you can safely, having added the cream and seasoning, leave the sauce for as long as half an hour, giving it an occasional stir, while it almost imperceptibly thickens; by this *bain marie* method, preferable to the ordinary double saucepan system, the sauce is surrounded by heat instead of merely cooking *over* heat, and so thickens more evenly. Lastly, remember that for a cold dish the sauce need not be so thick as for a hot one, for like a custard it thickens as it cools.

A chicken of the size given should serve six people, provided it has been carefully and neatly carved.

As to the tarragon, dried whole tarragon leaves are usually more effective than the powdered variety and, of course, fresh tarragon is better than either. Dried herbs in large bottles are, for a small household, a waste of money because the contents will have lost all flavour long before they can be used up.

Veal escalopes with brandy and cream sauce

This is a concoction which, in one form or another, seems to be in a fair way to becoming, with fried scampi, one of our most popular national dishes. I had a version of it a month or two ago prepared with tremendous verve by a Polish waiter in an otherwise stolidly British country inn. On this occasion, though, the effect was rather spoiled by the fact that the maestro of the chafing dish finished the sauce, as the chefs say, by sloshing in about half a bottle of tomato ketchup and a very generous dose of Worcester Sauce. There isn't any need for such complications, and you don't want your meat drowned in a thick soup. It's all as simple as ABC once you've caught your escalopes; but it *is* primarily a stove-to-table dish, so here I will give quantities for two people only. When such a dish is required for a party, the version made with *médaillons* of veal rather than escalopes, as explained in the next recipe, is more satisfactory.

First, season your escalopes, weighing between 3 and 4 oz each and cut very thin and flat, with a very little salt, pepper and lemon juice. Have hot plates and a hot dish ready, and near the stove all the necessary ingredients and implements—i.e., about 4 tablespoons of brandy, a ladle or a little pan in which to warm it, a quarter pint of thick fresh cream, a palette knife for turning the meat over and a wooden spoon for stirring the sauce.

In a 10 to 12 inch frying-pan heat 1 oz of butter until it is just foaming. Put in the escalopes; after a few seconds turn them over; while they are browning on the second side warm the brandy in the ladle or small pan. Catch light to it. Pour it flaming over the meat. Shake and rotate the pan until the flames die down. Reduce the heat and let the meat and sauce simmer gently for three or four minutes. Turn the escalopes again. Increase the heat and pour in the cream: almost instantly it will start bubbling; shake and rotate the pan again, lifting and spooning up the cream over the meat. Remove to the hot dish and continue cooking the sauce for a few more seconds until it is evenly thickened. Pour it bubbling over the escalopes and serve them quickly.

All this is what ought to happen and usually does. But sometimes the cream sauce either does not thicken or else it curdles. In the first case it is either because too small a pan is being used, so that the cream does not spread and heat properly, or perhaps because thin cream is being used. If you find yourself, therefore, with only single cream with which to make the sauce, thicken it by first cooking it in a separate pan with a teaspoonful of flour (I only recommend this system for use in an emergency). When the cream either separates or curdles it is because it is not fresh and the sudden heat causes it to curdle; as a precaution, therefore, it can be heated first in another saucepan. If it curdles on coming to the boil there is nothing to do about it. Make your dish without cream. If however the sauce, after cooking, separates into little lumps it is not necessarily curdled, it is probably because there was too much butter left in the pan (the flaming process usually eliminates this risk, however). The remedy is exceedingly simple. Having removed the meat to its dish, you add a few drops of cold water to the sauce and stir. Back it comes to life, smooth and elegant. It is an interesting point, what can be done in cookery with a little water.

Médaillons de veau à la crème

Médaillons of veal look rather like miniature fillet steaks: they are cut either from the fillet or from that strip of meat in the leg which corresponds to the roll of the silverside in beef. It is often easier to lay hands on this cut than on true escalopes, and in some ways they are more convenient, for after the preliminary cooking is done they can be left in a slow oven for half an hour; the cream sauce can then be made at the last minute.

Allow 2 little *médaillons,* cut about an inch thick and each weighing about 3 oz per person. Brown them in butter on each side, flambé them with warmed spirits as for the escalopes above, transfer them with all the juices to a small fireproof dish, cover with paper and a lid and leave them in a slow oven, Gas no. 1 or 2, 290 to 310° F. for 30 to 40 minutes. Immediately before serving, pour off all the liquid into a wide pan: stir in your cream (same proportions as for escalopes) and, when the sauce has thickened, pour it over and round the meat, ready in a shallow serving dish.

Celeriac with cream sauce

Once you know how to make a plain but really good and creamy cream sauce any number of excellent little vegetable, fish and chicken dishes can be devised on this basis and they are dishes which all English people appear to like very much; but don't make the mistake of thinking that the onion, bay leaf, carrot, mushroom stalks, and so on, which cooks add to a béchamel or a cream sauce will necessarily improve it. On the whole these flavourings are apt to falsify the taste of the finished dish and detract from that of the main ingredient.

For a celeriac root weighing about $\frac{1}{2}$ lb, the sauce is made as follows: melt 1 oz of butter in a thick saucepan. Off the fire add 1 tablespoon of flour. Stir it smooth. Return to the fire and gradually add a $\frac{1}{4}$ pint of warmed milk, stirring all the time. Season with a little salt. Put an asbestos mat under the saucepan, let the sauce gently cook at least 10 minutes; now add a generous $\frac{1}{4}$ pint of cream (single cream will do for this sauce). Continue stirring; in a few minutes the sauce will be ready, but if it is any thicker than thick cream it should be thinned with more cream or milk. The trouble with most English plain white sauces is not so much that they are not properly cooked but that they are too solid and pasty. Stir in also, for celeriac, a good teaspoon of strong mustard, either French or English.

The celeriac is prepared as follows: peel and rinse it, shred it on the fluted blade of the mandoline, or if you haven't one, on a coarse cheese grater. Blanch it half a minute in a big pan of boiling, salted and acidulated water (for this, add either lemon juice or a little white vinegar). Drain it, pressing it as dry as possible. Stir it into the prepared sauce.

Turn the whole mixture into a gratin dish, strew a few little nuts of butter on the top and leave it on the top shelf of a low oven for 25 to 30 minutes, but not much longer, for the celeriac will lose the crisp bite which is part of its charm.

This is a good vegetable dish to serve on its own, or with a meat dish instead of potatoes, and with poached eggs on the top and little triangles of fried bread all round it makes a lovely luncheon dish.

Soufflés

The most tricky part of soufflé cooking is getting the whites of the eggs to the right consistency. They must be stiff, but creamy rather than grainy. The utensil which all professionals used to keep especially for beating egg whites was a hemispherical, untinned copper bowl. There seems to be little doubt that in this bowl egg whites can be whipped quicker and to a better, more airy—and at the same time creamier—consistency than in a china bowl. I do not know exactly why this should be so, I only observe that it is. But these copper bowls are expensive and most people can do well enough with an ordinary kitchen mixing bowl, so long as it is roomy enough for the number of eggs with which you are dealing. See that it is scrupulously clean. Specks of grease may spoil the chances of the eggs rising in the proper way. For the same reason, take care to remove any yolk which may have broken into the whites.

Personally, I can come to terms with neither rotary nor electric whisks for egg whites; I can't control them, and they produce too solid a mass. I use an old sixpenny spiral whisk for small quantities, and a long looped wire whisk for anything over four or five whites. But if you are used to using a rotary or mechanical beater, and find it successful, then no doubt it is better to stick to it.

As to the oven, get it really hot before you put in your soufflé. Have a baking sheet ready on the shelf in which the soufflé is to stand. The heat from this metal sheet helps to cook the egg mixture at the bottom of the dish.

Don't worry too much about the correct soufflé dishes. The ones we use nowadays are quite different from those at one time considered suitable for soufflés, and which were usually oval and made of metal. These, when taken from the oven, were slipped inside another ornamental one

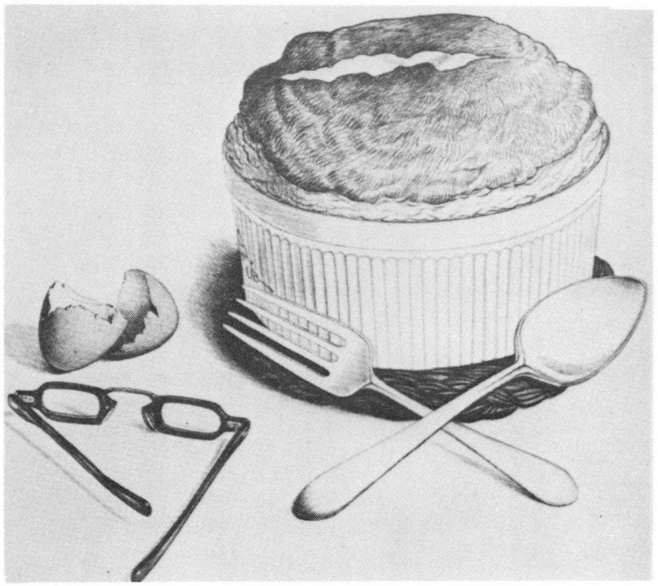

Edward Kasper

suitable for presentation at table. So you can use a pie dish or an old-fashioned metal entrée dish for soufflés, but the timing depends to a certain extent upon the depth of the dish and whether the mixture is spread out or piled up—a soufflé in a wide, shallow dish naturally cooks a good deal quicker than in a deep one.

I don't myself go in for tying paper collars round the dish; this system, except for cold soufflés, is a complication and a nuisance. If you fill your dish almost to the top with the mixture, and time it properly, all will be well. A terrific, towering soufflé is sometimes overcooked and empty inside. High and dry, as you might say, which is worse than one which is too liquid. The ideal, of course, is a well-risen, spongy soufflé which is still creamy in the centre as you dip into it. If it is cooked too dry to start with, it will be quite withered by the time it reaches the third or fourth person. But experimenting with different types of soufflé is more useful than theory. Here are five, each one made in a slightly different way. The obvious course is to find out which best suits your oven, your dishes, your own system of preparation and serving.

Lemon soufflé

This is the simplest form of soufflé, and the lightest. Separate the yolks and whites of 4 large fresh eggs. To the yolks add the grated peel and strained juice of 1 lemon. Stir in 4 tablespoons of caster sugar. Beat very thoroughly. (I allow about 5 minutes for this operation, which seems a long time, but it pays.) Whip the whites until they are creamy and stand in peaks. Amalgamate the two mixtures by tipping half the egg whites at a time on top of the yolks and folding them together very carefully and lightly, but thoroughly. A big metal spoon is what I use for this particular mixture, because a palette knife doesn't do the job so quickly, but the eggs should be lifted and folded rather than stirred, so that plenty of air gets in.

Turn into a 1½-pint soufflé dish (it isn't strictly necessary to butter it); spread the mixture level with a knife. Make two deep cross cuts right across the top, so that the soufflé is divided into four. Transfer the dish quickly to a baking sheet at the centre of a moderate pre-heated oven, Gas no. 4, 355° F. It will take just about 18 minutes to cook, but it rises quite quickly, so you can open the oven door after 12 minutes or so and see if it looks done: the test is whether the cuts you made across the top have split open. If they have not, shut the oven door gently and wait five minutes before you look again.

Vanilla soufflé

This is typical of the kind of soufflé made on a basis of a thickened white sauce, in this case a sweetened one.

Ingredients are: 1½ oz butter, 2 level tablespoons of flour, ½ pint of milk, 3 oz of white sugar, a vanilla pod, 4 whole eggs and 1 extra white.

Put the milk, sugar and vanilla pod into a saucepan and let it simmer gently for about 10 minutes. Melt the butter in a thick saucepan, stir in the flour, and when this is smooth gradually add the hot milk mixture. Cook over gentle heat, with a mat under the saucepan, for another 10 to 15 minutes until the sauce is quite smooth and thickish. Remove the vanilla pod and, off the fire, stir in the very well beaten yolks of the eggs. All these preparations can be done in advance.

When the time comes to cook the soufflé, preheat the oven to Gas no. 4, 355° F. and have ready a 2-pint soufflé dish.

Whip the whites, fold them into the main mixture, turn into the dish, make cuts as explained in the recipe above, strew with a little caster sugar and cook for 25 to 30 minutes.

This soufflé mixture can be used as a basis for flavourings such as grated lemon or orange peel or a sherry glass of liqueur (Curaçao, Grand Marnier, Kirsch, etc.) substituted for an equal proportion of the milk, and added to the basic mixture just before the yolks of the eggs are stirred in.

Chocolate soufflé

A chocolate soufflé is usually made on a somewhat different system, the melted chocolate itself being so thick that no other basic mixture is required. But it cooks very quickly and equally quickly becomes dry; so extra careful timing is necessary, for a chocolate soufflé which is not creamy and moist in the centre is just awful.

Ingredients are 4 oz of bitter chocolate, 2 tablespoons of rum, brandy or strong black coffee, 3 tablespoons of caster sugar, 4 whole eggs and 2 extra whites.

Break the chocolate into small pieces and put it with the liquid in a heat-proof plate or bowl to melt in a very low oven. Stir it smooth, quickly add the well-beaten yolks of the eggs. Turn the oven to hot, Gas no. 6, 400 °F. Whip the whites and fold them into the chocolate, taking great care that the two mixtures are very well amalgamated. Turn into a 2-pint soufflé dish and proceed as for the lemon soufflé. Cooking time is just about 18 minutes. I think, myself, that a chocolate soufflé is greatly improved by thick fresh cream served separately.

Cheese soufflé

There are dozens of different recipes for cheese soufflés. I give this particular one to show the system of cooking a soufflé slowly, so that it can be got ready in plenty of time, leaving you free to attend to other matters.

Start off with the same basic mixture as for the vanilla

soufflé, i.e., $1\frac{1}{2}$ oz butter, 2 level tablespoons of flour, $\frac{1}{2}$ pint of milk. The other ingredients are 2 oz of grated cheese, the ideal being a half-and-half mixture of Parmesan and Gruyère, although of course English Cheddar or mild Cheshire also make quite a good flavouring; salt, plenty of freshly milled pepper, nutmeg, cayenne, 4 whole eggs and 1 extra white.

Having prepared the basic sauce of butter, flour and hot milk, and simmered it for 10 minutes, stir in your cheese and seasonings and, off the fire, the well-beaten yolks. When cool, fold in the 5 whipped whites. Turn into a $1\frac{1}{2}$ to 2 pint soufflé dish. Have the oven heated to very moderate, Gas no. 3, 330° F., and, having made the cuts across the top of the soufflé (as explained for the lemon soufflé), cook it with the dish standing on a baking sheet in the centre of the oven for 30 to 35 minutes. A cheese soufflé nearly always smells cooked some while before it in fact is, so don't be taken in by this. And it is wiser not to sprinkle grated cheese on the top, as is often done for cheese soufflés, for during the long cooking it gets too browned.

Miniature cheese soufflés

It is a curious point about soufflés that the identical mixture which is enough for 4 people when cooked in one dish will serve more than double the number if divided into small dishes, each one holding about 2 oz. So if you serve soufflés frequently it proves an economy in the end to invest in a few miniature china or glass soufflé dishes. Soufflés are pretty filling and most people find one small one is quite enough, whether it comes at the beginning or the end of a meal. The disadvantage of these small soufflés is that they fall rather more rapidly than large ones, so perhaps they are only advisable for those whose dining tables are fairly near their stoves.

For six miniature cheese soufflés, then, make the mixture as above with *half* quantities, allowing 2 whole eggs and one extra white, and a little extra cheese to sprinkle on the top of each soufflé before it is put into the oven. This addition is advisable here because, being cooked for only 13 to 15 minutes at Gas no. 3, 330° F., the tops do not brown nicely without the grated cheese.

Anthony Denney

In Elizabeth David's house, French regional and classic cooking pots.

Top shelf; Norman cider carafe. Saffron yellow Provençal fireproof serving dish. White sauce-boat from the Creil factory (probably 18th century).

Middle shelf; A *diable,* for cooking unskinned potatoes or chestnuts without liquid. Tall glazed jar for storing goose or pork preserved in its own fat. Glazed jar for storing *rillettes.* A brown and yellow glazed terrine or pâté dish.

Bottom shelf; White glazed earthenware baking or gratin dish, and three *poêlons*—bowl-shaped earthenware pans with hollow handles—excellent for stews. A deep glazed hare terrine in earthenware, 19th century.

On the table, back row; Outsize straight-sided stock-pot for *pot-au-feu,* etc. Earthenware jug with wooden spatula and spoons. Traditional earthenware mould for *kugelhopf.* Brown and yellow glazed earthenware *tripière,* for slow baked dishes like the Norman *tripes à la mode.*

Front row; Four cream cheese drainers. A heavy oval unlined cast-iron *cocotte* with tight-fitting lid.

Menus from International Hostesses

—and one host— famous for their memorable food, with their favourite receipts

They come from France, England, Italy, America. We asked that the receipts should give ideal ingredients, regardless of shortages; we publish them in this first issue of 1952 as a reminder of perfection, a challenge to ingenuity.

MRS WILLIAM A. M. BURDEN, JUNIOR
New York City

LUNCH
Gazpacho
Pouilly Fuissé '49
Clafoutis au fromage
Vin rosé
Sliced raw mushrooms
served on lettuce, dressed with
fines herbes French dressing
Willemstadt freeze
(vanilla ice cream topped with grated
orange peel, cashew nuts,
orange Curaçao)

Clafoutis au fromage
Gruyère cheese
2 whole eggs
1¼ pints cold milk
salt, pepper, grated nutmeg
2 tablespoonfuls ground rice

Cut a number of thin strips of Gruyère cheese and place them at the bottom of a deep earthenware baking dish (buttered). Beat up the eggs, yolks and whites, adding a little salt and pepper, grated nutmeg, and 2 tablespoonfuls of ground rice, stirring well to avoid lumps. Pour it all into the cold milk, stir well and pour the lot upon the cheese in the dish. Leave in a moderately hot oven until custard is set (about 30 minutes).

LOELIA, DUCHESS OF WESTMINSTER
Surrey

SUNDAY DINNER
Homard frappé
White devil
Apples in rum

Homard frappé
With a fork shred the flesh of a well-cooked lobster finely. Make some very thin, well-seasoned mayonnaise faintly coloured with coral from the lobster. Add it to the lobster meat. Mix together so that it is quite loose. Pile it up in a dish, roughly, and sprinkle a little more of the coral over it. Place on ice and serve in a dish with cracked ice around the bowl containing the lobster. Serve sandwiches of mustard and cress with this.

White devil
Left-over chicken may be used for this. Cut into neat chunks. Place in a fireproof dish. Whip 1 cupful cream, about 1 teaspoonful Worcester sauce, the same of Harvey sauce, a little mustard, and salt and pepper. Mix this and pour over the chicken or game. Bake in hot oven for 10 minutes. Serve at once.

MRS ROLAND PENROSE
Muddles Green, Sussex

SUNDAY LUNCH
"Muddles Green" Green Chicken
Baking powder biscuits; fried parsley
Tossed salad
Cheese
Fresh fruit
English trifle

"Muddles Green" green chicken
2 or 3 5-lb chickens
6 heads of celery, green leaves and roots included
1 dozen parsley heads, with roots and leaves
3 big white onions or the equivalent
the white part of 6 leeks
6 slices of golden toast
veal stock
salt
1 dozen white peppercorns in a gauze bag
white wine (dry)
butter
cream
4 or 5 egg yolks

Rough chop the celery, onions, and leeks. Place them in a well-buttered pot or casserole big enough to hold not only the vegetables but also the chicken, later. Scatter butter over the top and bed down the parsley, tied in two bunches on top. Sprinkle with three wineglassfuls of dry white wine. Cover with greased cooking paper and a tight-fitting lid and simmer until the vegetables have "melted".

Meanwhile, cut up the chickens in serving pieces, scrub them with a cut lemon, and set aside. Scald and peel the feet, clean the head, and add these, with the neck, giblets, toast, bag of peppercorns, and carcass trimmings to the vegetables when they are soft. Cover with veal stock (not beef cubes—water would be better). Replace the lid without the paper, and simmer for four hours. Skim occasionally. Strain, reserve bouillon. Remove chicken bone debris, giblets, peppercorns, and pass everything else through a fine sieve, beginning with the parsley. This is best accomplished by putting the whole mass through a *moulin à légumes* and then bit by bit working it through a fine sieve with the back of a wooden spoon. Chicken bits which accidentally get puréed are an improvement, but not the dark giblets.

Add the purée to the bouillon, season lightly with salt, add the chicken, and simmer till tender but not falling off the bones. At this point, the whole thing can be set aside for the following day, or "whenever", to be gently re-heated and the soup thickened and smoothed by a liaison of at least a cupful of cream and four egg yolks, just before serving.

English trifle

Slightly dry sponge cake, raspberry jam, bananas, fresh peaches, Maraschino liqueur, sherry, egg custard (the pouring kind made with egg yolks, milk sugar, and vanilla pod), whipped cream, angelica for garnish. There should be a gentle English rain of sherry and Maraschino on each and every layer of this, especially the sponge cake. Line a huge crystal dish with sponge cake, spread thinly with raspberry jam, cover with a layer of sliced bananas and then a layer of peaches. Start again with sponge, repeat the fruit layers and end with sponge. It never stops raining. Cover with the custard and put in a not too cold part of the refrigerator to mellow until the following day. Before serving, garnish with huge blobs of cream, leaving space for the custard to show and be trimmed with the angelica and cherries. Please don't use crystallized violets.

VISCOUNTESS ROTHERMERE
London

SUPPER PARTY

Cold pea soup
Haddock au gratin
Poulet à l'espagnole
Currant leaf ice

Haddock au gratin

Divide a smoked haddock into flakes and mix with tinned sweet corn and a little cream (no salt). Cook slowly. When haddock is cooked, arrange in an entrée dish. Make a white béchamel sauce, mixed with one tablespoonful flour. Mix and cook for two minutes. Slowly add milk to make it as rich as cream, pour over dish and bake for about five minutes. Pass dish under grill to brown top lightly.

Poulet à l'espagnole

Cut a chicken into neat joints and fry in one wineglass of pure olive oil in a stewpan. When nearly cooked add some chopped onions and fry with it. Then add about four tomatoes cut into quarters (skinned first) and 1 teacupful of rice. Add a little broth and stew until the rice is cooked, and the broth dried up. Serve in a deep dish without a lid as steam must not be left in.

Currant leaf ice

Steep a handful of fresh blackcurrant leaves in cold water for about twelve hours. Remove leaves and ice the water until solid. Then crush and serve in glasses.

MRS GILBERT MILLER
Sussex

SUPPER

Consommé madrilène
Calves kidneys à la lyonnaise
Cold smoked turkey
String bean and tomato salad
Suprême au chocolat
(with vanilla cream)
Macédoine of fruits

Suprême au chocolat

3 *bars of sweetened chocolate*
1 *bar of unsweetened chocolate*
(or half and half)
4 *tablespoonfuls sugar*
4 *eggs*
$3\frac{1}{2}$ *ounces of butter*

Melt chocolate and mix in with a fork: the sugar, one by one the yolks of eggs, and then the slightly softened butter. Beat well for 20 minutes. Fold in the whites of eggs, which have been whipped with a wire beater till they are very stiff, and pour into an oiled mould, or if you prefer, pile up the mixture in the serving dish.

Allow to stand for several hours and serve with vanilla cream:

1 *pint milk*
3 *egg yolks*
2 *ounces sugar*
vanilla bean

Boil sweetened milk with vanilla bean. Beat yolks, add little by little the hot milk and thicken in double boiler, stirring constantly.

MME ELSA SCHIAPARELLI
Paris

SUNDAY NIGHT BUFFET

Bœuf à la mode en gelée
Salade
Fromages
Pear halves around
Gâteau Saint-Honoré

Salade

Mix together: romaine, tomatoes, watercress, celery. Prepare French dressing, with mustard added, also *fines herbes*, including thyme, sweet marjoram; then add crushed anchovy fillets to the dressing. Fry croûtons rubbed with garlic and mix with the dressing and at the last minute boil 4 eggs (3 minutes) and put them, crushed, in the dressing.

Pour the dressing over the salad and sprinkle grated Parmesan generously over it.

Watermelons, painted by Rufino Tamayo
July 1952

CHRISTIAN DIOR
France

LUNCH
Tarte à la tomate
Truites Denise
Pommes à l'anglaise
Sorbet à l'orange
Fromages et fruits

Truites Denise
Cook some crayfish in bouillon. When they are done, use the same bouillon to cook your trout. Serve with a crayfish sauce and a few crayfish as decoration.

COUNTESS ROBERTI
Rome

LUNCH
Gnocchi alla romana
Fritto misto
Salad
Macedonia di frutta

Gnocchi alla romana
(For 6)
1 *quart milk*
½ *lb hominy—finest ground*
2 *tablespoonfuls grated Parmesan cheese*
1½ *ounce butter*
Let the milk come to the boil, then sprinkle the hominy slowly into it, stirring constantly for about 15 minutes. Remove from stove and stir in butter, cheese, and a pinch of salt. Mix well, and pour hominy on marble slab slightly moistened with water—or onto large damp plate. Wet a big knife and flatten hominy to a thickness of about half an inch. Leave to cool for an hour.

Cut into rounds and place in Pyrex dish (which has been greased), one round overlapping the other.

Sprinkle abundantly with more grated cheese, and with another ounce and a half of melted butter. Place in hot oven until gnocchi are golden in colour. Serve at once in the same dish.

Fritto misto
Anything and everything can go into this—chicken croquettes, brains, sweetbreads, cheese or potato croquettes, fillets of fish, shrimps, thin slices of squash, cauliflower buds, onion rings, etcetera.

The vegetables are dipped into a thin batter of flour and water before frying, and all the other ingredients into beaten egg and then rolled in very fine breadcrumbs. Only a few pieces at a time into hot (not boiling) fat, so heat is not reduced. Each ingredient is put into separate piles and the dish garnished with fried parsley and lemon. (If thin slices of eggplant or squash are used, they must first be soaked in salt and water, and then the moisture is pressed out in a cloth.)

MRS DAVID BRUCE
Paris

LUNCH
Omelette Tipperary
Kidneys in white wine
Rice créole
Peas
Cheese
Meringues duchesse

Kidneys sautéed in white wine
Skin the kidneys and cut them into very fine slices. Sauté them over a hot fire in very hot melted butter. As soon as they are cooked, put them in individual dishes. Cool the frying-pan with some white wine and a shallot chopped very fine. Reduce the wine by half and add several spoonfuls of brown sauce, a generous piece of butter, and several chopped cooked mushrooms. Let it start boiling and then pour over the kidneys, which should not under any circumstance boil. Sprinkle with parsley and croûtons fried in butter.

Philippe Jullian

Anthony Denney, July 1956

Bounty of Britain

by Doris Lytton Toye

The Butcher *Penn*

Lancashire hot pot

To make this in grand style add 3 sheep's kidneys and a dozen sauce oysters to the other ingredients (2 lb best end of neck, 2 lb potatoes, 1 spanish onion, salt and pepper, ½ pint of gravy, 1 oz butter, stock). Divide the meat into cutlets and boil down any lean trimmings of meat with the short ribs and the onion for gravy. Grease a fireproof dish, lined with a deep layer of sliced potato, arrange the cutlets and on each place a slice or two of kidney and an oyster. Season and cover with the remainder of the potato. Add ½ pint stock, brush the top layer of potato with melted butter, cover with buttered paper and bake in a moderate oven for 2 hours. Half-an-hour before it is ready, remove paper to allow potatoes to become crisp and brown. When ready pour in a little gravy and send the rest to table in a tureen.

Boiled bacon with Cumberland sauce

When a piece of collar of bacon is available for boiling, add a cupful of cider and a few cloves to the water for the last hour and allow it to cool in its liquor. It will have a lovely flavour when cold. Skin it, cover with brown sugar and bake until the sugar forms a luscious golden brown surface. Baste every now and then with some of the cider liquid.

Cumberland sauce

This can be used for cold ham, tongue or any other cold meat. Dissolve ¼ pint redcurrant jelly in a small pan. When melted, add 1 small teaspoon of chopped, blanched and dried shallot, 1 large teaspoon of orange and lemon rind cut in fine shreds and blanched; a coffee spoon (level) of English mustard, ½ gill port, the juice of an orange and ½ lemon. Season with salt, cayenne and a pinch ground ginger.

Lemon flummery

To make this typically English sweet put ½ pint water with ¾ oz butter and the grated peel of 1 lemon on to boil. Mix in a bowl 1 oz flour and 4 oz castor sugar; make a well in the centre and pour on the hot liquid, whisking to avoid any lumps. Return to the pan. Put 1 yolk of egg (two if eggs are small) in the bowl, whisk in some of the hot liquid, then mix with the remainder in the saucepan. Bring slowly to the boil, and cook gently, stirring occasionally, for 10–12 minutes. Whisk the white or whites of egg to a stiff froth. Add the juice of the lemon to the pan, pour out into a bowl, fold in the whisked white and turn the mixture into serving dish. Cool. When cold, decorate with crushed macaroons and serve cold with cream or top milk.

Crab, Isle of Wight

Remove the meat from a medium-sized crab; flake it and beat into it 2 heaped tablespoons of fine breadcrumbs, freshly made; also ½ teaspoon dry mustard, a walnut of butter, a little black pepper, a tablespoon olive oil. When well blended, add 1 tablespoon fine vinegar and 2 tablespoons cream or top of milk. Rearrange in the shell or serve on lettuce leaves.

Other ideas for the first course are: Potted Morecambe Bay shrimps with lemon slices, brown bread and butter; smoked salmon with lemon quarters and pepper from the mill; smoked trout with tartare sauce, or with kipper butter or smoked cod's roe butter. To make these, mix together equal parts of sieved kipper meat or smoked cod's roe and margarine, add pepper and serve with crisp hot toast.

Cock-a-leekie soup, from Scotland

Wash well 4–5 large leeks, to eliminate all grit. Remove green part and cut them into small pieces. Melt 1½ oz margarine in soup pan, throw in the leeks, cover the pan and permit them to cook slowly over a low heat for 10 minutes, without colouring. Add 2 quarts of chicken stock, bring to the boil and sprinkle in 1 oz of fine oatmeal, a little salt. Stir, then simmer until the oatmeal is quite soft. Correct the seasoning with salt and pepper. This soup, they say, is much improved if warmed up a second time.

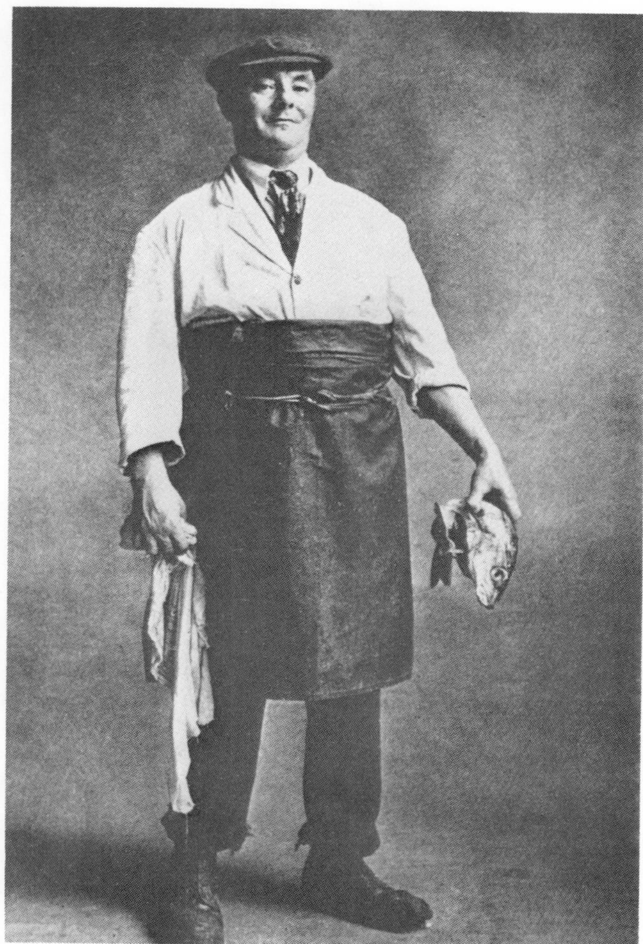

The Fishmonger *Penn*

Scotch barley broth
Blanch 2 oz barley, rinse thoroughly. Place it in a soup pan with a knuckle bone of veal. Cover with $1\frac{1}{2}$ quarts of water, a pinch of salt. Bring gently to boiling point, skim, and simmer for 2 hours. Dice a carrot, a small turnip, 2 stalks of celery and 2 medium onions; add to the broth at boiling point. Simmer an hour or so longer. Season to taste, scatter in a little chopped parsley. Bring again to the boil.

Fishermen's trout
Procure a fresh sea trout of $2\frac{1}{2}$–3 lb. Poach it slowly in salted water till the flesh leaves the backbone when tested with a knife. Lift it up, drain completely. Lay it on a folded napkin on a hot dish. Tuck a nosegay of parsley in the mouth, lay rashers of grilled bacon across its back. Serve plain melted butter flavoured with lemon juice separately.

Scotch whiting
Fillet some silver whiting. Toss the fillets in seasoned flour until it adheres. Melt some butter or margarine in a flat pan and cook the fish very slowly. They should not colour or become dry. Meanwhile, mince a few spring onions or shallots and a little parsley, mix them with a few tablespoons stock and an equal quantity of cream or evaporated milk, sufficient to give enough sauce for your whiting. Season the sauce if necessary. Pour over the fillets just before they are finished. Shake the pan as the sauce boils up. Lift the fish carefully on to a dish; pour over the sauce and serve.

Herrings baked in port
An old receipt from Hampshire, to be eaten cold. "Season the cleaned and decapitated herrings well with pepper and salt. Cover them with an equal amount of fine wine, vinegar and port. Bake them the same time as household bread—you may add two or three bay leaves." That is how the receipt runs, the cooking time is about 1 hour in a moderate oven (Reg. 4, 360° F.). (Cook them in a Pyrex or earthenware dish and cover them whilst cooking.)

Sussex game pudding
(Rich and rare). Remove the flesh in fillets from a pheasant, two partridges, or other game bird. Pigeons can be used, if plump. Soak the fillets with $\frac{1}{4}$ lb calves liver in a glass of port overnight. Have also $1\frac{1}{2}$ lb stewing beef, and $\frac{1}{2}$ lb sausage meat and suet crust made from 12 oz flour and 6 oz suet. Line a large basin with suet paste, not too thickly. Line again with the sausage meat, season, put half a bay leaf inside and little chopped parsley. Cut up the beef. Fill the basin with layers of beef, the game and the liver cut finely, seasoning as you proceed. Pour in the marinade and cover securely with suet crust. Cover basin with a floured cloth and boil if possible for 8 hours. Before sending to table, brown the top lightly in the oven, then wrap a clean napkin about the basin.

Note: A practical method for lining a basin with suet pastry. Roll out the paste to the thickness and size required, keep it as circular as possible. Next, cut out a wedge about one quarter of the circle. Roll this quarter out again for the top, the remaining three-quarters will fit easily into the basin. Moisten and press the edges well together so that no liquid can seep through.

Oxford hare (*Stuffed shoulder of mutton*)
Have a shoulder boned by the butcher. Make a little stock. Prepare a stuffing of chopped ham, some breadcrumbs, a little chopped onion, a crushed clove of garlic, a pinch of rosemary; season with black pepper. Remove any excess fat from the meat, lay the stuffing inside, roll up and tie. Melt some clear fat in a deep pan, toss some roughly sliced onion and carrot in this, sprinkle a little sugar over the carrot and onion. This gives the sauce a nice colour. Place the "hare" upon this bed, adding a few peppercorns, a bay leaf, a sprig of thyme. Turn the meat until browned on all sides and the vegetables slightly brown. Drain off any excess fat, pour in a little stock and a small wineglass of dark sherry. Cover pan and braise for about 3 hours in the oven very slowly (Reg. 4, 350° F.). (If you don't possess a pan that will go in the oven, continue on top of the stove over low flame or transfer the whole thing into a casserole. Whichever you do be sure the lid fits tightly or the good juices will evaporate.) Baste at intervals seeing that the stock does not dry up. When the "hare" is tender, baste with the essence, the lid off, until the meat is glazed and shines as if varnished. Remove the strings, set joint on a hot dish. Rinse out the pan with a little stock, boil up, season and strain into a sauceboat. Garnish the "hare" with bouquets of vegetables.

From a Scottish Kitchen

by Peter Pirbright and Gretel Beer

Cullen skink
1 Finnan haddock
1 onion
1 pint milk
1 dessertspoon butter
mashed potatoes
salt and pepper
Chop onion, skin haddock. Place fish in a saucepan, sprinkle with chopped onion and cover with boiling water. Simmer until haddock is cooked, remove flesh from bones, flake and return bones to stock. Boil for another hour. Strain stock, reheat and add flaked fish. Bring milk to the boil in a separate saucepan and add gradually, stirring well. Salt and pepper to taste. Just before serving, add butter and enough hot mashed potato to give a creamy consistency.

Partan bree
2 cooked crabs
5 oz rice
1 pint milk
½ cup cream
white stock
anchovy paste
salt and pepper
Pick flesh from 2 cooked crabs, putting the meat from the claws on one side. Boil rice in slightly salted milk until soft and pass through a hair-sieve together with the crab meat. Stir until smooth with a wooden spoon and add about 1 pint unseasoned white stock. The consistency should be slightly thinner than a purée. Season with salt, white pepper and anchovy paste. Reheat and add claw meat, but do not boil. Have cream ready in a soup tureen, pour hot soup over it.

Stovies
1 large onion
1½ lb potatoes
a little milk
salt and butter
Cut onion into rings and fry in butter. Add good quality potatoes and just enough water to cover the bottom of the pan. Sprinkle with salt, dot with butter and cover. Simmer until the potatoes are cooked through. Add a little milk as the water is being absorbed.

Potato scones
½ lb potatoes
about 2 oz flour
milk, butter and salt
Mash potatoes whilst hot, add a pinch of salt. Work in as much flour as they will take (about 2 oz) and just enough milk to make a soft dough. Roll out thinly on a floured board. Cut into triangles and prick all over with a fork. Bake lightly on a hot greased gridle (or thick frying-pan) for 5 minutes on each side. Butter immediately, roll up and serve on a hot plate.

Ayrshire shortbread
4 oz flour
4 oz rice flour
4 oz butter
4 oz castor sugar
1 egg
2 tablespoons cream
Sieve together flour and rice flour, work in butter and sugar. Bind with beaten egg and cream. Roll out to about ¼ inch thick and cut into strips. Prick with fork and bake on greased paper in a moderate oven until golden brown.

Urny pudding
4 oz butter
2 oz sugar
4 oz flour
2 eggs
½ teaspoon bicarbonate of soda
1 teaspoon milk
2 tablespoons strawberry jam
Cream butter and sugar, add well-beaten eggs. Fold in flour and finally jam and bicarbonate of soda dissolved in milk. Pour into a greased pudding basin which should be about half full. Cover with greased paper and steam for 1½ hours. Serve hot with custard.

Black bun
½ lb flour
½ teaspoon baking powder
6 oz butter
1 egg
1 egg yolk

Sift flour and baking powder, rub in butter, add egg and enough cold water to make a stiff dough. Roll out on a floured pastry board, line bottom and sides of greased cake tin with dough, reserving enough to cover filling:

½ lb flour
½ teaspoon cream of tartar
½ teaspoon bicarbonate of soda
1 lb raisins
1 lb currants
1 tablespoon mixed peel
1 teaspoon ground ginger
1 teaspoon cinnamon
2 tablespoons almonds
½ cup milk
½ cup brandy
pinch black pepper

Wash and clean raisins and currants, blanch and chop almonds. Sift together ½ lb flour, cream of tartar and bicarbonate of soda. Mix all ingredients for the filling, pile into the lined cake tin. Roll remaining pastry into a round and cover filling with this. Prick with a fork and brush with egg yolk. Bake at 350° F. or Regulo 4 for 2½ hours.

Roast grouse

young grouse
1 tablespoon cranberries or blaeberries per bird
bacon rashers
sprigs of heather
flour
lemon juice
salt and pepper

Wipe the grouse well with a damp cloth, inside and out. Put 1 tablespoon blaeberries or cranberries into each bird, rub with salt, pepper and lemon juice. Wrap first in bacon rashers, then in greaseproof paper, enclosing a sprig of heather (for tradition as well as luck). Place the birds breasts down in a baking tin and roast for about 20–30 minutes (450° F. or Regulo 7), depending on size. Ten minutes before serving remove paper, heather and bacon, sprinkle grouse with flour and return to oven. Cook livers for about 10 minutes, chop or mince finely and pound to a paste. If necessary add a little butter to give a spreading consistency. Salt and pepper to taste. Spread on slices of toast, remove all but a little dripping from the baking tin and place toast under the birds two or three minutes before serving.

Anthony Denney

Coronation Cuisine

Coronation celebrations will not stop short at the decorations. The kitchen will also want to celebrate and, knowing this, *Vogue* asked chefs of several well-known restaurants for a preview of some of the dishes they will star in Coronation week. Try them in your kitchen, and compare yours with the professional version which will be *à la carte* at the restaurants in the week of June 1 1953.

PÈRE AUGUSTE

Les œufs Elizabeth

2 eggs
1 large walnut of butter
¼ lb Gruyère cheese

Cut the butter into small pieces so that the whole of the bottom of a fireproof dish is covered. Slice half the Gruyère into fine wafers and make a layer over the butter. Place over gentle heat until cheese begins to melt. Separate the yolks of the eggs from the whites and put yolks into the dish without breaking, and leave on gentle heat until nearly set. While the yolks are setting, beat the whites until stiff, having added a pinch of salt, and place a layer of stiffly beaten white over the dish. Cover the egg white with a layer of finely sliced Gruyère and place in the oven until golden.

THE CONNAUGHT HOTEL

Œuf poché Britannia

1 lobster
6 tartlets made of rough puff, or short pastry
6 eggs
fresh asparagus tips and sliced truffles
Madeira cream sauce:
¼ pint béchamel sauce
1 egg yolk, a knob of butter
2 tablespoonfuls of cream
2 tablespoonfuls of Madeira

Arrange the lobster in the tartlets, lay a poached egg on top of each tartlet, coat with the Madeira Cream sauce, and garnish with asparagus tips and sliced truffles.

PRUNIER'S

Soufflé de filets de sole royal

6 small soles
½ bottle of white Bordeaux
stock made from fish cuttings
Cheese soufflé mixture:
made with 2 oz butter
2 oz flour
1 gill milk
6 eggs
2 tablespoonfuls grated Cheshire cheese
2 tablespoonfuls Parmesan

Cut the fillets in small strips, poach with the wine, and drain them. Add some fish stock to the cooking liquor, reduce it to a glaze, and roll the fillets in it. Prepare the cheese soufflé mixture, and when cool add the yolks of eggs, beating in one at a time. Add the cheese and fold in the whites of egg, stiffly beaten. Arrange this and the fillets of sole in alternate layers in a buttered timbale. Finish with a layer of the mixture and cook like an ordinary soufflé. Serve with a white wine sauce.

HUNGARIA RESTAURANT

Pojarsky de volaille regina

1 breast of roast chicken
¼ pint cream
½ oz butter
1 oz bread soaked in milk and squeezed out
breadcrumbs
salt, pepper, butter for frying
Smitane sauce made with:
1 teaspoonful chopped onion
1 bottle yoghourt, salt, pepper

Skin and bone the breast and cut in small pieces; season with salt and pepper; add bread and butter. Pass twice through a very fine mincer, or chop very finely. Put in basin and add the cream very slowly, beating it vigorously. Correct seasoning if necessary. Divide into cakes of the desired size: roll in breadcrumbs and flatten out into oval shape cakes. Fry in butter for about 10 or 15 minutes. Remove from pan, keep hot. Smitane sauce: fry chopped onion in pan, add yoghourt, simmer 10 minutes, season to taste and strain over the Pojarskys.

LEONI'S QUO VADIS

Filetto di pollo alla coronella

Breast of 1 chicken
tinned pimento
½ pint thick chicken stock
¼ lb of butter
4 tablespoonfuls of cream
Batter made with: 1 egg
2 tablespoonfuls cream
a little Parmesan

Skin and cut the white meat from the breast of an uncooked chicken, cut each side into two equal parts and beat flat as you would a veal escalope. Beat the egg and make a batter with the cream, add the Parmesan cheese and coat each fillet with this and fry in butter for four or five minutes. When cooked place on serving dish: garnish with strips of pimento and lady's fingers (okra). Cover with cream sauce. To make: mix the stock, butter and cream in a pot on the stove and thicken with a little potato flour.

With bunting, and tea, and hurrahs, and dancing, the Queen's loyal subjects express their glee *Edward Ardizzone*

QUEEN'S RESTAURANT

Grenadin de veau Elizabeth

4 escalopes of veal
$\frac{1}{4}$ lb sliced mushrooms
4 tablespoonfuls cream
butter for frying, a little stock, parsley

Fry the mushrooms in butter and when partly cooked add a little stock: bring to the boil and remove from the pan. Take four small escalopes of veal, season and dredge in flour, toss in foaming butter, bringing them quickly to a golden brown on both sides. Add half a measure of dry sherry, this will flare immediately, then the previously prepared mushrooms, and in addition the four tablespoonfuls of cream. This will all blend into a pleasant creamy sauce. Sprinkle a little finely chopped parsley before serving. This is cooked at table.

WASHINGTON HOTEL

Peach royal

6 peaches
4 egg whites
$\frac{1}{2}$ lb castor sugar
Maraschino
a few drops of lemon juice
$\frac{1}{2}$ bottle of sweet white wine
cocktail cherries and angelica

Split each peach in half. Place in a fireproof dish, sprinkle a little sugar on top with a few drops of Maraschino. Make the meringue mixture, whipping the whites of egg stiffly and folding in the castor sugar and the lemon juice. Pipe the meringue dome shape over the peaches and decorate with the cocktail cherries and the angelica cut into diamonds. Pour the white wine into the dish and cook in a slow oven until the meringue is golden.

Supper after the Theatre

by Robin McDouall

The poor dear housewife gets a lot of sympathy for having to prepare delicious meals to welcome back the breadwinner. We hear nothing about the poor dear bachelor who is both breadwinner and cook. How he envies the housewife with all the day before her—that jolly morning, pottering round Soho; that happy afternoon in the kitchen with pestle and mortar. He, on the other hand, is expected by his friends to leave his office at six and, dressed in his best, to produce a four-course dinner at eight.

Even worse than dinner at eight is that simple little supper after the theatre. This is the kind of thing that happens: one finds one has said, "Sweet of you to take me; you must come to supper with me afterwards"—and discovers that the party consists of eight. There is no time to go home from the office. Most of the cooking has to be done the night before, with a few dawn touches. The table-laying and a few simple preparations can, let us assume, be left to one's "daily". The rest is up to oneself.

Here is a menu I have worked out for a crisis of this kind—though the dishes can, of course, be eaten when there isn't a crisis, and can be cooked by a married man or even a woman.

I suggest chestnut soup to begin with—rather comforting if the night is cold and the hour late. This can, except for the hotting-up and the addition of cream, be made the night before. While you are out in the kitchen, let the guests help themselves to sherry or Italian Vermouth. If they must have hard liquor, leave whisky, soda, gin and tonic on the drink-tray—and, of course, ice. Don't mix them cocktails, as that will keep you from your kitchen chores.

Chestnut soup

Slit the tops of 1 lb chestnuts and boil them for twenty to thirty minutes—they should be cooked but not squashy. Drain them. As soon as they are cool enough to handle, skin them (the inside as well as outside skin must come off).

While they are cooking, chop two large onions coarsely and cook them gently in a little butter until they are soft but not brown. Add the chestnuts to the onions. Season with salt and pepper. Mash the chestnuts with a fork and moisten with a little stock (preferably chicken or veal) or milk. When the chestnuts are soft, put the whole mixture through a fine mill into a clean saucepan. Add more stock or milk so that there is a cupful of soup per person. Simmer gently for twenty minutes. The soup is then ready for the next day. All it needs is to be brought nearly to the boil. You then add half a cup of cream. Remember to have your own glass of sherry in the kitchen.

For the next course I suggest a chicken and tunny-fish salad. All the preparation can be done the night before, leaving nothing to do but combine the ingredients.

Chicken and tunny-fish salad

Roast one large or two small chickens in butter. Take the contents of one and a half tins of tunny-fish, break into medium-sized pieces and put into a strainer to let the oil drip away. Make nearly a pint of mayonnaise (putting it in a cold place, but not a refrigerator). In the morning, the "daily" can cut up the chicken-meat into medium-sized pieces and wrap them in greaseproof paper. She must also wash a lettuce, separate the leaves and hang them up to dry. On the night all you have to do—while the soup is being heated and the guests are having their pre-supper drinks—is to shred some lettuce and make a bed of it on a large plate. On this bed put pieces of chicken and pieces of tunny-fish. Just before serving, pour the mayonnaise over it. You can decorate the dish with tomatoes (blanched, peeled and quartered), and quartered hard-boiled eggs, prepared for you by the "daily".

You may think it necessary to have potato with this salad. A potato salad with *vinaigrette* is not practical, as it must be made fresh while the potatoes are still hot. And potato salad made with mayonnaise is unsuitable, as it is too much like the dish it is to accompany. I therefore suggest that, the night before the party, you bake eight medium-sized potatoes. When they are cooked, cut them in half lengthways. Scoop out the flesh, mix it with butter, pepper and salt, and put it back in the bottom half of the potato. Roughen the tops with a fork. Grate on them a little Parmesan. All you need do on the night is to put a small piece of butter on each potato and brown them in a hot oven while you are heating and eating the soup.

As a salad, I suggest *mâche* (lamb's lettuce)—bought and washed by the "daily" and hung up to dry—covered with a dressing made the night before from finely grated horse-radish, salt, sugar, a few drops of lemon juice and cream. This would be better eaten after the chicken and tunny-fish.

The next course, Welsh Rarebit, can be made in a chafing-dish in the dining-room to avoid the host disappearing again.

Welsh rarebit

Take a pound of best English Cheddar, very fresh and cut it in paper-thin slices. Put them in the chafing-dish with some made mustard, a generous dash of Worcestershire sauce, a dessertspoon of sherry and two tablespoons of beer. Stir it until it reaches the consistency of well-chewed chewing-gum. An obliging guest should, in the meanwhile, have made some toast. Put a piece of toast on each plate and spoon on to it some of the Welsh Rarebit.

Finish the meal with fresh fruit and coffee.

During supper I should recommend drinking several bottles of Bourgeuil, that delicious, slightly *pétillant* red wine from the Loire, which should be served iced.

It will, presumably, be quite late when all this is over. Instead of giving your guests the conventional whisky and soda, you could give them a glass of Atholl Brose just before they leave to give them courage to face the fog, snow and ice which will probably greet them on the doorstep.

Atholl brose

Take two or three handfuls of medium oatmeal and put them in a jug or basin with a quart of cold water. Allow it to stand overnight. In the morning, strain the liquid through a muslin. Warm a cupful of runny honey—preferably heather—and add it to the oatmeal. Stir in a cupful of cream. Add a bottle of whisky. Mix well, and pour through a funnel into clean bottles. Giving your guests Atholl Brose is not altogether without its dangers: one glass, and they may not want to leave; two, and they may be unable to.

John Ward

Week-end Cooking

by Robin McDouall

Country week-ends are supposed to be a pleasure and, indeed, for the guests they sometimes are. For the host or hostess who is also the cook, most of the pleasure is in anticipation: once the guests are actually there, the cook is riveted to the kitchen, turning out meal after meal for guests who do nothing but take exercise in order to develop their tucking-in power. Personally I am a fortunate week-ender; when I go away, I have a rest from cooking. But pitying the hostess-cook who is let in for a house-party, I have tried in this article to plan a programme of Friday-to-Monday eating which will allow him or her some time for hob-nobbing with the guests. (For those who dislike their guests I could devise an alternative that would keep the cook tied day and night to the stove.) I have chosen dishes which appear a second time, either cold or in a different form. I have assumed that the cook can devote the whole of Friday to cooking, and that a large refrigerator or a very cold larder is available. Here is my week-end programme:

Enough vichyssoise can be prepared on Friday for hot and cold. The gammon reappears cold and then as potted ham. The curry can be made on Friday and is none the worse for being hotted up. All the puddings can be made on Friday, though the cream for the banana trifle will have to be whipped on Sunday evening. Even the haddock for Saturday's savoury and Sunday's breakfast can go through the first stage of cooking on Friday.

I haven't the space to give recipes for all the dishes. In any case, *Vogue* readers do not need to be told how to roast beef or make an apple tart (zest of lemon, not cloves, please). The flageolets are simply tinned ones (little green beans), heated in a saucepan with, if you like, a touch of garlic and a little butter; the kidneys are baked in the oven in their own fat, the fat removed before dishing up and seasoning added; the horseradish cream is grated horse-radish, stirred into whipped cream; mulligatawny is the remains of the curry finely sieved, with stock added and a little cream; banana trifle is just banana cut up, left in a bowl of apricot jam and covered with whipped cream just before serving. By the way, a tip for scrambled eggs (made with butter, of course, not milk); when they are done, take them off the fire and stir in one raw egg.

Crème vichyssoise

Cut 2 pounds of potatoes into cubes and 2 pounds of leeks into slices and cook them gently in butter in a large, thick saucepan. Season with salt and pepper. Cover with stock (preferably chicken). Keep adding stock as it is absorbed by the vegetables. Then add more stock up to a total of two pints and also add two pints of milk. Simmer for half an hour. Strain off the liquor and put the vegetables through a mill, add the liquid again and divide it in two, keeping one half for hot and putting the other, when cold, in the refrigerator. With both lots add just before serving, cream and chopped chives.

Baked gammon

As the bacon is to appear hot, cold and then as potted ham, it is as well to buy 8 lb of gammon. Get your grocer to bone it for you. Fill the inside with brown sugar and three or four cloves. Tie it up firmly with string and spread black treacle over it. Make some ordinary shortcrust pastry and use it to wrap the gammon in, making the covering about half an inch thick. Bake it in a slow oven for four to five hours. Remove the crust and the skin. Spread on it some breadcrumbs, mixed with a little of the treacle. Keep it hot until you are ready. Serve with Cumberland sauce.

Curried beef

3 *onions*
2 *cloves of garlic*
2 *tablespoons of olive oil*
2 *tablespoons of curry-powder*
cinnamon and nutmeg
2 *tomatoes chopped*
salt and pepper
lemon juice
½ *an apple, sliced*
a handful of raisins
1 *tablespoon of desiccated coconut*
1 *tablespoon of mango chutney*
1 *pint of stock*
1 *lb rump steak*

Chop the onions coarsely and the garlic finely and cook them until they are soft, but not brown, in the olive oil.

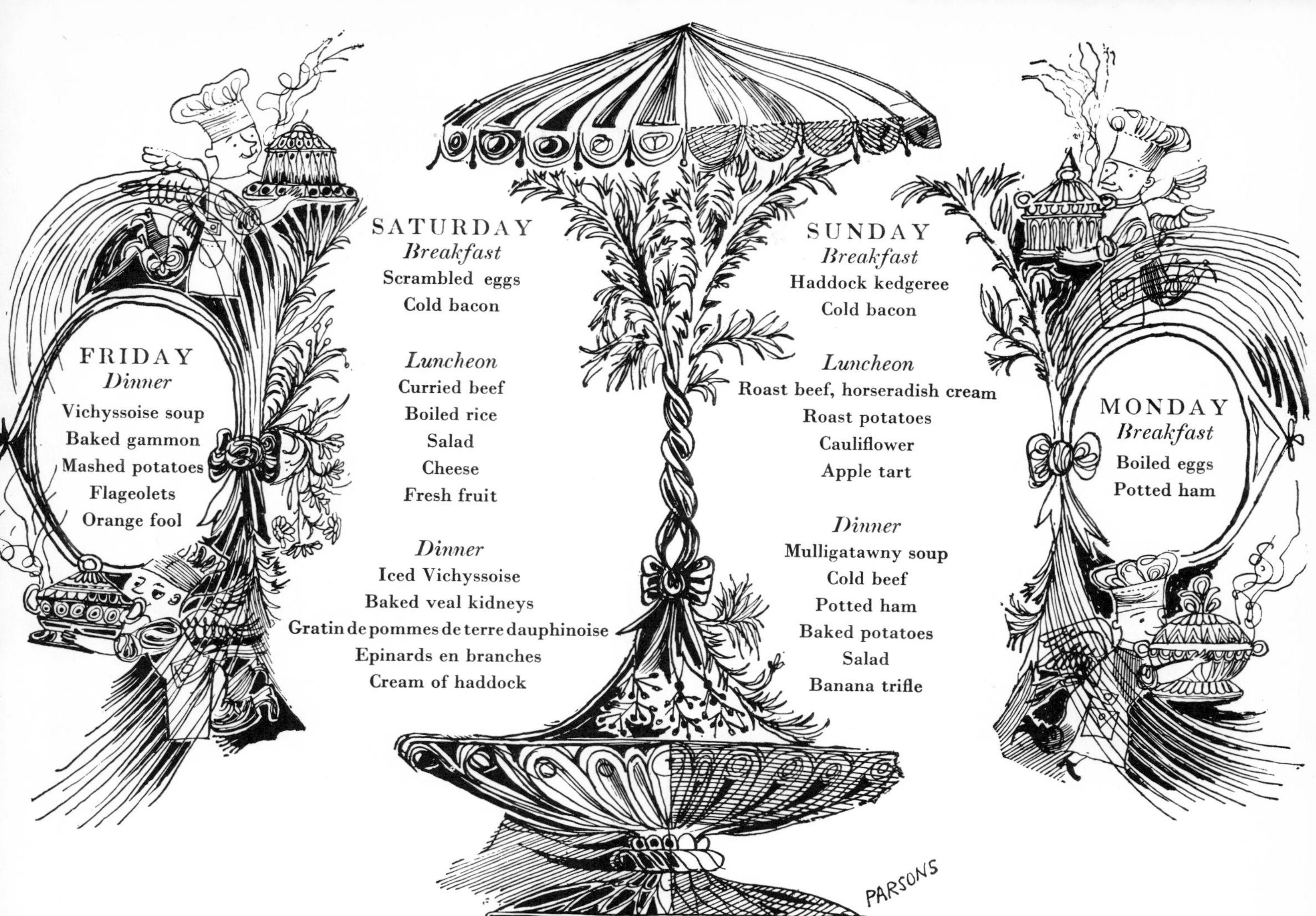

Add the curry-powder—less than two tablespoons, if you do not like a very hot curry. Cook very gently, stirring well, adding more oil (or butter), if necessary. Add the cinnamon and nutmeg, then the meat (from which you have cut off the fat), cut into cubes a little larger than lumps of sugar. Add the apple and tomatoes. Moisten with some stock. Add the coconut, raisins and chutney and the rest of the stock. Cook slowly over a gentle flame, adding more stock—or water—if the curry gets dry. Add salt, sugar and lemon juice if, after tasting, you think them desirable. Serve with boiled rice, Bombay duck and poppadums, dried in the oven, and mango chutney.

Potted ham

Take the remains of the gammon. Mince all the lean and about a quarter as much fat. Stir in some made mustard (English), some powdered mace and some nutmeg. Then add enough melted butter to bring it to the consistency of potted meat. Put it into a terrine, the terrine into a *bain marie*, and bake in a slow oven for half an hour. When cold, cover the top with more melted butter.

Cream of haddock

Cook a smoked haddock in milk until the flesh begins to fall off the bones. Remove the skin and bones and put the flesh through a mill. (This can be done on Friday.) When required, heat the haddock purée in a very little butter. Season with black pepper. Add some thick cream, but not so much as to make it runny. Serve it in an earthenware dish, garnished with large croûtons (one per person) and sprinkled with cayenne pepper.

Haddock kedgeree

Cook two haddocks in milk as in the preceding recipe. Remove the skin and bones and flake the flesh. Heat this in butter and add about the same quantity of cold boiled rice (from the curry). Add two hard-boiled eggs, cut in quarters. Season with a little salt, some black pepper and a good deal of cayenne. Add a raw egg and a cup of cream—not so much, however, as to make it runny.

Orange fool

Peel six or eight oranges so as to remove both pith and skin. Cut out the pips and save any spare juice. Make a syrup with a pint of water and half a pound of sugar by boiling them together for fifteen minutes. Pour the syrup over the oranges and their juice and let them simmer over a low flame for about five minutes. Put this through a sieve or the finest holes of a vegetable mill. When cold, stir in an equal quantity of cream or a mixture of cream and custard (the custard, needless to say, must be home-made and not out of a packet).

Luxuries for the Larder

by Peter Pirbright and Gretel Beer

Blackberry syrup
For this delicious thick syrup we present two recipes—an old family one and, in case this should frighten you, a more conventional one.

Put blackberries in a large bowl, cover with a cheesecloth and leave for eight days. By that time, to your horror, they will be covered in mildew. That is exactly as it should be. Remove mildew, place blackberries in a muslin bag and hang up over a bowl. Leave until all the juice has run out. Remove fruit, giving a slight squeeze to the muslin bag before doing so. Weigh the juice, add its own weight in sugar and simmer gently in an enamel pan. Remove any impurities that rise to the top and continue simmering until the liquid has thickened. This takes about 15 minutes. Be careful not to overcook. Remove from fire and pour into warmed bottles. Seal and store.

The second method is more conservative: 2 lb blackberries, 1 lb of sugar. In a deep bowl put alternate layers of blackberries and sugar. Cover and stand overnight in a cool place. On the next day cook gently for 15–20 minutes, pour into a muslin bag and hang up over a bowl. Leave overnight. Alternatively, have ready a large sieve with a bowl underneath and strain through that—but it is important that the fruit should be left for 12 hours in order to extract all the juice. Strain again if necessary, fill into bottles and seal. The remaining fruit pulp may be used for trifles, fruit tarts, and so on.

Bosnian plum preserve
This is excellent with cold meat, as well as with practically every type of sweet pudding. 2 lb plums (weighed after stoning), 7 oz sugar, 6 cloves and 1 small stick cinnamon in a muslin bag. Place plums, spices and sugar in a strong saucepan, simmer gently until the skin of the fruit begins to curl. Pour into warmed preserving jars, removing spices at the same time. Place a round of greaseproof paper, previously dipped in rum, on top of each jar, seal and sterilize by putting the jars into a pan filled with cold water and heating to 165° F. for 15 minutes.

Spiced marrow jam
1 lb diced vegetable marrow, 3–4 lb sugar, 2 cups vinegar, 3 cloves, 1 stick of cinnamon, 1 piece of ginger, grated rind of lemon. Put vinegar in a saucepan. Add cloves, cinnamon, ginger and grated lemon rind. Bring to the boil and quickly pour over the diced marrow. Cover and leave for two hours. Carefully drain off the liquid, return to the stove with sugar and simmer until sugar is melted. Bring to the boil, add marrow and cook until the marrow looks "glassy". Test for jam, fill into warm jars, seal and store.

Pickled peaches
About 4 lb peaches, 2 lb sugar (1 lb brown and 1 lb granulated or castor), 2 pints wine vinegar, a few cloves, 1 stick cinnamon, 1 bay leaf, 1 piece root ginger. Skin peaches carefully (the skin will come off more easily if they are dropped into boiling water for a moment). Depending on the size halve or leave whole but, if halving, leave the stone in. Put vinegar, sugar and spices into a saucepan, simmer until sugar is dissolved, then boil up once. Drop in the skinned peaches, simmer gently until fruit is tender. Lift out carefully and pack into hot jars. Boil up the syrup, pour over fruit and seal at once.

Pickled white cabbage
3 lb firm white cabbage, 1 lb green peppers, 1 lb green tomatoes, ½ lb onions, salt, sugar, about 1 pint wine vinegar. Shred cabbage, salt well and leave in a covered bowl for two hours. Chop onions and cut green peppers into strips. Slice tomatoes. Put vinegar with a pinch of sugar in a saucepan and bring to the boil. Remove from fire. Squeeze out all the liquid from the shredded cabbage, mix with the green peppers, onions and tomatoes. Pack tightly into jars. Pour the cold vinegar over the cabbage, seal and store.

Pickled mushrooms
1 lb fresh mushrooms, about ¾ pint vinegar, ¾ pint water, salt, pickling spice, 1 bay leaf, 3 shallots. Clean mushrooms. Mix together water and vinegar, add a good pinch of salt, spice and bay leaf and shallots. Bring to the boil, throw in the mushrooms and bring to the boil again. Remove mushrooms and drain on a sieve. Retain liquid and return to the stove to simmer for a few minutes. Pack mushrooms into bottling jars, pour over the cooled liquid, seal and sterilize in water bath for 10 minutes (165° F.).

Rich tomato sauce
4 lb tomatoes, ¾ lb onions, 2 tablespoons sugar, 2 cloves garlic, salt, 2 large green peppers, about 1½ pints vinegar. Crush garlic with salt under the blade of a knife. Slice onions and tomatoes, cut peppers into thin strips. Place all ingredients into a large saucepan and cook for 2–2½ hours. Taste for seasoning. Strain and pour into bottles and sterilise in water bath for 10 minutes (165° F.) Seal and store.

The great kitchen of the Royal Pavilion with its gleaming batterie de cuisine
Anthony Denney

The vegetable market at Cavaillon, in Provence

Anthony Denney

60s

The sixties in *Vogue* started as they meant to go on — bubbling with cooking talent. Elizabeth David in January 1960 began a series on The Markets of France. The first time, she says, that a cookery writer was sent anywhere "with expenses" and with a photographer—Anthony Denney—to take pictures especially for her. They went to Cavaillon, Yvetot, Martigues, Valence, Montpellier, where she found "the stalls massed with flowers; fresh fish shining pink and gold and silver in shallow baskets; cherries and apricots and peaches on the fruit barrows; one stall piled with about a ton of little bunches of soup or pot-au-feu vegetables—a couple of slim leeks, a carrot or two, a long thin turnip, tied with a rush, ready for the pot; another *charcuterie* stall, in the covered part of the market, displaying yards of fresh sausage festooned around a pyramid-shaped wire stand; a fishwife wrapping pussy's parcels of fish tidily in newspaper; an old woman at the market entrance selling winkles from a little cart shaped like a pram; a fastidiously dressed old gentleman choosing tomatoes and leaf artichokes, one by one, as if he were picking a bouquet of flowers, and taking them to the scales to be weighed (how extraordinary that we in England put up so docilely with not being permitted by greengrocers or even barrow boys to touch or smell the produce we are buying); a lorry with an old upright piano in the back threading round the market place trying to get out. These little scenes establish the character of Montpellier market in our memories. . . .

"When one tries to analyse the real reasons for the respect which French cookery has so long exacted from the rest of the world, the French genius for presentation must be counted as a very relevant point, and its humble beginnings can be seen on the market stalls, in the small town charcutiers' and pâtissiers' shops, in the modest little restaurants where even if the cooking is not particularly distinguished, the most ordinary of little dishes will be brought to your table with respect, properly arranged on a serving dish, the vegetables separately served, the object of arousing your appetite will be achieved and the proprietors of the establishment will have made the most of their limited resources. This in a sense is the exact reverse of English practice. We seem to exert every effort to make the least of the most."

Alan Cracknell

In 1961 "The rainbow sauces of Toulouse-Lautrec" included the artist's illustrated menus, to coincide with the Henri de Toulouse-Lautrec exhibition at the Tate Gallery. This was followed by a series from the Comtesse de Toulouse-Lautrec, "one of the greatest of world authorities on French cooking . . . wife of Vice-Admiral Guy de Toulouse-Lautrec, a second cousin of the painter and sister of Louise de Vilmorin, the novelist. Ideas for her recipes come from all over the world, for she is a compulsive traveller; each new dish is carefully studied, adapted and submitted to the critical judgement of her husband, children and friends before she advises it to readers. It is this rigorous home-testing that is the great and irreplaceable secret of her success."

And another series, this time on Greek food, from Lady Fleming, "beautiful Greek widow of Sir Alexander Fleming, herself a scientist and fabulous cook. Slim and elegant, she is the cousin of Jean Desses, the Paris designer. She frequently produces a four-course dinner for sixteen guests single-handed."

In November 1961 Robert Carrier and his famous cookery cards came to *Vogue* with Creative Cookery.

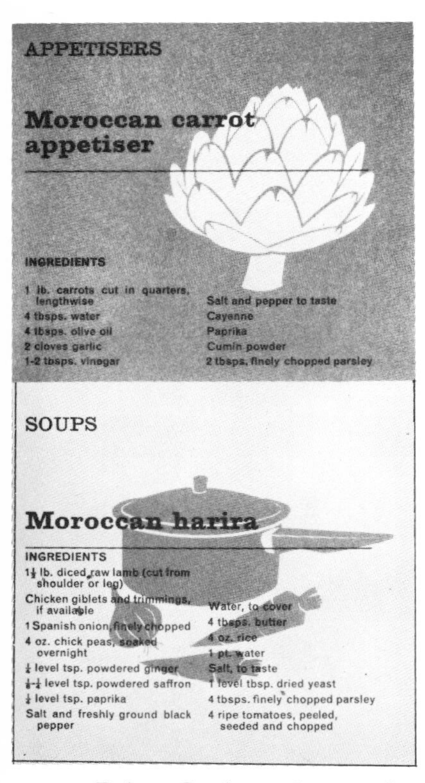
APPETISERS

Moroccan carrot appetiser

INGREDIENTS

1 lb. carrots cut in quarters, lengthwise
4 tbsps. water
4 tbsps. olive oil
2 cloves garlic
1-2 tbsps. vinegar
Salt and pepper to taste
Cayenne
Paprika
Cumin powder
2 tbsps. finely chopped parsley

SOUPS

Moroccan harira

INGREDIENTS

1½ lb. diced raw lamb (cut from shoulder or leg)
Chicken giblets and trimmings, if available
1 Spanish onion, finely chopped
4 oz. chick peas, soaked overnight
¼ level tsp. powdered ginger
⅛-¼ level tsp. powdered saffron
¼ level tsp. paprika
Salt and freshly ground black pepper
Water, to cover
4 tbsps. butter
4 oz. rice
1 pt. water
Salt, to taste
1 level tbsp. dried yeast
4 tbsps. finely chopped parsley
4 ripe tomatoes, peeled, seeded and chopped

Robert Carrier cookery cards

Like Boulestin, Robert Carrier drifted into writing about cookery. He had as a child discovered a talent for cooking and proceeded to develop it with professional and commercial verve: food accounts for his own public relations company; a new kind of eating club, the Pickwick Club; his instant-success cookery cards; his books, the first ever cookery books to reach best-seller lists; the Islington restaurant; Carrier cookshops; and Hintlesham Hall in Suffolk which he has carefully restored to be much more than a restaurant—which it superbly is—but also an arts festival and a gourmet dining club.

Robert Carrier was introduced to *Vogue* as "the most prestigious of a new generation of gourmets: he cooks for the sheer fun and pleasure of it, has the sophisticated palate of an epicure, and writes with as much wit and enthusiasm as he cooks. An American, he was making 'the best fried eggs in Connecticut' by the age of four, and soon after the war perfected his art in Paris, St Tropez, and all the gastronomic centres of Europe." He wrote in his introduction: "For the uninitiated to whom cooking with wine may seem as extravagant as it is difficult, the well-known author and gourmet, Paul Gallico, once set down this golden rule: 'The only difference between cooking with wine and not cooking with wine is that you pour some wine in.' It's as easy as that. During this new series of articles on food, drink and entertaining, I am going to dispel the maze of myths that surround *haute cuisine*. My aim? To make every phase of gastronomy as simple as cooking with wine."

From 1962 to 1966 Robert Carrier covered every aspect of cooking and entertaining from THE RETURN OF THE DINING-ROOM—"Today's accent on entertaining for the pure pleasure of it is bringing about the return of the dining-room and more intimate dinners for six to eight. Gone are the days when the dining-room was just an extra room used daily for family meals and the occasional dinner party" and TOEING THE PARTY LINE—"The conventional opening for a dinner party has always been clear soup, followed by fish, a hot entrée and a pudding. But why be conventional? And don't, I beg of you, be the hostess who over-reaches her own resources, who tortures the food to make it look fancy, who serves six courses when three or four would have been more agreeable, and who wears herself out preparing for the party and then has nothing left of herself to offer once guests have arrived" to such things as THE SECRETS OF SAUCERY, THE ART OF CHINESE COOKING, EGG TIMING and VINTAGE FOOD FOR PICNICS.

He created a special series of recipes to take advantage of the best of modern cooking equipment: an electric mincer, blender (see pages 205–9), spit, freezer

Lester Bookbinder, April 1966

Peter Rand

Robert Carrier's kitchen/garden/dining-room

and in 1966 was EATING ROUND THE WORLD. As a result—"I became two stone overweight. The correct weight for my build and height—6 feet—is 12½ stone. I kept it at an average of 14½ stone for the past year—with a dramatic rise to 15¼ after a six-week eating tour researching France's greatest restaurants." So *Vogue* published Robert Carrier's Gourmet Diet "the most delightful, easy to follow, diet plan I know and one which has brought a revolution into my life".

Robert Carrier stopped writing for *Vogue* in November 1966 to concentrate on his many other activities. His place as a cookery writer was taken by Arabella Boxer, whose passion for perfection had forced her into becoming a food expert, and whose ingenious *First Slice Your Cookbook* had brought a new dimension to cookery books. She started a HOW TO series: how to stop over-impressing your friends and alienating your family . . . how to plan ahead today and stop worrying about what to eat tomorrow . . . how to experiment with unusual vegetables and be more adventurous with the familiar ones . . . how to stop ruining vegetables and start treating them with the respect they deserve (these two with illustrations by Alan Cracknell formed *Vogue*'s Vegetable Calendar, see pages 222–5) . . . how to economise on food and stop thinking about the cost:

"Although it sounds paradoxical I find the only way to economise on food is to stop thinking about the cost. (In the same way, when on a diet people are unable to think of anything but the next meal, while if preoccupied with other things, they often find at the end of the day that they have forgotten to eat at all.) I always manage to be most economical when thinking of something else altogether. For me it comes down to this: I save money when I don't go to the butcher or the fishmonger. I don't like the cheapest cuts of meat; even for stewing I buy the best quality and prefer to go to a good butcher where the meat is properly trimmed rather than to one where it is cheaper. . . . Economy for its own sake is nothing to be proud of; anyone can buy last week's vegetables and a breast of lamb and make a disgusting meal out of them."

Lester Bookbinder, September 1966

Arabella Boxer's next series was "Entertainers in Vogue" . . . talking to Kathleen Tynan: "Ken has a passion for Lea & Perrins' Worcester sauce; he drinks it neat after the theatre"; Lady Birley—"Someone in India said a bad-tempered cook gives you indigestion, and I think it's true"; Edna O'Brien—"Cooking is my greatest daily pleasure. I love that hour about five-thirty when I come downstairs and put on an overall and know that for the next hour or two I am going to be cooking"; Diana Melly—"Once you get away from the very informal cheap way of entertaining the whole thing starts to escalate very quickly. From sausages and wine I went to pâté (bought of course) and a joint; then the next thing I know I'm doing a course at the Cordon Bleu"; and Cecil Beaton—"I prefer having dinner at home quietly with a few friends, not having to compete with the noise and hazards of a restaurant, which can so easily destroy a mood. I wish that we could all say when we are invited out, 'who is coming?' instead of taking that awful risk."

Other entertainers entertaining in *Vogue* included Lady Antonia Fraser: "My feeling for the theatrical and for appearances extends also to the food: I have a particular fancy for lovingly inspecting the panoramic buffet before a supper party in raptures at its prettiness, my ideal being the plaster doll's-house food which so enticed the eyes of the two bad mice in Beatrix Potter's story. Once my ecstasies actually carried me away and I prevented some early hungry guests from cutting a slice or two from a classically arranged smoked turkey on the grounds that this would spoil the whole look of the thing."

And Wenda Parkinson in Tobago: "I am not a born hostess—I don't have the special kind of vitality and force that are essentials, nor do I greet invitations from others with the joy they deserve. By nature I am an indolent and contented recluse and have too often wondered, gloomily and ungratefully, what entertaining is really all about."

So the sixties in *Vogue* turned into the seventies with Veronica Maclean's Menu of the Month—a year of her menus and excellent recipes start on page 227.

Arabella Boxer in her kitchen

John Goss

Sixties People and their Recipes

Lady Melchett's *"food to prepare in advance and save jangled nerves—all enough for eight people"*

FIRST COURSE

Egg, anchovy and caviar mousse

12 *hard-boiled eggs*
½ *pint whipped cream*
1½ *large tins consommé*
2 *dessertspoons anchovy essence*
1 *tablespoon sherry*
salt and pepper
1 *small tin Danish caviar*

Allow hard-boiled eggs to cool and then sieve. Add cream, consommé, anchovy essence, sherry, pinch of salt and pepper, and put in a serving bowl in the fridge. When set, cover the top with Danish caviar and serve.

Coupe caprice

2 *small melons*
1 *lb packet peeled prawns*
1 *pint well-flavoured mayonnaise*
2 *tablespoons tomato ketchup*
8 *tablespoons double cream*
2 *tablespoons finely chopped green peppers*
salt and pepper
dash of Tabasco
2 *tablespoons finely chopped tarragon*

Chill melons and prawns. Combine mayonnaise, ketchup and cream, stir in peppers and season to taste with salt, pepper and dash of Tabasco. Chill. Peel, seed and dice melon and mix together with prawns and sauce. Spoon into individual bowls and sprinkle with a little chopped tarragon.

SECOND COURSE

Lobster and chicken fiesta

1 5-*lb chicken*
1 *lb cooked lobster meat*
2 *onions*
8 *tomatoes*
oil or butter for frying
1 *dessertspoon flour*
½ *small bottle tomato ketchup*
1 *cupful chicken stock*
salt and pepper
1 *lb mushrooms*
rice

Roast the chicken and when cold cut into small pieces. Cut the lobster into pieces about one inch long. Make a sauce by frying the chopped onions and peeled tomatoes in butter or oil. Thicken with a dessertspoon flour then add ½ bottle tomato ketchup and chicken stock and seasoning to taste. Stir and bring to the boil, then add cooked chicken and lobster. Meanwhile cook the mushrooms in butter. Serve the lobster and chicken mixture with fluffy rice garnished with the mushrooms.

Lady Melchett *Henry Clarke*

Lamb cutlets in sweet and sour sauce

16 lamb cutlets
½ lb small mushrooms
4 tablespoons redcurrant jelly
2 tablespoons Worcester sauce
juice of 1 lemon
pinch of nutmeg
salt and pepper
flour
stock

Trim excess fat from 16 lamb cutlets cut from the best end of neck. Brown quickly in very hot fat. Transfer them to a casserole and add the mushrooms. Melt slowly in a saucepan the redcurrant jelly, Worcester sauce and lemon. Add pinch of nutmeg and salt and pepper to taste. Add flour to the fat in which the cutlets were browned to make a roux, then add the melted jelly mixture and a little stock to make a fairly thick gravy. Pour over the cutlets in the casserole and cook in the oven (Regulo 3) for about 1½ hours.

THIRD COURSE

Mango fool

2 tins mangoes
½ pint double cream
grated nutmeg

Put the flesh of the mangoes through a sieve keeping the juice separate. Stir in the double cream. Add a little of the juice and serve in glasses with grated nutmeg.

Cheese mousse

¼ pint milk
2 yolks of egg
½ packet powdered gelatine
white of 3 eggs
3 oz grated Parmesan cheese
½ pint double cream

Make a custard with the ¼ pint milk and 2 egg yolks (first add a little of the cold milk to egg yolks; boil the rest of the milk and when cool add to the mixture). Add ½ packet powdered gelatine, and allow to cool. Whip up 3 egg whites and when the mixture is about to set add the grated cheese, white of egg and cream. Serve with hot biscuits.

Lady Emma Tennant's Empanadas

"In Argentina they always had barbecues and you were given these to eat while the steaks were cooking. They were delicious and it was impossible to guess the filling."

Make a dough with 2 cups of flour, 2 tablespoons lard, ½ cup milk and a little salt. It should be very stiff. Knead it until it holds well together, then divide into 2 or 3 pieces. Roll out very thin, as thin as you possibly can without breaking it. Cut out rounds about 3–4 inches across. On each put 1 teaspoon coarsely grated Port Salut or similar cheese and 1 teaspoon icing sugar. Fold over, dampen the edges and pinch together like Cornish pasties. Heat plenty of lard in a frying-pan until very hot and fry them until golden brown and puffed up. Eat immediately. In Argentina they make tiny ones for canapés and eat the larger ones sprinkled with icing sugar for a first course.

Spiced chicken

Roast or boil the chicken in the usual way. Cut it up when cold and rub it all over with a mixture of butter and chutney and various curry-type spices. Put it in the fridge so that the butter becomes hard and cold, then put it under a hot grill so that it gets almost charred on the outside. Only grill long enough to char the outside and heat through.

Diana Phipps' Czechoslovakian fruit dumplings

2 cups self-raising flour
1 teaspoon salt
1 cup milk
¼ cup melted butter
1 egg
1 egg yolk
1–1½ lb fruit (cherries, plums, peaches, apricots)

Sift flour and salt into a bowl. Scald the milk with the butter and pour over the flour. Mix well. Blend in the egg and the yolk. When smooth take pieces of the dough and roll them out to a thickness of ⅛ inch. Wrap round the individual fruit (except in the case of cherries, which should be done three at a time). Drop into boiling water and poach for 5–7 minutes, turning once. Lift out the dumplings and drain. Holding them over the serving dish, prick each one two or three times with a fork, allowing the juice to run out. Serve with separate little bowls of melted butter, castor sugar, ricotta (or cottage) cheese, poppy seeds, and bread-crumbs fried golden in butter.

Caramel fruits

Fruits served with sour cream under a brown sugar crust are delicious, but to make the sugar crust requires careful watching at the last minute. To avoid this you can cheat by drawing the outline of the fruit-filled dish on a piece of silver foil, covering the silver foil liberally with butter and pressing brown sugar within the outline. Melt the sugar under the grill, watching it closely. When it has cooled, the paper can be peeled off and you will be left with a hard praline, the size of your bowl, which you put on top of your fruit in cream at the last minute.

Lady Birley's pâté irlandais

¾ lb gammon (previously boiled with 2 tablespoonfuls of honey, 1 tablespoonful of brown sugar, cloves, peppercorns, a bouquet garni of thyme, 1 bay leaf, mint and sage, and, if available, a large powdering of rosemary or, better still, a fresh sprig. Under-cook rather than over-cook); ½ lb sausage meat; 1 lb fresh salmon or the best tinned salmon; 2 tablespoonfuls of brown breadcrumbs; ½ lb butter; 1 clove of garlic; 2 onions; dash of allspice; dash of nutmeg; 2 whole eggs. Put all the ingredients gradually through a mincer, or failing this a blender, and grind, with enough sherry to keep the mixture a pliable consistency. When thoroughly blended, put into an oval-shaped bowl or soufflé dish or whatever you have. Tie a collar of greaseproof paper round the top of the dish. Place in a pan containing a little water, and cook gently in the oven for ¾ of an hour. Cool in the fridge. An aspic can be made with a good bouillon mixed with sherry, and be sure to have enough aspic to stiffen it. Take 2 to 3 small teacupfuls of this aspic and pour it into the pâté and mix it thoroughly. Leave the pâté in the fridge while the aspic gradually becomes turgid.

Before it becomes a jelly, line the bowl, bottom and sides, and let it settle. Finally, pour in the pâté, press it down well, and pour the rest of the aspic over the top to cover it thoroughly.

Potato cakes

12 oz mashed potato
4 oz self-raising flour
2 oz butter

Add butter to the potato while it is hot. When cold, blend in the flour. Roll on floured board. Cut into cakes about $\frac{1}{2}$ in thick and place on a greased griddle or thick frying-pan. Turn once, when brown, and cook other side. Re-heat in a cool oven and serve spread with butter. Sultanas may be added if liked.

Kathleen Tynan's smoked haddock

Make a béchamel sauce. Bake in milk six smoked haddock fillets, flake and add to béchamel. Add $\frac{1}{2}$ lb grated Gruyère and $\frac{1}{4}$ pint double cream before serving.

Chicken fricassée

1 3-lb chicken, cut up
1 tablespoon salted flour
3 tablespoons olive oil
1 large onion, finely chopped
4 tablespoons chopped almonds
2 cloves minced garlic
1 tablespoon minced parsley
$\frac{1}{4}$ teaspoon saffron
$\frac{1}{2}$–$\frac{3}{4}$ teaspoon salt
yolks of 2 hard-boiled eggs
1 cup chicken stock
$\frac{1}{2}$ cup of slivered ham

Dust chicken in salted flour and sauté in hot olive oil. Remove from casserole when browned; add chopped onion to casserole. When golden, add onions to chicken in baking dish. In a mortar pound almonds to a paste with garlic, parsley and saffron. Add salt and egg yolks, moisten with some oil from casserole and add one cup chicken stock. Pour over chicken. Bake uncovered for 30 minutes. Add ham during last five minutes.

Wenda Parkinson's chicken pilau

$3\frac{1}{2}$–4 lb chicken cut in serving pieces
1 cup large shrimps
wine vinegar; black pepper
2 cloves of garlic
2 tablespoons cooking oil
1 heaped teaspoon of sugar
2 cups rice
3 tomatoes, quartered
mixed fresh herbs, chopped
1 green pepper, sliced
1 onion, chopped
2 scallions, chopped
a little of a chopped small hot pepper
celery leaves, chopped

Wenda Parkinson — *Norman Parkinson*

Marinate chicken and shrimps in wine vinegar, black pepper and garlic. In an iron pan make the oil very hot and add the sugar; when it froths add the chicken. Let it brown and then cook slowly until it starts to soften. In the meantime parboil the rice and drain dry. Add tomatoes, herbs, green pepper, onion, scallions, hot pepper and celery leaves to the chicken. When nearly cooked add the rice, cover and put in the oven to finish cooking. Ten minutes before serving add the shrimps.

Banana flambé

4 large bananas
$\frac{1}{4}$ cup moist brown sugar
3 tablespoons lime juice
rind of grated orange
grated nutmeg
butter
$\frac{1}{2}$ cup of light rum

Cut the bananas lengthwise, put in a buttered fireproof dish, sprinkle with sugar, lime juice, orange rind, nutmeg, dot with butter. Pour over half the rum, bake for half an hour in a moderate oven. Baste and lower the heat if getting too brown. The bananas should be fluffy. Pour over the remaining rum and light as you serve.

The Rainbow Sauces of Toulouse-Lautrec

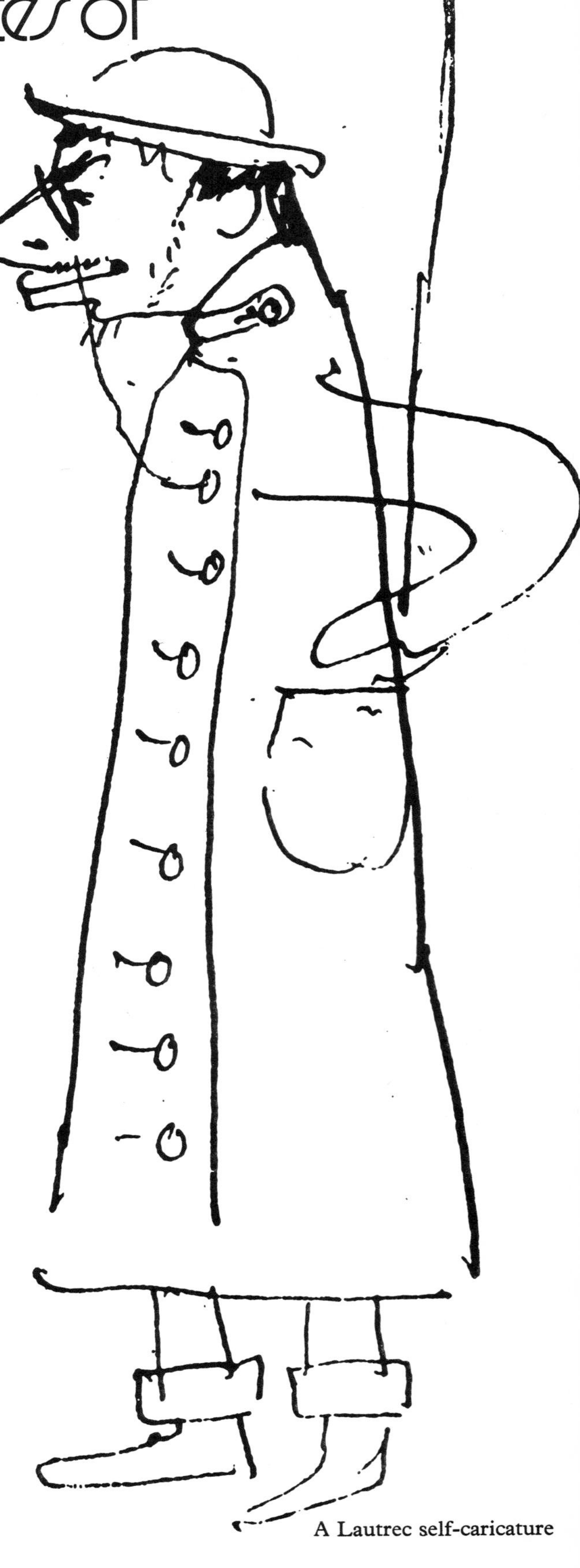
A Lautrec self-caricature

White sauce *(recipe from my grandmother)*
3 tablespoons unsalted butter
2 hard-boiled egg yolks
1 cup veal or chicken stock
1 tablespoon minced shallots
3 egg yolks, raw
1 tablespoon minced parsley
$\frac{1}{4}$ lb white mushrooms, sliced
1 cup heavy cream
1 lemon
salt
white pepper, freshly ground
Cook together in a casserole 2 tablespoons butter, the mashed egg yolks, the shallots, and the stock. Bind them with the raw egg yolks and add the parsley, the mushrooms previously sautéed in the remaining butter, and the cream. Stirring constantly, cook the sauce until it is thick and smooth. At the last moment, add the juice of the lemon, salt and pepper to taste, and serve lamb, veal, or other white meat in this sauce. It is also delicious poured over slices of mild pink ham, but for this omit salt and pepper.

Yellow sauce *(aïoli or garlic mayonnaise)*
2 egg yolks, raw
2 or 3 cloves garlic
salt
white pepper, freshly ground
1 teaspoon lemon juice
1 cup olive oil
Place the egg yolks, the garlic previously mashed, the salt, pepper, and lemon juice in a small bowl, and mash to a paste. Add the oil, drop by drop, stirring the mixture continuously in one direction with a wooden spoon. The sauce will become a thick paste. This sauce may be made more quickly in an electric blender, first mixing all ingredients but oil, then adding that a few tablespoons at a time. Serve the *aïoli*, a Marseillaise dish, excellent with cod, sardines, snails, mussels, with hard-boiled eggs, boiled or steamed potatoes, young carrots or cauliflower, artichokes, green beans, asparagus, turnips.

Yellow sauce
4 egg yolks
unsalted butter
tarragon
1 tablespoon wine vinegar
salt
pepper

18 Rue Clapeyron
Potage
Hors d'œuvre
Truite du Lac Michigan
Le Cuissot de chevreuil
Foie gras en Croute.
Salade
Entremets
Dessert.
Vins. grand Ordinaire Vouvray
Corton

Maurice Joyant

A Lautrec-illustrated menu for a dinner given in 1896 by May Belfort, a singer, who always carried a black cat

Put the egg yolks and a piece of butter the size of an egg in a small bowl, and stir gently with a wooden spoon over hot water until the mixture thickens. Remove from the heat and add another egg-sized lump of butter, stirring while it melts. Add a good handful of chopped fresh tarragon, the vinegar, and let the sauce thicken. Season with salt and fresh white pepper. Serve with all charcoal-grilled meats, kid, mutton, venison or beefsteak.

Yellow-orange sauce (*wine or sabaionne*)
6 *egg yolks*
6 *Madeira glasses of white Bordeaux, port, or cherry liqueur*
6 *heaping tablespoons of powdered sugar*
Put the egg yolks in a two-quart mixing bowl and beat them over hot water on the stove until light lemon-coloured. Add the 6 glasses of wine one at a time, beating constantly, then the sugar. Beat until thick and frothy, pile in dessert glasses, and serve at once.

Deep orange-yellow sauce (*curry*)
4 *tablespoons butter*
1 *onion, finely minced*
parsley bouquet
1 *tablespoon raw ham, finely chopped*
1 *tablespoon flour*
1 *teaspoon curry-powder*
1 *thread saffron*
1 *cup chicken bouillon*
2 *egg yolks*

Place 2 tablespoons of butter, the onion, parsley, and ham in a saucepan and cook until the onion is blanched. Add the flour, curry-powder, saffron, and bouillon, and cook for a quarter of an hour, then strain. Heat the sauce again and then, removing the casserole from the fire, bind it with the egg yolks and 2 tablespoons of butter. Serve over hard-cooked eggs, shrimps, chicken, or lamb.

Green sauce
To mayonnaise sauce, made from the recipe of *aïoli* but without garlic, add chervil, tarragon, parsley, shallots, watercress, all chopped and minced very fine in a mortar, or mixed with the mayonnaise in an electric blender. The sauce will be a lovely green. Serve with cold vegetables or fish.

Green and white sauce (*with capers*)
3 *tablespoons butter*
3 *tablespoons flour*
$\frac{3}{4}$ *cup fish stock*
$\frac{3}{4}$ *cup heavy cream*
2 *tablespoons capers*
1 *lemon*
1 *tablespoon finely minced dill*
salt
black and white pepper, freshly ground
Put the butter and flour in a casserole over a low flame. Gradually add the fish stock and cream, stirring and cooking until the sauce is thick and smooth. Remove from the flame and add the salt and pepper, capers, the juice of the lemon, and the dill. Serve with poached fish.

Dr. Gabriel Tapié de Céleyran, a cousin of Lautrec

Spring Lamb Menus

by Mapie de Toulouse-Lautrec

Lamb, roasted on a spit or in the oven, is a traditional spring dish accompanied by delicious young spring vegetables. These we shall simmer (and how French cooks adore simmering) or cook into special dishes because, except in *pot-au-feu*, plain boiled ones never appear on our tables. We don't pander to them in this way just to make life complicated. We are simply trying to get the best out of our raw materials and to vary their presentation.

Menu du déjeuner
Omelette aux coquilles Saint-Jacques
Navarin printanier
Salade
Fromage
Gâteau Basque

Menu du dîner
Soupe aux moules
Gigot d'agneau en croute
Carottes nouvelles Vichy, ou
Gratin de haricots verts
Gâteau de fraises

MENU DU DÉJEUNER

Omelette aux coquilles Saint-Jacques

16 *scallops*
16 *eggs*
4 *oz butter*
2 *liqueur glasses brandy*
2 *tablespoons flour*
½ *pint cream*
salt and pepper
and a court-bouillon made with: ½ *pint water*
¼ *pint dry white wine*
1 *each sliced carrot and onion*
1 *clove garlic,* 1 *sprig thyme,* 1 *bay leaf*
the juice of 1 *lemon*
salt and pepper

Simmer court-bouillon ingredients for 1 hour and then set aside to get cold.

If possible, buy unopened scallops and set them, round side down, in a baking tin over heat. When they have opened, remove them from the shell, cut off and throw away the black parts and wash the rest thoroughly.

Put them in the *court-bouillon*, bring to the boil then simmer for 5 minutes. Drain them and reserve the stock. Heat up half the butter, sauté the scallops in it for a minute or two then pour in the brandy and light it.

Make a béchamel sauce with the remaining butter, the flour and the strained stock, then add the cream and, if the sauce is too thin, reduce it by boiling, stirring all the time. Taste, add salt and pepper if necessary, then put the scallops into the sauce.

Beat the eggs thoroughly and make an ordinary omelette, slide it on to a hot dish and pour sauce and scallops over it.

Navarin printanier

Ingredients: 4½ lb (weight after boning) boned shoulder of lamb cut into pieces of about 3 oz, 4 oz lard, 1 heaped teaspoon caster sugar, 4 tablespoons flour, 3 tomatoes peeled and chopped, 1 clove garlic, a bouquet parsley, thyme and bay leaf tied together, 1 lb new peas, 20 each small young turnips, carrots and potatoes, salt and freshly ground pepper. Have ready some hot water or, better still, if you have it, some stock.

Melt the lard in a heavy stewpan, put in the lamb and sugar and season with salt and pepper. Brown the meat well all over then take it out of the pan and pour away three-quarters of the fat. Roll the meat in the flour until it is well coated, then put it back in the pan, sauté it for a minute or two while you stir, then add tomatoes and the bouquet and enough water or stock to cover the meat. Cover the pan and cook in a slow oven for 1 hour.

During this time, boil all the other vegetables in separate pans. Drain them when done and, at the end of the hour, add them to the meat, cover it again and cook on for a further 20 minutes.

Remove the bouquet, taste the gravy, add salt and pepper if necessary, pour in about ½ teacup cold water and if there seems excessive fat, mop it off with absorbent paper. Bring the *navarin* just back to the boil and serve very hot.

Gâteau Basque

For the dough:
1 *lb flour*
½ *oz yeast*
8 *oz butter*
8 *oz caster sugar*
3 *egg yolks*
1 *liqueur glass brandy*
the juice of ½ *lemon*

For the filling:
8 *oz caster sugar*
3 *egg yolks*
5 *tablespoons flour*
1 *pint milk*

Mapie de Toulouse-Lautrec, wife of Vice-Admiral Guy de Toulouse-Lautrec and, in April 1961, Principal of the cookery department of Maxim's Academy in Paris

Make the dough the day before it is wanted. Sieve the flour into a bowl and mix in the yeast. Make a well in the middle and put in the butter, softened but not melted, sugar, egg yolks, brandy and lemon juice. Mix thoroughly with your hands and work the dough until it no longer sticks to your fingers.

Make the filling. Put sugar, egg yolks and flour into a bowl, and stir (do not whisk) until thoroughly mixed. Bring the milk to the boil and add, little by little. Bring this mixture to the boil, stirring all the time otherwise it will stick to the bottom of the pan. Then turn the mixture out so that it will cool.

Line a flan tin with buttered greaseproof paper, then divide the dough into two equal parts and roll each one into a circle sufficiently large to overlap the tin all round. Put one piece of dough into the tin and if it tears (it is very fragile) press the torn edges together with the tips of your fingers. Put the filling into the case, cover with the other piece of dough and seal by rolling the pieces together with your fingers. Cook for 30 minutes in a hot oven, but if the tart is colouring too quickly, lower the heat.

MENU DU DINER

Soupe aux moules

4 *quarts mussels*
2 *chopped onions*
2 *bay leaves*
4 *sprigs parsley*
5 *oz butter*
1 *pint white wine*
2 *egg yolks*
½ *pint cream*
salt, pepper and, if possible, a handful of chopped fresh chervil for a garnish

Scrub and wash the mussels then put them in a large pan with onion, bay leaves, parsley, wine, butter, salt and pepper. Cover the pan and cook until the mussels open. Take them out of their shells and strain their stock through muslin.

Whisk the yolks into the cream and, off the stove, add to the mussel stock. Just before serving, put the mussels into the soup and heat up slowly, but do not let it boil. Scatter the chervil over it.

Gigot d'agneau en croûte

2 *half-legs of lamb each weighing* 2 *to* 2½ *lb*
1½ *lb short-crust pastry*
6 *oz butter*
2 *egg yolks*
salt and pepper

Warm the butter and rub it well all over the legs, then put them in a hot oven (preheated) for 20 minutes, and baste frequently adding a little salt to the gravy (don't sprinkle it directly on to the meat). Remove the legs and leave them to get luke-warm.

Pour a little hot water into the baking pan and boil it up while you stir and scrape to remove any bits of residue. Set this gravy aside.

Divide the pastry in half and roll out each piece fairly thin. Put one leg into each piece and cover it completely. Brush water under each overlapping part of the pastry and press it down firmly with your fingers. Brush the pastry all over with whisked egg yolk.

Put the legs back in a baking tin or on the baking sheet in a hot oven for 30 minutes (20 if you like the meat pinkish)—if the pastry is colouring too quickly, cover with paper. Serve and carve the lamb in the pastry. Boil up the gravy and serve in a sauceboat.

Carottes nouvelles Vichy

4½ *lb young carrots*
4 *oz butter*
1 *heaped dessertspoon caster sugar*
salt

Peel the carrots and slice them across as thinly as possible. Put them in a pan with just enough water to cover them, add the butter, sugar and a very little salt, then simmer, uncovered, over very low heat until practically all the water has evaporated and the liquid is the consistency of syrup. Let the carrots sauté gently in this until they glaze and are just beginning to brown.

Gratin de haricots verts

6 *lb French beans*
½ *teaspoon bicarbonate of soda*
¾ *pint cream*
5 *oz butter*
½ *lb button mushrooms*
salt and pepper

Throw the beans into plenty of boiling salted water, add the bicarbonate and cook, uncovered, until they are about three-quarters done—some varieties take longer than others so bite into one to test it.

While the beans are cooking, cut and throw away the earthy base of the mushroom stalks, wash and dry the mushrooms and chop them, then sauté them for 2 minutes in about 1 oz of the butter.

When the beans are ready, tip them into a colander and drain thoroughly then put them back into a pan with the cream, a very little salt and pepper and finish off their cooking over very low heat. Turn beans and cream into a buttered ovenproof dish, spoon the mushrooms over the top, melt the rest of the butter and pour it over. Add salt and pepper and set in a hot oven for 10 minutes. Serve these beans as a course on their own or with any roast meat.

Gâteau de fraises
Later in the season we make this in France with wild strawberries, but ordinary ones will do, or frozen ones completely defrosted and well drained. All but wild strawberries will have to be quartered.

Ingredients: 8 eggs, 14 oz caster sugar, a pinch of salt, ½ lb potato flour, ½ lemon, 3 tablespoons Kirsch, 2 to 2½ lb strawberries, 1 pint double cream, 4 oz vanilla-flavoured caster sugar (keep a tightly covered jar of caster sugar with a vanilla pod in it—it tastes so much better than when it is flavoured with essence), butter and flour.

Break the eggs and separate yolks and whites. Whip the yolks with the unflavoured sugar and pinch of salt until they become white and creamy then beat in the potato flour and juice of the lemon very thoroughly.

Whip the whites absolutely stiff and fold into the yolk mixture lightly but thoroughly, working with an upward movement all the time.

Butter the inside of a large mould (the mixture should only fill it by about two-thirds as the cake rises considerably while cooking), dust it with flour, shake out any surplus then put in the mixture, and bake in a fairly hot oven until a skewer or knife pushed into the cake comes out dry (about 45 minutes).

When the cake is cold, cut it horizontally into 3 slices. Sprinkle the first slice with 1 tablespoon of Kirsch, then put a layer of strawberries and then a layer of cream ready whipped with the flavoured sugar. Cover with the second slice, sprinkle with Kirsch, add strawberries and cream as before. Cover with the third slice, sprinkle with Kirsch then spread the remaining cream over the whole cake and stud the top all over closely with strawberries. Chill in the refrigerator for several hours.

Oranges and Lemons

by Mapie de Toulouse-Lautrec

Orange frangipane tart (*Tarte frangipane à l'orange*)
Ingredients for the tart:
10 *oz flour*
¼ *lb caster sugar*
½ *lb butter*
1 *egg*
1 *pinch bicarbonate of soda*
1 *pinch salt*

Ingredients for the frangipane:
1¾ *pints milk*
¼ *lb caster sugar*
4 *tablespoons flour*
5 *oz butter*
4 *eggs*
2 *oz chopped almonds*
1 *lb marmalade*

Make the pastry. Put the butter in a warm place to soften. Sieve the flour into a basin, mix in the egg, butter, sugar, bicarbonate and salt, and work it into a nice smooth dough. Set it aside in the cool.

Make the frangipane. Set aside about ¼ pint of the milk then warm up the rest slowly with the sugar, butter and almonds. Stir the cold milk gradually into the flour until you have a smooth cream, then beat in the eggs.

When the milk has just come to the boil, take it off the stove and cool it for a minute or two, then, whisking continuously, pour in the egg and flour mixture a very little at a time. Boil for a few minutes. Set aside to cool.

Roll the pastry as thin as possible and line a greased flan tin. Spread a layer of marmalade over the bottom of the pastry then fill up with the frangipane. Cut the surplus pastry into narrow strips, twist them and arrange criss-cross on the tart. Bake the tart in a hot oven for about 20 minutes and, when it is cooked, spoon more marmalade between the crossed strips of pastry. Enough for 6.

Frothy orange cake (*Gâteau mousseux à l'orange*)
2 *oz flour*
2 *oz butter*
2 *oz caster sugar*
1 *tablespoon cream*
4 *eggs*
5 *tablespoons milk*
1 *large orange*

Grate the rind of the orange on the finest grater and put it into a small bowl with the cream. Heat up the milk just short of boiling. Melt the butter in a saucepan over very low heat, and directly it has melted, add the sugar and stir with a wooden spoon for a minute or two, then stir in the flour, the cream and rind and the milk, and stir continously while the mixture thickens. Take the saucepan off the stove and let it cool while you get the eggs ready.

Separate yolks and whites and whip the whites very stiff. Beat the yolks, one at a time, into the cooled mixture, then fold in the whites lightly with an upward movement.

Grease a Charlotte mould, turn the mixture into it, put it in a *bain marie*. Set in a slow oven for 30 minutes. Let the cake get tepid before you unmould it and serve as it is or leave to get cold, whichever you like. Enough for 4.

Orange sponge (*Éponge à l'orange*)

3 eggs
8 very juicy large oranges
5 oz flour
1 pinch bicarbonate of soda
1 lb caster sugar
5 tablespoons rum

Beat the eggs in a basin, sieve in the flour and stir in 6 oz of the sugar and the bicarbonate. Grate the rind of 2 of the oranges, add this to the mixture and mix thoroughly. Grease a cake tin, put in the mixture and bake in a hot oven for about 30 minutes.

During this time, squeeze all the oranges and put the juice in a saucepan with the remaining 10 oz of sugar and the rum. Simmer into a syrup but do not let it boil. When the cake is done, turn it out on to a deepish dish and pour the hot syrup over it at once. Enough for 6.

Lemon and white wine cream (*Crème au citron au vin blanc*)

4 lemons
½ pint white wine
¼ lb caster sugar
12 egg yolks

Beat the yolks. Squeeze the lemons and put the juice into the top of a double saucepan with the sugar, wine and yolks. Put the double saucepan over moderate heat and whisk without stopping while the mixture thickens—this happens quite quickly, but the cream must not boil so lift the top of the saucepan out of the water occasionally while you continue to whisk. This is enough for 6 people.

Lemon four-quarters (*Quatre-quarts au citron*)

2 lemons
2 eggs
the weight of the eggs in flour
also in caster sugar
also in butter
1 teaspoon baking powder
6 oz icing sugar

Mix the baking powder into the flour. Squeeze the lemons. Put the butter in a warm place to soften.

Cream butter and caster sugar together until it is perfectly smooth then add one egg and beat the mixture for several minutes. Add the second egg and beat for several minutes more. Stir in 1 tablespoon of lemon juice then sieve in the flour and mix.

Turn the mixture into a greased cake tin and bake in a fairly hot oven for about 30 minutes. Leave the cake in the tin until cold and while it is cooling, stir the remaining lemon juice and 1 teaspoon of hot water into the icing sugar, and beat until it is smooth. Turn out the cake and ice it. Enough for 4.

Lime soufflé (*Soufflé au limon*)

2 limes
1½ oz candied orange peel
4 eggs
2½ oz lump sugar
4 tablespoons flour
2 oz butter
8 tablespoons milk
salt

Rub the pieces of sugar on the skins of the limes until they are thoroughly impregnated with the flavour, then put them into a basin with the milk and stir until the sugar has completely dissolved.

Sieve the flour into a saucepan, then, with a wooden spoon, stir in the milk little by little. Put the saucepan over very low heat and add the butter, stirring all the time. When the mixture is thick and smooth, add a pinch of salt and take the pan off the stove.

Separate yolks and whites of the eggs, grate the rind of the limes on a medium grater and finely chop the candied peel. Beat the egg yolks one after the other into the mixture in the pan and add the lime rind and candied peel. Whisk the egg whites very stiff and fold them into the mixture. Put this into a well greased soufflé mould and bake in a moderate oven about 30 minutes, serve immediately. Enough for 6.

Cold lemon soufflé (*Soufflé froid au citron*)

2 lemons
5 eggs
5 oz caster sugar

Squeeze the lemons and separate yolks and whites of the eggs. Beat the yolks thoroughly with the sugar then stir in the lemon juice. Put this into the top of a double saucepan and stir while it thickens but do not let it boil. Take the pan off the stove.

Whisk the egg whites very firm and fold them into the mixture. Turn into a fruit dish and set in the refrigerator to get very cold. Enough for 4.

Frosted oranges (*Oranges givrées*)

6 oranges
½ lb caster sugar

Cut a cap off each orange about a third down from the stalk end. Remove pulp, squeeze it and reserve the juice.

Put the sugar into a saucepan with ½ pint of water, heat up to 86 degrees on a sugar thermometer. Take the pan off the stove, and add the orange juice and put back on the stove until the syrup reaches 66 degrees. Leave the syrup to get cold, then put it into the ice tray of the refrigerator. When it is set but before it is ice-hard, fill the oranges with it. Enough for 6.

Orange ice cream (*Glace à l'orange*)

1½ pints of milk
4 whole eggs
8 egg yolks
10 oz caster sugar
1 pint double cream
3 oranges
8 tablespoons Cointreau

Finely grate the rind of the oranges and put it into a basin with the juice of 1 orange, the eggs and yolks and sugar, and whip it until the mixture is frothy.

Bring the milk to the boil, then stir without ceasing while you add it, little by little, to the egg mixture. Put all this into the top of a double saucepan over low heat and continue to stir all the time while the mixture thickens but on no account let it boil. Leave it to get cold. Whip the cream mix it into the egg mixture, add the Cointreau, mix again thoroughly, and put into the freezer. Enough for 8.

Take One Electric Blender

by Robert Carrier

There are three basic items in the kitchen that I simply could not do without: a butcher's chopping block, four inches thick, that I keep next to the cooker top; a small wooden chopping bowl with a knife with a curved blade specially designed to fit it; and a large pestle and mortar. I learnt to use this last ancient piece of equipment in France, and find it indispensable for pounding herbs to make a sauce, meat to make a pâté, or anchovies for a Provençal anchoïade. But of all modern electric equipment, I find the blender an absolute essential. This is a magic tool that takes much of the drudgery out of cooking. It takes over the time-consuming operations—puréeing, grating, chopping and the perfect blending which makes simple dishes taste like the work of a life-long professional.

Keep your blender where it is always available for instant use. I have had mine built compactly into the counter top in my kitchen, and it is measure-marked for accurate filling. It makes subtle soups, perfect mayonnaise, quick vegetable purées, blends rich creamy sauces and mixes refreshing fruit drinks in the Italian manner: just peel and core 1 apple and pear; add grapes, 1 banana and any other fruit of your choice; drop in a few ice cubes and fill three-quarters full with milk. Blend to a smooth creamy drink.

Use your blender to make all kinds of fruit fools: rhubarb, apple, gooseberry, plum. And to make delicious water ices: this blackcurrant ice is excellent, and frozen currants can be used when fresh ones are not available. Purée 1 pint topped and tailed blackcurrants in your blender, add the strained juice of 2 lemons to 3–4 oz granulated sugar and stir well. Add to the fruit purée and place in the freezing tray of refrigerator and freeze until almost stiff—about 1 hour. Put half the blackcurrant ice in the blender and blend until softened to sherbet consistency. Repeat with second half. Spoon into chilled glasses and serve at once.

When making thick purées, be careful not to overheat the motor of your blender. If you find that the mixture is not being drawn properly down into the blades of the blender as the motor whirls, stop the motor and stir the mixture with a rubber spatula to introduce air into it. If you find your mixture is a little too thick to blend easily, just add a few tablespoons of liquid. Never use your blender for raw meat or fish that has not first been minced. The fibres of raw meat and fish are too resistant for the blender to deal with efficiently, but once these fibres are broken down by mincing you will be able to blend the raw fish, poultry, game or meat quite easily. The following recipes all use the blender to achieve, quickly and effortlessly, the smoothly blended ingredients necessary for fresh-tasting vegetable soups, and the blender terrines.

Blender liver terrine

¾ lb liver sausage
2-4 *tbsps mayonnaise*
2-4 *tbsps cream*
1 *tbsp finely chopped onion*
finely chopped parsley
salt and freshly ground black pepper
lemon juice or brandy
toast, crackers, or thin slices of rye or pumpernickel bread
sieved hard-boiled egg yolks (optional)

Combine liver sausage, mayonnaise, cream, finely chopped onion and 1 tbsp finely chopped parsley in a blender and flavour to taste with salt, freshly ground black pepper, and lemon juice or brandy; whirl until smooth.

Serve on toast, crackers or thin slices of rye or pumpernickel bread, or pack into small individual crocks or a terrine, and decorate with sieved hard-boiled egg yolks or chopped parsley.

Blender spinach soup

2 *lb fresh spinach leaves*
4 *tbsps butter*
salt and freshly ground black pepper
½ pint double cream
½ pint chicken stock

Wash spinach leaves in several changes of water; drain. Put spinach in a thick-bottomed saucepan with butter, salt and black pepper to taste, and simmer, stirring until tender.

Whisk in the blender or put through sieve. Season to taste with salt and black pepper. Combine with cream, chicken stock; heat and serve. Serves 4.

Pea and cucumber soup

2 *pints chicken consommé*
1 *small packet frozen peas*
4 *tbsps butter*
½ cucumber, peeled and seeded
2 *egg yolks*
¼ pint double cream
Salt and freshly ground black pepper

Robert Carrier's summer kitchen at St Tropez
David Gentleman

Defrost peas and simmer in 2 tbsps each chicken consommé and butter until cooked. Drain and purée in blender or through a fine sieve. Cut cucumber into matchstick-sized slivers; simmer in remaining butter until tender.

Beat eggs; add cream and purée of peas. Heat chicken consommé; stir in purée mixture and cook over a gentle heat, stirring continuously, until green-tinted soup is smooth and thick. Do not let soup come to the boil or it will curdle. Just before serving, stir in *julienne* of cucumber sticks; add salt and black pepper to taste. Serves 4.

Creamy pea soup

½-¾ lb shelled peas
1 medium potato, sliced
1 medium onion, sliced
1 lettuce, cut into quarters
1 pint chicken stock
½ pint double cream
juice of ½ lemon
salt and freshly ground black pepper

Place peas, potato, onion, lettuce and half the chicken stock in a saucepan and bring to the boil. Cover and simmer for 15 minutes. Transfer contents of saucepan to the container of blender, blend until vegetables are puréed; or press through a fine sieve.

Return to saucepan; add the remaining stock and simmer for 5 minutes. Add cream and lemon juice and season to taste with salt and pepper. Serves 4.

Quick blender mayonnaise

2 eggs
¾ pint olive oil
4 tbsps lemon juice or vinegar
½ level tsp each dry mustard and salt
freshly ground black pepper

Combine eggs, ¼ pint olive oil, lemon juice or vinegar, dry mustard, salt and freshly ground black pepper, to taste, in electric blender. Cover the container and turn the motor to high. When blended, remove cover and add ½ pint olive oil in a thin steady trickle, blending continuously. Correct seasoning and use as desired.

Brandade de saumon

1½ lb fresh salmon
1 clove garlic, crushed
6 tbsps double cream
¼ pint olive oil
juice of ½ lemon
salt and freshly ground black pepper
toast triangles fried in olive oil or butter

Poach salmon until tender. Remove from water; drain and flake, removing bones and skin.

Place salmon flakes in electric blender with crushed garlic, 2 tbsps cream and 4 tbsps olive oil, and blend, adding remainder of cream and olive oil alternately from time to time until the oil and cream are completely absorbed and the brandade is creamy smooth. When ready to serve: simmer mixture in top of a double saucepan; stir in lemon juice and season to taste with salt and black pepper.

Brandade de saumon may be served hot or cold. If hot, place in a mound on a warm serving dish and surround with toast triangles fried in olive oil or butter. Serves 4.

Carrot ring mould

2-3 lb new carrots
4 tbsps butter
¼ pint chicken stock
1 tbsp sugar
salt
2 eggs
butter
6-8 tbsps grated cheese
freshly ground black pepper
cooked peas and button onions

Wash carrots; slice thickly and place in a saucepan; cover with cold water and cook over a high heat until water boils. Drain.

Simmer blanched carrots in butter, chicken stock, sugar, salt to taste, until carrots have absorbed liquid and are tender. Combine mixture with eggs, 4 tbsps softened butter, cheese, salt and black pepper to taste, in the blender: blend until smooth. Press into buttered ring mould and heat in a slow oven (325° F, Mark 3) for 15 mins. Turn carrot ring out on a heated serving dish: fill centre with cooked peas and onions. Surround with remaining peas and onions. Serves 6.

Purée St Germain

2 lb fresh or frozen peas
1 lettuce heart, shredded
12 tiny spring onions, or ½ Spanish onion, sliced
3 sprigs parsley
¼ lb butter
4 tbsps chicken stock or water
sugar
salt
2 boiled potatoes, puréed (optional)

Put peas in a saucepan with the shredded heart of a lettuce, spring onions, parsley, half the butter, chicken stock or water, and sugar and salt to taste. Bring to a boil and cook slowly until peas are tender. When cooked, remove parsley and drain, reserving juices. Blend to a fine purée in an electric blender (or press through a fine sieve) and reheat in the top of a double saucepan, adding a little of the strained juices and the remaining butter. If purée is too thin, add puréed potatoes to lend body. Serves 4.

Raspberry Bavarian cream

1 packet frozen raspberries (10 oz)
juice of 1 lemon
2 level tbsps gelatine
4 tbsps milk
2-4 tbsps sugar
2 egg yolks
½ pint double cream
1 cup crushed ice

Defrost raspberries in a bowl with lemon juice. Drain ¼ pt of the juices into a saucepan; heat to simmering point. Pour the hot juice into the container of blender. Add gelatine and milk; cover; blend at high speed for 1 minute.

Remove cover; add sugar, raspberries, egg yolks. Then cover and blend at high speed for 5 seconds. Remove cover, add cream, crushed ice and keep blending until smooth. Pour into a mould and chill until set. Serves 4 to 6.

Bob Brooks

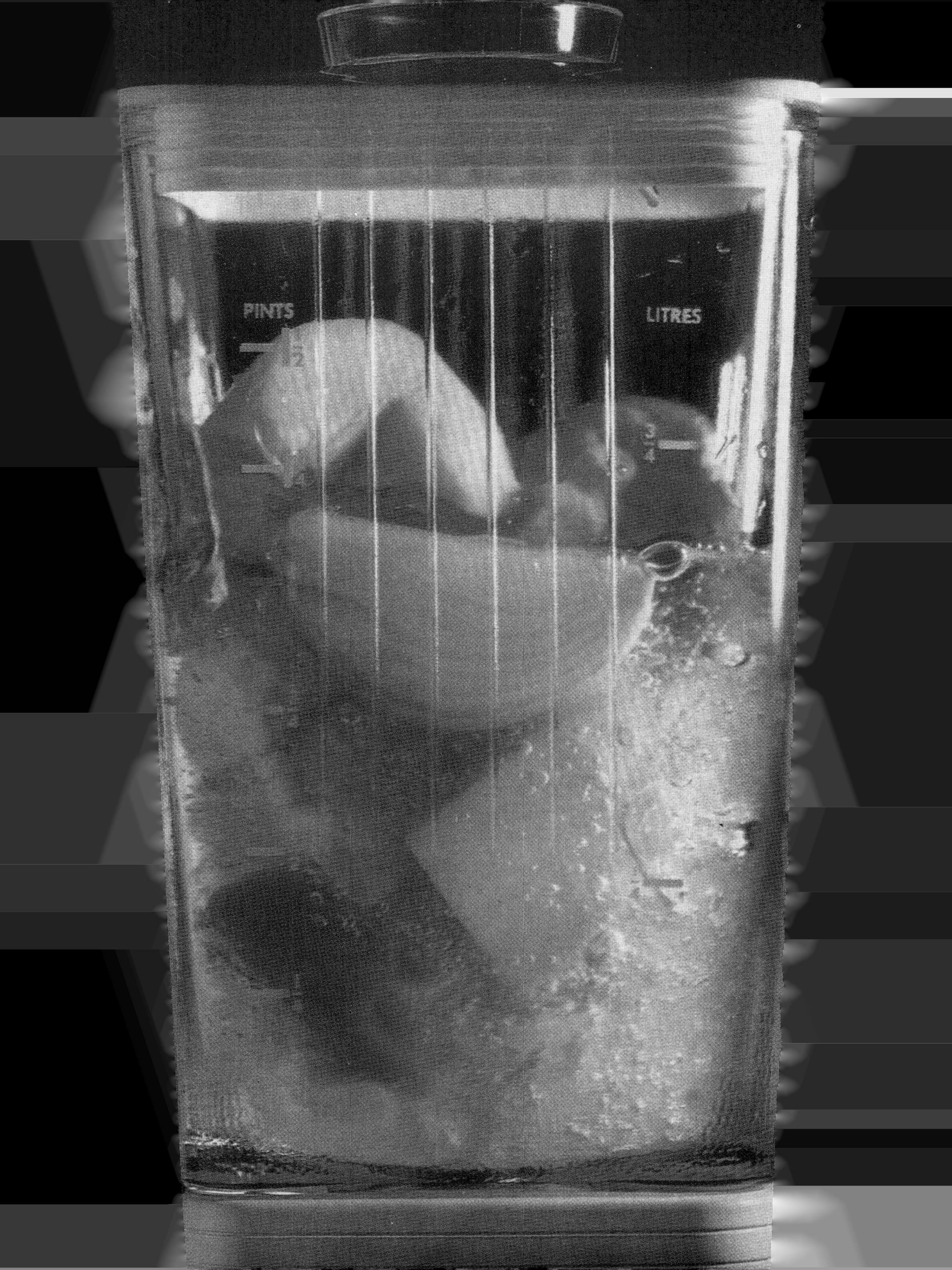
PINTS
LITRES

Taramasalata

1 jar smoked cod's roe (8 oz)
6 slices white bread
¼ Spanish onion, grated
1-2 cloves garlic, mashed
8 tbsps olive oil
juice of 1 lemon
1 tbsp finely chopped parsley
green olives
hot toast

Place cod's roe in a mortar. Trim crusts from bread; soak bread in water; squeeze and add to cod's roe. Pound mixture to a smooth paste. Combine in an electric blender with grated onion and garlic. Then add olive oil and lemon juice alternately in small amounts, blending well until mixture is smooth.

Serve in a salad bowl, sprinkled with chopped parsley, garnished with green olives. Serve with hot toast. Serves 4 to 6.

Salmon soufflé mousse

1¼ lb fresh salmon
4 tbsps cognac
6 egg whites
1 tsp onion juice
3 tbsps lemon juice
salt and freshly ground black pepper
cayenne pepper
¾ pt double cream
butter
prawn and lobster sauce

Remove bones and skin from salmon; dice and marinate in cognac for a few hours. Place 2 egg whites in blender, then add diced salmon, the marinade, onion juice and lemon juice; season to taste with salt, freshly ground black pepper and cayenne pepper, and blend at low speed until fish and eggs form a smooth paste. Turn to a high speed and blend until very smooth.

Put purée in a bowl surrounded with cracked ice; cool. Whip cream until thick and whisk into fish purée. Beat 4 egg whites very stiff but not dry, and gently fold into mixture; correct seasoning; remove bowl from ice and pour mixture into a buttered soufflé dish. Stand in a pan of hot but not boiling water and bake in a slow oven (325° F, Mark 3) until firm enough to turn out—45 to 60 minutes. Turn out on to a heated serving dish and serve with Prawn and Lobster Sauce. Serves 4.

To make Prawn and Lobster Sauce: Shell 1 small lobster and boil chopped shells in ¾ pt fish fumet or rich fish stock for a minute or two. Melt 3 tbsps butter in the top of a double saucepan; stir in 3 tbsps flour and cook over water for 3 minutes, stirring continuously until smooth. Strain fish fumet and add to roux, stirring continuously until sauce is rich and creamy. Simmer gently for 20 minutes; then add cream and continue cooking, uncovered, stirring from time to time to keep skin from forming, until the sauce is reduced to the desired consistency. Dice lobster meat and sauté with ½ lb frozen prawns, coarsely chopped, in 2 tbsps butter until heated through; season to taste with salt, freshly ground black pepper and cayenne. Flame with 2 tbsps cognac and add to sauce. Makes about 1 pt. Good for poached fish and fish and shellfish soufflés.

James Beard's clam soup

2 7-oz cans whole clams in juice
¾ pt double cream
2 tbsps butter
salt and freshly ground black pepper
paprika

In a blender, blend whole clams in juice until the mixture is thick. Pour it into the top of a double saucepan. Add double cream and butter, and season to taste with salt and freshly ground black pepper. Heat the soup to boiling point over hot water and serve it with a dash of paprika. Serves 4 to 6.

Prawn bisque

½ lb cooked prawns
¼ pt canned clam juice
¾ pt double cream
¼ tsp paprika
salt and freshly ground black pepper
4-6 tbsps dry sherry
1 tbsp finely chopped parsley
1 tbsp finely chopped chives

Place cooked prawns (saving one or two for garnish) and clam juice in the container of electric blender, and blend for 1 minute. Remove to the top of a double saucepan, add cream and paprika, and season to taste with salt and freshly ground black pepper. Cook over hot water, stirring from time to time, until soup comes to the boil. Thin to taste with additional clam juice. Add sherry, and serve immediately in individual cups, garnished with chopped prawns and finely chopped parsley and chives. Serves 4 to 6.

Artichokes with green mayonnaise

4 artichokes
salt
juice of ½ lemon
green mayonnaise
½ pt well-flavoured mayonnaise
1 handful each sprigs of watercress, parsley and chervil
1 tbsp finely chopped watercress leaves
1 tbsp finely chopped chervil
2 tbsps finely chopped parsley
1 tbsp finely chopped tarragon leaves
lemon juice
salt and freshly ground black pepper

Remove tough outer leaves of artichokes and trim tops of inner leaves. Trim the base and stem of each artichoke with a sharp knife. Cook until tender (30-40 minutes) in a large quantity of salted boiling water to which you have added the juice of ½ lemon. Artichokes are ready when a leaf pulls out easily. When cooked, turn artichokes upside down to drain. Serve cold with Green Mayonnaise. Pull off a leaf at a time and eat the tender base, then remove "choke" (fuzzy centre) and eat artichoke heart. Serves 4.

To prepare Green Mayonnaise: wash sprigs of watercress, parsley and chervil; pick them over carefully and put them in a saucepan with a little salted boiling water. Allow greens to boil for 6-7 minutes; drain and press as dry as possible. Pound greens in a mortar; rub through a fine sieve and add green purée to mayonnaise. Whirl green mayonnaise, finely chopped watercress leaves and herbs in blender, or blend well with a whisk; add lemon juice, salt and black pepper to taste. Chill.

Caradog Williams

Gourmet Diet

by Robert Carrier

This gourmet diet plan sheds pounds as easily as water from a duck's back, lets you eat in restaurants without any qualms and dine in other people's houses without becoming a problem to your hostess. It is the most delightful, easy to follow, diet plan I know and one which has brought a revolution into my life. One and a half stones lighter than my usual 14½, I am well on the way towards the ideal weight for my height (12½ stone). And all this in a matter of weeks. The gourmet diet starts off with one premise; protein turns into energy, carbohydrates into fat. So: limit your carbohydrates. This is easy to understand when it comes to breads, sugars, pasta, rice, sweets and puddings, but gets a little more complicated when we find that even fruits and vegetables are high in carbohydrate rating. We are helped, however, by the fact that our bodies only require a minimum of 30 grammes of carbohydrates which allows us to adjust our intake daily and thus painlessly to cut down our excess weight, enjoy as much and as many high protein foods as desired. This means you can have all the fish, shellfish, meat, poultry and game you want and still lose weight. One of my first gourmet diet meals was: a fresh crab salad dressed with one tablespoon of mayonnaise and one tablespoon of lemon juice, followed by two braised quails served with green vegetables. My companion and I split a bottle of Corton Grancey, then we each had a brandy with our coffees. That week-end I lost 5 lb. With this high protein, normal fat, low carbohydrates diet, all your meals can be as high powered if you want them to be. In the main, of course, you won't want to eat so richly. Plain grills and roasts, except when giving dinner parties or dining out, will be the answer. And you can drink spirits and wines within reason without affecting your loss of weight. Begin your new life with the following crash diet to start your weight loss. Breakfast: coffee, double cream (no sugar); two rashers grilled bacon or one poached egg. Lunch or dinner: first course, chicken or beef consommé; or smoked trout, salmon or eel; or grilled fish or shellfish. Main course, poached, grilled or baked fish or shellfish; or grilled steak or chop or grilled or roast lamb, veal or beef; or grilled or roast poultry or game (add one serving of green vegetables). Salad or cheese, coffee (no sugar). From this crash diet, go on to the dietary additions. Below are 15 menus you can enjoy and still lose weight.

Breakfast
Coffee with double cream (no sugar)
your choice of any of the following:
2 *rashers of bacon and* 1 *egg (poached, soft boiled, scrambled)*
2 *eggs (poached, soft boiled, scrambled)*
1 *kipper (or* 1 *serving smoked haddock)*
2 *sausages*

Robert Freson

Lunch or dinner menus
First course; main course (with green vegetable); salad or cheese (no bread); coffee

Lunch and dinner first courses
Chicken or beef bouillon or consommé
Oysters on the half shell
Smoked trout, salmon or eel
Potted shrimps
Prawn cocktail
Lobster cocktail
Lobster mayonnaise
Fresh crab mayonnaise
Grilled sole
Poached or grilled turbot or halibut
Grilled herring or mackerel
Grilled scallops
Grilled lobster with sherry
Moules à la marinière
Salami
Parma ham

Lunch and dinner first courses
If no green vegetable with meal
Artichokes à la vinaigrette
½ *avocado pear à la vinaigrette*
Broccoli hollandaise
Brussels sprouts appetiser
Leeks à la vinaigrette

Lunch and dinner main courses
Roast, grilled, braised meat (beef, lamb, veal, pork)
Sweetbreads, kidneys, brains
Roast, grilled, braised poultry or game
Poached, grilled, baked fish, shellfish

Salads
4–6 *lettuce leaves and* 6 *slices cucumber,* 1 *stalk celery with French dressing*

Cheeses: one of the following
Cheddar, Camembert, Gruyère, Roquefort

Drinks
1 *Pre-lunch or dinner: Dry sherry*
Dry Martini
Whisky, gin or vodka on the rocks, with soda or water
Dry white wine
2 *Lunch or dinner drinks:*
Dry white wine or rosé wine
Red wines

Fifteen Gourmet Diet Menus

1

Chicken consommé
Grilled lamb chops
Puréed green peas (small portion)
Salad or cheese

2

Smoked fish platter
(smoked salmon, smoked eel and smoked trout)
Chicken paprika
Steamed spinach
Cheese

3

Parma ham
Veal chops
Green salad

4

Raw green vegetables (cucumber, celery and green pepper)
Ham and beef burgers with anchovy sauce
Cheese

5

Taramasalata
Lamb stew with courgettes
Salad or cheese

6

Fresh crab with mayonnaise and lemon dressing
Roast pheasant
Buttered spinach

7

Whitebait
Grilled steak or chops
Cauliflower and green beans hollandaise

8

Brussels sprouts appetiser
Italian veal cutlets au gratin
Green salad
Cheese

9

Baked eggs
Lamb's kidneys en brochette
Puréed spinach
Cheese

10

Prawn or lobster cocktail
Steamed chicken
Chinese green beans

11

Brochettes of cod and sole with mustard sauce
Beefsteak with Roquefort butter
Buttered broccoli
Green salad

12

Salami
Baked fish with mustard sauce
Raw cabbage salad
Cheese

13

Grilled lobster with sherry
Veal with rosemary
Braised chicory
Cheese

14

Potted shrimps
Lamb steaks with béarnaise sauce
Spinach
Salad or cheese

15

Oysters on the half shell
Roast beef Redbridge
Leeks in butter

Chinese green beans

1 lb green beans
2 tbsps peanut oil or lard
1 level tsp salt
$\frac{1}{4}$ pt water
1 tbsp soy sauce, sake, or dry sherry

Wash and trim beans; break them into sections about 1-inch long. Heat oil or lard in the wok (or frying-pan): add beans and cook over medium heat for 1 minute, stirring continually.

Add salt and water; cover pan and cook beans for 3 minutes; remove cover and simmer, stirring from time to time, until all the water has evaporated (about 5 minutes). Add soy sauce, sake or dry sherry, to taste.

Brussels sprouts appetiser

1 lb small Brussels sprouts
salt and freshly ground black pepper
$\frac{1}{4}$ pt well-flavoured vinaigrette dressing
lettuce leaves
2 tbsps finely chopped onion
4 tbsps finely chopped parsley

1. Prepare and cook Brussels sprouts in the usual way.
2. Place Brussels sprouts in a bowl; pour over well-flavoured vinaigrette dressing; toss well and leave to marinate in this mixture for at least 2 hours.
3. To serve: Line a salad bowl or hors d'oeuvre dish with leaves of lettuce and arrange marinated Brussels sprouts in centre. Sprinkle with finely chopped onion and parsley and serve. Serves 4.

Roast beef Redbridge

4 thick slices rare roast beef
2 tbsps butter
meat juices left over from roast (fat skimmed)
1 tbsp Dijon mustard
4-6 tbsps red wine
freshly ground black pepper
finely chopped chives

Melt butter in large frying-pan. Sauté beef-slices in this until warmed through. In the meantime, combine meat juices with mustard, whisking well until blended. Pour over meat in pan and let sizzle for a moment; then pour in red wine and turn up heat to reduce sauce. Season to taste with a little freshly ground black pepper and finely chopped chives. Serves 4.

Grilled steak with Roquefort butter

1 rump steak (about 1$\frac{1}{2}$ inches thick)
freshly ground black pepper
2-4 tbsps softened butter
salt
Roquefort butter:
1 oz Roquefort cheese
2 oz butter
juice of $\frac{1}{2}$ lemon
2 tbsps finely chopped parsley, chervil or chives
salt and freshly ground black pepper

Remove steak from refrigerator at least 30 minutes before cooking and slit fat in several places around side to prevent meat from curling during cooking. Pre-heat grill for 15 to 20 minutes. Sprinkle both sides of steak with freshly ground black pepper and spread with softened butter.

Rub hot grid with a piece of suet; place steak on grid and grill for 8 minutes on each side for a rare steak; grill a few more minutes if you prefer steak to be medium rare. Sprinkle with salt to taste.

To make Roquefort butter

Cream Roquefort cheese and butter with lemon juice and finely chopped parsley, chervil or chives. Season to taste with salt and freshly ground black pepper.

To serve: Transfer steak to a heated serving platter and top with Roquefort butter. Serves 4.

Ham and beef burgers

1 lb freshly ground beef
French mustard
salt and freshly ground black pepper
4 thin slices ham
butter and olive oil
Anchovy butter:
2 tbsps softened butter
anchovy paste

Form beef into eight thin, oval-shaped patties. Spread four patties with French mustard and season generously with salt and freshly ground black pepper. Place a slice of cooked ham on each patty, trimming away excess ham. Place ham scraps on top of ham slice and top with remaining patties, pressing meat well together.

Sauté patties in equal quantities of butter and olive oil for 2 to 3 minutes on each side. Serve with a knob of anchovy butter on each. Serves 4.

Brochettes of cod and sole with mustard sauce

2 thick cod steaks
2 small sole, filleted
salt
flour
oil for frying

Mustard sauce

1 tbsp butter
1 tbsp olive oil
1 onion, coarsely chopped
1 bunch parsley stalks
salt and freshly ground black pepper
1 tbsp flour
$\frac{1}{2}$ pt tinned clam juice
$\frac{1}{4}$ pt dry white wine
1 tbsp mustard

To make mustard sauce

Heat butter and oil in a saucepan; add chopped onion and parsley stalks and salt and freshly ground black pepper, to taste, and sauté, stirring continuously until onion is transparent. Sprinkle with flour, stir until well blended: add clam juice and wine, and simmer gently for 20 minutes.

Place mustard in the top of a double saucepan and strain stock over it, pressing onion and parsley stalks well against sieve with a wooden spoon. Mix well, over water, and continue to cook until sauce is thick and smooth.

When ready to serve: Cut fish into 1-inch squares and arrange them on small skewers. Salt and flour them and deep fry in very hot oil until golden. Serve brochettes immediately, accompanied by sauce. Serves 4.

Baked fish with mustard sauce
½ pt dry white wine
¼ pt water
2 *tbsps olive oil*
3 *tbsps finely chopped parsley*
6 *tbsps finely chopped shallots*
2 *tsps dry mustard*
salt and freshly ground black pepper
1 3-*lb white fish*
Combine dry white wine, water, olive oil, finely chopped parsley and shallots with dry mustard that has been mixed with a little hot water. Add salt and freshly ground black pepper to taste and pour liquid over a 3-lb fish which has been cleaned and scored. Bake in a slow oven (325° F, Mark 3) for ½ hour or until the fish flakes easily at the touch of a fork, basting it every 10 minutes. Remove the fish to a heated serving platter, pour the basting sauce over the fish and serve. Serves 4.

Lamb steaks with béarnaise sauce
3 *tender lamb steaks, cut from leg of baby lamb*
salt and freshly ground black pepper
2 *tbsps butter or lard*
watercress
béarnaise sauce
Ask your butcher to cut 3 tender lamb steaks, about 1 inch thick, from the large end of a leg of lamb. (The remainder, boned and cut into 1-inch cubes can be used for a curried lamb dish with rice.)

Flatten lamb steaks with a cleaver and season with salt and freshly ground black pepper; melt butter or lard in a thick-bottomed frying-pan; place lamb steaks in and sauté them in the hot fat for 6 minutes per side. Transfer to a heated serving dish; garnish with sprigs of fresh watercress and serve immediately with béarnaise sauce. Serves 6.

Lamb stew with courgettes
2½ *lb boned lamb shoulder, cut into 2-inch cubes*
4 *tbsps olive oil*
1 *Spanish onion, finely chopped*
1 *large tin Italian peeled tomatoes*
2 *tbsps tomato concentrate*
2 *tbsps finely chopped parsley and oregano*
salt and freshly ground black pepper
2 *lb courgettes*
4 *tbsps butter*
Heat the oil in a thick-bottomed heatproof casserole and brown lamb on all sides; add chopped onion and cook until lightly browned. Add tomatoes, tomato concentrate dissolved in a little water and chopped parsley and oregano, salt and freshly ground black pepper, to taste.

Bring to the boil; reduce heat; cover casserole and simmer gently for 1 hour. Brown courgettes in butter; add to casserole and continue cooking for 30 minutes or until meat and vegetables are cooked. Serves 4-6.

Steamed chicken
1 *roasting chicken*
½ lemon
salt and freshly ground black pepper
4 *tbsps butter*
4 *tbsps chicken stock*
2 *tbsps finely chopped onion*
parsley, celery or velouté sauce
Rub cleaned and trussed chicken with cut side of ½ lemon; sprinkle with salt and freshly ground black pepper, to taste; place it in a gratin dish just large enough to hold it. Add butter, chicken stock and finely chopped onion and place gratin dish in a large double steamer, over 3 inches of rapidly boiling water and steam for 1 to 2 hours, according to size of chicken.

Serve with pan juices, parsley, celery or velouté sauce. Serves 4.

Chicken paprika
2 *young chickens, about 2½ lb each*
salt and freshly ground black pepper
¼ lb butter
1 *large onion, chopped*
1 *tbsp paprika*
1 *tbsp flour*
¾ pt good white stock
1 *tbsp tomato purée*
¼ pt thick cream
juice of ½ lemon
Rinse chickens and pat dry. Cut in serving pieces and season with salt and freshly ground black pepper.

Heat butter in a flame-proof casserole or large iron frying-pan; add onion and cook until transparent; stir in paprika. Add chicken and cook slowly until pieces are golden; then cover and cook 20 minutes longer, or until chicken is almost tender. Sprinkle with flour; add stock and tomato purée, stir well and cover. Bring to the boil and simmer for 20 minutes. Remove chicken to warmed serving dish. Stir cream and lemon juice into pot; stir and cook for 5 minutes. Pour over chicken. Serves 4-6.

Italian veal cutlets au gratin
8 *thin escalopes of veal*
¼ pt double cream
2-4 *tbsps freshly grated Parmesan*
¼ lb mozzarella cheese, diced
¼ lb sliced cooked ham, diced
2 *eggs*
salt and freshly ground black pepper
2 *tbsps butter*
Combine cream, grated Parmesan and diced mozzarella and ham in the top of a double saucepan and cook over hot water, stirring until cheese melts.

Beat eggs in a bowl; then whisk in the hot cheese mixture and season to taste with salt and freshly ground black pepper.

Melt butter in a thick-bottomed frying-pan and brown veal escalopes on both sides. Season with salt and freshly ground black pepper; place 2 escalopes in each gratin dish and spoon cheese mixture over each. Place under a hot grill until sauce is well browned and bubbling. Serves 4.

Edgell

CREAM

Hostess Pages

by Elizabeth Kendall

Orange halva cake

An unusual recipe adapted from a Greek one. Make it a day or two before it's wanted so that the syrup soaks well in, and use a little brandy in the orange juice if you like. The cake is best baked in a ring tin so that the hole can be filled with whipped cream. You need for the cake:

6 *oz butter*
6 *oz caster sugar*
1½ *teaspoons grated orange rind*
5 *tablespoons orange juice*
3 *eggs*
9 *oz fine semolina*
3 *teaspoons baking powder*
4 *oz ground almonds*

For the syrup you need:

6 *oz caster sugar*
5 *tablespoons water*
2 *dessertspoons lemon juice*
3 *tablespoons orange juice*
1 *tablespoon finely sliced candied orange peel*
1½ *inch piece cinnamon stick*

Beat butter, sugar and orange rind to a smooth fluffy cream. Beat in orange juice. Whip eggs and beat in gradually. Stir in semolina, baking powder and almonds. Turn into greased tin and cook in preheated oven at mark 7 for 10 minutes. Reduce heat to 4 and cook for another 30 minutes. A few minutes before the cake is cooked make up the syrup with all ingredients except orange juice and peel, and boil until it thickens. Add the orange juice and peel and boil for a second. Turn out cake carefully and pour over hot syrup.

Sauce from New Zealand

For lending variety to the Sunday lamb. It takes no longer than plain gravy to make. You need:

½ *oz dripping*
2 *tablespoons vinegar*
1 *teaspoon cornflour*
2 *teaspoons brown sugar*
½ *teaspoon paprika*
1 *tablespoon Worcester sauce*
5 *tablespoons stock*
1 *tablespoon redcurrant jelly*

Melt the fat, add the sugar, jelly, paprika, vinegar and sauce. Blend the cornflour with the stock, add and bring to boil. Simmer for five minutes.

Old-fashioned ginger pop

Children used to thinking that everything to drink is bought in a bottle, may find some home-made ginger pop refreshing. It's simple to make with only one snag: you must remember to make it three days before it's wanted. For enough for twenty glasses you need:

2 *large lemons*
1 *oz bruised root ginger*
1 *teaspoon cream of tartar*
5 *quarts boiling water*
1¼ *lb granulated sugar*
1 *teaspoon caster sugar*
½ *oz yeast*

Peel lemons very thinly, removing all the pith. Cut into thin slices, discarding the pips. Put lemons and peel into a large bowl, add granulated sugar, ginger and cream of tartar. Pour the boiling water over, cover and allow to cool until luke-warm, stirring occasionally to dissolve the sugar. Cream the yeast with the caster sugar, add this to the mixture and leave in a warm place for 24 hours. If necessary skim off any scum. Strain and bottle, tying the corks down securely.

Rhubarb with pleasure

1 *lb rhubarb*
4 *oz sugar*
2 *oz quick oats*
½ *teaspoonful ground ginger*
3 *oz butter*
2 *oz flour*

Cut rhubarb into ½-inch pieces and put into buttered pie dish. Sprinkle with the ginger and half the sugar. Dot with ½ oz of the butter. Mix flour, oats and rest of sugar, then rub in the rest of the butter. When the mixture is like coarse breadcrumbs, sprinkle over the rhubarb, making sure the fruit is completely covered. Bake at mark 5 for 30 minutes. You can add a little chopped ginger to the mixture, but some children hate it. Serve with thick cream or a scoop of dairy ice-cream.

And with a real glut of rhubarb, make this excellent preserve: For 6 lb fruit you need 6 lb sugar and 6 lemons. Cut fruit into small pieces, slice the lemons very thin. Put the fruit in a large bowl, cover with the sugar and leave to stand until the juice has drawn. Then boil for 45 minutes (do not stir so that it breaks up), then put into warm jars with a scented geranium leaf in each as a fragrant refinement.

Elizabeth Kendall's kitchen in Kensington

Tod Draz

Mackerel and herbs
Recipe adapted from a notebook dated 1826 suggests an excellent way of dealing with them. Clean fish, carefully slitting underside no more than is necessary, and make a mixture of the following: a handful of parsley, a tablespoon of capers or chopped nasturtium seeds, 2 oz melted butter, a little finely chopped lemon peel, seasoning, and enough breadcrumbs to firm the mixture. Put a tablespoon or so into each fish. The old recipe says "broil"; a more convenient way, now, is to wrap each fish securely in buttered paper or metal foil and bake for half an hour. Turn on to a hot dish and garnish with lemon. This makes a good start to a cold supper as the fish can be prepared beforehand and will come to little harm by a short wait.

Harry More Gordon

Mushroom necklaces
Field mushrooms generally have more flavour for this purpose. Merely thread the mushrooms, with stout needle and linen thread, and hang in a warm place until they are dry and brittle. Store in an airtight tin and simply pour boiling water over them five minutes before you want to use them. For pickled mushrooms use the small button kind. Put them in a saucepan with a nut of butter and sprinkle liberally with salt. Simmer until tender, put in jars and pour in the liquid from the pan to not more than two-thirds up the jar. Then top each jar with boiled spiced vinegar (6 peppercorns and a bay leaf to each pint). Seal jars and keep at least a week. A pound of mushrooms fills a pound jam jar.

Try a new pancake
8 *oz plain flour*
1 *teaspoon sugar*
½ *oz fresh yeast, or* 1 *teaspoon dried yeast*
½ *pint warm milk*
1 *egg*
½ *teaspoon salt*
a little lard
Mix flour, sugar, yeast and milk to a batter and let it stand 20 minutes. Add egg yolk. Whisk egg white and salt to stiff froth and fold in. Grease a heavy frying-pan and fry spoonfuls of the batter, turning to brown both sides. Turn on to sugared greaseproof paper. Serve piled in threes with a pat of butter on top. Other finishes might be some juicy slices of orange or lemon, *or* spread the layers with warmed black cherry jam, *or* warm a spoonful of rum, set it alight and pour over.

For holiday teas
A home-made loaf. This one is simple. You need:
½ *lb flour*
4 *teaspoons baking powder*
½ *teaspoon salt*
1 *oz sugar*
2 *tablespoons of the crunchy kind of peanut butter*
3 *oz melted butter*
2 *eggs*
¾ *cup milk*
First mix all dry ingredients, then add milk, butter and beaten eggs. Stir in peanut butter, put in loaf tin and stand half an hour in a warm place. Bake at gas mark 4 for 45 minutes.

Coolest ice of all
The fresh clean taste of a real lemon water ice is particularly nice at the end of a summer meal. Here is a recipe that is hardly any trouble at all. You need, for four people:
3 *lemons*
2 *envelopes of gelatine*
1 *egg white*
sugar
1 *tablespoon of hot water*
½ *pint cold water*
Dissolve the gelatine in the spoonful of hot water, then add the rest of the water, the finely grated rind and the juice of the three lemons. Sweeten to taste, then put in freezing part of refrigerator. Stir every ten minutes until nearly frozen, then beat in stiffly beaten egg white. Return to fridge and freeze. Serve in glasses decorated with fragments of fresh fruit.

Washington cream pie
One of America's favourite puddings. First make an uncooked "shell" with 6 oz digestive biscuits, crushed, and 3 oz melted butter. Use the mixture firmly to line an 8-inch tin and leave to cool. In the meantime make a lemon jelly but make up only to ¼ pint, and whisk a small tin of Carnation milk with the grated rind and juice of half a lemon until thick. When jelly starts to set, whisk into the creamy mixture and pile mixture into shell. When set, sprinkle with grated bitter chocolate.

Aubergine hors d'œuvre
For four people bake four aubergines until tender, then scoop out the flesh with a silver spoon. Into a stout frying-pan put two tablespoons of olive oil and in it fry a finely minced onion and clove of garlic. Add four tomatoes, peeled and chopped, and the aubergine flesh. Cook all together until soft, adding seasoning and a little marjoram or oregano; the mixture should be homogeneous and smooth. Serve cold with crisp French bread, curls of unsalted butter and black olives.

Seven herb cheese
A combination of two old recipes, one from America, the

other from Cumberland. You need: 1 lb grated sharp English cheese, 1 tablespoon of chopped fresh parsley and the same quantity of thyme, sage, savory, tarragon, chervil and chives, a gill of cream, a gill of sherry. Blend all together by hand or with a mixer, and leave in the fridge for up to three days. Force through a strainer and, if possible, whirl again in a mixer. A new addition for a cheese board, it also makes delicious cocktail party mouthfuls, particularly if spread on small pieces of pumpernickel.

Fruit and nut conserve
A sweet and luscious preserve, delicious in pies and tarts. You need:
1½ *lb seedless raisins*
grated rind and juice of 3 *oranges*
grated rind and juice of 1 *lemon*
8 *oz chopped walnuts*
8 *oz chopped blanched almonds*
1 *lb sugar*
½ *pint of pineapple juice*
Stir all together and simmer over a low heat, stirring occasionally, for an hour. Pour into sterilised jars, and seal.

Family fudge pudding
A pudding that turns into two layers, a light cake mixture at the top, a fudge sauce at the bottom. You need:
2 *oz caster sugar*
1 *oz cocoa*
¼ *level teaspoon cinnamon*
pinch salt
2 *oz fine semolina*
1 *level teaspoon baking powder*
1 *oz melted butter*
¼ *teaspoon vanilla*
2 *eggs well beaten*
1 *tablespoon chopped walnuts*
½ *pint hot water*
3 *oz brown sugar*
½ *oz extra cocoa*
Sift the first six dry ingredients. Blend melted butter, vanilla and beaten eggs, and stir into dry mixture. Add walnuts. Turn into buttered pie dish. Blend hot water, brown sugar and extra cocoa and pour over top. Bake at gas mark 5 for 30 minutes.

Supper after the show
As a change from bacon and eggs, try a new kind of omelette. You need for two people: four eggs, separated, 8 oz cottage cheese, seasoning, butter. Beat egg yolks until creamy and season. Beat in cottage cheese. Whisk egg whites and fold in yolks. Melt butter in stout 10-inch pan, pour in eggs and cook slowly for 10 minutes, loosening sides with palette knife. Serve with mushroom sauce made, for speed, thus: heat small can of condensed mushroom soup and stir in a gill of cream and a little lemon juice.

The classic pudding
A steak and kidney pudding is one of those things it's almost impossible to have a failure with provided the meat is good. This recipe makes enough for six people. You need, for the pudding: 8 oz self-raising flour, 4 oz shredded suet, salt, water. For the filling: 1 lb steak, three lambs kidneys, seasoning, stock. Cut the meat into thin pieces, chop the kidney, mix and roll lightly in flour. For the pudding, mix dry ingredients and add enough water to make a firm paste. Line a greased basin with pastry, keeping enough for the cover. Put in the meat, sprinkling with a little more seasoned flour. Pour in stock just to reach the top of the meat. Put on lid, sealing edges well. Cover with greased paper and seal with foil, then steam for 5 hours. Additions to the pudding may include chopped mushrooms, bearded oysters, chopped onion.

Stuffed aubergines Washington
A good hot first course or, in more generous quantities, an attractive luncheon dish. Cut the eggplants in two lengthwise and criss-cross the flesh with a knife without damaging the skin. Moisten with oil, cook in oven until flesh is tender then take out the flesh with a spoon and chop. Mix it with an egg yolk, a little white sauce, and a tablespoon of grated Parmesan cheese. Now line the bottom of the aubergine skins with creamed sweetcorn, fill up with the mixture, sprinkle with more grated cheese and brown in the oven or under the grill.

Harry More Gordon

Quick railway pudding
With the children home from school again, a quickly-made, no-fiddling pudding is in demand. This one, served in the dining-car of the crack Mancunian, appeals to schoolboys as much as to the businessmen who demand it regularly. It takes:
1 *pint milk*
½ *lb breadcrumbs*
6 *oz butter*
4 *oz sugar*
3 *eggs*
lemon juice
apricot jam
Bring the milk to the boil, add crumbs, stirring well. Take pan off the heat, add sugar, and butter cut into smallish pieces, and stir until melted. Finally beat in eggs and lemon juice. Butter a pie dish, put in a layer of apricot jam, spoon in the mixture and bake for 30 to 40 minutes at mark 6. Serve with hot apricot sauce.

Greek Food

by Lady Fleming

Taramosalata

Taramasalata is made with the smoked roe of fish. In London I usually make it with smoked cod roe. *Ingredients*: 1 jar of smoked cod roe, 1 teacup of breadcrumbs (which have been well soaked in water and most of the water squeezed out), 1 teacup of olive oil, the juice of one or two lemons (more or less according to taste), 1 grated small onion (optional), ¼ teacup finely chopped parsley (optional), salt.

If you possess an electric mixer or an emulsifier it takes a couple of minutes to make *Taramosalata*. Put in the mixer all the ingredients together (except the salt and half the olive oil) and switch on. In a few seconds the mixture takes the consistency of a smooth creamy paste. Taste, add salt and the rest of the olive oil. Mix. Taste again, add lemon juice and salt if necessary.

If you have not got an electric mixer, crush well in a mortar the smoked roe, the moist breadcrumbs and the grated onion. Add slowly and alternately the olive oil and the lemon. Work the mixture till thoroughly blended and of a creamy consistency. Add the parsley and adjust salt and lemon juice to taste.

Melitzanosalata (Aubergine salad)

This, much less known in England, is a delicious salad. *Ingredients*: 2 lb aubergines (the large roundish kind), ½ teacup of olive oil, 1 teaspoon of wine vinegar, the juice of one lemon (or more or less according to taste), one small grated onion rinsed well in cold water (optional), two green pimentoes (optional), ½ lb firm tomatoes (optional), salt and pepper to taste.

Bake in a hot oven the aubergines and the pimentoes till soft inside (same result can be obtained with slow grilling, or by putting the aubergines and pimentoes on the hot plate of the cooker and turning them over constantly). Remove skin of both while hot. Put in the mixer all ingredients together except the pimentoes and tomatoes (or crush well in a mortar) and blend well. The mixture turns creamy. Cut the tomatoes in tiny pieces, remove seeds, and leave to drain well. Chop the pimentoes and remove seeds. Add tomatoes and pimentoes to the mixture and add salt and lemon to taste. Chill in the fridge; it keeps well.

Dolmathes avgolemono

Vine leaves stuffed with minced meat and covered with thickened egg and lemon (avgolemono sauce). They make a delicious main dish.

Ingredients for six: 1 lb lean minced meat of half lamb and half veal, 1 coffee cup rice, 1 medium size onion, 2 oz butter, 1 cup of milk, about 10 oz of fresh vine leaves or 1 tin of the canned ones, parsley finely chopped, mint, salt, pepper to taste.

Grate the onion and cook it slowly in the butter till translucent (do not brown). Remove from fire and add all the ingredients except the vine leaves. Mix well. Parboil vine leaves, strain them, and when cool, put one leaf at a time on the kitchen board, with the shiny side down, and place on it one heaped teaspoonful of the mixture. Starting from the stem, roll the vine leaf round the meat mixture. Push the two ends in, so that you have rolls of about an inch and half long, and half an inch in diameter. Lay any vine leaves which are left over, or were too torn to be used, on the bottom of a saucepan and line and pile the *dolmathes* one by one close together. Add boiling stock to cover. Add the juice of one lemon. Cover with grease paper and place a plate on the *dolmathes* so that its weight will keep them still. Cook slowly for half an hour. When ready, pour out all the stock which has not been absorbed in a saucepan, holding the plate tightly on the *dolmathes*, so that they are not disturbed. This fluid will be used in the avgolemono sauce. One teacup will be necessary; if it is not, add water.

Avgolemono sauce

Ingredients. The stock from the *dolmathes*, 2 eggs, the juice of one lemon (more or less according to taste), 1 dessertspoon of butter, 1 dessertspoon of flour.

Beat whole eggs thoroughly. Add slowly, while beating continuously, the lemon juice and then the boiling stock.

Make a roux with the butter and flour. Pour in the egg mixture and cook slowly till boiling point (do not boil), adjust salt and pepper, lemon according to taste. Dish out the *dolmathes* and pour the sauce on them. Serve hot.

Artichokes a la polita

Ingredients (for six): One large tin of *fonds d'artichauts* (there are about 12 large ones), 24 small onions or shallots, 24 small cubes of potatoes (about half a square inch), carrots cut into 12 half-inch pieces, half a teacup of olive oil, 1 teaspoon flour, juice of 2 lemons, salt to taste, dill.

Partly cook the onions and the carrots in a little water (because the artichokes are already cooked; with fresh artichokes this is not necessary). Place the *fonds d'artichauts* in a saucepan being careful not to break them. Add the partly cooked onions and carrots with their water, and all the remaining ingredients, thickening with a little flour. Place a plate on them to keep everything still. Cook on a strong heat until onions are tender. Do not disturb until cold.

Satziki

Ingredients: 8 oz yoghourt, 1 cucumber, 4 cloves of garlic, 1 teaspoon of olive oil, vinegar, salt, pepper to taste.

Chill the yoghourt and cucumber and just before serving grate the peeled cucumber, mince or crush the garlic and mix all ingredients together. Serve as a salad or as a sauce.

Fish plaki

Ingredients for eight: 4 to 5 lb fish (I use a whole fish, choosing a sea bream or a sea bass, which are both delicious and cheap, but any other fish from cod to turbot or halibut would do, and the fish need not be whole but can be in slices). 1 large tin of peeled tomatoes (about $1\frac{1}{2}$ lb), $\frac{1}{2}$ lb onions, 1 coffee cup of chopped parsley, 1 small teacup of olive oil, 1 clove garlic, 1 wine glass of white wine, 2 tablespoons of toasted breadcrumbs, 1 tablespoon of sugar, salt and pepper to taste.

Wash fish thoroughly, dry in a cloth, put in a fireproof dish and sprinkle with salt.

Mash the tomatoes coarsely, grate the onions, mince or crush the garlic, add sugar, salt and pepper, mix and cook in olive oil till almost all the water from the tomatoes has evaporated. Add the chopped parsley and the wine and pour over the fish. Sprinkle with breadcrumbs and cook covered for about an hour in a moderate oven.

This dish is invariably eaten cold in Greece.

Aubergines moussaka

Ingredients for eight: $2\frac{1}{2}$ lb aubergines, $\frac{1}{2}$ lb minced veal, 1 lb tinned peeled tomatoes, $\frac{1}{2}$ lb cheese (Parmesan, Gruyère or Cheddar), enough olive oil (or any other frying fat) to fry the aubergines, 1 medium size onion, 3 oz butter, 1 tablespoon sugar, salt and pepper to taste.

Cut aubergines in $\frac{1}{4}$-inch slices, sprinkle them with salt and leave overnight in a colander. Press the aubergines in a dry cloth to remove fluid and fry them in hot olive oil till lightly golden. Put minced meat in a frying-pan with the butter, grate the onion, mash the tomatoes and mix well with meat adding the sugar, and salt and pepper to taste. Cook till meat is tender and only a little fluid is left.

Arrange in a deep fireproof dish half the aubergines in layers, cover with the meat mixture, arrange the remaining aubergines in layers to cover the meat. Top with béchamel sauce.

Souvlakia

Ingredients for eight: 2 lb of fillet steak, or *noix de veau* or lean meat from a leg of lamb, 3 large green pimentoes (or one small tin of red pimentoes), marinade, for which you need: 1 wine glass of white wine, 1 coffee cup of olive oil, 1 medium onion grated, 1 tablespoon of oregano, 2 bay leaves, the grated rind of one lemon, the juice of half a lemon, 1 teaspoon sugar, freshly ground pepper, salt. Mix all ingredients of the marinade together in a bowl.

Cut meat in 1-inch chunks. Put in marinade, mix well and leave overnight. Remove the meat from marinade. Cut the fresh green pimentoes or the red tinned ones in 1-inch squares. String meat and pimentoes alternately on skewers allowing 6 to 8 chunks of meat for each individual skewer. Grill till cooked as required, turning over the skewer a few times.

Souvlakia are served in Greece with French fried potatoes and a salad. I prefer them with rice pilaf and tomatoes glacées.

Tomatoes glacées

Choose small round tomatoes allowing one or two for each person. Scoop the top to allow insertion of a little knob of butter and one teaspoon of sugar. Sprinkle with salt and pepper and cook them in a moderate oven till they are soft.

Arrange the tomatoes on a serving dish so that they surround the rice pilaf, and stick the skewers in the middle.

Use the marinade from the souvlakia as a sauce: remove the bay leaves, add a glass of water and a teaspoon of flour and boil till onions are soft and thoroughly cooked and fluid is greatly reduced till it becomes the right thickness.

Barbara Karban

Alan Cracknell

by Arabella Boxer

How to experiment with unusual vegetables and be more adventurous with the familiar ones

Although not as immediately tempting as the "primeurs" of the early summer, autumn and winter vegetables are more varied than you might think. The first English leeks, button sprouts, small turnips, and the early cabbages are at their best in September and October, but during the long months that follow they lose something of their first charm. This would seem to be the moment to experiment with some of the more unusual vegetables like fennel, kohl-rabi, celeriac, and Jerusalem artichokes, sea kale and salsify.

I have included some unusual vegetables because I want to encourage people to try them. I am afraid that unless we keep demanding them and bothering the greengrocers, who will in turn I hope bother the growers, they will disappear from the market. As far as I am concerned, vegetable cookery falls into two distinct groups. Either they are intended to be served in their own right, or to accompany meat or fish. As for the latter, I prefer them to be cooked as simply as possible, in most cases in a covered pan in the minimum of boiling salted water which should have almost vanished by the time the vegetables are tender, after which they need only a knob of butter and a sprinkling of salt and pepper.

January

The variety of fennel I am writing about is properly called Florence fennel, or finocchio. As well as the feathery leaves and branches (see page 225), which are similar to those of common fennel, it also produces a white bulbous root, somewhat like celery in appearance and in its uses. It can be eaten raw in salads or braised slowly in the oven. I sometimes serve it in a cheese sauce as the main course for a light meal, since it is quite filling.

Fennel in cheese sauce
6 heads fennel
2 oz butter
2 tablespoons flour
salt and pepper
2–3 oz grated cheese preferably Gruyère
½ gill cream
Trim the fennel, cutting off any discoloured leaves and washing well. Bring a pan of salted water to the boil and drop them in. Simmer until they are tender, about 30 minutes. Lift them out and drain them, cut each one in half, and lay cut side down in the serving dish. Boil up the cooking water until it is reduced to a good flavour; do not let it get too salty. Make a cheese sauce with the butter and flour and about ½ pint of the strained cooking liquid. It should be thick enough to mask the fennel, like fairly thick cream. Season well with salt and pepper, stir in the grated cheese off the fire; when quite smooth add the cream and pour over the fennel.

February

Seakale is a particularly delicious vegetable that is available in February and March. It used to be popular before the war but is quite rare now; I suspect that it is difficult to grow, but could not be simpler to cook. The delicate white stalks need only to be washed and trimmed at the roots, then thrown into boiling salted water and cooked for about 20 minutes. After draining they can be served with melted butter flavoured with lemon juice, or a sauce of thin cream flavoured with lemon juice, salt and pepper. They can also be deep fried in the same way as salsify.

Another treat to come into the shops in February is purple sprouting broccoli. It deserves to be eaten as a course in its own right with a sauce hollandaise, or simply melted butter. Kohl-rabi is also to be found now; it is a decorative vegetable that is very popular in Austria and Switzerland. Both the root and the leaves can be eaten. I think the best way is to slice the roots and braise them in stock and a little fat, then to chop the best leaves and toss them briefly in butter and pour them over the sliced roots before serving.

March

Celeriac is a rewarding vegetable that I only recently discovered. It has all the delicious flavour of celery without its annoying stringy consistency. It can be eaten raw in salads, either grated or finely chopped; or boiled and made into excellent soups and purées. A good hors d'œuvre can be made by shredding it coarsely and mixing it with flakes of tunny-fish in a vinaigrette sauce with chopped parsley. A purée of celeriac and potatoes goes well with game, and with grilled and roast meat. An excellent soup can be made by diluting the purée with stock or milk, or, better still, a mixture of both.

Celeriac purée
1 celeriac weighing about 1 lb
½ lb potatoes
2 oz butter
½ gill cream
salt and pepper
Peel the celeriac and the potatoes. Cut them in pieces and cook them in separate pans until they are soft. Drain both well, reserving the celeriac water for use later. Push them through the food mill and mix in a heavy pan over gentle heat. Beat well with the butter and the cream and season with salt and plenty of ground black pepper. If the purée seems too thick, thin it with a little of the water that the celeriac was cooked in.

April

In April the first English asparagus appears in the shops but at an astronomical price: so also do the first English tomatoes, the first crop of spinach, and the first horseradish. Tomatoes and horseradish can be combined in an unusual and delicious dish to serve with cold beef or lamb; it is particularly good with boeuf à la mode.

Tomatoes in horseradish sauce
Peel 1 lb small tomatoes and arrange in the serving dish. Whip ½ pt cream very lightly, so that it will still pour, and fold in four or five tablespoons of grated horseradish. Season with lemon juice and chill both the tomatoes and the sauce. At the last moment pour the sauce over the tomatoes.

May

In May the first English new potatoes appear, as opposed to the foreign ones that have been in the shops for some time which are impossible to scrape and have much less flavour than our own. The first of the green peas and baby carrots make it an important month for those with their own vegetable gardens. These tender young vegetables are so good that they should be served as a course in their own right, two or three of them boiled quickly in the minimum of water and arranged on a flat dish with a little melted butter poured over them. For a party, a more elegant dish can be devised by serving them in pastry.

Spring vegetable flan
Make a good short pastry enriched with an egg yolk and flavoured with a few drops of lemon juice, and line a flan ring. Bake until crisp and golden, filled with dried beans for the first 15 minutes to weigh it down, then for 5 minutes empty. Have the peas and carrots cooked separately—if larger than one's little finger, the carrots should be cut in halves or sliced—then at the last moment toss them, still separately, in a little butter or cream and pour into the pastry case in two rings, so that each slice will contain some of each. Serve immediately.

June

Mange-tout peas, one of the greatest delicacies among vegetables, come into the shops for only two short weeks about now. They are quick and simple to cook and although expensive they go far and need practically no preparation. The peas are almost non-existent (unlike the illustration facing p. 224), and the whole pod is eaten. Runner beans start now, and a few early broad beans may be found. If really young, these may be cooked and eaten in the same way as the mange-touts, but they require longer cooking. Tarragon is available now, so this is the moment to make that most delicious of summer dishes, poulet à l'estragon. (Only the true French tarragon has the necessary flavour. It is a delicate plant and does not always survive the winter, but even for one season it is worth the trouble to cultivate.)

Mange-tout peas
Just cover the bottom of a broad heavy pan with water, salt it lightly and bring it to the boil. Throw in the peas which only need washing and the pod end cut off, and a piece of butter and cover the pan. Cook quickly for 5 minutes then try one; if they are really fresh this will be enough as they should retain their crisp consistency and over-cooking makes them slimy. Serve with their juices poured over them, preferably on their own, or with simply cooked escalopes of veal and a few new potatoes.

July

Asparagus should be more reasonable in price by now and can be cooked and served in a variety of ways, although plainly boiled, with melted butter, is still most people's favourite. It is good cold for a change, with a vinaigrette sauce, while a dish of creamy scrambled eggs with a bit of butter added to them at the last moment and surrounded with freshly boiled asparagus tips, makes a perfect start to a summer meal.

Sorrel is now ready to be picked, and makes an unusual soup with a fresh slightly tart flavour. It can also be made into a purée and served with veal escalopes, or poached eggs laid on the top. The domestic sorrel has larger leaves than the wild plant, and a less bitter flavour. Broad beans should be freely available by the beginning of this month; when still very young they are good eaten raw, as are most new vegetables. A selection of them can be served with a mayonnaise sauce lightly flavoured with garlic.

Alan Cracknell

Sorrel soup
Wash ½ lb sorrel; if it is still young there is no need to remove the stalks. Chop it coarsely and cook gently in 2 oz butter for 10 minutes, stirring now and then. Heat 1½ pts light stock (chicken or veal), and pour it on. Simmer very gently for 20 minutes then thicken with 2 egg yolks beaten into ½ gill cream and added to the soup off the heat. If you do not have enough sorrel, it can be combined with an equal amount of spinach, lettuce, or potato, or a mixture of all three.

To make a sorrel purée, proceed as for spinach, remembering that it will reduce in the same way.

August

The vegetable marrow is often unfairly criticised: I have always found it a delicious vegetable so long as it is cooked with care and not allowed to degenerate into a mush. I think it is particularly good combined with tomatoes, which are cheap now, as the sharpness of the tomato contrasts well with the blandness of the marrow. The vegetable marrow makes a good main dish filled with a stuffing of meat and rice, baked in the oven and served with a fresh tomato sauce, it also makes a good vegetable dish to serve alone or with plainly roasted or grilled lamb.

Marrow and tomatoes
Peel the marrow and cut it in pieces about 1 inch square. Melt 2 oz butter in a heavy sauté pan with a lid, and put in the marrow. Cover the pan and cook gently for about 8 minutes, shaking it now and then. At this point throw in ½ lb peeled and roughly chopped tomatoes and continue cooking for another 8 minutes, or until the marrow is tender. Sprinkle with a little chopped parsley before serving. This is also good made without the tomatoes but more parsley.

September

This is the month of the globe artichoke; although so many of these are imported at different times of the year, this is the moment when they are to be found in our own gardens. and are therefore at their freshest, best and cheapest. They are nourishing and easy to cook and seem to be universally popular, except with children. They should be cooked in plenty of fast boiling salted water, and left upside down in a colander to drain. Artichokes are best served cold with a good thick vinaigrette sauce, but can also be eaten hot with melted butter. More elaborate dishes can be made by cooking them as above and using only the bottom, which seems wasteful, but if you are inundated with them, it is well worth trying.

Artichoke soufflé
Cook 4 artichokes in the usual way, and drain them reserving their cooking water. When cool enough to handle, pull off all the leaves and remove the choke, then push the bottoms and the fleshy part of some of the leaves through a coarse sieve. Make a thick sauce with 1½ oz butter and 1½ oz flour and a scant half pint of equal parts milk and the cooking liquor, reduced till it has a good flavour. Mix with the artichoke purée, beat in 3 egg yolks and fold in 4 stiffly beaten egg whites. Pour into a soufflé dish and bake in a moderate oven (350°, or gas mark 4) for 25 minutes.

October

This is the best time of the year to eat those Provençal dishes made from aubergines, peppers, courgettes and tomatoes, such as ratatouille, piperade and moussaka. Too heavy for the hot weather, and hard to get later in the winter, they seem ideally suited to the autumn. Here is a recipe for ratatouille that can be served hot with garlic

APRIL

MAY

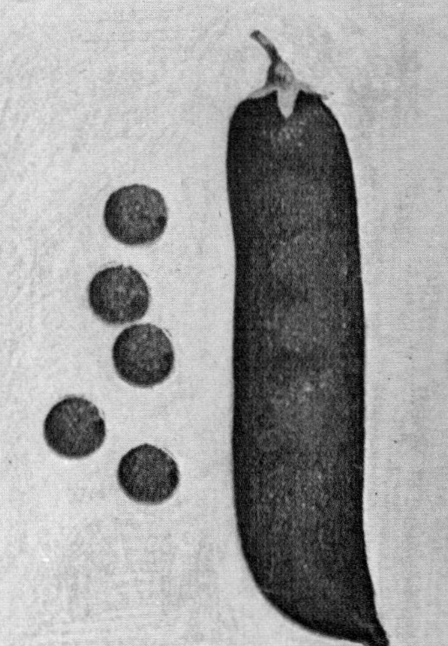
JUNE

JULY

AUGUST

Alan Cracknell
SEPTEMBER

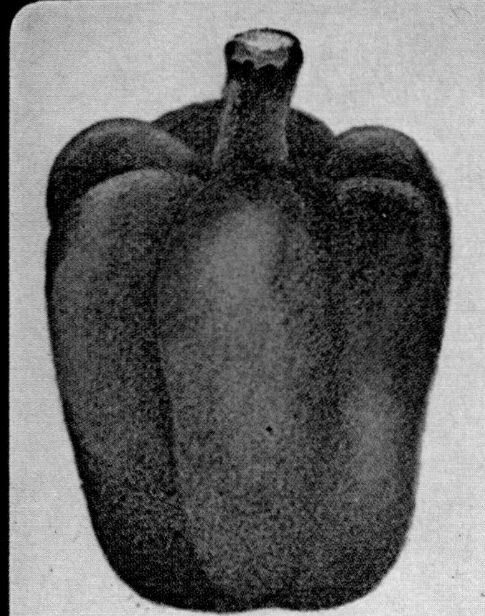

OCTOBER
PEPPER

NOVEMBER
ARTICHOKE

DECEMBER
SALSIFY

JANUARY
FENNEL

FEBRUARY
SEAKALE

MARCH
CELERIAC

bread for a really delicious, fattening meal. Or cold as an hors d'œuvre.

Ratatouille
2 aubergines
2 medium or 4 tiny courgettes
2 large green peppers
2 onions
4 tomatoes
½ pint olive oil
1 clove garlic
2 tablespoons chopped parsley
salt and pepper

Chop the aubergines and courgettes and sprinkle with salt. Leave to drain for 30 minutes. Chop the peppers, removing the seeds, and the onions; skin and de-seed the tomatoes and chop coarsely. Heat the oil in a large sauté pan and cook for a few more minutes, then put in the dried aubergines, and courgettes. Cover and simmer gently for 30 minutes, then add the tomatoes and the crushed garlic and cook for another 10 minutes. Stir in the chopped parsley and serve, or leave to cool.

November

Jerusalem artichokes make their first appearance this month, and can be made into a good and unusual soup.

Jerusalem artichoke soup
1 lb Jerusalem artichokes
1½ pints chicken or game stock
salt and pepper
1 egg yolk
½ gill cream
Peel the artichokes and cut them in equal sized pieces. Just cover them with salted water and cook till soft (about 8 minutes).

Drain them and push through the medium mesh of the mouli with the heated stock. Reheat and season well with salt and plenty of pepper.

Mix the egg yolk with the cream and add a little of the soup, mix again, then return to the pan and heat without allowing it to boil.

The first of the savoys appear now, which are my favourite among the cabbages, also the first winter crop of spinach, and the first cranberries, which can be made into sauce to serve with venison.

December

Salsify is about the only new vegetable to appear in December, and its delicate and unusual taste makes a welcome change from the other winter vegetables. There are two varieties, one with white skin, and the other which is more correctly called scorzonera, with a black skin and the better flavour. The only difference in the cooking is that the white-skinned one should be peeled before cooking, and must be put immediately in a bowl of water with a little vinegar to prevent it going black, while the black-skinned variety should be peeled after boiling. The white one is cut into lengths about three inches long, thrown into boiling salted water and cooked for about 30 minutes, or until just tender; it should then be well drained and served with a sauce of melted butter flavoured with a little lemon juice and a few chopped herbs. Alternatively, it can be accompanied by a good béchamel or cream sauce, although I prefer the first. The black-skinned variety should be cooked whole if possible, for instance in an asparagus pan, and peeled and cut up after boiling, then served with any of the above sauces. Salsify can also be made into fritters by drying after boiling, then dipping each piece in batter and frying in deep fat.

The new crop of dried vegetables come into the shops in mid-December, so this is a good time to stock up.

Alan Cracknell

Menus of the Month

by Veronica Maclean

January

Cœurs de palmier diana

2 10 *oz cans palm hearts*
6 *thin slices bread*
2–3 *oz butter*
little chopped parsley
Béarnaise sauce:
$\frac{1}{8}$ *pint wine vinegar*
$\frac{1}{8}$ *pint dry vermouth or dry white wine*
5 *shallots finely chopped*
2 *tablespoons fresh tarragon finely chopped* (1$\frac{1}{4}$ *tablespoons if dried*)
3 *egg yolks*
2 *tablespoons cold water*
$\frac{1}{2}$ *coffee spoon arrowroot (optional)*
salt and pepper
1 *oz cold butter*
4–5 *oz melted butter*

Warm gently, then carefully drain and arrange about a dozen palm hearts (obtainable from any good grocer) on six thin croûtons of bread that you have fried in a little butter, then cooled. Cover with a thick béarnaise sauce, sprinkle with chopped parsley and serve.

Béarnaise sauce: Use a heavy copper-bottomed saucepan if possible. Boil the vinegar, wine, shallots and 1 tablespoon tarragon briskly over high heat until liquid has almost entirely evaporated. Remove from heat. When quite cool add egg yolks, 2 tablespoons cold water, optional arrowroot, pepper and salt, beating vigorously all the time with a wire whisk over a *bain-marie*. Add half the cold butter and whisk continuously until the eggs thicken, then the other half, and finally the melted butter, drop by drop, whisking all the time, until the sauce reaches the consistency of thick mayonnaise. Sprinkle in the second tablespoon of chopped tarragon and the sauce is ready.

Note: It is quite legitimate to add $\frac{1}{2}$ a coffee or small teaspoon (not more) of arrowroot to the egg yolks when you start beating. It prevents the sauce curdling. Serves 6.

New year brown devil

6–9 *large pieces cold turkey*
2 *tablespoons flour*
butter utter
2 *teaspoons made English mustard*
2 *teaspoons French mustard*
2 *tablespoons green tomato chutney, or any soft chutney that is not too sweet*
1 *tablespoon Harvey sauce*
little paprika
salt and pepper
dash of Tabasco
The sauce:
5 *tablespoons good gravy*
devil paste
2 *oz butter*
1 *tablespoon cream or yoghourt*
The Chinese fried rice:
6 *slices bacon*
1 *large onion*
3 *cups cooked rice*
1$\frac{1}{2}$ *teaspoons soy sauce*
bacon fat or 2 oz butter and 1 tablespoon olive oil

Make some *beurre manié* by working 2 tablespoons flour into the same amount of butter in a bowl with a wooden spoon. Add the two mustards, the chutney, the sauce and seasonings. If the paste is too thin work in a little more flour. Put aside one third of the paste and cover your neatly cut turkey joints with the rest, spreading it on liberally with a flat knife. When your sauce and rice are nearly ready grill the devilled joints under a pre-heated grill for three to five minutes each side and pile on to one end of a large hot ashet. Pour the devilled sauce round them and heap the rice at the other end of the dish.

The sauce: Melt some good gravy in a pan, work into it the reserved devil paste, and butter in small pieces; stir vigorously and simmer until the flour is cooked, about

Robin Jacques

12 minutes, then take off the fire and add the cream or yoghourt. Taste and correct seasoning.

The Chinese fried rice: Fry bacon in fat until crisp; remove and drain on paper napkin. Fry finely chopped onion until brown. Add rice, stirring constantly, until also golden brown. Add crumbled bacon and soy sauce and seasoning. You can also add 1 tablespoon chopped green pepper *or* chopped bamboo shoots and 1 tablespoon cooked chopped mushrooms if you wish to, but don't overdo it.

Lady Jekyll's orange sorbet

The syrup:
7½ *oz granulated sugar*
cold water
The juice:
3–4 *large oranges*
6–7 *sugar cubes*
The Italian meringue:
4 *oz granulated sugar*
4 *tablespoons water*
2–3 *egg whites*

Put the sugar into a pint measure and add enough water to make up a pint. Pour into a saucepan and heat slowly until sugar melts. Bring to the boil and, without stirring, simmer gently for 20 minutes. Cool.

The juice: Wash and dry the oranges. Rub their skins with sugar cubes to extract the oily essence. Squeeze the juice from the oranges and sieve. There should be half a pint. Add the impregnated cubes. Chill.

The Italian meringue: Dissolve sugar and water slowly in a small pan over low heat. Raise heat till syrup bubbles but do not stir. The syrup is ready when a little of it dropped in cold water forms a firm ball (445–450 deg F. on a saccharometer). Remove from heat and slowly pour the syrup on to the whites that you have already whisked into a firm white snow, whisking all the time. Whisk until all the syrup has been used and the mixture is firmish. Chill.

To combine: Have ready a large chilled bowl and in it combine the first syrup and the fruit juice (stir the latter to make sure the sugar cubes have dissolved). Add the cold Italian meringue. Use a spatula and carefully fold the liquid up and over the meringue to combine. Pour the mixture into refrigerator ice trays or put the bowl into the deep freeze. When the sorbet is half frozen and mushy stir again to blend the two mixtures together. When frozen cover with foil and store in freezer or deep freeze until required.

To serve: Fill six scooped-out oranges with the sorbet just before serving and stick a lemon geranium leaf into the top of each orange. Remember to slice a little bit of skin off the bottom of each orange or they will roll over. A lemon sorbet can be made in the same way, substituting at least six lemons for the oranges.

February

Mushrooms with green garlic sauce

18 *mushrooms*
6 *slices bread*
2 *oz butter*
little salt
Green garlic butter:
1 *clove garlic*
½ *oz shallots*
½ *oz chopped parsley*
4 *oz butter*
salt and black pepper
½ *teaspoon demi-glace*
Green garlic sauce:
1 *oz fat bacon*
1–2 *cloves garlic*
tender part of 3 *spinach leaves*
1 *tuft parsley*
1 *tuft chervil*
1 *wineglass white wine*
stock
pepper and salt
walnut oil
1 *egg yolk*

Take 18 fine fresh mushrooms, *not* the button kind, but the open, flat variety, like field mushrooms. Remove the stalks carefully, without damaging the cap, and wipe caps with a damp cloth. Do not peel. Sprinkle with a little salt and cook for 3 minutes only in the butter. Lift out and keep hot. Sauté 6 thin slices of bread in the same pan, adding more butter if necessary. Drain the croûtons and arrange them on a serving dish. Put 3 mushroom caps on each croûton and fill the stalk cavity with the green garlic sauce you have already prepared. I give two versions: a quickly made butter, and a more elegant sauce.

Alan Cracknell

Green garlic butter: Pound and sieve chopped garlic and shallots which you have first blanched by having put them into cold salted water, brought to the boil, boiled for one minute, and drained. Blend this purée with the very finely chopped parsley, the butter and seasonings. Add half a teaspoonful of meat glaze (demi-glace) if you have any of the real stuff available.

Green garlic sauce: Chop the first five ingredients very finely. Put them in a saucepan with the wine, 4 tablespoons stock and seasoning. Boil the sauce for 40 minutes or so until it is reduced to half its former quantity. Make a liaison by mixing 2 tablespoons of walnut oil with the yolk of egg, slowly, in a bowl. Stir this sort of mayonnaise into the sauce, which you have sieved and cooled. It will make it smooth and creamy and easy to drop into the centre of each mushroom.

Françoise's bœuf en daube
(to be eaten cold)
3–3½ *lb silverside or topside rump*
little pork back fat or fat bacon for larding
2–3 *cloves garlic*
2 *tablespoons olive oil*
2 *tablespoons fresh pork lard*
12 *little onions*
handful of shallots
1 *good piece pork fat or unsliced bacon cut into dice*
2 *large wineglasses white wine*
2 *tablespoons brandy*
salt and pepper
nutmeg
bouquet garni
few cloves
1 *calf's foot*
2 *lb fresh good carrots*

If your butcher will not oblige, lard the beef yourself with a few strips of pork or bacon fat. Then make incisions with the point of a sharp knife and stick in the garlic that you have cut into slithers. Melt the lard and olive oil in a heavy iron casserole and when sizzling put in the meat and sear it, turning carefully from side to side. When it is brown all over add the onions, shallots and diced pork fat. Flambé (heat and set alight) the wine and brandy in a small pan. As soon as the flame has gone out pour over the meat. Add 1 or 2 glasses of water to the casserole, salt, pepper, nutmeg, bouquet garni and the largest onion stuck with 3 or 4 cloves. Then the calf's foot, well cleaned and cut into 4 pieces, or split down the middle.

Now wash and scrape 2 lb carrots; cut them into thin circles, add them to the casserole and cover it tightly. If the lid does not fit well then seal it with flour and water. Simmer gently and evenly for 5 hours without opening.

When quite tender degrease the daube firstly by tilting the casserole and skimming off the surplus fat with a spoon, and then mopping up the remainder with some kitchen tissues. Let the meat cool a while, then pour a little of the sauce into a china pudding basin. Line the sides of this bowl with the sliced rounds of carrot. Place the meat, which you can slice if you wish or leave whole, in the middle of the bowl and fill it up by pouring in the rest of the juices (removing the calf's foot, bouquet garni and cloves).

Leave the daube in the fridge overnight. Dip bowl for a second or two in hot water before turning out on to a serving dish. Accompany with sauté potatoes and a green salad or vegetable.

Peaches Empress Eugénie
6 *fine fresh peaches*
little sugar
wild strawberries
2–3 *tablespoons Kirsch and Maraschino mixed*

Choose ripe peaches. Dip them in boiling water and then into iced water and remove skins. Remove stone by pushing it through the stalk end with a larding needle, or you can core both ends with an apple corer and push stone out of one end. Cut a slither off bottom of peaches, if necessary, and sit them in a ring in a shallow glass bowl. Sprinkle with a very little sugar and fill each cavity with wild strawberries which you have sprinkled liberally with the Kirsch-Maraschino mixture. Pile up the rest of the strawberries in the centre of the bowl, and keep on ice until required. Serve with Crème Brûlée and iced Kirsch, in little liqueur glasses, handed separately.

March

Gratin of endives au jambon
8 *heads of chicory*
lemon juice
crust of bread
4 *large thin slices cooked ham*
breadcrumbs
For the mornay sauce:
1½ *oz butter*
1 *oz flour*
1 *cup of milk*
2 *oz grated Swiss cheese*
seasoning
pinch nutmeg

Wash and clean the chicory removing any damaged leaves. Cook uncovered in boiling salted water to which you add the juice of a lemon and a crust of bread (to prevent chicory losing its colour). Do not boil too fast; 25 minutes should be enough but test for tenderness by sticking in a silver fork. Then strain thoroughly and dry carefully on a cloth. Keep ½ a cup of the drained off liquid.

Mornay sauce
Melt 1 oz butter in a heavy saucepan over low heat. Blend in 1 oz flour and cook slowly for 2 minutes without colouring. Remove from heat and pour in milk and chicory liquid that you have heated to boiling point in a small pan. Beat

vigorously with wire whisk to blend, and then return to heat and bring to boil, stirring hard. Boil for a minute or two, stirring, then once more remove from heat and beat in three-quarters of the cheese, salt and pepper to taste and nutmeg. Wrap each head of chicory in half a slice of ham. lay in buttered fireproof dish and pour sauce over. Sprinkle with breadcrumbs and remaining cheese. Dot with remaining butter and put in a hot oven for about 10 minutes, until top is golden brown, or reheat under moderate grill.

Spiced chicken

1 4–5 *lb roasting chicken*
1 *carton natural yoghourt*
salt to taste
1 *level tablespoon paprika*
4 *tablespoons good cooking oil*
1 *medium onion, finely grated*
2 *cloves fresh garlic, chopped*
1 *bay leaf*
$\frac{1}{2}$ *teaspoon ginger powder*
2 *one-inch pieces of cinnamon stick*
1 *small tin of tomatoes*
water or chicken stock

Disjoint the chicken into ten pieces. Wash and clean. Mix yoghourt, salt, paprika together and marinade chicken in it for at least one hour. Heat the oil in a heavy saucepan or enamelled cast-iron casserole, add the onion, sauté till golden brown, add the garlic, bay leaf and ginger and bits of cinnamon. Sauté for a little longer, till the onions are darker but not burnt, then add the tomatoes. Stir and cook for five minutes, then add the marinated chicken with all its marinade, plus one cup of water or good chicken stock. Cover and cook on medium heat for $\frac{1}{2}$–$\frac{3}{4}$ of an hour until the meat is tender. (Or put in preheated oven Regulo 4 for a little longer.) If it becomes too dry add a little more water or chicken stock. Serve with plain boiled rice and chappatis. This is not a hot but a spiced and fragrant curry and it needs no accompaniments.

Elizabethan rhubarb tansy

1 *lb young rhubarb*
$\frac{1}{4}$ *lb fresh unsalted butter*
2 *tablespoons sugar*
2 *egg yolks*
$\frac{1}{4}$ *pint cream*
1 *lemon*

Cook chopped rhubarb in butter until tender. Add sugar and blend well. Take off fire to cool. Beat the egg yolks and cream together and add to rhubarb. Reheat to the point when cream thickens but do not boil, then take pan off fire and place in bowl of cold water. Stir occasionally while cooling and when cold pour into individual dishes. Sprinkle copiously with the juice of a lemon and a little brown sugar. If you wish Tansy to look pink, add a few drops of cochineal while it is cooling. Serve chilled, with home-made sponge fingers.

Avocado mousse

2 *cups mashed avocado*
1 *teaspoon salt*
a little mustard
1 *teaspoon Worcester sauce*
1 *teaspoon grated onion*
$\frac{3}{4}$ *cup heavy cream, whipped*
$\frac{1}{2}$ *cup mayonnaise*
1 *envelope gelatine* (1 *teaspoon*)

Use a silver fork to mash avocado pulp. Mix seasoning and Worcester sauce with pulp and grated onion. Whip the cream and fold it in with the home-made mayonnaise. Soften gelatine in $\frac{1}{4}$ cup cold water, and dissolve in $\frac{1}{4}$ cup boiling water. When cool fold into avocado mixture. Turn into a quart tin mould (rinse it out in cold water first) and chill for six hours. Unmould on to a serving platter and garnish with watercress and sliced raw mushrooms; or, if you prefer, black stoned olives and fresh shrimps.

Spring chicken with green grapes and almonds

2 *young roasting chickens*
2 *large cups rice*
$\frac{1}{4}$ *lb butter*
a little cream
1 *tablespoon grated Gruyère*
2 *small onions*
1 *lb good green grapes*
3 *oz blanched and peeled almonds*
olive oil

Roast the two young chickens carefully. Carve and only use breasts and wings cut into portions. No skin or brown meat.

Cook two cups of well-washed rice in twice its volume of boiling, salted water for 20 minutes. It should be dry, separate and not too soft. (If you find this tricky, use a safer method: boil rice in large amount of boiling water for 13–14 minutes, turn into tambour sieve, rinse under cold water, and dry out in cool oven or hot cupboard for $1\frac{1}{2}$–2 hours, turning occasionally.)

Sauté rice in a large heavy frying-pan with $\frac{1}{4}$ lb butter, a tablespoon of cream, a tablespoon of grated Swiss Gruyère cheese and one of the onions, which you have chopped very fine and sweated a little in butter until transparent, but not coloured.

Turn the rice on to a very hot flat dish and arrange pieces of chicken on top. Garnish with clusters of peeled and seeded green grapes, and blanched whole almonds that you have salted and sautéed very lightly in olive oil. If you like onion, you can also add to the garnish thinly sliced onion rings from the second onion, fried crisp in hot oil or deep fat. To do this you dust them with salt and flour, blanch them the first time in the hot oil for 4–5 minutes, remove, and then re-plunge for a few seconds to crisp and colour just before serving. Make a sauce suprême, pour a little over the top of the chicken, and hand the rest in a sauce boat.

Sauce suprême
4 oz butter
2 oz flour
2 pints chicken stock
little mushroom liquor
½ pint cream
pepper and salt
Make a white roux of 2 oz butter and 2 oz flour, and before it colours add 1 pint boiling chicken stock, stirring constantly. Bring to the boil again and cook slowly for 10–15 minutes. Remove fat and strain into another pan. Add another pint of strained hot chicken stock, two tablespoons mushroom liquor, and bring once more to the boil. Keep on boiling over fierce heat stirring vigorously until it is reduced by half. Then lower heat and add the cream gradually. Season well, remove from heat and stir in the remaining 2 oz butter. If not quite smooth, strain.

No accompaniment is necessary to this dish, but a plain green salad with a French dressing would be nice.

Apple anka
An apple torte from the Dalmatian Island of Korcula
The pastry mixture:
a mean 5½ oz butter
a mean 5½ oz ground almonds
a generous 4 oz icing sugar
a generous 4 oz sifted flour
juice of a lemon
Mix all ingredients together. Knead well, divide into two and roll both parts lightly into two rounds, florin thickness. Bake both halves in well-greased and floured cake tins about 8 inches across, one if possible fairly deep and both with loose bases, in a moderate oven (375° F. or gas mark 5). Leave the deep cake tin with the pastry in it when it is cooked; turn the other one out carefully.
The filling:
1. *Crème Pâtissière*
¾ pint milk
vanilla pod
4 egg yolks
4 oz caster sugar
a mean 2 oz sifted flour
1 tablespoon rum
1 teaspoon butter
Simmer the milk with the vanilla pod in it. Meanwhile beat egg yolks and sugar together. When pale add the sifted flour, still beating. Bring milk to the boil and strain on to the eggs, stirring vigorously; return custard to saucepan and bring to boil again, stirring with a whisk all the time. Continue cooking for a little while it thickens. Leave to cool and then stir in rum and a teaspoonful of butter.

2. *Apple mixture*
2 lb tart eating apples
2 tablespoons rum
1 tablespoon sugar
Peel and coarsely grate apples. Stew lightly with the sugar and the rum. Leave to cool.
Combine by covering the pastry in the deep cake tin with crème pâtissière, putting the second pastry round on top of this and then the cooked grated apple mixture. Refrigerate for at least two hours. Then turn out carefully. Do not attempt to remove the metal loose base of the cake tin, which makes a good base when cutting the torte.

Meringue:
4 fresh egg whites
8 oz very fine caster sugar (if possible vanilla flavoured)
Beat the egg whites very stiff. Whisk in half the sugar. Stop whisking and sprinkle in rest of sugar which you fold in very quickly with a palette knife. Cover the whole cake with the meringue. Smooth over with a palette knife, leaving a few peaks here and there. Put it into a moderate oven to set for a few minutes only. Do not let it colour. Replace in refrigerator until just before serving.

May

Fillets of sole Colette
4 *Dover soles weighing about ¾ lb each*
½ pint dry white wine
a few mushroom stalks
1 small chopped onion
lemon juice
parsley
bay leaf
a few shallots, finely chopped
¼ lb butter
tarragon
Ask your fishmonger to fillet the sole for you, and to make another parcel of the remains. Make a fish stock by putting 1 pint cold water and the ½ pint dry white wine into a saucepan with mushroom stalks, chopped onion, a few drops lemon juice, parsley stalks, bay leaf and the washed bones and trimmings of the sole. Cover partially, bring to boil and skim; then reduce heat and simmer slowly for 20 minutes. Strain through muslin. To poach the fish: cut your fillets in two lengthwise; tie each in a single knot and place carefully (with tails sitting up perkily) in a fireproof baking dish that has been buttered and sprinkled with 1 oz finely chopped shallots. Season well and half cover the fish with the stock; put a buttered paper over the dish and place in a warm oven (350° F. or gas mark 4) for 8–10 minutes.

Sauce: you can now either drain away excess liquid (but keep it) or transpose fish to warm serving dish. Then pour over melted butter into which you have squeezed the juice and grated rind of half a lemon and added a teaspoonful of both chopped parsley and tarragon.

Saddle of lamb printanier
weighing about 3½–4 lb
Spring lamb is at its tender best at 6–12 weeks old, and should be eaten from the end of April till the middle of June. Roast in a warm oven (350° F. or gas mark 4) for 2–2½ hours, allowing 30 minutes per lb once it has begun

cooking. Baste every 15 minutes. Carve in the kitchen and re-form back on to the bone. Serve a gravy made from pan juices in one sauce boat and some redcurrant jelly, or better still, crab-apple jelly, in another.

It should be accompanied by a large platter of spring vegetables.

Château potatoes

potatoes
butter
parsley

Fill up the middle of the dish with the château potatoes, which are potatoes cut to the shape of large olives, put on to boil in cold water, but only boiled for a minute, then cooled immediately in cold water and dried. Afterwards they are half roast, half sautéed very slowly in a large sauté pan or roasting tin in hot butter till a nice golden colour. (Shake pan occasionally while roasting.) Sprinkle with chopped parsley and check salt. Surround these with small piles of any fresh vegetable that is young and tender and available. Baby carrots and baby onions look nice. So do steamed and buttered beans or baby courgettes.

Glacéed carrots

2 lb small carrots
a bouillon meat cube
1 oz sugar
a large nut of butter

Just cover carrots with bouillon, made up from meat cube or paste. Add sugar, butter and salt, and cook slowly until liquid has reduced to a syrup and they are tender. Shake them about in this to glaze.

Glazed onions

Prepare the same way, blanch the onions first.

Best of all would be an outer ring of fonds d'artichauts and petit pois.

Fonds d'artichauts Clamart

12 small artichokes
1 lb shelled peas
3 oz butter
3 oz flour
12 small cooked carrots

Cut off the leaves of the artichokes. Trim the bottoms and plunge in cold salted water. Bring to boil and cook for about 20 minutes, till rest of leaves and the choke come away easily and the artichoke bottom is tender but not too soft. Simmer peas in butter until tender, then bind with the butter and flour that you have cooked together for a few minutes. Scoop out a very little from the artichoke bottoms and fill with this mixture. You can add a buttered carrot in the middle if you like. Arrange on a platter and put in the oven for a few moments to reheat.

Stone cream

1 pint good cream
a little sugar
1 leaf gelatine
a few drops vanilla essence or ratafia
3 tablespoons apricot jam
wineglass medium dry sherry
1 lemon, a little grated lemon peel

This is a very old Lancashire dish. You need a stepladder in the kitchen to make it and a lot of newspaper on the floor.

Boil the cream for a few minutes with a little sugar, the melted gelatine and a few drops of vanilla or ratafia. Have ready a deep glass dish, cover the bottom with apricot jam (the tinned kind is best), a wineglassful of sherry, the juice of a lemon and a little grated lemon peel. When the cream has cooled a little, pour it into this dish, which you have placed on newspaper on the kitchen floor, from as high as you can. Let it stand overnight in a cool place. In the morning the cream will be all bubbly and aerated.

June

Pâté in aspic

1 lb liverwurst (or homemade liver pâté)
1–2 tablespoons Worcester sauce
3 oz cream cheese
3 tablespoons brandy
1 small onion, grated
salt, black pepper

Beat ingredients together well and season to taste. For the aspic: 2 pints of good homemade Madeira aspic, which involves boiling calves' feet and vegetables for 3 hours, clarifying and flavouring, then straining. Take a small ring or savarin mould and place it in a large bowl of crushed ice. Pour in the liquid but syrupy aspic. As soon as it starts to set at the sides pour off the liquid in the centre and your mould will be evenly lined. If you think it needs a thicker layer, reheat aspic, re-cool and repeat. Chill a little more. Then fill the centre of mould with the creamy pâté. Smooth it over and cover with remaining aspic. Aspic should, ideally, be just over $\frac{1}{4}$ inch thick on the sides and just under $\frac{1}{2}$ inch thick at the bottom of mould. Set in fridge.

Unmould before serving by dipping mould rapidly into a bowl of hand warm water and shaking mould. Turn out onto serving dish and fill centre with a bunch of watercress. Decorate with a few slices of black truffle and white of egg.

Halibut Strachur

$3\frac{1}{2}$–$4\frac{1}{2}$ lb halibut
6 oz butter
iuice 2 lemons
$\frac{1}{2}$ pint cream
1 tablespoon Worcester sauce
salt, black pepper

Get your fishmonger to give you a well shaped piece of halibut weighing at least 3 lb. Half a small fish looks better than a slice from a large one. Remember it will be a lot smaller when cooked. Clean and trim halibut but do not skin or bone it. Cook it in the butter in a large frying-pan, with one of the lemons squeezed over it while it is cooking.

Cook it until it is golden brown on both sides and till the flesh comes away easily from the backbone. Turn the fish very carefully so as to keep it whole. It will need about 15 minutes gentle cooking on both sides. When ready, remove fish from pan, skin and collect as many bones from edges of fish as you can: transfer it to a shallow entrée dish and keep hot. Add the cream to the juices in the pan, then the Worcester sauce (if liked), salt, pepper and more lemon juice. Correct seasoning and pour sauce over the fish. Serve with deep fried straw potatoes in little bundles round the edge of fish.

Fraises à la russe

2 lb strawberries
4 tablespoons caster sugar
juice 2 oranges
2 tablespoons orange Curaçao
2 tablespoons cognac
Chantilly cream: *1 pint whipped cream*
1 white of egg
sugar to taste

Clean, hull and dry 2 lb fine fresh strawberries. Pile them in a silver, or better still, a pretty porcelain bowl. Sift caster sugar over them and sprinkle with the orange juice to which you have added Curaçao and cognac. Refrigerate for at least 2 hours, then cover with chilled Chantilly cream (beat cream and egg white separately, combine and add a little sugar). Try and show some strawberries through the cream here and there, to give colour. Serve with Tuiles d'Amandes biscuits.

Cold egg mousse

6 eggs
1 pint double cream
French mustard
Worcester sauce
a little mayonnaise
1 tomato
1 lettuce flower
chicken aspic

Hard boil the eggs. Sieve the yolks through a wire sieve. Chop the whites coarsely. Whip the cream fairly stiff. Mix the eggs into the cream, first the yolks, then the whites. Season well and correct flavour with a little mustard, a dessertspoonful of Worcester sauce, a little mayonnaise. The egg by itself is an uninteresting taste but it must be left to the individual how much of each seasoning is used. Turn into a white soufflé dish, smooth off top and decorate with a flat tomato and lettuce flower, then cover with $\frac{1}{4}$-inch thick top of chicken aspic and put in fridge to set. Aspic that is made from real chicken stock is best.

Vitello tonnato

rolled roast of veal
8 oz tin tuna fish without the oil
1 large chopped onion
2 chopped carrots
2 chopped celery stalks
2 large cloves garlic, finely minced
1 tin anchovies without the oil
1 cup dry white wine
2 bay leaves
parsley sprig
salt
freshly ground black pepper
mayonnaise
lemon juice
rice
capers

This is one of the best summer luncheon dishes in the world, but a much abused one as many disastrous imitations are served under its name. I got this recipe from a gourmet friend in Geneva, who got it from a famous Italian restaurateur in New York, and I think it is the nearest to the real thing that can be eaten outside Italy.

Brown a rolled roast of veal in a very little oil, not too dark a colour because of the sauce, in a very heavy cast-iron pan, so that it cooks slowly. Add to it the tuna fish, onion, carrots, celery stalks, garlic, anchovies, white wine, bay leaves, parsley, salt and black pepper. Cook slowly in a moderate oven for 2 hours, closely covered.

Remove the meat and chill it. Reduce the sauce by half by boiling fast, and put it in a blender (remove parsley and bay leaves, all other ingredients will have infused). When chilled, mix this sauce with a cup of mayonnaise, and season with lemon juice. Arrange cold rice on a serving dish. Cover with finely sliced veal. Spread sauce carefully over and sprinkle with capers.

Raspberry mess

$1\frac{1}{2}$ lb fresh raspberries
1 pint double cream
3 oz sugar
sponge cake (less than $\frac{1}{2}$ in thick) or 10 sponge fingers
little Maraschino
1 or 2 in green angelica
1 lb fresh raspberries
$\frac{1}{2}$ lb granulated sugar

Squash $1\frac{1}{4}$ lb raspberries slightly with a fork. Whip cream very stiff. Combine with sugar and raspberries. Put sponge at the bottom of a glass bowl and sprinkle with a little Maraschino. Heap up cream and raspberry mess onto this (it should be quite stiff) as high as you can, and decorate with the remainder of the raspberries, hulled but whole, and bits of chopped angelica that you push in sideways to look like leaves. Serve a raspberry sauce separately.

Raspberry sauce: Force the raspberries through a sieve to make a purée. Put this in an electric liquidiser with the sugar. Cover and whirl at top speed for 2 to 3 minutes. Take out and chill.

Harry More Gordon

Iced pea soup

I *dessertspoon butter*
2 *small shallots*
I *lettuce heart*
$1\frac{1}{2}$ *pints peas (older ones will do)*
salt
$\frac{1}{2}$ *teaspoon sugar*
$\frac{1}{4}$ *pint chicken or veal stock*
$\frac{1}{4}$ *pint milk*
$\frac{1}{4}$–$\frac{1}{2}$ *pint cream*
black pepper
a little skinned chopped cucumber
few small mint leaves

Melt the butter in a fairly large saucepan. Sauté the finely chopped shallots and roughly chopped lettuce in it until golden but not brown. Add the peas, together with a few pea pods, salt and sugar, cover with cold water and bring to the boil. Simmer gently for about 20 minutes. Remove pea pods, drain peas, reserving $\frac{1}{4}$ pint cooking liquid. Put the peas through a mouli or fine sieve—a liquidiser is apt to make the soup too bland—and reheat the purée. Add the strained stock, the vegetable water you have kept, the milk and finally the cream. Do not boil. Correct the seasoning and add black pepper. Pour into a bowl and chill in the fridge for at least two hours. Serve in chilled soup cups with a little chopped cucumber, and a small fresh mint leaf or two floating on top.

Fitz's lobster risotto

2 *medium freshly boiled lobsters (about* $1\frac{1}{2}$ *lbs each)*
2 *tumblers rice*
about 4 *oz butter*
a little olive oil
salt
black pepper
a little paprika
$\frac{1}{4}$ *pint sour cream*
4 *hard-boiled eggs*
I *tablespoon freshly chopped tarragon*
I *tablespoon freshly grated Parmesan cheese*
I *wineglass medium dry sherry*

When lobsters are cold, crack claws, cut tails in two and remove all meat. Skim the water in which the lobsters were boiled. Bring once more to the boil and throw in two tumblers of rice. Boil briskly for about 12 minutes (start testing after 11, it should be *al dente,* or firm not hard) and when ready turn immediately on to a large sieve or colander and run cold water over the rice until starch is washed away and water runs clear. Leave to drain and dry in a very cool oven, with door open, or on top of cooker; it will take from 1–2 hours. 15 minutes before serving melt 4 oz butter and a little olive oil in a large sauté pan. Turn in rice and cut lobster into convenient pieces. Add the lobster coral and any bits you can scrape from shell, then salt, pepper, paprika, cream, hard-boiled eggs, tarragon, Parmesan and sherry. Mix together carefully, adding more butter and oil if necessary to prevent sticking. Correct seasoning and turn on to a very hot serving dish.

Charlotte russe with compote of fraises des bois

I *pint double cream*
I *teaspoon vanilla*
$\frac{1}{2}$ *cup sugar*
little Kirsch
I *dessertspoon gelatine*
$\frac{1}{4}$ *cup cold milk*
$\frac{1}{4}$ *cup warm milk*
5 *egg whites*
I *lb alpine strawberries*
juice I *lemon*
I *pint water*
I *tablespoon vanilla*
$\frac{3}{4}$ *lb granulated sugar*
I *lb alpine strawberries*

Whip the cream until it is stiff, add the vanilla and sugar, then add Kirsch to taste. Soften the gelatine in cold milk, and dissolve it in warm milk. When it is cool add it to the cream, beating all the time. Then fold in carefully the stiffly beaten egg whites. Pour into a china mould or pudding bowl and set in the fridge. Unmould in glass serving bowl and surround with the strawberries that you have cleaned, sprinkled with sugar and marinated for a few hours in lemon juice and Kirsch. Decorate top with a few strawberries and whipped cream.

Compote of fraises des bois: Simmer water, vanilla and sugar in a saucepan until it has dissolved. Add cleaned strawberries. Bring again to simmering point and then maintain at just below the simmer for 5 minutes. Remove pan from heat and allow strawberries to cool in syrup for 20 minutes. Pour into glass serving dish and chill.

September

Mushrooms à la grecque
$1\frac{1}{4}$ lb mushrooms
olive oil
1 tablespoon finely chopped onion
$\frac{1}{4}$ pint dry white wine
juice 2 lemons
teaspoon salt
pinch of pepper
teaspoon mustard
pinch coriander
chopped fennel and parsley
1 bay leaf
Wash and dry the button (or small field) mushrooms carefully, but do not peel. Trim the stalks and cut into two or more suitable portions. Heat a generous cupful of oil in a large enamel saucepan; add all the ingredients putting in the mushrooms last of all. Cover and cook for 3–4 minutes. Turn the mixture into an earthenware serving dish and leave to cool in the marinade for at least six hours. Serve cold in the same dish. If you wish you can make this dish one day to serve the next.

Strabane groundnut and chicken casserole
1 large plump chicken, or 2 small ones
2 medium onions finely chopped
2 tablespoons butter
1 jar peanut butter
1 pint chicken stock
pepper
salt
Worcester sauce
10 rashers thin streaky bacon
Cut the chicken(s) into joints. Sauté them in butter with the chopped onions until golden brown. Transfer them to a casserole and add the contents of a jar of peanut butter and enough chicken stock to make a thick creamy sauce. Have some chicken stock in reserve. Season to taste and add a spoonful of Worcester sauce. Simmer until the chicken is tender. If the sauce gets too thick add more stock. It should take about 35 minutes, depending on the age of the chickens. Before serving sprinkle with the bacon which you have fried in hot fat, drained on paper and crumbled. Spinach en branche or a green salad goes well with this dish.

Green grapes caramel
3 lb green grapes
8 oz sugar
$\frac{1}{4}$ pint water
a little green Chartreuse liqueur
pouring cream
Fill 6 goblet-shaped glasses with carefully peeled and seeded white grapes. If you plunge the grapes into boiling water for a few seconds first it makes the peeling process much quicker.

Make a caramel by putting water and sugar into a heavy pan and shake or swirl it over gentle heat until the sugar is quite dissolved, then turn up the heat and allow sugar to boil and boil on for about 3–4 minutes or until it turns a light nut brown. Remove from heat and pour on to a metal tray or enamel plate or plates, as caramel layer must be only $\frac{1}{8}$ in thick. When it is cold and set, break it up into small pieces with a hammer or mallet and sprinkle fairly thickly on top of the grapes. Add a few drops liqueur and chill until time to serve. Hand cream separately.

Oranges, carefully peeled so as to leave no pith and sliced in thin circles, can be used for this dish instead of grapes, in which case the liqueur should be Grand Marnier or Orange Curaçao.

October

Salmon cutlets en papillote
6 salmon cutlets 1 in thick
2 oz mushrooms
chopped parsley
pinch of chopped dill
3 oz butter
salt, pepper
juice of 1 lemon
wineglass of sherry
Chop the mushrooms, add parsley and dill and work into butter. Season salmon cutlets well on both sides and trim them. Spread one side with the butter paste. Sprinkle with lemon juice. Lay each salmon cutlet on oblong piece of greaseproof paper and twist ends of paper tight to make a papillote. Pour a little sherry into each and bake in a hot oven for about 40 minutes. Serve in their paper cases. These salmon cutlets are also very good cold, taken out of their paper cases and laid on a thin piece of rye bread that has been buttered with watercress butter. Cover with a rather thin mayonnaise made with lemon instead of vinegar.

Cold grouse pie
5–6 grouse (old or young)
1 lb lean pork
a little pork fat
1 medium onion
3 black truffles (optional)
salt
peppercorns
bay leaf
dash of Worcester sauce
1 lb streaky bacon, thinly cut
3 pints stock, made with grouse carcases and/or chicken bones or cracked veal knuckle
Use only breasts of grouse. Remove all tough fibres and

skin, and cut into pieces. Lay each piece of fillet between two layers of greaseproof paper and beat flat with a wooden mallet or a wine bottle if you haven't got a mallet. Mince the lean and fat pork, add finely chopped onion and coarsely chopped truffles, salt, peppercorns, bay leaf, Worcester sauce. Take a fireproof pie dish and line it with overlapping rashers of bacon. Spread grouse fillets with mince mixture and lay one on top of the other until you cannot fit any more in. Cover with more rashers of bacon and pour in a good strained grouse stock until dish is half full. Cover pie dish with foil and a lid and stand in a roasting tin with water to come halfway up its sides. Cook in slow-medium oven for two hours. Do not let it run dry. Reduce the remaining stock by boiling rapidly and when the pie is ready fill it up with this. When cool put a sheet of greaseproof paper on top and some weights. When quite cold remove these and scrape off fat which will have risen to top of pie. Garnish with parsley. Serve with a tossed green salad and baked potatoes in their jackets.

Whisky bananas

9 *bananas*
3 *tablespoons butter*
4½ *tablespoons sugar*
4½ *tablespoons whisky*

Sauté bananas, skinned but left whole, in butter with the sugar sprinkled thickly over them. Turn carefully. When sugar begins to caramelise and bananas are well cooked heat the whisky in a little saucepan. Set it alight and pour it over the bananas. Serve at once.

November

Barbara Karban

Quiche aux poireaux

1 *lb whites of leeks*
2 *oz butter*
2 *large eggs*
½ *pint cream*
pepper, salt
pinch of nutmeg
an 8 *inch partially cooked short-crust pastry flan*
1 *tablespoon grated Gruyère* or *Emmenthal cheese*
little extra butter

Slice leeks thinly, using only white part; blanch for 5 minutes in boiling water. Pour off water, leaving only a spoonful, then simmer gently in 2 oz butter and a little salt with the lid on saucepan. In about 30 minutes the leeks will be very tender and the liquid all absorbed. Beat eggs (use either 2 large or 3 small ones), cream, pepper, salt and nutmeg together. Cool the leek purée and add to cream gradually; correct seasoning and pour into partially cooked pastry case. Sprinkle with grated cheese and dot all over with small flakes of butter. Bake for about 25 minutes on top shelf of oven (375° F. or gas mark 5) until puffed up and golden brown.

Cutlets on brown rice

8 *cutlets, lamb or mutton, trimmed*
2 *eggs*
white breadcrumbs
2 *oz butter, tablespoon oil* or *cooking fat*
pepper and salt
1½ *cups rice*
2 *oz good dripping*
3 *rashers bacon*
1 *medium onion, chopped*
1 *clove garlic*
6 *small mushrooms*
6 *chicken livers*
2¼ *cups stock* or *water with bouillon cube*
¼ *teaspoon browning*

Cutlets: Beat eggs, dip each cutlet in them, then roll in breadcrumbs, patting gently. Fry in hot fat for about 7–10 minutes each side, but do not brown too much. Season to taste and serve on bed of savoury brown rice.

Brown rice: Prepare rice. Melt dripping in a heavy pan. Add cut-up rashers of bacon, chopped onion, very finely chopped garlic and cut-up mushrooms. Cook gently until onion and mushrooms are soft but do not burn. Sauté chicken livers separately and chop into small pieces. Add rice and chicken livers; stir, season well and cook together for a few minutes. Add the stock and a little browning. Stir all together again and put in hot oven with lid on (375–425° F. or gas mark 5–7) for 20 minutes. Look at it occasionally and stir a few times with a fork during the cooking time. Add a little stock if necessary but this quantity of rice should absorb all liquid and cook to the al dente point without going mushy.

Nun's pudding

½ *pint milk*
4 *eggs*
4 *leaves gelatine or just over* ½ *oz of powdered kind*
2 *tablespoons apricot jam*
2 *tablespoons powdered cinnamon*
½ *pint cream*

Make a custard with the milk and the 4 yolks of eggs. Add 4 leaves of melted gelatine, which you obtain by melting leaves or powder very slowly with a spoonful of hot water in a bowl over hot water. Pour into the dish in which it is going to be served—a glass one looks best—and let it set. Then mix a dessertspoonful water with the apricot jam and spread carefully over the custard. Sprinkle the cinnamon over the jam, and cover with a fairly thick layer of whipped cream.

December

Truffles in champagne
6 large truffles
1 pint dry champagne
1 pint lightly seasoned veal stock
bread for toasting
Wash and peel six good-sized truffles. Put side by side in a large saucepan and just cover with about one pint of champagne and one pint of very lightly seasoned veal stock. Cover pan. Bring to boil and simmer gently for a bare five minutes, then remove from heat and leave to cool by side of stove for a further ten minutes. Take truffles out carefully with a perforated spoon and arrange on a hot serving dish. Reduce the cooking liquor by two thirds by boiling rapidly, then strain it over the truffles and serve at once with hot thin toast.

Côtes de porc with rosemary
about 3 lb boneless loin of pork
black pepper
1 teaspoonful salt
2 tablespoons bacon fat or cooking oil
1 oz butter
3 or more sprigs of rosemary
1 lemon
¼ pint or ½ cup dry white vermouth
The marinade:
3 tablespoons lemon juice
3 tablespoons olive oil
6 sprigs of fresh rosemary
1 clove mashed garlic (optional)
Ask your butcher for about 3 lb boneless loin of pork. Get him to trim it and cut it into 6–8 chops about one inch thick. Rub pepper and salt into the pork and marinate in a covered enamel or china bowl for at least four hours, if possible overnight.

Turn over and baste meat several times during marination. Discard marinade, dry meat thoroughly, then heat the fat or oil in a large sauté pan which has a lid until it is nearly smoking. Sear the chops quickly, in two lots, cooking them on each side for about 3 or 4 minutes or until brown, then take them out of the pan and keep warm. Pour away fat, then put a good ounce of butter and the second lot of rosemary, which you shred a little, into the sauté pan. Return the chops which will slightly overlay each other, reheat until sizzling, then cover the pan and simmer gently for another 20–25 minutes, basting with the butter and juices every now and then. Remove chops to a hot serving dish and squeeze the juice of the lemon over them, and scatter with as much rosemary as you can collect from the pan. Skim off some of the fat from the pan juices, pour in the Vermouth, boil rapidly to reduce and pour over the chops. Serve with a smooth potato purée and a simple green salad.

Monte Bianco or chestnut Mont Blanc
The chestnuts:
1 lb dehydrated chestnuts
About 1 pint milk
Pinch of salt
2 tablespoons vanilla sugar

The whipped cream centre:
1 pint double cream
½ cup caster sugar
1 level dessertspoon powdered gelatine
4 tablespoons cold milk
4 tablespoons hot milk
1 teaspoon vanilla extract
5 egg whites

The Crème Chantilly:
½ pint chilled cream
1 tablespoon caster sugar
½ teaspoon vanilla extract
To decorate:
1 small jar of "Marrons Debris"
Soak the dehydrated chestnuts in water overnight. They can be bought in ½ lb packets at any good Italian grocers and save hours of tiresome shelling without losing out on flavour. Cook them gently in milk, with a pinch of salt, until they are tender. Drain, and where necessary skin, rub through a wire sieve or Moulinette on to a large plate, being careful not to compress the chestnut "worms". Sprinkle with two tablespoons vanilla sugar. Lift the chestnut "worms" carefully with two silver forks and pile them round a central whipped-cream mousse (a not too stiff Charlotte Russe) that you have already unmoulded on to a flat serving dish. Heap up the chestnuts until they entirely cover the cream. The cream centre is made thus: whip 1 pint double cream until stiff, fold in the caster sugar. Soften the gelatine in the cold milk and dissolve it in the hot milk. When it is really cool add it to the cream, beating all the time, and flavour with vanilla. Fold in the 5 egg whites that you have beaten into peaks. Spoon into a cylinder mould or china pudding bowl and set in fridge. Make a Crème Chantilly by beating the other ½ pint of chilled cream (it should be refrigerated for 5–6 hours before use) until it is moderately thick, then folding in the sugar. Flavour with a few drops of vanilla and cover the top of the chestnut "mountain" with the cream, letting it dribble down the sides so that it covers most of them too. Decorate the base of the Mont Blanc with a few spoonfuls of Marrons Glacées Debris. Refrigerate for an hour before serving.

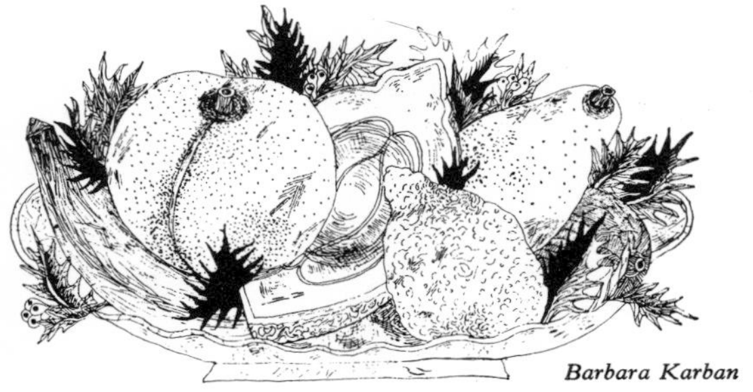
Barbara Karban

TEA
RICE
SUGAR

70s

The seventies began with *Vogue's Food Gazette*. For this feature Pamela Harlech contributed an amazing variety of recipes culled from family and friends and her own numerous notebooks. Then came a series of people "talking to Pamela Harlech" about food: the Earl of Gowrie—"When I was in New York with the United Nations I was overweight and having to do quite a lot of eating out so I decided, when by myself, to eat in Japanese restaurants. This is really the best inexpensive way of going on a diet because the Japanese have a far higher protein and a far lower cholesterol, animal fat, and carbohydrate intake then we do, so one ate marvellously. In two weeks I lost 15 lb and got an insight into Japanese life and culture at the same time." Viscount Eden: "Cooking first interested me in 1954 when I bought a house in Rutland Street. There was an M.P.—who wasn't an M.P. then—who did the washing up, a doctor who cleaned the *moules* and I did the cooking. Of the three jobs it seemed to me the most attractive. . . . My idea of a kitchen is to have as much space as possible and a very simple stove. I think three sinks is an absolute minimum—one for washing the vegetables, one for washing up as one goes along, and one you can pour the dregs of anything down." Anthony West: "I was brought up on the outer fringes of Bloomsbury, in the 'converted country farmhouse' syndrome so I have always done that kind of cooking, using lots of country food. I suppose the centre of it all is the rough country bread that I get a great deal of pleasure out of making. It is the key to the whole kind of cuisine I like, a cross between English and French country cooking. My interest began years ago when Marcel Boulestin began trying to save England by teaching the English how to cook." Mrs Peter Hall: "In the holidays feeding the children is like having a lot of cuckoos with imploring eyes and open mouths leading to bottomless stomachs. But pleasurable all the same because they are vociferous in their approval."

James Mortimer

Lady Harlech and her daughter Pandora in her country kitchen

In October 1974 Arabella Boxer summed up the changing attitude to cooking: "As meat grows ever more expensive, my enthusiasm for it has waned still further. Contrary to the general propaganda, urging us to experiment with cheaper cuts and to learn to make them into sustaining meals, I find that I have done the

Duc

opposite, and now think of meat as a luxury. I resent the time spent on transforming unattractive pieces of flesh into eatable dishes, and am only prepared to make this sort of effort during the bleakest winter months. During the rest of the year I prefer to buy the best meat, which requires only grilling or roasting, once or twice a week in small quantities, rather than make a time-consuming economical meat dish each day.

"I have come to think of fish in the same way. Except for the occasional dish of kedgeree or smoked haddock, I prefer from time to time to buy halibut or turbot, salmon trout or bass without resenting the price, rather than cod or haddock two or three times a week. Poultry is one of the few foods that has come down in price, and this I buy more often, partly because chicken combines so well with vegetable dishes, and partly because I rely on a regular supply of good chicken stock.

"The rest of the time I live on dishes made from combinations of vegetables with pastry, rice, noodles, cheese or eggs, gnocchi or pancakes. I do not claim to save time or money by eating in this way, for accumulating a varied selection of vegetables is not always cheap, and there is quite a lot of work involved, but the preparation is pleasant, does not smell and provides a series of dishes that are tempting and never monotonous."

Tessa Traeger

The following year, in May 1975, *Vogue* started a special Food and Drink section, *A* rabella *B* oxer *C* ooking, with Pamela Harlech's Notebook, Henry McNulty Drinking in Vogue and Quentin Crewe writing about restaurants. Tessa Traeger photographed the covers for each supplement, a superb series, each picture a delight and a surprise. She worked closely with Arabella Boxer whose new series had explanatory titles such as "Arabella Boxer Kneads Dough", "Arabella Boxer Spills the Beans", "Arabella Boxer has a Freezing Day/a Baking Day . . ." Opposite and overleaf are Tessa Traeger's photographs for "Arabella Boxer Tosses a Salad" and "Arabella Boxer Goes to the Country" with their recipes. This is how Arabella Boxer introduced her first recipes: "I find my cooking has become much simpler. The general shortage of money has contributed to this, but in a surprisingly constructive way. I find I work best within limitations, and whether these are imposed by lack of cash or of materials does not matter. It is in times of comparative affluence that I start to panic, when I feel people's standards have become too high, and we have been spoilt by restaurant meals, too many invitations, and so on. A few years ago I remember hearing one guest complain that he could not face another salmon trout, and recommended a "filet de boeuf en croute" as ideal picnic food. In this sort of atmosphere I quickly become defeatist; when anything is within the bounds of possibility, nothing seems good enough . . .

"I think part of the trouble was that many of us were still trying to live according to a pattern laid down by our grandparents in an era of prosperity. We were living in large houses without the help they were originally planned to have, giving dinner parties that would have kept a staff of two or three fully occupied for a couple of days; in short, we were trying to keep jobs, bring up children, run houses, maintain gardens, and entertain in a way that was far too demanding for most of us to accomplish without a degree of strain. I find it a relief that we have been forced to abandon all this, and to find a simpler way of living, more within our reach."

Now, in the mid-seventies, it looks as though the future pattern is already taking place: a more individual and simplified approach not only to entertaining but to family cooking, too. Fruits and vegetables treated in their own right, salads an accepted part of British diet, national dishes appreciated and family recipes exchanged. Cooking has become not only a necessity but a pleasure. But while meals are reduced to one or two courses, a far cry from the 15-dish menu in *Vogue* over fifty years ago, recipes are more precise and imaginative than ever.

Tessa Traeger, June 1975

GRANDS
PARIS

Arabella Boxer Goes to the Country

I haven't lived in the country since the age of ten, yet the thought of returning to it still tantalizes me. Perhaps it was those early years that were responsible; as the Jesuits are supposed to say, "give us a child till the age of seven and he is ours for ever", or words to that effect. Or perhaps the yearning would still exist, independent of any actual experience.

As must happen to many other parents, the feeling was intensified by watching one's children grow up in the city, playing in adventure playgrounds rather than forests, rowing on the Serpentine rather than on lochs and rivers. For many of us, the situation has been improved by compromise: the country cottage, easily accessible for weekends and holidays.

I think the most important thing is to make country life as unlike one's urban life as possible, to take advantage of the country in every way. The most extreme way of doing this would be to try to live entirely off wild food, gathering nuts and berries, looking for plants with edible leaves and roots, even picking the flowers to use as a garnish. What could be more appealing than a salad of blanched dandelion leaves and wild sorrel, with primroses scattered over the top?

But I fear I am both too lazy and too pragmatic to attempt such an ambitious scheme in full. I also feel that most wild foods, however pure and nutritious, are hardly very sustaining, and the leaves of wild plants, watercress, sorrel, and so on, are much smaller than those of their cultivated cousins, so it would be hard work to find them in sufficient quantities.

I have worked out a compromise, however, which I plan to try out at the next opportunity. This would consist of living off local produce, either from one's own garden, or the gardens of near-by cottages who hang out signs saying "runner beans for sale, eggs, lettuces", and so on. This, together with milk and butter from a friendly farm or the nearest dairy, and a supply of flour and yeast laid in beforehand, would assure the basis of good solid meals. One would then have the confidence to experiment, using as much wild food as one could find. To a salad made from one's own lettuce, for instance, I would add wild watercress and dandelion leaves, with crushed wild garlic in the dressing, and the chopped leaves scattered over the top.

Young nettles are to my mind the most useful of wild foods, largely because they are so easy to find. Not only are they abundant, they are also easy to cook and quite delicious. They must be gathered with gloves and scissors, using only the tips, the first four or five leaves, of the young spring nettles, and cooked exactly like spinach. You need to pick masses, for they shrink as spinach does. They can be eaten as a vegetable: in leaf form, chopped or puréed; or as a soup.

Wild dandelions should be blanched—this removes any bitter taste and makes them more digestible—and again only the young spring plants should be used. Blanching is done by putting an inverted flower pot, or two slates, over the whole plant, and leaving it thus shaded from the light for a week to ten days. The pale leaves then make an excellent salad, either alone, or mixed with other leaves.

Wild watercress should be treated with caution, and one must know the whole course of the stream it grows in before being sure it is safe; if at any point it runs through pastures where cattle graze it can be dangerous. It is only really safe in high places, where the stream flows through rocks rather than fields.

Blackberries are another plentiful and delicious food. I love berries of all sorts, especially when very lightly cooked indeed, just until the juice starts to run, then left to cool and served with home-made yoghourt or cream. I rarely make them into pies, as I find the baking of the pastry over-cooks the fruit. We find wild raspberries quite often in the woods, but never in sufficient quantities to contemplate cooking them.

Rose hips are full of goodness from a nutritional point of view, but like all things that remind me of the war, when we used to be made to pick them for rose-hip syrup, they depress me as a food, although I love their appearance. Elder-flowers are much used in Central Europe; usually deep-fried, they are eaten either as a vegetable fritter, or with sugar as a pudding. They make a delicious and subtle

Tessa Traeger, August 1975

flavouring for jams, and the best of the home-made wines.

Cobnuts and filberts abound in the Sussex woods; here the problem is how to leave them long enough on the trees to ripen, without letting the squirrels get them first. I love to eat them plain, or chopped and scattered over salads of raw vegetables, or in yoghourt. Spanish chestnuts are also plentiful; these I like best roasted over the fire. The smell alone is delicious, and more nostalgic than any other. They can also be cooked, as vegetables, sauces, soups, or stuffings for birds. For those who like it, there is the classic sweet dish of puréed chestnuts topped with whipped cream.

In late September the first sloes appear. These fruits, like tiny damsons, purple-black and bitter to taste, are easily found in the woods and are well worth the picking. They can be made into sloe gin, ideal for presents or for drinking at home.

Never having lived by the sea, I am totally ignorant of wild sea-food, but Tessa Traeger, has often eaten the shellfish and seaweeds like those in the illustration. She has eaten laver fried with bacon and eggs, for example, a dish I had never heard of, and tells me it is sold in barrels at Barnstaple market, possibly at other similar seaside towns. It is rich in iron, like all seaweeds, and should be tried, although it has a strange taste.

One piece of equipment I consider vital for country life is the yoghourt machine. Not only is good yoghourt difficult to buy, but one often has surplus of milk, and fresh yoghourt makes a perfect complement to meals of this sort. It is also a useful way of using small amounts of fruit; a tiny bowl of redcurrants from the garden, or wild strawberries, is plenty to flavour four or five bowls of yoghourt.

The recipes I have given are all for very simple dishes; things that can be made either from the most basic of ingredients, or from easily found wild foods. The quantities are for four people only, as I thought it unlikely that anyone would cook this sort of food for other than their immediate family.

Wild garlic soup

a bunch of wild garlic, or
2 bunches spring onions and
1 clove garlic
2 oz butter
2 large potatoes
1½ pints chicken stock
sea salt and black peppercorns
chopped parsley or chervil,
chives or dill

Wild garlic is much milder than ordinary garlic, with a fresh juicy flavour more like a very strong spring onion. Chop the little bulbs finely and stew gently in butter for 4–5 minutes, being very careful not to let it burn. Peel the potatoes and cut in slices. Add to the garlic and stir around while the stock is heating in another pan (use a cube if none is available). Pour the hot stock onto the garlic and potatoes and stir until well mixed and just simmering. Cook gently with the lid on for 20–25 minutes. Put through the coarse mesh of the vegetable mill, add salt and pepper to taste, and sprinkle with whatever fresh herbs you have to hand. (Spring onions and 1–2 cloves of cultivated garlic can be substituted for the wild garlic. In this case, only add the minced garlic with the potatoes.)

Nettle purée with poached eggs

1½–2 lb young nettle tips
1½ oz butter
sea salt and black pepper
½ gill thick cream, or sour cream
4 eggs
croûtons:
2 slices stale bread
butter
1 clove garlic

Throw the nettles into a large pan of boiling water lightly salted and cook briskly until tender. Drain them very well, forcing out as much water as possible in a colander with the back of a wooden spoon. Chop as finely as possible on a wooden board with a long knife, backwards and forwards. Return to the clean pan and add the butter and cream over gentle heat, adding salt and pepper to taste. Poach the eggs and drain well. Make the croûtons by frying the bread, each slice cut in four triangles, in butter until golden, then rubbing with a cut clove of garlic. Pour the nettles onto a serving dish, lay the poached eggs on top, and surround with the croûtons. (Spinach can be substituted for nettles.)

Potage santé

1 lb potatoes
2 lettuces, or 1 lettuce and a bunch of sorrel
2 oz butter
1½ pints chicken stock
sea salt and black pepper

Peel the potatoes and cut in cubes. Shred the lettuces by cutting across in thin strips. Boil the potatoes for 10 minutes in lightly salted water and drain. Melt the butter in a casserole and stew the lettuces gently for 10 minutes. Heat the stock and pour onto the lettuce. Bring to simmering point, add the potatoes and cook gently for another 10 minutes. Put through the coarse mesh of the vegetable mill and re-heat, adding salt and pepper to taste.

This soup can be made quite simply as it is, or used as a base for any wild greens you may like to add: sorrel, watercress, dandelions, etc. It is also very good made with a mixture of lettuce and garden sorrel, which gives a sharper taste.

Mussel or cockle soup

3–4 pints mussels or cockles
1 onion
1 clove garlic (optional)
1 bay leaf
a few sprigs parsley
sea salt and black peppercorns
¾ pint water
¾ pint dry white wine (if available)
¼ pint thick cream

The cleaning of mussels and cockles picked from the seashore is exactly the same as for mussels bought from the fishmonger. Throw them immediately into a large bowl of cold salted water until ready to prepare. Then go through them, discarding any that are broken or half-open. Under a running cold tap, scrape the shells with a strong sharp knife, and scrub well with a hard brush. Leave to soak for at least 15 minutes in a bowl under a running cold tap, or change the water several times until it is quite clear and free from grit.

Put the cleaned shellfish in a pan with a finely chopped onion, a clove garlic if liked, a bay leaf, the stalks of the parsley (reserving the heads), some salt and a few black peppercorns. Add the water and wine—instead of wine you can use water with a couple of spoons of white wine vinegar added—and bring quickly to the boil. Simmer for 10–15 minutes; cockles take about 10 minutes to cook, mussels from 12–15 according to size. When cooked, lift out the shellfish and remove from their shells. Keep them hot in a tureen while you strain the cooking liquor into a clean pan, and reheat, adding the cream and some chopped parsley. Taste for seasoning, then pour over the shellfish.

Bean salad

½ lb runner beans
sea salt
black pepper
olive oil
½ lb dried haricot beans, or tinned (well rinsed)
1 onion, or a few bulbs wild garlic
lemon juice, or white wine vinegar

Using young runner beans, trim away only the thinnest string from the edges if necessary. Cut the beans in 1-inch chunks diagonally. Throw into salted boiling water and cook until only just tender, leaving them still definitely crisp rather than soggy. Drain well, and add olive oil and salt and pepper while still hot. Leave to cool, then mix with the haricot beans which you have already cooked and add finely chopped onion or wild garlic, salt and pepper, more oil and lemon juice or vinegar to taste. (Whole string beans can be substituted for the runner beans, and are even better, although not so easily come by in the country.)

Eggs and potatoes with yoghourt

1½–2 lb potatoes
sea salt and black pepper
1 oz butter
¼ pint yoghourt
¼ lb shelled peas
4 eggs (poached)

Boil the potatoes and drain well. Push through the vegetable mill and dry out over gentle heat, adding the butter and plenty of salt and pepper. Stir in the yoghourt and add the peas, which you have cooked separately. When all is hot and well mixed, pour into a shallow dish and lay the poached eggs on top.

Wild green salad

a good bundle of mixed wild green leaves: sorrel, dandelion, watercress, etc. (garden lettuce, spinach, and sorrel can be added as needed)
sunflower-seed oil, or nut oil
lemon juice
sea salt and black pepper
a handful of cob nuts, or wild primroses according to season

Mix the greens in the salad bowl, leaving them whole. Dress with a light oil and lemon juice in the usual way, adding a light sprinkling of salt and pepper. Chop the nuts and scatter over the top, or, in spring time, scatter some primroses (flowers only) over the top.

Jonvelle

Arabella Boxer Tosses a Salad

In the days when I used to cook proper meals of two or three courses it always annoyed me that I did not have enough time to spend on the salad. There were always other more important things to attend to. Now, for a variety of reasons, I prefer to do the opposite. I like to take one thing which used to be considered as a mere part of the meal, a detail, and by spending a lot of care and thought on it, turn it into a meal in itself. I started to do this with cooked vegetable dishes; now I do it with salads. A salad can be a whole course in microcosm; it can contain poultry, fish, cheese, eggs, nuts, as well as a huge variety of vegetables, both raw and cooked.

Although a salad is by its nature a mixture of things, it must be a carefully chosen mixture, not just a heap of remains. The cooked part must be freshly cooked, and should be either just one thing, or a group of closely related things; a mixture of shellfish, for example, or a combination of new vegetables. There are a few exceptions: hard-boiled eggs go well with fish, or with a mixture of cooked vegetables; fried bacon and mozzarella cheese make a delicious combination with finely shredded summer spinach and sliced avocado. The ingredients should be cut in similar sized pieces; whereas in a simple lettuce salad I leave the leaves whole, in a mixed salad of this sort I usually cut them in strips.

As far as I am concerned, a salad is composed mainly of raw vegetables, most of them green and leafy; raw spinach or sorrel, lettuce, endive, batavia, chicory, watercress, cucumber, fennel and radish. The numerous Italian dishes of cooked vegetables dressed with oil and lemon are sometimes called salads, but, good as they are, they do not really fit in this category.

Lastly there is the choice of dressings. With a quite elaborate salad, one containing chicken or fish, I think the best solution is to have two dressings: one very simple to mix with the dish itself, possibly a little beforehand; the other quite different, more of a sauce, creamy and quite thick, which is handed separately. If a thick sauce of this type is poured over the salad it spoils the appearance and gives a slightly gluey consistency; another advantage in keeping it separate is that those on a diet can avoid the richer sauce altogether. With a shellfish salad, for instance, I would first marinate the fish in lemon juice for an hour before serving, then I would dress the assembled salad with the best olive oil and more lemon juice. When serving, I would have a mayonnaise in a separate bowl. With a chicken salad, I would marinate the chopped chicken briefly in lemon juice, then dress the assembled salad with a light sunflower seed oil and more lemon; I would accompany it with a creamy white sauce flavoured with fresh tarragon, or dill.

With the simpler salads, those containing dried bread, cheese or nuts, a creamy sauce is not wanted; but with salads of mixed cooked vegetables, or of hard-boiled eggs, it can be an optional extra. The addition of the second sauce will, however, turn the whole dish into something more special, quite elegant enough for a lunch party.

Shellfish salad

1 *lb hake or other firm white fish*
6 *scallops*
6 *crawfish tails or giant prawns*
½ *lb prawns or shrimps*
2–3 *lemons*
1 *crisp lettuce, Webb's or Iceberg*
1 *large green pepper*
1 *cucumber*
4 *hard-boiled eggs*
6 *tablespoons olive oil*
sea salt
black pepper
½ *pint mayonnaise*

Poach the hake gently, and leave to cool in its court-bouillon. Remove the skin and bones and break into large flakes. Pour over the juice of 1 lemon and leave for about 30 minutes. Poach the scallops for 5 minutes in the same court-bouillon; cool, then marinate in lemon juice also. Shell the crawfish tails, prawns and shrimps and soak for 10 minutes in a bowl of very cold salty water. Make a mayonnaise with 2 egg yolks, ½ pint of olive oil and a mixture of lemon juice and wine vinegar. Wash the lettuce and break up the leaves into neat pieces; you will probably need only half of it. Cut the pepper and the peeled cucumber into strips. Put the lettuce in a large salad bowl and cover with the pepper and cucumber. Pile the white fish in the centre, and arrange the shellfish over the top. Surround with the halved hard-boiled eggs and pour over a vinaigrette made with 6 tablespoons olive oil and 2 tablespoons lemon juice, sea salt and black pepper. Mix the salad at the table, and hand the mayonnaise separately. Serves 6.

Chicken salad

1 *chicken*
lemon juice (1–2 *lemons*)
1 *crisp lettuce, Webb's or Cos*
1 *cucumber*
1 *large green pepper*
1 *bunch watercress*
1 *head celery*
1 *head fennel*
1 *bunch spring onions*
sunflower seed oil (*or nut oil*)
sea salt and black pepper
Herb sauce:
¼ *lb Philadelphia cheese*
¼ *pint buttermilk*
2 *teaspoons lemon juice*
2 *tablespoons chopped tarragon, or dill*

Poach the chicken and leave to cool in its stock. Chop in pieces, removing skin and bone. Sprinkle with lemon juice. Shred the lettuce. Cut the peeled cucumber in sticks. Cut the pepper in thick strips. Chop the watercress, reserving the best leaves. Slice the celery and reserve any leaves. Mix all the vegetables with the chopped chicken and dress with sunflower seed oil and lemon juice, sea salt and black pepper. Prepare 1 hour before serving. Use the reserved leaves as a garnish. To make the herb sauce: put the cream cheese in the blender with the buttermilk and blend till smooth. Add lemon juice, salt and pepper, and stir in the herbs. Serve separately. Serves 6.

Mixed vegetable salad

1 *round lettuce*
½ *lb new potatoes*
¼ *lb new carrots*
¼ *lb shelled peas or broad beans*
1 *small cauliflower*
½ *lb tiny tomatoes, or medium ones quartered*
1 *bunch spring onions*
4 *hard-boiled eggs*
sea salt and black pepper
4 *tablespoons olive oil*
2 *tablespoons white wine vinegar*
½ *gill thin cream*
3 *tablespoons chopped chervil, when available*

Wash the lettuce. Cook the unpeeled potatoes, carrots, peas or beans, and cauliflower separately until just tender; leave to cool. Before they have completely cooled, peel the potatoes and slice them thickly. Mix them with the other cooked vegetables in a bowl and pour over half the oil and vinegar. Put the lettuce leaves in the salad bowl; add the peeled tomatoes and the spring onions, bulbs only. Shell the eggs and cut in half, lay around the edge of the bowl. Add the cooked vegetables and the remaining oil and vinegar. Season with salt and pepper and mix lightly, without breaking the ingredients. Pour on the cream and mix again. Scatter over the chervil and serve. Serves 4.

Spinach, bacon and mushroom salad

6 *oz summer spinach*
6 *oz small mushrooms*
½ *lemon*
4 *oz streaky bacon rashers*
2 *slices dry bread*
a little butter
1 *clove garlic* (*optional*)
sea salt and black pepper
6 *tablespoons olive oil*
2 *tablespoons white wine vinegar or lemon juice*

Wash the spinach and drain well. Discard the stalks and cut the leaves across in thin strips. Wipe the mushrooms, remove the stalks and slice the caps. Squeeze the juice of half a lemon over them. Fry the bacon slowly until crisp, drain on soft paper, and break into small pieces. Remove the crusts and cut the bread in small cubes. Fry until golden brown in butter with the whole peeled clove of garlic. Mix all together in a bowl, discarding the garlic. Add salt and pepper to taste, and dress with olive oil and vinegar or lemon juice. Serves 4.

Pitta salad

1 *cucumber*
1 *lb tomatoes*
1 *green pepper*
1 *flat loaf or "pitta"*
sea salt and black pepper
¼ *lb "feta" cheese*
olive oil
lemon juice

Peel the cucumber and cut it in strips like thick matchsticks. Peel the tomatoes, slice them thickly, and cut in similar strips, discarding the seeds and juice. Cut the pepper in strips likewise. Toast the *pitta* briefly. (It can be cut in half and put in an electric toaster). Cool, then tear in pieces. Mix all together in a bowl and season with sea salt and black pepper. Chop the cheese roughly and scatter over the salad. Dress with oil and lemon, using about two parts oil to one of lemon. This salad can be prepared in advance, as there is no lettuce to become limp. Serves 4.

Pine kernel salad

1 *cucumber*
1 *heart of a crisp lettuce, Webb's or Cos*
1 *green eating apple, i.e., Granny Smith*
1 *bunch watercress*
1 *bunch radishes*
2 *oz pine kernel*
sea salt and black pepper
sunflower seed oil
lemon juice

Peel the cucumber and cut in small dice. Chop the lettuce heart, the unpeeled apple and the watercress, stalks and all. Slice the radishes finely and mix all together in a large bowl. Scatter in the nuts and season with sea salt and black pepper. Dress lightly with sunflower seed oil and lemon juice, just enough to moisten. This pretty salad—green and pink and white—is delicious with cheese. Serves 4.

Seventies People and their Recipes

by Pamela Harlech

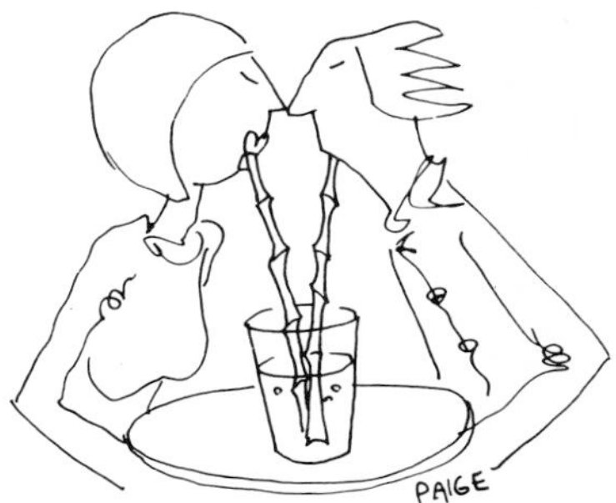

Mrs George Axelrod's mushrooms à la grecque
2 lb small button mushrooms
1 cup water
1 cup good white wine
1 cup olive oil
1 clove crushed garlic
½ teaspoon black pepper
pinch of salt
1 bay leaf
lettuce
8 pieces endive
4 oz red or black caviar
8 slices thinly cut smoked salmon
4 oz cream cheese
horseradish sauce
Put the mushrooms in an enamel saucepan with the water, white wine, olive oil, garlic, pepper and salt, and bay leaf. Bring to the boil, simmer for 7 minutes and cool. Marinate in its juice overnight in the refrigerator. When ready to serve, place the greenest, freshest lettuce you can find on 8 individual dishes. Then fill the endive with black or red caviar, and roll the slices of smoked salmon filled with a mixture of cream cheese, and horseradish sauce to taste. Place one of each either side of the mushrooms â la Grecque. Garnish with watercress. Serves 8.

Mrs Charles Douglas Home's apple snow with a difference
for 6–8 people
7 cooking apples
2 tablespoons water
1½ tablespoons brown sugar
2 teaspoons cinnamon
juice from 1 orange and 1 lemon
3 egg whites
double cream
Peel and core cooking apples, cut up and put into saucepan with 2 tablespoons water. Boil for 5 minutes, then put into liquidizer, adding brown sugar, cinnamon, and orange and lemon juice. Whip egg whites and fold into purée. Serve in a bowl with double cream. Note: this can also be made with raspberries or strawberries.

Mrs Tony Curtis's French vanilla ice cream
4 large egg yolks
½ cup honey (mild, light)
⅛ tsp salt
2 tsps vanilla extract (pure)
1 pint heavy cream whipped
Beat egg yolks lightly. Add honey, salt and vanilla. Fold in whipped cream. Turn into bowl or freezable container and put in freezer. When mixture freezes ¼ in around the edges of bowl, beat with beater and put back in freezer. Repeat this partial freezing about 4 times. Then freeze and serve (freezing time about three hours).

Lady Dacre's apples with red wine
Peel 4 Golden Delicious apples, cut into halves and take out hearts. Put into a Pyrex dish with a little redcurrant jelly in each half apple with a little butter. Mix ¾ cup of wine with ¼ cup of water and put in each half apple with a mixture of 1½ oz grated almonds and 5 oz castor sugar. Put in a moderate oven (325–350 deg. Mark 3–4) for about 15 minutes, covering the dish with silver paper. Take off the paper and leave apples to cook until light brown. Serve at once with cream.

Madame Correa da Costa's shrimp loaf bossanova
1 unsliced loaf of white bread
mayonnaise
1 lb shrimps
½ lb liver pâté
chopped parsley
½ lb chopped ham
1 oz butter
½ lb chopped walnuts
tomato purée

Trim the bread and slice lengthways into five slices. Spread a little mayonnaise on each slice. On the first put two-thirds of the shrimps, sautéed and minced. Cover with the second slice which has been spread with the liver pâté mixed with the parsley. Cover with the third slice which has been spread with the ham, butter and walnuts mixed together. Spread the fourth slice with the tomato purée (or any other filling you like) and cover with the last slice of bread. Cover the entire loaf with mayonnaise and garnish, using the remainder of the whole shrimps. Chill and serve.

Lady Elizabeth von Hofmannsthal's cabbage in cream

1–1½ *white cabbages finely shredded*
1 *oz butter*
1 *gill sour cream*
salt and black pepper
dill seed

Blanch cabbage in fast boiling salted water for 5–7 minutes. Drain well and dry as much as possible. Toss in melted butter, stir in cream and bring to simmering point. Add dill seeds, pepper and more salt if needed.

The Earl of Gowrie's cold cucumber soup

2 *cucumbers*
¾ *pint single cream*
½ *pint sour cream*
fresh chopped chives

Peel one of the cucumbers and chop both into coarse chunks and put in a blender. Stir cream and sour cream into the purée, chill and decorate with chives and a little parsley if you like it. Season. Serves 4.

Viscount Eden's devilled chicken or turkey

8 *oz salted butter*
2½ *tablespoons mango chutney*
2 *tablespoons lemon juice*
1 *tablespoon French mustard*
1 *teaspoon English mustard*
2 *teaspoons curry powder*
freshly ground pepper
8 *legs of chicken or* 4 *of turkey*

Soften the butter and combine all ingredients except the chicken legs in a bowl. When mixture is almost smooth, spread over the legs; these can be scored first so the mixture gets into the flesh. Warm in a gentle oven and finish under a hot grill so that the sauce is bubbling and even burnt in places.

Anthony West's cucumber soup

Take 2 good cucumbers, peel them and cut into thin slices before putting them on a large dish and salting. When the salt has drawn the water for about an hour, drain them and rinse before cooking in butter until cucumber begins to soften. Be careful not to brown them or the butter. This can very well be done in the casserole in which the soup is going to be made. If so the next stage is to pour 2–3 pints of chicken stock onto the cucumber, flavouring the liquid with any herbs you fancy. Mrs. Beeton recommends chopped sorrel and chervil; my own taste is for chopped green dill, fine shavings of celery, a small quantity of lemon juice and salt and pepper. The soup should simmer gently for about 40 minutes. Just before serving add 3 egg yolks beaten into ½ pint of cream.

Nathalie Hambro's poulet bamako

1 *big chicken cut into pieces*
12 *slices of bacon cut very thin*
2 *tablespoons olive oil*
juice of 2 *lb of lemons*
rosemary, thyme, powdered bay leaves, sage, tarragon, parsley, salt and pepper
wooden cocktail sticks

Marinate the chicken pieces overnight in the lemon juice which will help to "cook" the chicken. In the morning leave them to drain. Put all the herbs on a plate and roll each piece of chicken in the mixture. Wrap chicken pieces in one or two slices of bacon and fix in place with a cocktail stick. Lay on a flat dish and brush each piece with olive oil. Cook in a medium oven for 40–45 minutes. Take chicken pieces off stick and serve with brown rice with thyme, walnuts, sultanas and sliced bananas, which should be wrapped in foil and warmed in the oven for 15 minutes. Serves 6.

Mrs Rupert Hambro's sardine pâté

2 *large packets Philadelphia cream cheese*
2 *large or* 4 *small tins sardines, drained*
juice of 2 *lemons*
pepper and salt to taste

Put all ingredients in blender until creamy. Put in a container and serve with hot Melba toast.

Mrs Rupert Hambro's ginger soufflé

4 *medium tart green apples*
½ *cup powdered ginger snaps*
3 *tablespoons butter*
1½ *cups sweet cider*
4 *tablespoons sugar*
2 *egg yolks*
6 *egg whites*
½ *teaspoon cream of tartar*
For the poaching syrup:
2 *tablespoons apple brandy*
2 *tablespoons chopped crystallized ginger*
1 *teaspoon lemon juice*
2 *tablespoons sugar*
2 *tablespoons water*

Peel, core and thinly slice the apples. Make a syrup with the brandy, ginger, lemon juice, sugar and water and poach the apples for a few minutes until soft. Take out the ginger and put it with apples and 2–3 tablespoons syrup in the bottom of a buttered and sugared 2-quart soufflé dish and keep warm. Place crisp ginger snaps in the blender and run until powdered. Melt butter in the top of a double boiler over boiling water. Stir in the powdered ginger snaps and cook for a few minutes until smooth. Then pour in cider and sugar, stir constantly and cook for about 5 minutes until mixture is smooth and thick. Remove from heat, cool and beat egg yolks into mixture. Beat egg whites into stiff creamy peaks. Sprinkle cream of tartar over them as you beat. Spoon a third of the whites into ginger snap sauce and combine vigorously. Dribble this over remaining beaten egg whites and fold carefully until all is combined. Pour sauce over the warm apple slices in soufflé dish. Bake in preheated oven 350 deg F., Mark 4. Should be done in 25 minutes, but test it.

Lady Warner's green tea ice cream

$\frac{1}{2}$ pint milk
2 eggs
sugar
3 teaspoons powdered green tea
$\frac{1}{2}$ pint double cream

Heat the milk. Beat together the eggs, sugar and powdered green tea and pour on the milk, stirring. Return mixture to pan and cook without boiling until custard coats the back of a wooden spoon. Cool a little, add whipped double cream. Cover and freeze.

Lady Warner's veal with tuna sauce

1 lb roast or boiled veal thinly sliced
1 $9\frac{1}{4}$-oz tin of tuna fish
3–4 anchovies
2–3 tablespoons olive oil
$\frac{1}{2}$ pint mayonnaise

Flake the tuna and add chopped anchovy. Mix with mayonnaise. Put some sauce on a serving plate and put the meat on top. Add more sauce and meat. Repeat several times. If you pour a little olive oil between the meat and the sauce it helps the taste of the sauce to go into the meat. Decorate with parsley and capers.

Lady Victoria Yorke's crab en croûte

2 finely chopped shallots
1 oz butter
1 lb crab meat
salt and pepper
paprika
2 egg yolks
1 lb frozen puff pastry
2 tablespoons milk

Cook chopped shallots in butter until transparent and add to crab with salt, pepper and dusting of paprika. Pound together with yolk of 1 egg. Cut puff pastry into 4 pieces and roll out into four sheets 8 in square. Put the crab mix into the centre of each and fold once envelopewise. Brush pastry envelopes with mixture of egg yolk and milk using flat brush. Cook in the middle of a hot oven, 450 deg. F., Mark 8 for 20–30 minutes.

Sauce: Make a sauce with $\frac{1}{4}$ pint roux with $\frac{1}{2}$ tablespoon tomato purée, 1 teaspoon paprika, finely chopped garlic clove, tomatoes, paprika and garlic. Strain through a sieve. Heat. Add $\frac{1}{2}$ gill double cream, grated zest of 1 lemon, juice of $\frac{1}{2}$ lemon and 4 drops of Tabasco at the last minute.

Mrs Peter Hall's chicken in the pot

1 3–4 lb chicken, or 4 baby poussins
$\frac{1}{2}$ orange
$\frac{1}{2}$ apple
2 onions
1 lb carrots
4 leeks
$\frac{1}{2}$ head celery
2 pieces of bacon
garlic to taste
fresh herbs and/or bouquet garni
salt and pepper to taste

Put the half orange and apple and half an onion inside the chicken. Put the chicken in an ovenproof casserole which has a lid. Surround the chicken with the rest of onions and cut up vegetables, put bacon pieces over the breast. Add garlic, herbs and seasoning. Sometimes I roll the livers in bacon, skewer with a toothpick and add these. Bake at 325 deg. F. (Mark 3) for two hours. Serves 4.

Mrs Peter Hall's chicken with apple

1 chicken, jointed
sage leaf
carrot and onion
butter and oil for frying
4 apples
1 onion, finely chopped
1 tablespoon flour
$\frac{1}{2}$ pint apple juice
$\frac{1}{2}$ pint chicken stock
small carton double cream
chopped parsley

Boil chicken carcass with sage leaf, carrot and onion for stock. Fry chicken pieces in butter and oil and put aside. Core apples but don't peel, and cut in rings. Fry with the onion until cooked. Keep warm. Add flour to make a roux. Add apple juice and stock and stir until it thickens. Season. Add chicken pieces. Simmer $1\frac{1}{4}$–$1\frac{1}{2}$ hours. Put chicken in serving dish and arrange apple rings around the edge. Whip the double cream and put a blob in the centre of each ring. Sprinkle liberally with chopped parsley. Serves 4.

Conversion Tables

Metric and American Measures

Our original units were anthropometric, based on body size and needs. A pint is a good measure of drink, a foot the length of a grown man's feet, a stone a sizeable weight to carry. The metric system is decimal and to convert English units into metric units we need precise conversion factors. We need to *think* metric. While we are getting used to the idea, remember that a pint is about half a litre, a kilogramme is about two pounds, 200 grammes not quite half a pound.

Weights

British ounces	*Metric grammes*
1	30
2	55
3	85
3½	100
4	115
5	140
6	170
7	200
8	225
9	255
10	285
11	310
12	340
13	370
14	400
15	425
16	455

Liquid Measures

British and Metric
1 quart = 2 pints = 40 fluid oz = 1·1 litres
1 pint = 4 gills = 20 fluid oz = 6 decilitres (dl)
½ pint = 2 gills = 1 cup = 10 fl oz = 3 dl
¼ pint = 8 tablespoons = 5 fl oz = 1·5 dl
1 tablespoon = just over ½ fl oz = 15 ml
1 dessertspoon = ⅓ fl oz = 10 ml
1 teaspoon = ⅛ fl oz = 5 ml

Metric and British
1 litre = 35 fl oz = 1·75 pints
½ litre (5 dl) = 18 fl oz = 0·875 pt
¼ litre (2·5 dl) = 9 fl oz = 0·437 pt
1 dl = 3½ fl oz = 0·175 pt

American Liquid Measures

1 quart = 2 pints = 32 fl oz
1 pint = 2 cups = 16 fl oz
1 cup = 8 fl oz
1 tablespoon = ⅓ fl oz
1 teaspoon = ⅙ fl oz

Approximate Equivalents

British	*American*
1 quart	2½ pints
1 pint	1¼ pints
½ pint	10 fl oz (1¼ cups)
¼ pint (1 gill)	5 fl oz
1 tablespoon	1½ tablespoons
1 dessertspoon	1 tablespoon
1 teaspoon	⅓ fl oz
1½ pints + 3 tablespoons (32 fl oz)	1 quart
¾ pint + 2 tablespoons (16 fl oz)	1 pint
½ pint − 2 tablespoons (8 fl oz)	1 cup

Metric Temperatures

This conversion chart shows the comparison between Fahrenheit, Centigrade and Gas Marks. A rough guide for converting existing recipes to the metric settings is to think of °C cooking temperatures as being roughly one half of °F.

Fahrenheit	*Centigrade* (approximate)	*Gas Mark*
150	70	
175	80	
200	100	
225	110	¼
250	120	½
275	140	1
300	150	2
325	160	3
350	180	4
375	190	5
400	200	6
425	220	7
450	230	8
475	240	9
500	260	
525	270	
550	290	
575	300	

Index of Recipes

Q

R

S